Luminos is the Open Access monograph publishing program
from UC Press. Luminos provides a framework for preserving and
reinvigorating monograph publishing for the future and increases
the reach and visibility of important scholarly work. Titles published
in the UC Press Luminos model are published with the same high
standards for selection, peer review, production, and marketing as
those in our traditional program. www.luminosoa.org

The publisher and the University of California Press Foundation
gratefully acknowledge the generous support of the
Simpson Imprint in Humanities.

# Placing Islam

ISLAMIC HUMANITIES

Shahzad Bashir, Series Editor

Publication of this Luminos Open Access Series is made possible by the Islam and the Humanities Project of the Program in Middle East Studies at Brown University.

# Placing Islam

*Geographies of Connection in Twentieth-Century Istanbul*

Timur Hammond

UNIVERSITY OF CALIFORNIA PRESS

University of California Press
Oakland, California

Suggested citation: Hammond, T. *Placing Islam: Geographies of Connection in Twentieth-Century Istanbul.* Oakland: University of California Press, 2023.
DOI: https://doi.org/10.1525/luminos.153

Cataloging-in-Publication Data is on file at the Library of Congress.

ISBN 978–0-520–38743-0 (pbk. : alk. paper)
ISBN 978–0-520–38744-7 (ebook)

32   31   30   29   28   27   26   25   24   23
10   9   8   7   6   5   4   3   2   1

*For my parents, my first teachers*

# CONTENTS

# ILLUSTRATIONS

## MAPS

## FIGURES

# ACKNOWLEDGMENTS

Books—like places—are always products of the relationships that made them possible. Whether people know this place as Eyüp or Eyüp Sultan, I am grateful to everyone who has welcomed me. Several people have become especially central to my understanding of Eyüp. My deepest thanks to Ayla Gökçen Eren, Fatma Sevil Malcıoğlu, Nidayi Sevim, Deniz Sökmen, Şenol Tanju, Şener Türkmenoğlu, and Semra Zorluer. My research about this place was also facilitated by the tremendous efforts that the municipality has made to document and organize its own history. Between 2011 and 2013 I benefited from the regular use of their library collection; after it opened, I also worked at the Eyüp Sultan Research Center (EYSAM). My particular thanks to İrfan Çalışan and Hülya Yalçın for their efforts to make that center possible.

This book began as a dissertation at the University of California, Los Angeles. Lieba Faier saw this project take shape and helped me imagine it as a book. She continued to read drafts, offer suggestions, and encourage me to cross disciplinary and theoretical boundaries as this book has developed. Even though our paths cross less frequently today, my dissertation committee's writing and thinking has continued to stay with me: Michael Curry and John Agnew both helped me think differently about place, and Susan Slyomovics modeled how to link area studies scholarship with disciplinary traditions. I was first drawn to UCLA to work with Denis Cosgrove; after he passed away, Irene Bierman helped me find my footing in graduate school. I mourn them both.

I was blessed with departmental colleagues at UCLA who were brilliant, funny, and supportive. I am especially grateful to Abigail Cooke, Nicholas Lustig, and Alice Huff, who have provided feedback at every step of the way. I worked as an adjunct for one year at the University of Vermont. My colleagues there helped me rekindle a sense of curiosity in my work. My thanks to Pablo Bose, Meghan Cope, Harlan Morehouse, Cheryl Morse, and Ingrid Nelson in particular.

The Department of Geography and the Environment at Syracuse University has been a welcome place to complete this book. For their guidance, feedback, and support, I am especially grateful to Jacob Bendix, Natalie Koch, Matt Huber, Tom Perreault, Bob Wilson, and Jamie Winders. Joseph Stoll graciously helped me prepare one of the maps. Margie Johnson and Debbie Toole have patiently handled all the paperwork.

I have also been sustained by friendships and collaborations across campus. Amy Kallander and Rania Habib both helped me with transcriptions from Arabic. My special thanks to the Humanities Center and the Central New York Humanities Corridor for cultivating a collegial and supportive environment at Syracuse and beyond. For sharing conversations and support, my thanks to Lawrence Chua, Nicole Fonger, Vivian May, Tessa Murphy, Brice Nordquist, Romita Ray, Sascha Scott, and Sarah Workman. Glenn Peers very generously read a chapter draft and offered suggestions. Organizing a writing group helped to finish my book while (mostly) avoiding the cycles of boom and bust. Although our numbers fluctuated, Patricia Roylance and Robert Terrell have been key companions. It was Patty who described her writing process as something akin to spelunking with a candle; we spend a lot of time groping about in the dark, but sometimes the light catches on a surface and the world gleams.

I shared a draft of my book with graduate students in my Spring 2022 cultural geography seminar. Their feedback helped me see some of the flaws in the book but also gave me the confidence to completely rewrite much of the preface and the introduction. My sincere thanks to Lauren Ashby, Amanda Beavin, Bella Corieri, Jamie Fico, Yeryun Hong, Molly McConnell, Larry Morgan, Avia Nahreen, Gabrielle Reagan, and Gabriel Smith. Dominic Wilkins provided immensely valuable and careful feedback. Alex Michel produced three lovely maps.

Biray Kolluoğlu and Dikmen Bezmez helped me arrange letters of affiliation as a graduate student. Fellowships from the Fulbright Foundation and the American Research Institute supported my dissertation research. Dissertation writing was supported by the Institute of Turkish Studies and a dissertation completion fellowship from UCLA. At Syracuse University, a faculty leave in fall 2019 and a Humanities Center fellowship in spring 2020 also provided more space to revise the book.

For a variety of reasons, in-person research in Turkey has often been difficult over the past decade. My work has been made possible by the ongoing expansion of online archives. I am grateful to SALT Research, the Islamic Research Center (İSAM), the Marmara University Open Access archive, and the online scholarship repository DergiPark for making their materials accessible.

In the decade that I have been working on this project, I have been blessed with supportive friends and colleagues. For almost a decade, Kate Elizabeth Creasey has been a steady and generous interlocutor. My thanks for past conversations and looking forward to many more. Nicolas Howe helped me to better frame the initial book proposal. Caroline Jennings worked with me to edit a sample chapter for my initial book submission. Ilaria Giglioli has helped me track my time and keep myself accountable over the past four years. Lâle Can read through drafts of the introduction and several chapters; I am grateful for her friendship, generosity, and inspiration. Anand Taneja provided feedback on a draft chapter. Christiane Gruber has provided both encouragement and an ever-expanding list of new sources. Vincent Artman generously shared articles on short notice. During my final push to finish the manuscript, both Diana Davis and Veronica della Dora helped me maintain a sense of excitement about my project.

I have been lucky to share conversations, classes, and conferences with friends, teachers, mentors, and colleagues while working on this book. My thanks to Ceren Abi, Elizabeth Angell, Reem Bailony, Josh Carney, Eray Çaylı, Zeynep Çelik, Brittany Cook, Feray Coşkun, Nick Danforth, Sarah el-Kazaz, Banu Gökarıksel, Ali Hamdan, Rezzan Karaman, Hikmet Kocamaner, Avital Livny, Amy Mills, Nilay Özlü, Christine Philliou, Janell Rothenberg, James Ryan, Armando Salvatore, Zeynep Simavi, Sarah-Neel Smith, Danielle van Dobben Schoon, Kent Schull, İpek Türeli, Özlem Ünsal, Fabio Vicini, Jeremy Walton, Murat Yıldız, and Seçil Yılmaz.

I am delighted that this book will be published as part of the Islamic Humanities series at the University of California Press. Shahzad Bashir has offered encouragement and advice at every step of the way. His enthusiasm helped me immeasurably. The initial version of the manuscript benefited from two anonymous reviewers. Although they evaluated the book in very different ways, their comments helped the book's arguments grow and develop. It has been a pleasure to work with Eric Schmidt and LeKeisha Hughes. Their timely responses and clear feedback—even amid a pandemic—made this project possible. Sharron Wood copyedited the final version of the book; the book is much better for her careful attention.

My parents, Ayshe Ege and Doug Hammond, have always supported this project. Among many other qualities, they are models of curiosity and empathy. My thanks to my brother Altay for always encouraging me to think bigger. When I lived in Istanbul between 2011 and 2013, I was lucky to live with my grandmother, uncle, and aunt. My grandmother, Muazzez Ege, passed away in 2014. She is buried next to her mother, İhsan Parlakses, in Karacaahmet Cemetery in Üsküdar. My uncle, Husseyin Ege, was an indelible part of my life in Istanbul. Our conversations, meals, and Istanbul adventures are woven through this book. He passed away in 2020, but I hold my memories of him close. My aunt, Atiye Yalçın Ege, has been a friend, a mentor, a teacher of Turkish, and a sustaining presence.

Kirsten Schoonmaker has lived alongside this project from the very beginning. I continue to be so grateful that we share a life; it's even better for the presence of Ollie and Riker. May we continue to grow into more generous versions of ourselves. Without fully understanding the process, we stumbled into a remarkable community in Syracuse. My thanks to friends and neighbors who have helped this place become home.

Like Eyüp, Syracuse has been made by many histories, above all the histories that tie the Haudenosaunee people to this land and its waterways. Central New York remains home to the Haudenosaunee. I acknowledge the ongoing history of dispossession across the Confederacy and am grateful to live and share place on these lands.

Throughout the book I use standard modern Turkish spelling for Turkish and Ottoman names and terms. This is complicated by the fact that the vocabulary of Turkish has changed considerably over the past century, most notably following the 1928 Alphabet Reform, which installed a modified Latin script in place of the modified Arabic script that had been used for Ottoman Turkish. Many religious terms in Turkish are cognates of their versions in Arabic (e.g., *sahabe* and *sahaba*), although some may be less recognizable (*namaz* and *salah*). In general, I use the Turkish version of religious terms. The index generally provides the Turkish word first but includes translations in English and Arabic where necessary. For names specific to this context, I also preserve their "standard" Turkish spelling (so, *Halid bin Zeyd* instead of *Khalid bin Zayd*). With the exception of İrfan Çalışan, who would be identifiable by his role in the local municipality, I use pseudonyms for my other interlocutors. For those who are older than me, I also use the terms "Bey" (Mr.), "Hanım" (Ms.), and "Amca" (uncle, often used as a mark of affectionate respect).

Place names are an especially complicated issue in this book, as they have been shaped by both linguistic shifts and different naming conventions. For the sake of consistency, I refer to the place at the center of this book as "Eyüp." However, people refer to it by many names and spellings, including Eyüb, Eyyub, Eyoup, Ayoub, Ayyub, Eyüp Sultan, Eyüpsultan (the district municipality's current name), and Belde-i Hazret-i Halid (the town of His Excellency Halid), among others. Where possible, I seek to retain the specificity of my ethnographic and archival interlocutors and use their versions when quoting.

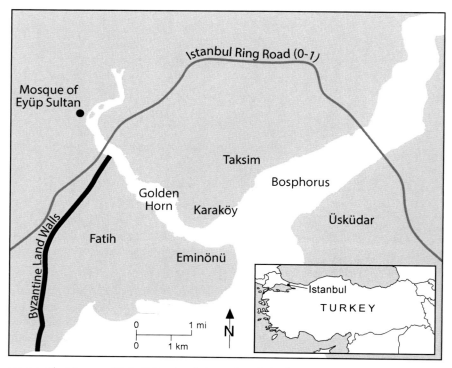

MAP 1. The Mosque of Eyüp Sultan in relation to Istanbul today.

While most consonants in Turkish are pronounced similarly to English, there are several exceptions:

c is pronounced as j in James or jami' (*cami*)
ç is pronounced as ch as in chair (*çarşı*)
ş is pronounced as sh as in shift (*şube*)
j is pronounced as in French (*jön*)
ğ is typically silent, lengthening the previous vowel (*ağaç*)

Modern Turkish has eight vowels:

a is pronounced as the a in cat (*kitap*)
e is pronounced as the e in bet (Eyüp)
ı is pronounced as the i in cousin (*hakkında*)
i is pronounced as the ee in seem (*kitap*)
o is pronounced as the o in goal (*bol*)
ö is pronounced as the i in bird (*göz*)
u is pronounced as ou in you (*umur*)
ü is pronounced as ew in few (*türbe*)

# Welcome to Eyüp

## WHERE IS EYÜP?

This is a book set in the Istanbul district of Eyüp, home to one of the city's most important Muslim tombs.

If you had never visited Istanbul, much less Eyüp, you might begin where many searches begin: Google. A few keystrokes later and you might see a screen with a range of information. A blurb from Wikipedia tells us that Eyüp or Eyüpsultan is a district of Istanbul without commenting on the difference between those names; another panel juxtaposes a view of the Golden Horn with a map of the district municipality; we are given points of interest, destinations, questions that people ask (Which prophet is buried in Turkey? Who was Ayub Sultan? Where did Eyup come from?). Each of those pieces of information is partial, but at first glance searching for Eyüp on Google enacts a particular kind of place: one where facts and stories can be coordinated, presented, and located in a transparent, legible way.

But there are other ways of locating Eyüp. Some longtime residents, for example, make Eyüp a place of social relationships and shared memories. Their Eyüp is located not just somewhere but *somewhen*. Their stories would take you from central Eyüp to the constellation of neighborhoods that extend in all directions: Akarçeşme and Defterdar as you head back toward the Byzantine land walls; Nişancı extending up the ridge leading to Edirnekapı; Düğmeciler tucked into the valley beneath the ridge of Rami; İslambey as you head up the old streambed toward the hills beyond; the old fields and meadows of Çırçır, Karyağdı, and Gümüşsuyu; and, along the shore of the Golden Horn as it narrows, there is Silahtarağa and Alibeyköy. While each of these neighborhoods has its own history, what matters

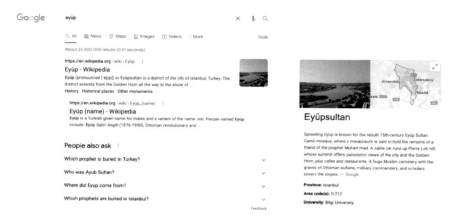

FIGURE 1. Screenshot of a Google search for "Eyüp" from Syracuse, New York, May 10, 2022. Photo of Golden Horn posted to Wikipedia by Jl FilpoC is licensed under CC by 4.0.

is less the exact boundaries between them and more the way that they organize a sense of place. Their Eyüp is enacted through everyday acts of neighborliness, phone calls and text messages, social media posts, and special events.

For these residents, many of these relationships and memories are linked to material sites like schools, factories, gardens, bakeries, coffeehouses, the open-air cinema. Were you to visit today, you would find a few of these sites still standing, such as the school endowed by and located just beside the tomb of Sultan Reşad (Mehmed V). Although that school's name has changed—from the Reşadiye Model School (Numune Mektebi) to the Eyüp Mixed Middle School (Muhtelit Orta Mektebi) to the Eyüp Middle School to the Eyüp High School (*lise*)—the building still serves as a reference point for those born and raised in the district.[1] Yet despite these buildings and ongoing efforts to maintain connections to those shared social relations, other longtime residents also look at the district where they live and say, "Eyüp is gone" (*Eyüp yok olmuş*). They experience this place as a site of loss, one where the built environment and its contemporary urban life mark absence and change. These two positions are not mutually exclusive; markers of continuity can exist alongside evocations of absence.

But other residents—many of whom have also lived in this place for decades—define Eyüp as that which is unchanged. Returning after years away, I might run into an old acquaintance. "How is Eyüp?" I ask. "Eyüp is the same," they shrug. And then there are still others who describe Eyüp not in relation to a changing city but in relation to the person buried at the district's center, the person whose story is so tightly interwoven with this place: Halid bin Zeyd Ebû Eyyûb el-Ensârî, a Companion (Tr. *sahabe*, Ar. *ṣaḥaba*) of the Prophet Muhammad.[2] As many would explain to me, "If he [Halid bin Zeyd] hadn't existed, this"—meaning the mosque and its density of visitors, the neighborhood of Eyüp, even Istanbul as a Muslim

FIGURE 2. Sketch of central Eyüp viewed from the opposite shore, drawn from memory.

city—"would never have been" *Olmasaydı burası olmazdı*. This phrase locates Eyüp not as a place that changes but as a place unchanged.

And then there are those who are visiting Eyüp for the first time. Some might have searched online; some might be traveling as part of an organized tour; but many others might be traveling with friends or on the recommendation of friends, most often to visit the Mosque of Eyüp Sultan. Sometimes these visitors know a great deal about the mosque and the person buried at its center. They might have learned that Halid bin Zeyd hosted the Prophet Muhammad when he fled Mecca for Medina; that he was one of the Prophet's most devoted and pious companions; and that because of that devotion, he was inspired to join the Muslim army that besieged Constantinople. Some might have learned that he died of sickness, others that he was martyred in battle. Others may know even more details. But other visitors might know only that Halid bin Zeyd was an important figure, someone important enough to have a tomb built of silver filigree, mother-of-pearl, and turquoise tile. They might simply follow the crowds of other visitors, doing as their neighbors do. They know Eyüp, but their Eyüp is not that of a longtime resident or a Google algorithm.

In short, there are many ways to answer the question "Where is Eyüp?" These many possible answers pose a puzzle: whose perspective is correct? One approach pushes us to search for the "right" answer. That answer is there, existing out there in the world, if only we could gather the correct facts. Another way of answering that question—a more nuanced approach—would tell us that there are many perspectives on Eyüp: where people locate Eyüp has much to do with their own histories and positions in the world. But there is a third way of answering that question: locating Eyüp depends on the practices through which different people enact this place.[3]

This book argues that places are not distinct, singular objects but *multiple*.[4] In the case of Eyüp—home to one of Istanbul's best-known Muslim shrines—this means that there is no single Eyüp. Rather, different groups and individuals have defined Eyüp—and thus placed Islam—in diverse, overlapping ways. In many cases, these enactments of Eyüp coincide; it is precisely when different ways of knowing Eyüp coincide that people arrive at a shared understanding and experience of Eyüp.

In other moments, it is possible for two different enactments of Eyüp to be physically proximate and yet in totally different places. For example, tourists from France visit Eyüp, passing through the mosque briefly before walking up the road to the café named for Pierre Loti; they might brush by two high school students—perhaps from a relatively distant district like Avcılar or Esenyurt—visiting the mosque to pray for success with their upcoming exam. Both the tourists and the students know Eyüp, but their modes of using and defining this place never coincide or align.

But there are also moments when different enactments of Eyüp clash: when a longtime resident talks about feeling like a stranger in the mosque; when a tourist and a religious pilgrim rub shoulders during Ramadan; when a religious scholar looks at a changing city and mournfully observes, "We don't even know how to say a Fatiha." In these moments there are often attempts to police the "correct" Eyüp, to draw boundaries between what should and should not be done, said, or known, or to instruct a public in the "true" meaning of this place.

Where is Eyüp? It depends on how people make this place through various modes of articulation, encounter, and inhabitation. These modes are linked to how people see themselves and others in and in relation to this place, the histories that are woven through it, and Eyüp's relationship to the city, nation, and world beyond. This book's approach thus extends one of geography's core insights: where we are shapes who we are; but through our complex and often contested forms of social life, we are always remaking the worlds in which we live.

This book studies how different individuals, groups, and institutions have sought to place Islam by making and transforming Eyüp. Although there are many possible places of Islam, Eyüp—or Eyüp Sultan, as some of my interlocutors would insist—provides an especially rich object of analysis. Focusing on the district's transformations over roughly the past hundred years, *Placing Islam* examines how understandings of history, urban life, cultural identity, and piety have been woven together.

This is a century of far-reaching transformations in and beyond Eyüp: constitutional revolution in 1908; the catastrophic wars and violence of the 1910s; occupation, revolution, and the uneven project of making "modern" Turkey; industrialization and urbanization; political strife and cultural change; military coups in 1960, 1972, and 1980; globalization, deindustrialization, and neoliberalization; the emergence of a conservative religious political coalition in the 1990s; long-standing and ongoing debates over the boundary between the "religious" and the "secular"; and an ongoing process of rapacious urbanization. These dynamics transform Eyüp and shift how "places of Islam" come to matter. At the same time, Eyüp's story is not simply a smaller version of those "big" dynamics.

Rather than use Eyüp as a footnote for a story to which we already know the ending, this book seeks to develop a different approach for studying *how* people make places of Islam. They do so in diverse ways that are deeply embedded in the lived and felt specificities that make this place *the* place. But as I also hope to show, this approach is not merely what Shahid Amin has termed "an evocation of a world fiercely local." Instead, it is an effort to make a place whose geography and history may be unfamiliar to many readers, "intelligible outside its particular location of space and time."[5] So I begin not with a story about power and politics but instead with another act that defines this place: welcome.

## WHERE ARE YOU FROM?

My first encounter with a place named Eyüp came in the form of Orhan Pamuk's memoir *Istanbul: Memories and the City*. In it, Pamuk uses a visit to the district as an opportunity to narrate his own sense of self, caught between worlds and ways of living. He described taking the small ferry up the Golden Horn to the last stop. There, he found himself frustrated:

> My trouble with Eyüp is that this small and perfect village at the end of the Golden never seemed genuine [*gerçek*] to me, it always appeared like a fantasy [*hayal*]. As a turned-in-upon-itself, "Eastern," mysterious, religious, picturesque, mystical fantasy, Eyüp was so perfect that it seemed to me like someone else's dream of the East embroidered upon Istanbul, like a sort of Turk-East-Muslim Disneyland existing in Istanbul.[6]

Even though I knew almost nothing about Eyüp when I read Pamuk's account, his version struck me as incomplete. There were no voices of people who lived in or visited Eyüp. Describing the village—which would have been a working-class district when Pamuk was a teenager—as "a sort of Turk-East-Muslim Disneyland" seemed to deny the possibility of change and transformation. Identifying what Pamuk missed about Eyüp became one of the goals that took me into this project. As I would come to learn, Pamuk's vision of Eyüp was also foreign to both Eyüp's longtime residents and its recent arrivals.

When I moved to Istanbul in 2011, I tried to learn about Eyüp in the way that was most comfortable to me: through books. On one of my first visits to the center of Eyüp, I wandered into a bookstore and asked in halting, accented Turkish, "Um, do you have books about Eyüp?" The bookstore's only employee—Şenol, who would become a friend—responded not by answering the question but by asking the question that is always reserved for people assumed to be out of place: *Nerelisiniz?* Where are you from?

I grew up in Los Angeles during the 1980s and 1990s with a first name that was different enough to be an object of humor in middle school but not so different that I ever felt "foreign." My Turkishness, insofar as it existed at all, came in the form of my grandmother's köfte and pilaf along with a handful of phrases she taught me. I came to learn Turkish only as a graduate student, the unfamiliar edges of its suffixes and syntax barely softened by my family acquaintance. When I first began my fieldwork in Eyüp in 2011, my vocabulary was stilted and halting, an awkward mix of Arabic cognates and formal classroom instruction. Over time, however, my Turkish grew more pliable.

As my fieldwork went on, the question "Where are you from?" took on a different form. I could often speak with someone for several minutes before my accent or phrasing marked me as belonging to a different place.

"So where are you from?" my interlocutor would ask.

"*Amerikalıyım*," I would reply. "I'm American."

They might compliment my Turkish before asking, "So what's your name?"

"Timur," I would answer.

"But that's a Turkish name."

"My mother's side of the family is Turkish," I would explain. "My grandmother was from Izmir, my grandfather Tatar."

That family history would help them locate me, as they continued with "Ah, so then you're Turkish" (*o zaman Türksün*) or "So you're one of us" (*bizdensin*).

Yet that shared connection was tenuous, especially if the person with whom I was speaking was especially pious: "Are you Muslim?"

Here, and in contrast to the questions I was comfortable answering and the compliments I was comfortable accepting, my answers often stumbled. In fact, I often resented being asked at all. Growing up in Los Angeles, religion was something that other people did. Although questions of belief and faith had come to play a more prominent role in my life as a I grew older, I almost never made my own views public.

As I carried out my fieldwork, I was fully aware of the irony of the situation: I wanted to learn more about other people's geographies of belief but chafed at being asked the same questions. In my field notes, I often wrote about my frustration at feeling like the question was an attempt to push me into someone else's narrative. My first thought on being asked was often, "What's it to you?" (*Sana ne?*) Out of politeness, I usually tried to answer their question with a noncommittal response: "I'm a human" (*insanım*).

At the same time, I fasted during Ramadan, sometimes joined in Friday prayers, recited the Fatiha when it was appropriate, and repeated *Amin* as clearly as those around me when someone prayed for health or good fortune. Yet when measured against some of my friends born in Turkey—who would likely never have been asked "Are you Muslim?" because that identity was legally designated on their ID cards—I knew more about Islam and Eyüp and Arabic than they did.

What was at stake in these introductory conversations was not just *who* I was but *where* I existed in relation to my interlocutors. As my Turkish improved and as I spent more time in Eyüp, negotiating the question of where I was from changed. For two years I taught free classes in English at a small community school a stone's throw from the Mosque of Eyüp Sultan and attended classes in Ottoman Turkish. On most days I would stop by the bookstore where Şenol worked, often dropping in on the long conversations that took place there. These regular routines came to define my experience of this place, but they also helped to reorient how people knew me in relation to Eyüp.

I forged friendships with some people, developed passing acquaintances with others, and have—in the decade since I first began to learn about Eyüp—fallen out of touch with many more. The bookstore where I once spent so much time has been turned into yet another shop selling plastic toys and religious paraphernalia. The community school where I used to teach is only a shadow of its former self. As a friend wrote to me on Facebook in 2020, "It's become a melancholy place" (*hüzünlü yer oldu*).

But there are things that stay the same: The small restaurant just off the main square is still there, and when I last visited in 2019, they welcomed me back with a smile. A few streets down is the barbershop where I first began to try to meet people in Eyüp. The barber has known me for over a decade, and our conversations have ranged from Eyüp's history to education to the politics of the war on terror to Ottoman history to Islam, all the while interspersed with the regular rhythms of his work. These relationships—and the contexts in which they played out—matter because they shaped my sense not only of how Eyüp has changed but also of how certain parts of it continue to stay the same. They also remind me that my access to these places might well have been different were I perceived by my interlocutors as a different kind of person in this place.

## WHERE ARE YOU FROM, DIFFERENTLY

The act of placing others was woven into the encounters that make Eyüp. A story from one afternoon in June 2013 provides one example. That day a woman and her young son entered the courtyard of the community school where I used to teach several days a week. Those who frequented the school called this place the *sıbyan mektebi* (primary school), a name that acknowledged its former use during the nineteenth and early twentieth centuries. The school sat on a narrow road that stretched between the mosque and a busy four-lane boulevard. In contrast to the busy square that defined the mosque's opposite side, this side of the mosque was often quiet and relatively deserted. Apart from the handful of people who deliberately visited the building, most visitors stumbled in by chance, perhaps drawn in by the hand-lettered signs displayed around the gate, perhaps reading the curious name displayed on a plastic sign: Tefekkür Bahçesi, the Garden of Contemplation.

On entering the courtyard, visitors found a cluster of seemingly mismatched objects. There were several fraying nylon tents set up in the middle of the courtyard; clusters of plastic chairs; a few benches; a wooden playground set; and several tall plane trees that shaded most of the courtyard. All around the courtyard there were chest-high walls that protected hundreds of Ottoman-era gravestones, and finally, at the near end of the courtyard, there was a small building fashioned of thick-cut stone. The director of this place was a man named Mehmet Emin Hoca.

Whenever visitors entered, he would welcome them and introduce this place as the *sıbyan mektebi*. Because many visitors didn't know that term, he would tell them that the *sıbyan mektebi* had been the system of primary education that existed before the Turkish Republic, under the Ottoman Empire. This school had been endowed at the end of the eighteenth century by Mihrişah Valide Sultan, one of the wives of Sultan Mustafa III and the mother of Sultan Selim III.[7] The school was one part of a broader complex that included her tomb, an *imaret* (public kitchen), and a *sebil* (public fountain), all located immediately across the road.

The school was a marker, Mehmet Hoca would continue, of Mihrişah Valide Sultan's piety and generosity and a reminder of the key relationship between education and religion that existed under the Ottoman Empire. That empire was, of course, in the past, but if you were to sit in the courtyard under the spreading plane trees, surrounded by carved marble gravestones and beneath the minaret of the nearby mosque, it was easy to feel the persistence of something.

Following the collapse of the Ottoman Empire and the establishment of the Republic of Turkey, state authorities reorganized the educational system and closed this system of primary schools.[8] Deprived of its function as a school and its funding, the building fell into disrepair and later was used as someone's home until a fire broke out. The building was restored in the 1990s. When I taught there between 2011 and 2013, the complex was used by a branch of the Association for the Dissemination of Knowledge (İlim Yayma Cemiyeti).[9] Mehmet Hoca was proud that the complex was being used as a school again. For him, the school's activities linked education and religious devotion in a manner that corrected the error of the Republic and honored the example of the Ottoman past.

The woman who walked in that afternoon wore pants and a modest blouse but was not wearing any sort of head covering. She would have blended in with the crowd in many of Istanbul's other districts that were not known for their religious identity, such as Taksim, Beşiktaş, or Kadıköy. Although people dressed in a variety of ways in Eyüp, her choice nevertheless signaled something different than those of women who came to visit the Mosque of Eyüp Sultan and its tomb of Halid bin Zeyd Ebû Eyyûb el-Ensârî while wearing long, loose-fitting coats and carefully knotted head scarves.

As he did for almost every visitor, Mehmet Hoca bounded up from where he had been sitting. Ah, welcome, welcome. *Hoş geldiniz.* Where are you from? *Nerelisiniz?*

We're longtime Eyüp folk, the woman replied. *Eski Eyüplüyüz.*

No, he corrected them, we don't have the right to say Eyüp. *Eyüp demeye hakkımız yok.* You're from Eyüp Sultan. *Eyüp Sultanlısınız.*

Eyüp or Eyüp Sultan? I knew from experience that Mehmet Hoca insisted on the latter because it stressed the importance of Halid bin Zeyd and Islam to this place. By insisting that we didn't have the right to say Eyüp, he was signaling a broader argument about how people should relate to this place. Yet Mehmet

Hoca's stress on "Eyüp Sultan" was itself relatively recent, largely the product of debates that crystallized in the 1990s.[10]

The woman understood his critique immediately and replied in a tight voice: Well, if you mean we're from the vicinity of the place where the Companion of the Prophet Halid bin Zeyd Ebû Eyyûb el-Ensârî is buried, then yes, we're from here, *biz buralılıyz.*

She and her son walked out of the courtyard and passed up the road in the direction of the mosque itself.

In one respect, this brief encounter follows the familiar fault line between "secular" (Eyüp) and "religious" (Eyüp Sultan) claims to place.[11] But the woman's response was not so much a rejection of Islam as it was a different enactment of it. Both she and Mehmet Emin Hoca shared a knowledge of the person buried at the mosque's center and both explained that person's importance in terms of his status as a Companion of the Prophet Muhammad. In that, their stories about this place coincided. But where they clashed was in the way that those stories were linked to being *of here*, being *buralı.*

Welcoming people to Eyüp—or not, as the case may be—involves both judgments about where Eyüp is and where people are from. These acts of welcoming help bring us into the wider histories that this book explores: how people create places of Islam amidst a changing city, nation, and world.

# Introduction

How do people share a place? Answering that question involves negotiating many linked issues: what defines these places, where those places are, and which people, histories, practices, and meanings are linked to them. Because of Istanbul's historical, social, and cultural complexity, these questions are especially urgent. Alongside the specificities of Istanbul, shared understandings of place are also relevant to the geographies of Islam because places are woven into the traditions, identities, and broader worlds that define how Muslims understand themselves as Muslim. Sharing a place involves far more than mere location.

*Placing Islam* argues that rather than beginning with a definition of what Islam is, we ought to begin by examining the practices by which people enact the *where* of Islam. This book focuses on how people have made one especially rich and textured place of Islam: Eyüp. Here, these practices include how people tell stories, how they write and publish popular and academic histories, how they visit mosques and tombs, how they evaluate the other people visiting alongside them, and how they engage with and move through the urban landscape. We can follow municipal restoration and redevelopment projects, seminars hosted by civil society organizations, and tourism companies advertising Eyüp as a destination. These practices are undertaken by people who define themselves (or are defined by others) in many ways: as Muslim and non-Muslim; as local, native, or foreigner; as Turk, European, American, Arab, Kurd; as rich or poor; as observant in their religious practice or not; as man or woman; and as educated or ignorant.

Making places is central to an experience of being in the world.[1] Although places are made through human activity, they are not simply reducible to human intention or activity.[2] Rather, they are sites of "mediation . . . at which we come to be who we are through the detour of something alien to ourselves."[3] Places of Islam emerge through the practices of social life, but miracles, dreams, and worlds beyond human agency also play a role in placing Islam.[4] Precisely because many of these materials and substances are distinct from a world of mundane human activity, they can serve as powerful and charismatic agents. At the same time, the capacity of these places to mediate between humans and the divine also makes them sites of contestation and debate.[5]

Making places of Islam is not simply a question of defining *where* they are; it also involves defining *when* they are.[6] Again, however, there are many temporalities that come together to make Eyüp. There is, for example, the way that most Sunni Muslims understand the unchanging and unchanged nature of God's revelation.[7] There are the stories that link Halid bin Zeyd to the Prophet Muhammad, as well as the chronicles that narrate—albeit inconsistently—the discovery of Halid bin Zeyd's tomb. There are mosques, tombs, and graveyards, built and rebuilt upon each other over centuries. There are lived stories of families, the memories of Sufi lodges, the echoes of factories along the Golden Horn. There are the rhythms of the natural world, ranging from the waters that flow through Eyüp to its storks and pigeons. Taken as a whole, the temporalities of Eyüp—this place of Islam—require that we imagine place and time as something other than a neat, bounded envelope.

Places of Islam are where people develop a sense of themselves as Muslim, articulate definitions of Islam, and encounter Islam as something in the world distinct from their own subjective experience. These places take many forms, ranging from homes to dormitories to shrines to mosques to cities, nations, and even the world. These places are made through the work of different actors engaged in diverse practices, but some places—like Eyüp—are especially important because they seem to be permanent, stable, and separate from the flux and instability of an unstable world.

Rather than simply *read* places or *consume* them, people *reckon* with them. Extending Donald Preziosi's apt phrasing, even as people inhabit places, places inhabit them.[8] Places are not merely "local" contexts or neutral backdrops but "articulated moments in networks of social relations and understandings . . . where a large proportion of those relations, experiences and understandings are constructed on a far larger [geographical and temporal] scale than . . . the place itself."[9]

How do we recognize those articulations? We follow multiple forms of connection. In Eyüp we might begin with Halid bin Zeyd, whose tomb connects Istanbul to Medina by means of his body, or the precious objects that adorn the tomb, whose giving linked givers with this place and cemented their power and authority. There are water and power lines that connect the mosque to a wider urban infrastructure; we can listen to stories of belief, visitation, and even miracles that circulate through various media and modes of communication; and then there are the people who visit the mosque from innumerable other places, their bodies materializing social positions, religious affiliation, political allegiance, citizenship, and more.

Places of Islam are also defined by a generative contradiction. On the one hand, places of Islam are immutable, sites whose force is directly related to their unchanged and unchanging nature. On the other, places of Islam are also mutable, enacted through practices and necessarily in dynamic relationship with other places, peoples, and times.[10] This tension is especially important to Eyüp, where appeals to its unchanged significance and observations about its wholesale transformation exist side by side. While geographers and others have long grappled with these discussions of relational place, *Placing Islam* develops a specific analytic to examine how Eyüp has been enacted as a place of Islam: *building stories*.[11]

At first glance, those two terms seem to operate in mutually exclusive ways: where buildings are often encountered as static objects, deeply rooted in specific locations, stories are imagined to be mobile, circulating widely across time and space. If buildings are concrete, tangible, and durable, stories are fleeting, ephemeral, the stuff of dreams and rumor and fiction. Yet as a range of scholars have helped us understand, stories and buildings are in fact closely linked.

*Building stories* call our attention to the way that people bring themselves into relation with their material environments. In Eyüp, stories about Halid bin Zeyd are also almost always stories about the urban landscape. This mode of storytelling echoes countless other forms of the "texted past" throughout the Muslim world.[12] Through stories, elements of the built environment—mosques and tombs, but also homes, squares, avenues, graveyards, and even factories—come to be meaningful.[13] In telling stories, people communicate judgments about how a building should be used and by whom; they justify its construction, repair, redevelopment, or even destruction; they link buildings to other places and other times. In the process, the built environment comes to mediate everyday life, serving as one key medium through which people develop a sense of themselves, their community, and their position in the world.

At the same time, thinking in terms of *building stories* also calls our attention to the material dimensions of storytelling: just as buildings are storied, so too are stories built. Stories are inscribed on and transmitted through materials that both enable and constrain their meanings.[14] The practice of storytelling plays out in those "messy, material, placed contexts [where] . . . relations are continually made and remade."[15] In telling stories, people come to articulate a relationship with the land that sometimes—but not always—aligns with the legible lines of the map.[16] Stories are material practices, told by people and through things in ways that reshape material relations and thus remake the world.[17]

This book's interest in building stories benefits from a rapidly expanding scholarship on material culture and material religion.[18] This scholarship challenges simple summary. However, one key commitment is its focus on material objects (and the world more generally) not as incidental to a purified world of belief but as entangled.[19] Focusing on the role that media plays in "connect[ing] people with each other and the divine,"[20] and showing how changing media reshape "the conditions of existence that make the expression of religion possible,"[21] these scholars show how mediation helps to make places of Islam.

Building stories have different shapes. For example, when asked to explain why Eyüp is important, some of my interlocutors would return to the person buried at its center: Eyüp is sacred because of Halid bin Zeyd, they would say. This mode of storytelling could be termed a chronotope of origins.[22] In these chronotopes, something—a person, an event, an idea, or a location—serves as the essential core of the world.[23] This core thus comes to explain the shape and the trajectory of the world's history.[24] Because these chronotopes of origin tend to underpin exclusive claims to place, they are often used to justify a broader politics of exclusion. These chronotopes are by no means unique to Eyüp, Istanbul, or even Turkey, but Eyüp (as a person, a tomb, a mosque, and a district) has come to function as one particularly durable example. Yet this way of explaining Eyüp's essential meaning in which Halid bin Zeyd defines the center of a "neat and tidy 'envelope of space-time'" is incomplete for two linked reasons.[25]

First, origin chronotopes ignore the work of transmission through which different actors and institutions have sought to define and communicate Eyüp's significance and meanings over time and place.[26] Assigning agency to a time and point of origin ("If he hadn't existed, this would never have been") elides the complicated and often contested practices through which people establish, document, communicate, instruct, and narrate traditions over time. Crucially, this mode of storytelling can underpin a politics whereby those in power represent themselves as always having been there.[27]

Second, these origin chronotopes are also poorly equipped to explain the importance of transformation and change. As Çiğdem Kafescioğlu has noted, even "Ottoman" Eyüp was always a "palimpsest of additions, alterations, restorations, and reconstructions."[28] Precisely because this mode of storytelling depends on "pure" essences threatened by transformation, we should look for alternative forms of building stories. Indeed, Eyüp provides a remarkable opportunity to consider how change and continuity can be co-present.

The chronotope of origins is one of many possible shapes for a building story. This book traces instead a chronotope of conjunctions. My invocation of "placing" Islam is not designed to offer a single interpretive framework for understanding the geographies of Islam. Rather, and in the spirit of Shahzad Bashir's recent critique of "Islamic history," *Placing Islam* seeks to provide an opportunity for "expand[ing] the interpretive possibilities" both within and beyond Islamic studies.[29] Emerging out of geography's core conceptual debates, this book also seeks to expand an interdisciplinary conversation between geographers and a range of scholarship on

Islam. Its conceptual intervention—focusing on place as multiple—is less a radical shift in approach and more a reworking of three long-standing debates.

## PLACE AND GEOGRAPHIES OF CONNECTION

One central challenge for scholars of Islam has been negotiating the relationship between a "universal" Islam and its "local" contexts and practices. There is a clear throughline from Dale Eickelman's call for a "middle ground" between village locales and "the Islam of all times and places"[30] and Talal Asad's conceptualization of Islam as a "discursive tradition"[31] to Shahab Ahmed's recent call to focus on "the local Muslim's idea and perception of being a member of the diverse and differentiated universal ummah of Islam [because] local islams conceive (even if differently) of universal Islam and of themselves by reference to it."[32]

Scholars have taken up the challenge of negotiating between the local and the universal in a variety of ways. Working both archivally and ethnographically, some have followed the routes and networks through which Muslims move.[33] Others have examined how different Muslims imagine their worlds, helping us understand that the *ummah* (communities of believers) is a flexible and contingent geography.[34] Another approach reminds us that the religious significance of ostensibly local sites and spaces depends upon relationships to elsewhere.[35] Finally, others have offered the "ecumene" as an alternative to concepts like "civilization" and "community," arguing that it can "[represent] the overlapping . . . dimensions of a potentially global, cohesive nexus."[36]

Despite the richness of this scholarship and the spatial vocabulary that informs much of it, this scholarship often begins with a definition of *what* Islam is rather than *where* it is. As Samuli Schielke and Georg Stauth argue, however, formulations of "discursive traditions" can efface local specificity because they primarily highlight elements that are able to travel between different sites. They offer "locality" as an alternative framework for understanding "Islam [as] only one of the many parameters that are important when people relate to cities, villages, landscapes, and the place of the sacred and saintly within them."[37] However, even terms like "local" and "location" tend to take for granted an image of space as a grid "within which objects are located and events occur."[38] Despite these terms' analytical richness, the close etymological linkage between "locality," "local," and "location" can lead us back to the familiar oppositions between local/global and particular/universal. I build upon this work but argue that we need a term that captures both these deeply sedimented and complex relationships between people and specific locales and the engaged universals that move across and between localities and cultures.[39] One such concept is *place*.[40]

Alongside debates about the relative merits of "local" and "universal" Islam, a second debate has turned on the relative emphasis on what is "inside" or "outside" Islam. This debate has taken many forms. For example, scholars once told "arrival stories" about Islam, focusing on how the worlds of Islam—typically assumed to be traditional, unchanging, static, and rooted—were transformed by the arrival of capitalism, Westernization, and modernization from "outside." Challenging the idea that Islam was only transformed by "outside" processes, Asad insisted instead on the historically dynamic nature of Islam as a discursive tradition, calling us to begin with the "instituted practice[s] (set in a particular context, and having a particular history) in which Muslims are inducted *as* Muslims."[41]

These scholars thus provide a way of understanding change within traditions not as the result of an "outside" acting upon Islam but as the result of reasoned decisions and deliberation within the tradition of Islam.[42] In the process, this scholarship has also undercut the assumption that modernness is essentially "Western." By looking at the "daily enmeshments" of Islam and everyday life, scholars have helped us think about the role that "comparison, boundaries between groups, relations of power, identity, similitude, and difference" play in defining one's sense of being Muslim.[43]

Recently, however, scholars have refined these discussions of "inside" and "outside" in two linked ways. First, recent scholarship has critically engaged with the framework of "self-cultivation" because it can overemphasize the coherence of "inside" and "outside" in the first place. Instead, scholars have examined how practices and communities can exist within overlapping and sometimes ambivalent networks of signification,[44] how dreams and miracles create other dimensions of religiosity,[45] and how urban landscapes are authenticated and experienced.[46]

Second, *where* is "inside" and "outside"? Geographers have also been especially attentive to the projects of boundary making that create "inside" and "outside" in the first place.[47] By focusing on the contingency of these boundaries—how they are made, transformed, and policed—they demonstrate the historicity of categories like the religious and the secular and their distinctive *geographies*.[48] Such approaches help us understand how geographies and religious identities come to be defined in mutually constitutive but contingent ways.[49]

Mobilizations of "inside" and "outside" tend to assume a particular kind of spatiality, in which space is imagined to be a container within which a tradition exists. These containers can be many sizes, ranging from the "local" to the "national" to the "civilizational." Left unexamined is the idea that being "in space" is the only possible way of imagining space and place.[50]

*Placing Islam* provides one alternative by shifting metaphors from "space-as-container" to "places-of-connection," where places are defined by the nature of their connections and relationships.[51] To share a place involves sharing the "connection[s] . . . established between two elements," where those elements can be people, objects, histories, or other places.[52] Thinking in terms of places-of-connection serves not as a substitute for space-as-container but as a vital complement. When we imagine locations as existing in space—a room inside a house, for example, or a building in a neighborhood—mapping inside and outside largely consists of identifying walls and boundaries. Proximity is primarily defined in physical terms. When we begin with place-of-connection, by contrast, we begin by considering different kinds of connection.[53]

Extending Enseng Ho's phrasing, places help to give "representational shape" to a given tradition.[54] Being part of a tradition—and a place—thus involves more than simply existing within a given space and requires cultivating relations that mutually define traditions, communities, and the places where they emerge. Both traditions and places are always connected elsewhere, and their geographies do not trace neatly onto the map. This approach complements recent conceptualizations of the "Islamic ecumene."[55] Similarly, it builds on recent critiques of "thinking about Islam [and] hajj . . . as things or objects" simply managed or instrumentalized, instead drawing our attention to the simultaneously embodied and imagined relations that define geographies of pilgrimage.[56]

The third and final debate upon which I build involves the places of sacredness. In addition to the debate's extensive tradition within the discipline of geography,[57] scholars in anthropology, religious studies, and sociology, among other fields, have also been deeply invested in these questions.[58] In parallel with scholarship on material religion, geographers have also explored how the meanings of landscapes, spaces, and places are not static representations but instead emergent, in flux, and assembled through a range of human and nonhuman practices.[59] Across much of this scholarship, metaphors of "networks" and "webs" help geographers capture the relational and dynamic dimensions of religion.[60]

In addition to its interest in networks, recent geographical scholarship has been especially interested in the concept of the "postsecular." At its best, this approach asks us not to take the "religious" and "secular" as given and stable categories but instead to examine "the maintenance, contestations, and meanings attributed to these divisions" in the first place.[61] However, I find Veronica della Dora's discussion of the "infrasecular" a more useful concept, a paradigm "able to capture the complexity of multi-layered coexistences and materialities [and] able to bring to light 'the stuff in-between.'"[62]

Geographers, however, should deepen their engagement with scholarship on the materiality of Islam.[63] In many ways, this disciplinary divide also reproduces a geographical divide. As Amy Mills and Banu Gökarıksel have noted, geographical scholarship on Islam and Muslim life has tended to focus on Muslim-minority contexts,[64] with the notable exception of scholarship on Muslim urbanism and Islamic cities.[65]

*Building stories* and their geographies of connection provide one framework for expanding an interdisciplinary conversation between geography and other disciplinary traditions. Attentiveness to language, cultural practice, and all the other hallmarks of humanistic scholarship challenge geographers—and not just geographers of religion—to broaden the intellectual worlds within which they work. Similarly, although concepts of space, place, and landscape have a long history outside geography, I see new opportunities for humanistic scholarship to think differently about the implicit geographies that underpin their work. *Placing Islam* offers one model for building these linkages in a new way.

## EYÜP: BEYOND THE CONTAINERS OF ISLAM, ISTANBUL, AND TURKEY

In both academic and popular conversation, the Republic of Turkey is usually considered through the lenses of religion and secularism. There are good reasons for this. Particularly in the first two decades following the establishment of the Republic of Turkey in 1923, state authorities sought to materialize a specific vision of secular modernity. This project was most obvious in the new capital of Ankara, in new urban centers in provincial cities, and in Istanbul districts like Taksim.[66] When many of these areas were "Islamized" beginning in the 1990s, their transformation precipitated fierce debates.[67] Over the past two decades, the fault lines over Islam have been transformed. While a debate between "Islamist" and "secular" positions still matters, we have also come to see growing struggles between different self-identified Muslim groups, most notably the struggle between the movement associated with Fethullah Gülen and communities affiliated with the current government.

These debates—while urgent and important—look different when considered from an "out-of-the-way" place. Eyüp was imaginatively and physically distant from the centers of secular spectacle, but it did not remain unchanged. Rather than assume that Eyüp's importance is somehow fixed and frozen in time, *Placing Islam* opens a way of understanding the changing, overlapping relationships that tie Eyüp to the world beyond in multiple ways. In doing so, it departs from three perspectives that underpin scholarship on Islam in Istanbul specifically and Turkey more generally.

First, the book reconsiders a frame that defines Istanbul's differences in terms of its specific districts. For anyone familiar with Istanbul, this may seem counterintuitive. After all, Istanbul's urban geography correlates ethnic, cultural, economic, political, and religious difference with a mental map of the city's districts: rich ones, poor ones, cosmopolitan ones, insular ones, traditional ones, modern ones, secular ones. This mental map helps us see how social difference can be spatialized. At their best, writers who mobilize this trope help us to imagine the mosaic of Istanbul's stories, ways of life, social norms, and imaginaries of the past and future.[68] They push us to think about the kinds of mobility and accessibility that shape who can move through the city, and why and how they do so.

But this frame can also flatten our sense of the city's differences, reducing them to a mere function of geography. Fatih is conservative because it is Fatih, Kadıköy is liberal because it is Kadıköy, Eyüp is religious because it is Eyüp, and so on. As a result, we spend relatively less time engaging with the complex ways that people experience these districts. Moreover, we miss the multifaceted means through which those meanings are transmitted over time and place. *Placing Islam* attends both to powerful continuities and moments when Eyüp's meaning has been reconfigured. Emphasizing these contingent continuities seriously challenges claims to authority based on an unchanged Islam.

The second frame I reconfigure is that of Istanbul as a "Muslim" city. While relatively rare within academic writing, characterizations of Istanbul as a Muslim or Islamic city tend to recur throughout the Turkish-language and English-language popular press. These stories take multiple forms but often conflate two observations. First, they link the visual prominence of mosques throughout Istanbul and its historic peninsula with an assumption that Islam is an ideology or belief system. The (hyper)visibility of some buildings obscures how people come to learn about and use the city around them. Second, these Muslim city stories tend to place an essential event, person, or landmark at the center of their narrative and then use that "core truth" as the reference against which the present is defined. This rhetorical move erases how geographies are made.

My critique of this frame is not designed to place another narrative at the city's center (e.g., Istanbul is "really" a Greek city or a Christian city). It is similarly incorrect to represent cities as essentially modern, capitalist, nationalist, or any other -ist. Rather than locate an unchanging essence at the core of a city, we ought to be asking how a given city—its diversity, built environments, economies, and other attributes—provides possibilities, opportunities, and challenges for residents and visitors to develop a sense of being Muslim.

Accordingly, Istanbul is a Muslim city for many and sometimes contradictory reasons: because people who live in the city develop a sense of themselves as Muslim in relation to sites ranging from its spectacular mosques to their intimate, domestic environments; because authorities, experts, and academics draw distinctions between what is Muslim or Islamic and what is not; because religious associations and Sufi orders organize their activities by means of the city's landscapes; and because visitors arrive in Istanbul with certain expectations about what Islam is and where it should (and should not) be found.[69] These uneven encounters with the city transform both the built environment and the stories that different groups tell about what Islam is. In turn, these place-based encounters shape how later audiences make sense of being Muslim.

The third frame I reorient is that defined by the linkage between nation, Islam, and politics. The simple version of this story begins with the founding of the Republic of Turkey in 1923. Leaders of this new nation established their authority through linked projects of secularization and modernization that helped to demarcate the secular modern from a religious, traditional past. However, scholars have complicated this story over the past three decades.[70] They have shown that the establishment of Turkey in 1923 was not a break from the Ottoman past but in fact was made possible by powerful lived continuities.[71] They have demonstrated that being Muslim and being modern were not mutually exclusive choices but often interwoven in myriad ways.[72] They have examined how the making of the "secular" actually involved the redefinition, incorporation, and institutionalization of Islam.[73] They have challenged static oppositions of state/society and center/periphery and instead pushed us to consider more complicated topographies and temporalities of experience and identity.[74] Finally, they have provided careful analyses of the architecture and spatial politics of Islam.[75]

Yet despite these careful analyses of religion in contemporary Turkey, much of this scholarship depends explicitly or implicitly on the "nation" to frame its analysis. Although these scholars help us understand the historical contingency of both the nation and Islam's position with it, they nevertheless privilege the nation as the geography that matters. There are good reasons that "Turkish" Islam continues to an object of study, but in assuming that "Turkish" Islam necessarily maps onto the territory of "Turkey," we miss other forms of geography. Thinking in terms of place provides one approach for understanding the forms of imagining, making, and maintaining geographies that exceed or otherwise elude the nation.

Thinking in terms of place provides a way to analyze Islam without assuming that all discussions of Islam are necessarily about "official" politics. While recent scholarship has done much to shift our attention from the "nation" to the uneven terrains of the vernacular, the local, and the everyday, much of this scholarship continues to emphasize how practices of Islam are (or are not) linked to the politics of state institutions. As a result, nuances in how people's political subjectivity and sense of themselves as Muslims are either flattened or assumed. Beginning from the question of place—and not Islam or politics—becomes one opportunity to explore how individuals come to understand themselves in geographies that don't necessarily sit neatly within the containers of national politics or a global Muslim solidarity.

## STUDYING PLACE MAKING

*Placing Islam* has elements of both ethnography and history, although it is not precisely a work of either.[76] It draws on methods of reading the landscape and archival fieldwork, but the book's core arguments are shaped by participant observation carried out between August 2011 and September 2013, when I lived full-time in Istanbul. I would visit Eyüp several days a week, traveling by a combination of ferry, bus, and foot from my home in Üsküdar to the district. Much of my time was spent at the *sıbyan mektebi* (primary school) described in the preface. Affiliated with the Association for the Dissemination of Knowledge (İlim Yayma Cemiyeti), it hosted a variety of free events, including courses in reciting the Qur'an, instruction in Arabic, classes for learning to read Ottoman Turkish, instruction in playing the *ney*, and public lectures, among other events. The school was a diverse place, visited by a mixture of the young and the elderly, some as families and others as individuals. Many of the residents lived nearby, although few identified as "Eyüplü."

In addition, I would regularly attend classes in reading Ottoman Turkish offered at the nearby Language and Literature Association (Dil ve Edebiyat Derneği). In contrast to the *sıbyan mektebi*, this latter location drew a more educated audience, who often lived in districts other than Eyüp. The relationships that emerged through these iterative, everyday activities helped me understand Eyüp's religious identity not simply through the lens of a particular religious community but as a texture of urban life. They also provided contexts to negotiate my relationship to the people, histories, expectations, and assumptions that defined Eyüp.[77]

My gender, social class, educational background, and citizenship status all shaped the questions I felt able to ask and the answers I received. For example, being male made it easier for me to wander through various public spaces. At the same time, my gender also shaped expectations for how, when, and where I was able to interact with friends, acquaintances, and interlocutors in Eyüp and beyond. The fact that I was able to live in Turkey without any apparent work other than research set me apart from many of the people I interacted with daily in Eyüp. My association with universities in the United States and Turkey as well as the "proper" character of my Turkish marked me as a kind of "educated" body. It also meant that the people I was most comfortable interacting with spoke similarly "educated" forms of Turkish, relatively unmarked by regional accents or slang. My American citizenship was—for some—a marker of my fundamental difference, a reminder that however much time I spent in Eyüp I would always be an outsider.

Although this project is deeply grounded in Eyüp, its sites of research are not limited to Eyüp. After first learning about Eyüp in Orhan Pamuk's memoir, my next encounter with Eyüp came in the form of conference proceedings published by the Eyüp Municipality that had passed into the holdings of the UCLA Library. I looked for Eyüp in periodical collections housed at the Atatürk Library near Taksim Square, in municipal correspondence at the Prime Minister's Ottoman Archives, in books stored at the National Library in Ankara, and in the papers of the Council for the Preservation of Antiquities.[78] After I finished my primary fieldwork in 2013, I continued to benefit from the digitized collections hosted by SALT Research, the Center for Islamic Studies (İslam Araştırmaları Merkezi, or İSAM), Şehir University, and Hathitrust. I have also benefited from the Islam Encyclopedia (*İslam Ansiklopedisi*), published by the Foundation of the Turkish Ministry of Religious Affairs.

Extending over a decade of research in and beyond Istanbul, this project links "side-glancing with settling in: taking time to learn about the fullness of what was going on in particular times and places, not just the fragments surfaced among search results."[79] Yet in turning to these archives, I remain acutely aware of their absences and blind spots; in particular, the overwhelming majority of my primary and secondary sources were written by men. The place of Islam that emerges through my research is only one of many multiples. That there are other ways to study place and map a cultural geography of Islam should be taken in the spirit suggested by Taymiya Zaman's recent observation: our fields of research and our sites of writing are "animated by registers of truth we have yet to consider."[80]

## BOOK OVERVIEW

While places of Islam—like places more generally—are made through a range of practices, I organize this book in relation to two practices that are especially important to twentieth-century Eyüp: storytelling and building. Each section begins with a short conceptual introduction. Before turning to those two practices, however, I provide a short historical introduction to Eyüp to furnish readers less familiar with Istanbul and its histories a basic orientation. Its citations also offer a point of departure for those interested in further reading.

After that orientation I begin part 1 with the story at the center of Eyüp, that of Halid bin Zeyd, Companion (*sahabe*) of the Prophet Muhammad.[81] The chapter juxtaposes three moments that his story has been told, moving from the 1920s to the 1950s to the 2010s. As I explain, there are powerful continuities in how this Companion's story has been told, but there are also small, important shifts. Contextualizing the practice of storying the *sahabe* shows how multiple social, political, and urban contexts have shaped the possibility and the urgency of his story.

From there, I shift to a key decade for Eyüp (and Istanbul more generally), the 1950s. A decade when the city was reshaped by far-reaching political, urban, and social shifts, the 1950s were also a key period of generational transition as writers and intellectuals who came of age in the final decades of the Ottoman Empire began to pass away. I trace how new publics were articulated in relation to an old Islam. Paying attention to this geography helps us describe a topography shaped by debates over history, religious practice, cultural memory, and changing urban norms.

I close part 1 with a speculative chapter that examines the place of water. Water is everywhere in Eyüp, delivered and channeled by means of multiple infrastructures. Focusing on this fluid geography, the chapter further develops the book's argument for attending to the ways that places are made through connection. However, water's capacity to be shared and to leak through boundaries of proper Islamic practice also make it an object of contestation. Mixing ethnographic observation and archival sources, the chapter thus helps us consider how many possible traditions continue to coexist in Eyüp.

Part 2 shifts focus from stories and those who tell them to buildings and those who build them. It begins by examining a key period in Eyüp's twentieth-century history: the district's transformations following the 1994 municipal election that brought the Welfare Party to power. Examining projects of public history and restoration, the chapter argues that Eyüp was made Ottoman in a new way during this period. Rather than see this project as a recovery of an untouched essence at Eyüp's core, it shows how the past came to be placed through new connections and associations.

The next chapter analyzes the "rules of place" that operate in and around the Mosque of Eyüp Sultan. Although one might assume the rules of a given building—and especially a mosque—are consistent, coherent, and clearly demarcated, the rules are in fact more flexible than they first appear. Because the mosque complex functions today as both a devotional site and a tourist destination, how people move through the mosque often emerges as an object of debate. Paying attention to these rules, their different but overlapping audiences, and their uneven forms of enforcement shows that the mosque is not a sacred space sealed off from the world around it, but rather a place embedded within broader networks of signification, circulation, and tradition.

I finish part 2 by focusing on the geography of Ramadan, the month of fasting that is one of the most important temporal markers of Muslim life. Eyüp's urban landscape has become one especially popular center for the public observance of Ramadan in contemporary Istanbul. Focusing on a series of debates that played out in 2012 and 2013, I show how the temporal observance of Ramadan also involves contested forms of place making that elevate the position and power of some groups while marginalizing others. In the process, the chapter helps us see how making place for Ramadan can bring bodies and buildings into new relationships.

In the conclusion, I summarize some of the major changes that have played out in Eyüp since 2013, when I moved from Turkey to the United States. I then return to the book's conceptual arguments and close with a brief story about hospitality in a changing city.

# 1

## Sites and Histories

Because this book focuses on Eyüp's twentieth-century transformations, the district's Byzantine and Ottoman histories are largely peripheral. However, knowing some of that history will help readers who are otherwise familiar with the book's reference points. This chapter sketches out the rough outlines of Eyüp's histories and geographies. It also aims to provide readers less familiar with Istanbul with a general picture of the city and highlight scholarship for further reading.

The central neighborhoods of Eyüp discussed in this book are located along or near the Golden Horn.[1] This waterway runs roughly northwest from the Galata Bridge, where it meets the Bosphorus, until it reaches Eyüp. At this point the gulf bends roughly ninety degrees to the northeast. If you were traveling by ferry along the Golden Horn, Eyüp is where the boat would make its final stop.

Here several hills surround the central neighborhoods. The best known—and the closest to the water—rises directly beside the Golden Horn. Many people call it Pierre Loti after the French Orientalist who was reputed to have frequented a café at the top of the hill.[2] Others, however, insist that the hill should be called by a more appropriate Turkish Muslim name. They often use names like Karyağdı Hill, İdris-i Bitlis Hill, or simply Eyüp Sultan Hill.[3] Today the hill's slopes are filled with graves, serving as one of central Istanbul's largest cemeteries.

Were you to stand at the ferry station in Eyüp, face west, and turn slowly from west to south, you would see three prominent ridges, first Rami, then Topçular, and then—looking roughly in the direction of the land walls—Nişancı. Valleys sit between each of those ridges: İslambey Boulevard traces the valley between Pierre Loti and the slopes ascending to Rami, and Düğmeciler is tucked between Rami and Topçular. In the past, many of these small valleys were also streambeds, although those waterways are largely invisible today.

Constantinople was the capital of the Byzantine Empire between 330, when the Emperor Constantine renamed the city of Byzantium after himself, and 1453, when the Ottoman sultan Mehmed II captured the city and declared it his capital.[4]

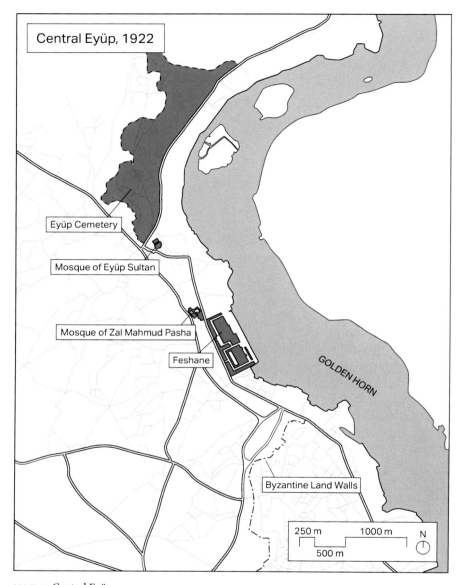

MAP 2. Central Eyüp, 1922.

At one point when Constantinople served as the capital of the Byzantine Empire, this area was known as Cosmidion, after the cult of the Saints Cosmas and Damian based in the area. A small church, to which a monastery was later added, sat somewhere near the center of what is now Eyüp. In addition to that church there were several other churches in the district, and evidence suggests that it was

FIGURE 3. The Mosque of Eyüp Sultan and the Eyüp Ferry Station as seen arriving via the Golden Horn, November 2012.

once a Christian religious center.[5] Because of these saints, the area came to be an important Byzantine healing shrine.[6] The shrine seems to have survived the Latin conquest of the city in 1204, although the last mention of the shrine comes in the early 1400s.[7]

The shrine in Cosmidion was only one node in the broader Byzantine devotional geography. The Hagia Sophia was at the center of that network, but the city was filled with churches, monasteries, and convents both within the city walls and beyond. Hagiographies and itineraries helped to instruct pilgrims and residents alike in how to move through this religious landscape.

In the fourteenth century Constantinople's religious legacy and political symbolism made it an alluring but contested target for the emerging Ottoman Empire. After weathering two sieges in 1394 and 1422, the city was finally captured in 1453 by Ottoman forces commanded by Sultan Mehmed II. Following the city's conquest, Sultan Mehmed II embarked upon an ambitious and sometimes contentious project of rebuilding the city.[8] For some, the city's capture consolidated the political rule of the Ottoman Empire. There were others, however, who wondered why an empire of Islam would establish its capital in one of the world's most important centers of Christendom.[9]

Echoing patterns of encounter that had played out in Anatolia, the Balkans, and the Levant since the first arrival of Muslim armies, many of Constantinople's most important Christian shrines were transformed into places of Islam. Eyüp's transformations thus followed similar events across other mixed confessional landscapes.[10]

Discovery stories were important to many of these transformations; here, it was the miraculous rediscovery of the tomb of Halid bin Zeyd. Details vary among different accounts,[11] but the rough outline of the story is as follows: Upon the Prophet Muhammad's death, Halid bin Zeyd joined one of the Umayyad armies that besieged Constantinople in the second half of the seventh century. He was motivated by a desire to realize a hadith of the Prophet: "Constantinople will absolutely be conquered. The commander who conquers it [will be] a great commander and that army [will be] a great army."[12] He died during the siege, and at some point between the seventh and fifteenth centuries his tomb was lost from view. Nevertheless, there are accounts that suggest that Halid bin Zeyd's tomb sometimes served as a place of pilgrimage for Christians as well, reminding us of the dense devotional geography that characterized this district.

During the siege Sultan Mehmed II tasked his spiritual adviser, the Sufi shaykh Akşemseddin, with discovering the grave of Halid bin Zeyd. Akşemseddin secluded himself and prayed for guidance. In that moment—in what might have been a dream—he saw the place where Halid bin Zeyd had been buried. He indicated the spot and said, "This is the place." After testing his adviser, the sultan commanded that his soldiers dig where the shaykh had indicated. At a depth of two arms' lengths they found a gravestone inscribed in Arabic: *Hadha qabir Abā Ayyūb.* This is the grave of Ebâ Eyyûb.

The sultan ordered the construction of a tomb and mosque complex on the site where the grave had been discovered. The complex became the first mosque built by the Ottomans in the conquered city and marked one of the first steps in making Constantinople into İslambol, a place where Islam was plentiful.[13] However, the complex's location outside the city walls and not in the city's center suggested that there were still unresolved debates over the place of Islam in Constantinople in those first decades of Ottoman rule.[14] As Çiğdem Kafescioğlu has observed, "The site that sanctified Ottoman conquest of and rule over the city remained outside, embodying the tensions between the ruler's centralizing, imperial vision, in which Constantinople represented the natural seat of power, and the ghazi vision, in which the city was no more than a target of conquest and expansion."[15] Regardless, in the decades and centuries that followed, Eyüp became a thriving center for religious, cultural, and social life.[16] Over time, the mosque complex and the neighborhoods that surrounded it came to be known by a variety of names, sometimes Eyüp, sometimes Eyüp Sultan. Eyüp was also referred to by names that stressed its religious importance, including "town of His Excellency Halid" (*belde-i Hazret-i Halid*) and the "sacred district" (*semt-i mukaddes*).

Eyüp became one of the three distinct suburbs that existed in relationship to the city of Istanbul proper: Üsküdar, on the Anatolian shore; Galata, on the northern shore of the Golden Horn where it met the Bosphorus; and Eyüp. As a mark of its importance, Eyüp also came to house a *kadı* court (*kadılık*), whose jurisdiction stretched from the Byzantine land walls to the villages of Çatalca and Silivri in the west.[17]

The district's religious significance was established and communicated in a variety of ways. Beginning with the rule of Sultan Ahmed I (r. 1603–17), new sultans were publicly girded with the Sword of Osman to mark their public ascendance to the throne and signal their commitment to a project of holy war (Tr. *gaza*).[18] From the mosque, the new sultan would return to the palace by land, tracing a dynastic geography that linked Topkapı Palace with Eyüp and the sequence of imperial mosques and tombs in central Istanbul.[19] The mosque complex was also linked to a broader geography of Islam in other ways, such as through the circulation of the woven covering of the Kaaba (*sürre*), which was returned from Mecca, ceremonially draped over the tomb of Halid bin Zeyd, and then paraded through the streets of Istanbul.[20]

Eyüp also became a center for architectural and religious patronage.[21] Key figures within the Ottoman court, including Grand Vizier Sokollu Mehmed Pasha (1505—79),[22] Vizier Zal Mahmud Pasha (d. 1580),[23] the Chief Harem Eunuch Hacı Beşir Ağa (d. 1746),[24] and Sultan Mustafa III's daughter Şah Sultan (1761—1803)[25] all endowed major complexes near the mosque complex of Eyüp Sultan. During the sixteenth century in particular, the immediate environs of the mosque were transformed by new tombs, madrasas, libraries, and graveyards.[26] It was also during this period that Eyüp became one of the most developed cemetery complexes in the city.[27] Eyüp's Sufi lodges were also an important part of the district's religious life.[28]

Yet Eyüp was not simply a religious destination removed from the everyday rhythms of the city. It nurtured a vibrant community of craftspeople, farmers, and shopkeepers and was especially known for its toy makers.[29] Perhaps not surprisingly given its proximity to the fields and pastures west of Istanbul, Eyüp was also known for its dairy products.[30] Many of these fields were also sites for recreation (*mesire alanı*), such as the Fields of Daffodils (Fulya Tarlası) above the valley of Gümüşsuyu. In addition to the daffodils for which the fields were named, roses, hyacinth, narcissus, and tulips were all grown there and sold in a flower market in Eyüp's center.[31]

Meanwhile, members of the Ottoman elite—particularly women within the imperial family—built palaces and mansions along the shoreline of the Golden Horn until the eighteenth century.[32] As the center of elite Ottoman cultural life shifted from the Golden Horn to new waterfront palaces along the Bosphorus in the early nineteenth century, however, many of these palaces and mansions were repurposed as some of the Ottoman Empire's first factories.[33]

The principal Mosque of Eyüp Sultan was completely rebuilt at the end of the eighteenth century. Around the same time, Mihrişah Valide Sultan (1745—1805) endowed the construction of an extensive complex (*külliye*) immediately adjacent to the mosque.[34] That complex included a large tomb, a primary school (*sıbyan mektebi*), a public fountain (*sebil*), and a public kitchen (*imaret*). Beyond the complex's social and religious functions, it also served as one of Istanbul's most notable examples of "Ottoman baroque" architecture.[35]

During the nineteenth century, the expansion of factories like İplikhane and Feshane along the Golden Horn also spurred Eyüp's transformation into a workers' district.[36] Migration at the end of the nineteenth century and the beginning of the twentieth century—particularly following the Ottoman Empire's defeat in the Balkan Wars (1912–13)—led to an influx of Muslim migrants from many parts of the Balkans. Although Eyüp had been important to dynastic ceremonies for centuries, it was only with Sultan Reşad (1844—1918) that a sultan chose to build his imperial mausoleum in Eyüp. Designed by Mimar Kemaleddin, the mausoleum and an adjacent school marked an especially noteworthy example of Ottoman neoclassical style.[37]

Although Eyüp always existed at some distance from the centers of Istanbul's political, social, and economic life, that distance became even greater following the 1923 establishment of the Republic of Turkey. The new government instituted new limits on religious life, closing many tombs, nearly every Sufi lodge, and the system of Islamic education that had existed during the Ottoman Empire.[38] These reforms were experienced unevenly in Eyüp, as they were everywhere else in Turkey.

As Islam was becoming less visible during the 1920s and '30s, however, Eyüp's industrial activities became more visible. Feshane was nationalized, renamed the Defterdar Factory, and became an important textile factory for Sümerbank, the state bank and industrial holding company established in 1933.[39] Meanwhile, much of the shoreline between the Byzantine land walls and Alibeyköy was filled in with a patchwork fabric of warehouses, mills, workshops, and small factories.

The modernization of broader Istanbul produced uneven impacts in Eyüp.[40] For example, a 1943 report submitted to central authorities of the Republican People's Party (CHP) stressed Eyüp's distance from the "modern" resources of Istanbul, something that posed challenges for the local party organization.[41] At the same time, there is also evidence that, because of the density of mosques, madrasas, and tombs in the district, urban planners sought to protect Eyüp from some of the modernization projects that were transforming the rest of the city.[42]

In 1956, Eyüp's relationship to the rest of Istanbul was profoundly reshaped by the building of new major asphalt boulevards that linked the center of Eyüp to the Edirne Highway (Edirne Asfaltı) on the ridge above and to the shore road that paralleled the Golden Horn. The construction of these roads led to the destruction of both the market complex that once stood in front of the Mosque of Eyüp Sultan and much of the nearby Toy Makers' Avenue (Oyuncakçılar Caddesi). These interventions helped to turn the square into an important transportation hub linking central Istanbul and the growing peripheral districts of Alibeyköy and Gaziosmanpaşa.

Like the nearby districts of Balat and Alibeyköy, Eyüp's shoreline was filled in with factories and workshops, particularly those specializing in textile production. This industrial landscape helped to draw new migrants to Eyüp. While some settled in the district's core neighborhoods, others were drawn to the informal housing districts (*gecekondu*) that emerged on the margins of Eyüp's core. Eyüp came to be home to a vibrant social life, with restaurants, cafes, cinemas, and more.[43] Eyüp's mosques and tombs continued to be important devotional sites, but factories' whistles coexisted alongside the call to prayer.

During the 1970s, Eyüp became a site of urban struggle between factions on the left and the right.[44] Its factories, workshops, and even old monuments were inscribed with competing slogans, showing how the materials of the city itself could be enrolled in the decade's political struggles. The coup d'etat of September 12, 1980 brought these conflicts to a violent end. In the coup's aftermath a slew of new changes reshaped Eyüp's relationship to the world once more.

A new system of municipal governance, designed to devolve planning authority to local municipalities, led to the establishment of the Eyüp Municipality in 1984. Meanwhile, the factories and workshops that had once lined the Golden Horn and sustained Eyüp's social and economic life were bulldozed and moved away from the shores of the Golden Horn. Some longtime Eyüp residents left during this decade, following those who had already moved to more developed and cleaner districts of Istanbul in the 1960s and '70s. What would Eyüp be without its factories? It was in this moment of flux that Eyüp's "historic" character became a renewed object of interest and debate. The district became one key site where wider debates about Ottoman heritage, public Islam, and shifting political alliances came to ground. These debates, as you will learn, continue today.

# PART I

# Storytelling (*Rivayet*)

*According to what has been storied* [rivayet olunduğuna göre], *as a result of* Hâzâ kabr-i Ebî Eyyûb [sic] *being written on the stone discussed above, the building of a holy tomb was immediately commenced and upon its completion a holy mosque was appended, and it is still famous as the Mosque of Eyüp.*

—AYVANSARAYÎ HÜSEYIN EFENDI, *THE GARDEN OF THE MOSQUES*

*Because he died during the siege, this warrior was buried in Eyüp. When Sultan Mehmed the Conqueror seized Istanbul in the year 857* hicri *(1453), it is storied* [rivayet olunuyor] *that from among the* ulema *Akşemseddin Efendi saw in a dream that Ebâ Eyyûb el-Ensârî was buried in Eyüp and that a* kitabe *inscribed in Hebrew was found atop his grave.*

—AVRAM GALANTI, *YENI MECMUA*, JULY 13, 1918

IMAGINE THAT YOU WERE TO WELCOME PEOPLE TO YOUR HOME. You might begin by pointing out some preliminaries—the washroom, where they might leave their coats and shoes, where they should sit—but at some point your conversation might turn to stories. There are the stories we tell about where we're from, where we grew up, went to school, found work, and fell in and out of love. These stories are never simply just stories; they are part of the physical texture of one's home. Homes are never simply the material objects that define them. Adapting Divya Tolia-Kelly's phrasing, stories and material cultures "become nodes of connection in a network of people, places, and narration."[1] Through storytelling, people create accounts of "what constitutes a place, of what in a place is possible and what is not possible."[2]

Geographers, like those in many other disciplines, have become increasingly interested in stories and storytelling over the past two decades.[3] Where cultural geographers once drew on concepts of discourse, that concept has largely been eclipsed by that of stories.[4] As Emilie Cameron notes, this shift has been "part of a project to reclaim what [was] lost, overlooked, or otherwise poorly served by geography's [conceptualization of] narrative, power, knowledge, and discourse through the 1990s."[5] Stories, she points out, are never simply abstract texts but "ordering strategies" that are practiced in specific times and places, bound up with "the materials in which they are carried."[6] In telling stories, people bring other people, places, and things into relation. Instead of assuming that these stories simply play out on an already existing "stage," we should consider how stories make those places in the first place.[7]

This interest in storytelling has often overlapped with a careful attention to the texture of things. Things travel, decay, and matter unevenly.[8] Studying storytelling is thus not simply an exercise in looking *at* stories but in working *through* them, considering how their materialities shape the meanings and the places that they come to define.[9] Such insights align with—and have emerged out of—a rich tradition of scholarship on the worlds of Islam. This interest also overlaps with studies of public culture that examine how everyday media like newspapers, penny novels, and postcards create identities.[10]

However, beginning from the traditions of Islam also provides a productive critique of how geographers have thought about stories. This section focuses on the practice of *rivayet*, a term that I translate as "storytelling," although the term's meaning is considerably richer. In its simplest sense, it designates the act of transmitting something heard or witnessed.[11] It also carries a more specific meaning in the context of hadith scholarship, referring to the act of transmitting a hadith from a shaykh (*mervî*) to a student (*râvi*).[12]

My interest in the term was first sparked by its use in accounts of Eyüp's history, but I came to realize the term is also closely linked to the role that Companions like Halid bin Zeyd played in transmitting hadith. Following the term helped me begin to think about the multiple ways that places of Islam could be defined. In English, "story" is often juxtaposed with "history," yet working in Turkish calls our attention to a different range of possibilities for creating relations across time and place. Comparing genres like *rivayet, hikaye, tarih, roman, masal, siyer, efsane, kısas, menkıbe,* and more challenges us to broaden the familiar English-language opposition between history and story.[13]

In pairing *storytelling* and *rivayet*, this book acknowledges a rich and growing body of geographical scholarship on stories but argues that we would benefit by widening the languages, histories, and disciplinary traditions within which we work. Similarly, this book is indebted to careful scholarship on Islam and Islamicate worlds but suggests that we should move beyond seeing textual traditions as simply *representing* the world to examining how they make places of Islam in multiple ways. The chapters that follow take up these conceptual concerns by tracing some of the twentieth-century acts of storytelling that have made Eyüp a place of Islam.

# Storying the *Sahabe*

In its basic contours, the story of Halid bin Zeyd is simple enough.[1] He lived in a modest house in Medina and was fortunate enough to host the Prophet Muhammad in his home upon the Prophet's flight from Mecca to Medina. He was a devoted Companion of the Prophet and participated in all the major battles of early Islam.[2] Halid bin Zeyd joined the Umayyad siege of Constantinople in the late seventh century, where he died and was buried.[3] There are differing accounts of how his grave was venerated by the Byzantines. In many accounts, the grave was protected and even became a devotional site for Constantinople's residents.[4] Others relate that a Byzantine threat to defile his grave was only forestalled by a warning that Christians and their churches living under the rule of Muslims would suffer.[5] Similarly, there are a range of opinions about how well known his grave was and at what point—if at all—it was lost from view.[6] The miraculous discovery of his grave confirmed the religious significance of Constantinople's capture in 1453. Ever since, the story goes, this place has been venerated by Muslims.[7]

Yet stories always require an act of storytelling. Their messages can never fully be separated from the materials and contexts of their telling.[8] In ways large and small, storytellers emphasize some details while obscuring others. They can emphasize their position as storyteller or undercut it, and the choice of which story to tell and which to withhold often depends upon questions of audience, incentive, and goal. To focus on storytelling helps us to consider "the relations between personal experience and expression and its broader context, and upon the interpretation of those relations."[9]

Scholars of medieval Islam and the Ottoman Empire have already shown us that the politics and practices of telling this story varied over time.[10] This chapter focuses instead on three twentieth-century tellings of this story. It does so to develop two linked arguments. First, situating acts of storytelling in their urban and temporal context provides us with a richer sense of the modes of transmission through which people develop a sense of themselves as Muslim.[11] Second, reading stories in this way challenges a tendency to extract certain stories from their context and hold them up as "essential truths." By historicizing the practice of storytelling (and, by extension, place making), we can better understand the work that these stories do and their complexity. Storying the *sahabe* can do many kinds of work.

This is especially important in the context of twentieth-century Turkey, as stories of Islam are often flattened or simply folded into political stories. The political dimensions of these stories matter, but we need a richer account of how Islam is enacted in the world. The Muslim-ness of these stories does not simply follow from the fact that they're told by self-ascribed Muslims; these are stories about Islam because they engage in acts of place making that establish relations between the present and the past that are oriented toward the future.

I begin with Yahya Kemal (Beyatlı)'s essay, "The Eyüp That We Saw in a Dream," originally published in May 1922, when Istanbul was still occupied by a combination of British, French, and Italian forces.[12] I read his essay against a rapidly shifting political, cultural, and urban context involving the collapse of the Ottoman Empire, a shifting geopolitical and religious map, a still uncertain War of Independence in Anatolia, and debates about the precise relationship between national, ethnic, and religious identities.[13] In a moment when past, present, and future had become new objects of public debate, Yahya Kemal's act of storytelling wove popular narratives with the genre of the city letter to define Eyüp as a new "national" place of Islam.

I then turn to the 1950s, focusing on Hacı Cemal Öğüt's two-volume book about Halid bin Zeyd. Blending biography with hadith commentary, Öğüt tells a story of Halid bin Zeyd that focuses much more on a doctrinal religious account that relies on textual commentary and the transmission of hadith. His book centers on the practice of *rivayet*, a term that refers both to the practice of transmitting events across time and place and to the specific act of hadith transmission. Reading Öğüt's discussion against the rapidly changing social and material landscape of 1950s Istanbul helps us to consider the practices, politics, and anxieties that surrounded Islam in a modernizing city. In his account, storying the *sahabe* becomes a way to establish a kind of continuity amid far-reaching urban and demographic change.

I end the chapter in 2013, listening to Muhammad Emin Yıldırım deliver a public lecture to an audience crowded into the Mosque of Eyüp Sultan. Organized by the religious foundation of which he was the head, Yıldırım's lecture calls our attention to the changed context for stories of Islam in Istanbul in the early 2010s. These changes included both a new political relationship between civil society organizations and local municipalities and a reconfigured definition of Islam that linked what Lara Deeb has called "authentication" with an affective register and experience of place.[14] Following these acts of storytelling helps us understand the generative tension that defines Eyüp, between its powerful story linking person and place and the always changing context in which that story has been told.

## CITY LETTERS FROM OCCUPIED ISTANBUL

In May 1922 there might have been many reasons for Istanbul residents to pick up a daily newspaper like *Tevhid-i Efkâr*. The city itself was under occupation by British, French, and Italian forces. The victors of World War I were busy negotiating a postwar settlement. And, above all, there was a war in Anatolia between Turkish forces, led by Mustafa Kemal (Atatürk), and their Greek opponents. But were they to turn past those events, they would have found an essay situated closer to their homes:

> Eyüp, the Turks' city of the dead, lingers verdant like an Islamic garden of paradise on the shore where Europe ends. Do those who enter this city of the city, when they felt lost in a dream of cypress trees and tiles, know that they are truly in a dream? Because Eyüp was a dream that the Turkish army that had come to conquer Istanbul in the spring of the year 857 saw before the walls.[15]

In a city under occupation, one in which many ostensibly certain truths were up for debate, Yahya Kemal's choice to begin his essay with a retelling of the city's conquest thus made a particular claim about Eyüp and Istanbul more generally in a period of rapid change.

Istanbul had been under the joint occupation of British, French, and Italian forces since November 1918.[16] For some, the city's occupation was experienced as a cause for celebration. For others, it was an occasion for despair. Yet regardless of residents' evaluation of the city's occupation, the cultural geographies of the city's everyday life were reconfigured in far-reaching ways.[17] Although the Ottoman Empire still existed as a political entity in 1922 and was ostensibly governed by Sultan Mehmed VI and a succession of cabinets from Istanbul, it was clear to everyone involved that the future of both Istanbul and the empire would bear no resemblance to the empire that entered World War in 1914.

What would the city's complex social, religious, economic, and linguistic landscapes look like in the event of a nationalist victory? What would the city's future look like in the event of a nationalist defeat? In newspapers, the satirical press, and the broader urban culture of 1922, writers, intellectuals, artists, residents, refugees, and visitors alike both critiqued the city's present and imagined many possible futures.[18] The city was home to nationalists, internationalists, liberals, conservatives, refugees, exiles, itinerant Sufis, South Asian migrants, Islamists, Communists, pan-Turkists, and more.[19] Newspapers were published in Ottoman Turkish, French, Greek, Armenian, and English, addressing a multilingual audience across the city. There were fliers pasted to walls, a vibrant magazine trade, bustling coffeehouses and reading rooms. Live music and records connected Istanbul's streets—and above all the bustling center of Beyoğlu—to the world.[20]

Although these debates were especially urgent in 1922, they were by no means new to the city. Istanbul had long been a city located at the intersection of multiple geographical imaginaries, but the nature of their intersection shifted markedly over the course of the nineteenth century. Political, cultural, social, religious, and economic changes helped to place Istanbul in relation to the world in a new way. For example, the articulation of new "traditions" across Europe during this period spurred projects within the Ottoman Empire to define a new kind of relationship between citizen and state.[21] The expansion of communication and transportation networks provided new opportunities to move and reimagine themselves.[22] In this context of migration, transformation, dispossession, and exclusion, the connections that defined the worlds of Islam also shifted in profound ways.[23]

These new translocal forms of imagination and identification intersected with new efforts to claim the past through projects of archaeology, conservation, preservation, and research.[24] This was a period when some sought to redefine an "Ottoman" architectural style.[25] Still others called for a new attitude toward "Ottoman" monuments in Istanbul, often imagined to be distinct from a Byzantine world.[26] Crucially, that engagement with the past was happening as other parts of Istanbul were being modernized and new forms of "modern" urban life were emerging.[27]

Istanbul's relationship with the broader world had been changing over the course of the nineteenth century, but the period between the Second Constitutional Revolution in 1908 and Yahya Kemal's 1922 essay was even more consequential. The Balkan Wars of 1912–13 and the utter devastation of World War I called into question what the empire was, what it meant to be Ottoman, what it meant to be Turkish, and what it meant to be Muslim.[28]

In 1922 Yahya Kemal was one of Istanbul's best-known writers and public intellectuals. He drew inspiration from a range of sources over the course of his life, including everything from French symbolist poetry to Greco-Roman antiquity to a tradition of Divan poetry. Following the Balkan Wars and World War I, however, his views crystallized.[29] Articulating a position in which Turkishness and Islam were tightly woven together, he set out to explain his present as the outcome of a historical struggle. He brought that interest to bear in his essays during the early 1920s. Later in his life he described these essays as an attempt to "to comment [*teşrih*] on nearly all old Istanbul's spiritual districts [*ruhani semtler*]" in order to tell "a story of the making of this land [*tevekkün edişi*] the 'land of the nation' [*vatan toprağı*]."[30] Most of these essays were published in the newspaper *Tevhid-i Efkâr*, which was known for its support of the National Movement led by Mustafa Kemal in Anatolia.[31]

In one sense Yahya Kemal's writing in 1922 built upon the well-established genre of the "city letter," which had emerged during the latter part of the nineteenth century and flourished following the 1908 Constitutional Revolution.[32] These letters usually shared a consistent set of tropes: the writer—almost always male—would visit some section of the city and use a passing observation or encounter to comment on contemporary urban mores.[33] These columns drew upon and helped to reproduce "an imagined cultural geography that located various social groups by emplacing their identities and histories in different areas."[34]

But in a city under Allied occupation, the question of locating oneself took on new importance. Choosing to ground himself in Istanbul's "spiritual districts" in the midst of Istanbul's occupation and war in Anatolia signaled Kemal's politics.[35] He sought to tell a story about Istanbul that both recentered its margins and used Turkishness and Islam to make Istanbul the "land of the nation." Leaving Istanbul's central districts for its margins signaled an attempt to tell a story about Istanbul that linked Turkishness and Islam in a particular way.

Eyüp occupied a curious position in the first decades of the twentieth century. As it had been for centuries, the Mosque of Eyüp Sultan continued to be an important religious pilgrimage destination. It also played a role in court protocol, most notably when the new sultan assumed the throne, as Sultan Reşad (Mehmed V) did in 1909 and Sultan Mehmed VI did in 1918.[36] The district was also an important center for Sufi brotherhoods, most notably the Bahariye Mevlevi Lodge on the shores of the Golden Horn and the Kashgari Tekke on the hill that rose from behind the mosque. But in a city whose cultural, economic, and social center had shifted to the Bosphorus and the newer districts of Beyoğlu and Pera, Eyüp existed on the margins, uneasily positioned between new factories being built on the shoreline and a crumbling religious landscape. Kemal's choice to address his audience from Eyüp was to make a claim about what kind of place Istanbul was and should be: a Turkish Istanbul (Türk İstanbul) with Eyüp at its center.[37]

In "The Eyüp That We Saw in a Dream," Kemal developed this argument in two linked ways. First, he did so rhetorically, structuring the essay as three nested containers of space-time.[38] This was a form of place making that relied on "core truths." Nested one inside the other, these three envelopes placed Eyüp at the new homeland's center; in turn, the nation's essence was rendered simultaneously Turkish and Muslim.

The "outer" envelope began by imagining a visitor lost in contemplation of Eyüp's cypress trees and the tiled Mosque of Eyüp Sultan. This visitor,

> waking from Eyüp's dream of cypress trees and tile, might say, "Where am I?! This place where I'm found recalls a verdant Garden of Paradise. And yet how strange it is that the ruins of the famous palace which the Greek Caesars named 'Blachernae' are here! These walls which stretch in either direction were those Caesars' line of defense. Here, by the name of Ebâ Eyyûb Halid, lies a Companion, one born in Medina, who spoke and conferenced with Muhammad! Where is Medina? Where are the towers of the Byzantine palace? What connection [*münasabet*] is there between them?"[39]

FIGURE 4. Detail of tiles in the Mosque of Eyüp Sultan, September 2019.

That rhetorical question—"What connection is there between them?"—connected Kemal's essay to a fierce debate: to what extent did Istanbul owe its character to the Byzantine past? The final decades of the nineteenth century and the first two decades of the twentieth century were a period in which a growing number of archaeological projects delving into the city's Byzantine past were used as "proof" that the city's foundations were essentially Byzantine.[40] In response, others found a "pure" Ottoman identity in the city's many monuments and architectures.

In the "middle" envelope, Kemal turned to the moment of the city's conquest in 1453, a historical reference with obvious resonance given the city's occupation and the growing strength of nationalist forces led by Mustafa Kemal (Atatürk). However, Kemal made the noteworthy choice to include a second event when he narrated the city's conquest: the doubt of Sultan Mehmed II's grand vizier, Çandarlı Halil Pasha. After this apparent digression, Kemal turned to the central story of Halid bin Zeyd.

Kemal's story echoes most of the other versions that would have been circulating at the time in Istanbul: Upon fleeing Mecca, the Prophet Muhammad arrived in Medina. Reluctant to disappoint the residents of Medina who wished to host him, the Prophet instead let his camel decide. The camel, guided by divine providence, knelt in front of the house of Halid bin Zeyd. Halid bin Zeyd became known as the *mihmandar*, the host of the Prophet Muhammad. Like many other writers, Kemal also emphasized Halid bin Zeyd's participation in the Battle of Badr and then followed him to the walls of Constantinople, where Halid bin Zeyd died in 669 in one of the first Umayyad sieges of the city.

Yet Kemal's essay was not simply repurposing the story of Istanbul's conquest to rally his readers for the support of the nationalist cause. In making Eyüp the "land of the nation," he also addressed two other debates that were playing out in the city around him. First, what was the proper practice of Islam? And second, what was the relationship between a Muslim identity and other forms of ethnic, linguistic, racial, social, or national association?

As they did in many other contexts around the Muslim world in the early twentieth century, debates about "proper" Islam intersected with global discourses of progress, modernity, and rationality. In that, many writers in the late Ottoman Empire sought to redefine Islam by criticizing what they held to be "traditional" religious institutions and practices such as Sufi orders and tomb visitation.[41]

Even assuming that one was able to agree on a definition of proper Islam, those debates were entangled with fierce arguments about the relationship between a Muslim identity and other possible identities, above all one founded on Turkishness.[42] For some writers and intellectuals, such as Şeyhülislam Musa Kazım Efendi and (Babanzâde) Ahmed Naim, Islam provided a common foundation for community that could and should transcend ethnic, racial, and national difference.[43] Others, however, argued for a political identity grounded first and foremost in Turkishness.[44] For example, writers like Ziya Gökalp and Ahmet Ağaoğlu imagined a world in which Islam continued to matter but ceded precedence to a Turkish exceptionalism.[45]

Kemal's essays in *Tevhid-i Efkâr* thus sparked a critique from Ahmed Naim. In 1922 both men were teachers in the Darülfünun (what would later become Istanbul University), but their religious and political positions often brought them into tension. From Ahmed Naim's perspective, Kemal's choice to write evocative essays about these Istanbul sites of pilgrimage associated with "traditional" or superstitious practices like tomb visitation served to "[spoil] [*tahrif*] the tenets and foundations of Islam."[46] In other words, there was a vigorous debate in the early 1920s about what and where Islam should be. Kemal's celebration of Eyüp and the city's other "spiritual districts" was thus only one of many possibilities.

Read against these two debates, Kemal's decision to highlight the Battle of Badr and the wavering enthusiasm of Çandarlı Halil Pasha in 1453 was noteworthy. The Battle of Badr occurred in 624 between the Prophet Muhammad and a much larger opponent army, castigated by Kemal as "idolators" (*müşrikler*).[47] The "crushing defeat" of the idolators helped to consolidate the Prophet's control over the cities of Medina and Mecca. In the case of Çandarlı Halil Pasha, the grand vizier (*sadrazam*) and his supporters were Muslim as well, but many would be executed soon after the conquest of the city.[48] Kemal's choice to emphasize these two small details thus suggests that his goal was not simply to rally Turkish Muslims against foreign occupation of Istanbul but also to castigate those Muslims in Istanbul deemed insufficiently enthusiastic about the independence movement led by Mustafa Kemal.

After taking his readers to the core of Eyüp's dream, Kemal ended the essay by returning to his present and answering the rhetorical question with which he began: what connection was there between this district and Mecca? Now, having presented his readers with a story that mapped out that connection, Kemal ended with an evocative encounter with the landscape: "I gazed in a trance at the turbaned gravestone of those conquering soldiers beside the Companion Halid; that steadfast stone, which marked the body of an aged soldier, had lost its turban in death but stood lost in thought, as though seeing still the dream of conquest. And isn't Eyüp the extension of that dream, shaped of earth?"[49] Dreams—like stories—are never simply ephemeral and immaterial. Rather, they acquire their force from their linkage to specific material sites. These linkages help to establish a set of connections that link multiple places, from Mecca to Medina to Istanbul, and multiple histories, from the time of the Prophet Muhammad to the occupation of Istanbul.

The years following World War I were an especially tumultuous moment in which phrases like "Islamic unity" and "the Muslim world" came to be defined, mapped, and deployed in new ways. For example, the Khilafat movement in India articulated its political vision for the subcontinent not just in relation to its immediate context but "on behalf of the imagined Muslim world."[50] Powerfully, theirs was a vision of Islam not bound to a specific locale or ethnicity but instead conceived as a form of global solidarity. Yet Kemal's essay, written contemporaneously with that movement, reminds us that there were also imaginaries of Islam could connect the world differently through the materials of places like Eyüp.

Approaching Kemal's essay as an act of place making also challenges the tendency to decontextualize his writings. Removed from their urban context, Kemal's essays seem to stand for a timeless and unchanging "Turkish Istanbul." Rather than take them as general truths about Istanbul, I have offered one way of reading "The Eyüp That We Saw in a Dream" that sees it as one way of making Eyüp a place of Islam, enmeshed with the shifting city and the world beyond. We move now from the 1920s to the 1950s, a shift that helps us see both the continuities in Halid bin Zeyd's story and the changed possibilities and politics of making a place of Islam.

## *RIVAYET* IN A CHANGED CITY

It is the early 1950s. An old man in a young Turkey surveys the traces of Islam left in a rapidly changing Istanbul: mosques, madrasas, tombs, libraries, and fountains sitting awkwardly beside and between new boulevards, apartment buildings, shantytowns, and transformed ways of life. "We don't even know," he writes, "how to recite a Fatiha for our ancestors. We visit some of them, saying only, 'May God have mercy on them.'"[51] That brief passage introduced and framed Hacı Cemal Öğüt's two-volume book, *The Famous Eyyûb Sultan* (*Meşhur Eyyûb Sultan*).[52]

Given the fundamental role of the Fatiha—the opening chapter of the Qur'an and a central part of every ritual prayer—Öğüt's mournful observation critiqued the changed geographies of being Muslim in Istanbul after three decades of urban, political, and cultural change. Where Yahya Kemal storied Eyüp to make a place of Islam in occupied Istanbul, Öğüt's practice of storytelling responded to a new challenge: the erosion of religious knowledge about Eyüp. Though the person at the center of Eyüp—Halid bin Zeyd—remained the same, Öğüt's project established Halid bin Zeyd's importance based not on apocryphal details and popular narratives but in terms of the hadith that this Companion of the Prophet Muhammad had helped to transmit. Written by a differently positioned author, addressing a different audience, mobilizing an alternative set of genres, and published in a radically changed context, *The Famous Eyyûb Sultan* draws our attention to the shifting relationships and institutions within which this place of Islam was embedded.

Three decades after "The Eyüp That We Saw in a Dream," Istanbul was a city transformed, albeit unevenly so. In 1923 the declaration of the Republic of Turkey ushered in a series of far-reaching changes, beginning with the removal of the capital from Istanbul to Ankara. Some of these changes also included the establishment of the Ministry of Religious Affairs; the passage of the Unification of Education Law (1924); the banning of fezzes and turbans in favor of brimmed hats (1925); the closing of all tombs and Sufi lodges, along with the abolishment of the position of tomb attendant (*türbedar*) (1925); the promulgation of a new civil code that mandated marriage in front of a civil official (1926); the substitution of "international" numbers in place of the Arabic ones that had been used (1926); the replacement of Ottoman Turkish's modified Arabic and Persian orthography with a Latin orthography (1928); the banning of titles like efendi, pasha, and bey (1934); and the banning of other forms of religious dress (1934). There was also the abolition of the Caliphate (1924), the closing of the sharia courts (1924), reforms in modes of timekeeping involving new definitions of the weekend and the renaming of the hours and months (1925–26), the removal of the *tuğra* (the sultan's calligraphic seal) from official buildings (1927), the removal of the phrase "The religion of the state is the religion of Islam" from the constitution (1928), and the removal of Arabic and Persian from the educational program (1929).[53]

The consequences of these changes were not a foregone conclusion and played out in uneven ways. Some religious networks were incorporated into reconfigured cultural networks.[54] Other religious networks reorganized themselves in provincial spaces.[55] There were also instances in which religious networks were actively suppressed by the government. But then there were also figures—like Öğüt—who came to operate within the new institutional structure provided by the Ministry of Religious Affairs (Diyanet İşleri Başkanlığı).[56]

Alongside this transformed institutional context for Islam, Istanbul's urban and social fabrics had changed in far-reaching ways. If the city had been neglected between 1923 and the 1930s, a series of planning efforts sought to redefine Istanbul as a "modern" city.[57] With the end of wartime austerity and the expansion of international programs like the International Monetary Fund and the Marshall Plan, the large-scale migration of rural migrants to Turkey's major cities generated new urban problems.[58] Both longtime residents of Istanbul and its new migrants thus encountered a city of patchwork modernity. Major new boulevards redefined the city's contours during the 1950s while new architectural forms—both formal apartment buildings and informal *gecekondu*—created a patchwork urban fabric.[59]

Religious buildings like mosques, madrasas, tombs, libraries, and cemeteries occupied a complicated position in this.[60] On the one hand, the relationship of religious buildings to their surroundings had been changed by the secularizing reforms of the 1920s and 1930s. Access to some of these sites had simply been curtailed; in other instances, such as libraries attached to religious endowments, their collections were often moved and consolidated; and in a handful of instances, religious buildings were closed outright, left to crumble through neglect or entirely repurposed.[61] On the other hand, and despite these reforms, the meanings and uses of some religious buildings continued. These buildings were thus simultaneously out of place in a secularizing nation and embedded in place, sustained by their long-standing social relations. Because of Eyüp's dense network of religious buildings, and especially on account of the presence of Halid bin Zeyd's tomb, the district served as an especially durable marker of Islam in a churning city.[62]

Öğüt was born in 1887 in the village of Alasonya (now known as Elassona, Greece). He moved to Istanbul around the turn of the century, graduating from the Faculty of Law at the Darülfünun in 1913.[63] He worked first as a müezzin in the Pertevniyal Valide Sultan Mosque in the central district of Aksaray before being appointed the mosque's preacher (*vaiz*) in 1915.[64] He would also work for a period in the Mosque of Eyüp Sultan. Following his participation in the War of Independence, he declined to stand as one of Istanbul's parliamentary representatives in the first Republican People's Party governments. Instead, he traveled through parts of the Muslim world to learn how Turkey's transformations were perceived in other Muslim countries. On returning to Turkey he fell into disfavor with state authorities, likely because of his relationship to other religious leaders. Nevertheless, he continued to deliver lectures in public mosques and to private groups in his home.[65] Famously, in December 1950 he joined the first memorial program organized for soldiers from Turkey who had died during the Korean War.[66] He was an active writer, publishing thirteen books on a variety of religious topics.[67]

Although *The Famous Eyyûb Sultan* is not precisely contemporaneous with (Bediuzzaman) Said Nursi's *Epistles of Light* (*Risale-i Nur*), it is useful to read Öğüt's book as a similar project. Like Nursi, Öğüt connected a range of authoritative texts, thus "bridg[ing] differing times and situations [to] shape new senses of community and society."[68] But where Nursi's work was focused primarily on producing a shared social identity and became central to the formation of religious networks organized in relation to his work, Öğüt's book focused on place. Above all, he sought to transform how his audience would encounter Eyüp.

Like Yahya Kemal, Öğüt explained his book was needed because of the ignorance of his audience. Yet where the imagined visitor in Kemal's essay encountered Eyüp as a gap in historical knowledge, Öğüt's book was framed much more explicitly as a response to a lack of knowledge about Islam:

Quite some number of people are encountered who know neither the value and honor of Hazreti Halid (R.A.A.) nor his elevated position. We encounter such ignorant and undeserving [*nasipsiz*] people—both those from out of town and locals from the area—that are found doing such things that suit neither our national manners nor our traditions. There's no feeling of respect nor of affection in these poor people's hearts for these great individuals. We've seen with our own eyes that even foreign travelers visit Ebu Eyyûb's tomb, when they visit Istanbul and while touring the Turks' national works that they've seen on their maps. But the surprising fact is that while foreigners, showing their respect according to their own manners and feelings, take off their hats and hold them in their hands before this great figure while they visit the tomb, some of our ignorant and careless Muslims stroll through the tomb, their hands clasped behind their backs and whistling while they pass through, or sing songs and ditties, cigarette dangling from their lips, swinging a chain around and around, while they come and go.[69]

*The Famous Eyyûb Sultan* sought to transform how its readers would interact with this place. Öğüt did so by providing his readers with an authorizing and authoritative discourse. This marks the first significant difference between Kemal's essay and Öğüt's two volumes. Kemal drew upon the genre of the "city letter," even as he reworked its site and perspective to ground a nationalist politics. In contrast, Öğüt's work emerged out of a genre of hadith writing and commentary. This difference mattered not only to the way that each writer established the authority of his storytelling but also to the ways that time and the city were enmeshed with Eyüp.

Öğüt's use of *rivayet* makes this clear. On the one hand, *rivayet* can carry multiple meanings, including story, account, rumor, tale, and report. Although some of these meanings seem to be in tension (in English, for example, a report and a rumor make very different claims about truth and verifiability), they share something common: an emphasis on *transmission*. Something becomes a *rivayet* when it is transmitted from person to person, from place to place, or across time.

As Öğüt observed, the act of transmission raises a problem: transmission can go awry. Öğüt began his text by acknowledging his sources but critiquing some for "never having shown their source," thus resulting in a work based on "opinion and belief."[70] In contrast, Öğüt emphasized his practice of documenting all sources to establish a firm foundation for his work. Part of his critical practice involved gathering as many "documented" (*mevsuk*, Ar. *mawṯūq*) sources as possible.[71] At the same time, Öğüt also stressed that one's relationship to these sources was interrelated with one's devotional identity. After evaluating the various documents that established the truth of how Halid bin Zeyd's tomb was discovered, he declared that a "sincere believer and true Muslim" would not object to the tomb's location; only a "restless and spiritually ill" person would not understand the truth of his proof.[72]

Öğüt also emphasized how his project about Halid bin Zeyd was distinct from other genres of history circulating in the 1950s. Part of this difference stemmed from his subject matter. "In truth," he wrote, "I know that writing the biography [*tercüme-i hal*] of His Excellency the Mihmandar [Halid bin Zeyd] does not resemble writing an ordinary history book [*alel'ade bir tarih kitabı*]."[73] Elsewhere, he asked his readers to make a similar distinction. Just as one shouldn't visit a grave casually, he wrote, one should also avoid reading this book like a "story [or] novel."[74] Both writing and reading the book were embodied projects of self-cultivation, acts of "using and being used by language . . . expressing and attending to bodily movement and sound."[75] Öğüt hoped that his book would help his readers live more attentively and carefully as Muslims.[76]

*Rivayet* were thus both a source and an epistemological problem for Öğüt, something to be gathered but evaluated with care. However, Öğüt's use of *rivayet* also functioned in a second, linked register that highlighted a tradition of hadith transmission. Hadith refer to the sayings and deeds of the Prophet Muhammad. For many Muslims, hadith form a key part of the tradition through which they define what it means to be Muslim. Crucially, hadith often require interpretation and evaluation, practices that have varied widely over time and space.[77] The act of *rivayet* designates the transmission of hadith from a teacher to student.[78]

The Companions of the Prophet are inextricable from the body of hadith because they helped to transmit these hadith across place and time. Evaluations of the strengths and weaknesses of specific hadith can hinge upon the veracity of the Companion who first transmitted the report. Not surprisingly, Öğüt stressed Halid bin Zeyd's piety, humility, and commitment to Islam.

He collected these hadith and transmitted them to his readers to address a gap that he observed in the Mosque of Eyüp Sultan. Despite the presence of the building, and the number of people who prayed there and visited the tomb, people "did not know Halid bin Zeyd's biography nor were his hadith recited [*hadisi şerif okunmuyor ve tercümei halini . . . bilmiyormuş*]."[79] Referencing examples of several Companions buried in Cairo whose hadith were recited or taught in the mosques linked to them, he called for something similar to take place with Halid bin Zeyd in the Mosque of Eyüp Sultan. Two points follow from Öğüt's account.

First, his definition of Islam was embedded in a system of authoritative and authorizing discourses, but it was only one of many possible definitions. His passing reference to the other ways that people visited this place of Islam reminds us that storytelling helps to "[create] an account of what constitutes a place, of what in a place is possible and what is not possible."[80] Second, Öğüt's imagined geography of Islam was not confined to the territory of Turkey. Here and elsewhere, Öğüt's book stressed a history of connection, tradition, and transmission that linked Eyüp to Mecca, Medina, Cairo, Damascus, and elsewhere. Although he made no direct reference to the projects of secularization and nationalization that defined the 1920s, '30s, and '40s, we should read Öğüt's book as an alternative way of enacting a shared geography of Islam through language, genre, and practices of citation. Although Öğüt's book does not precisely follow the translation of the hadith compendium *Sahih al-Bukhari* and its commentary in twentieth-century Pakistan, *The Famous Eyyûb Sultan* also demonstrates how "connectedness across time and space was so vital to the function of the text and the authority of its exegetes that . . . temporal and spatial difference appeared to collapse."[81]

Even as Öğüt's book helped to link Istanbul to a wider geography of Islam, this geography was deeply woven into Eyüp. In an oft-repeated phrase, he described Halid bin Zeyd as "[this] land's [*memleket*] first mujahid, Istanbul's spiritual conqueror [*ma'nen fatihi*], and, in the afterlife, this world's standard-bearer [*diyarın alemdarı*]."[82] Öğüt's use of *memleket*, in contrast to more abstract terms like province (*il*) or city (*şehir*), emphasized that the geography of this relation was one where Halid bin Zeyd and this place were bound by relations of obligation, history, affection, and hospitality. Belonging to this place, in other words, was not simply about a physical location but about the imagined, devotional, and affective relations that connected people to places and vice versa.

Elsewhere, Joel Blecher has observed how "Deobandi scholars spoke to their present by maintaining a connectedness with a conception of the Islamic past."[83] In some respects, Öğüt's *The Famous Eyyûb Sultan* is similar: through a practice of *rivayet*, he sought to connect his readers with a tradition of Islam. At the same time, Blecher's observation might be extended. What was at stake in Öğüt's project was an effort to connect his readers with both a *when* of Islam and a *where* of Islam. This place of Islam was enacted through Halid bin Zeyd, beloved Companion of the Prophet Muhammad. While there were overlaps between Yahya Kemal's "The Eyüp That We Saw in a Dream" and Öğüt's history, Öğüt established his authority and the truth of Eyüp in a very different way. There are no references to politics, the government, or the contested legacies of Turkey's secularizing reforms in *The Famous Eyyûb Sultan*, but that absence is also, in its own way, a choice. Read against the backdrop of the 1950s, Öğüt's book asks us to consider the endurance of religious networks woven in and through Istanbul. Alongside important discussions of figures like Said Nursi, Necip Fazıl Kısakürek, or Samiha Ayverdi, Öğüt offers one more point of entry into these multiple worlds of Islam.[84]

## TELLING *SIYER*: NEW GRAMMARS
## FOR CIVIL SOCIETY

One evening in early June 2013, Muhammed Emin Yıldırım stepped into the preacher's pulpit (*vaiz kursu*) in the Mosque of Eyüp Sultan. He was not the imam of the mosque, a position that would have made him an employee of Diyanet, the Ministry of Religious Affairs. He was instead the director of the Siyer Foundation (Siyer Vakfı), a religiously oriented civil society organization.[85] He shifted his robe around his shoulders, looked out at the crowd of men who filled the congregational space under the dome, and began to speak in measured, elegant Turkish:

> I knew that I was going to have difficulty speaking today, because I knew that I was going to be in the presence [*huzur*] of this exalted *sahabe*, Halid bin Zeyd Ebû Eyyûb

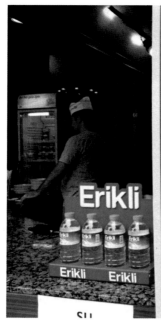

FIGURE 5. Flyer advertising a lecture sponsored by the Siyer Foundation, June 2013.

el-Ensârî. And I know that that Ebû Eyyûb el-Ensari who—on the path of Allah, in the name of Allah—carried the banner of the Divine Word of Allah [*Allah yolunda, Allah namına i'lâ-yi kelimetullah sancağını getiren*] from Medina to here is here among us tonight, and I'm fearful because of that.[86] My hands shake, my tongue is tied. *Rabbim!* Let my plea be this: let my *nefis* not be mixed with my words![87] Let what is told be one with those who listen.[88]

On the one hand, Yıldırım's opening address echoed a familiar way of telling Halid bin Zeyd's story, using his life and person to draw a connection between Medina and Eyüp. On the other hand, however, both the event itself and small details in Yıldırım's lecture speak to the changed possibilities for making a place of Islam in contemporary Istanbul. In other words, even if the story of the *sahabe* was largely unchanged in its core details, its context—and thus the possibilities for creating a place of Islam—has continued to shift.

Beginning in the late 1990s, a set of cultural, economic, political, and religious changes reshaped the fields within which Islam was practiced. First was the emergence of new cultural markets, productions, and opportunities, something that involved new television channels, retail environments, and forms of consumption.[89] Second, following the military intervention of 1997, religion was redefined less as a matter of state control and more as a matter of individual belief. This redefinition was linked to the emergence of new religious actors who took to describing their field of action not as the "state" but rather as "civil society."[90] At the same time, the Justice and Development Party's consolidation of power following their electoral victory in 2002 signaled not so much the withdrawal of state power as a transformed modality, one in which the state ostensibly reflected rather than dictated how its citizens understood Islam. Instead of "controlling" religion, government policy and judicial decisions have instead highlighted its "freeing."[91] At the same time, these debates over Islam in Turkey are not simply constituted in relation to "secular" actors or the "state" but also in relation to a set of "internal" traditions as well.[92]

The Siyer Foundation was established in 2010 with the declared goal of bringing people into a closer relationship with the Prophet Muhammad and thus "furnishing the possibility of living with Him [*sas*] once more, no matter how great the difference in time and place extends."[93] While many religiously oriented organizations in Turkey today are connected to specific religious communities, the Siyer Foundation insists that their work stands apart from any other "community, party, group, or gathering" (*cemaat, hizb, grub, fırka*).[94] However, they do form one part of a emergent landscape that has sought to instill in their audiences more "authentic" forms of Islamic knowledge and practice. Putting the political and economic relationships woven into these groups to one side, many of these groups are organized around self-conscious and reflexive debates about the sources and methods for defining correct Islam. In Turkey today these groups thus participate in the formation of an "enchanted modern" linked to specific sites, texts, and social relationships.[95]

The foundation's name, *siyer* (derived from Ar., *sirah*, pl. *siyâr*), refers to a distinct genre in which stories of the prophets and other exemplary figures are used to communicate a manner of conduct.[96] The goal of these stories is to help people model their behavior on the Prophet and so perfect their own practice of Islam. In its name, mission, and activities, the Siyer Foundation deploys a particular form of storytelling to refashion the relationship between its audience and their vision of Islam.

Yet the lecture in June 2013 depended on the conjunction of several factors beyond the mission of the Siyer Foundation. The first was the Ministry of Religious Affairs, which was responsible for the administration and use of the mosque. Yıldırım's lecture would not have been possible without their permission, pointing to the way that the line between religious institutions of the "state" and institutions of "civil society" has become quite permeable in practice in contemporary Turkey. Indeed, the lecture was introduced by Muammer Ayan, the Eyüp District Müftü (Eyüp İlçe Müftüsü). The second was the Eyüp Municipality, which provided logistical support for hosting the event (for example, helping to erect a portable video monitor in the square outside the mosque). The institutional context for the lecture thus involved much more than the foundation itself; this context was itself a historically specific one, linked to the changing configurations that have come to define a public for Islam in contemporary Turkey. Acts of storytelling help to make places, but their capacity to forge connections also depends upon a set of political, social, and economic relationships.

The lecture in June 2013 was the fifty-second lecture in the Siyer Foundation's project 82 Provinces, 82 Companions (82 Il, 82 Sahabe). The project's title speaks to the decidedly contemporary context for this storytelling. The eighty-two provinces in the project's title refer to the eighty-one provinces that make up Turkey and the province of Cyprus. The nation thus figures as the invisible framework for this story. At the same time, their decision to narrate the history of the nation through the Companions challenges conventional narratives organized around Turkey's 1923 founding and key figures like Mustafa Kemal (Atatürk).[97] Strikingly, however, the Siyer Foundation's project also largely bypasses alternative Ottoman histories deployed in opposition to Republican histories.[98] Using the Companions to tell the stories of Turkey's provinces—and using Halid bin Zeyd to retell Istanbul's story— makes visible alternative connections across time and place that redefine Istanbul from a city of cosmopolitan encounter into one in which claims for belonging are articulated primarily in terms of Islam.[99]

Yıldırım told a story that would have been familiar to anyone with a passing knowledge of Halid bin Zeyd, the Prophet Muhammad, and the history of Eyüp Sultan. In its general contours, his story echoed that of Yahya Kemal and Cemal Öğüt. Similarly, his description of Halid bin Zeyd as an exemplary model of piety for his audience largely paralleled Cemal Öğüt's presentation of Halid bin Zeyd in the 1950s. However, it differed in two important respects.

First, Yıldırım's lecture emphasized an embodied, affective understanding of Islam in ways that were decidedly contemporary. Yıldırım did not simply want his audience to hear his words. Both through his delivery (itself mediated through his own embodied performance) and the content of his lecture, Yıldırım worked to make his audience *feel* the truth of his words. For example, he stressed the embodied physicality of the Companions, who "[taking] only their horse, their *cübbe*, a single sword . . . traveling without crushing any flowers, [crossing] from geography to geography all the way to these lands, [planted] the message of Islam . . . in the hearts of humankind." He also referred repeatedly to the *nefis*—both his own and a more general collective. *Nefis* carries a complex set of meanings, but Yıldırım's use of the term referenced a tradition in which the *nefis* was the desiring, impulsive self that turned away from Allah.[100]

This desiring self was fallible but could be instructed through stories. As Yıldırım evoked his own fallibilities, he argued for the value of reading the stories of the Companions: "Whenever I'm bored (we're human) . . . I read the life of a blessed Companion and I tell my self (*diyorum nefsime*), are you a man, look at these men!" His point was precisely that engaging with these stories provided a way for him and his audience to cultivate in themselves a proper practice of

Islam. Halid bin Zeyd's five qualities become the model and goal for Yıldırım's lecture: (1) The blessings in his life (*hayatındaki bereket*); (2) his certainty of purpose (*hedefindeki istikamet*); (3) the affection in his heart (*yüreğindeki muhabbet*); (4) the truth of his knowledge (*ilmindeki selimiyet*); and (5) the continuity of his service (*hizmetindeki devamiyet*).

The second difference involved a subtle but important grammatical shift. Instead of narrating Halid bin Zeyd's life in the simple past tense (*Halid bin Zeyd welcomed the Prophet and then came to Istanbul*), he repeatedly used an unfulfilled conditional (*If Halid bin Zeyd had not come to Istanbul*). This grammatical shift turned the present into the evidence for the past: *If Halid bin Zeyd had not come to Istanbul, none of this would be here; because we are here, Halid bin Zeyd must have come.*

He addressed Halid bin Zeyd directly: "Ey Ebu Eyüp el-Ensari, if you hadn't come what would our state have been? Some of us Zoroastrian, some of us who knows what, some of us Christian, some of us idolators, we would have died bereft of faith [*imandan mahrum olarak ölüp giderdik*]." Implicit in this formulation was the notion that the audience was *not* "bereft of faith"; it was a Muslim audience whose position in both time and place was guaranteed by the truth of Halid bin Zeyd.

This grammatical tense also provided a way for Yıldırım to exhort his audience to be more like Halid bin Zeyd. "Had we been more like him [*Eğer . . . olsaydık*]," he closed the lecture, "we wouldn't find ourselves in the world we now live in, a world of faithless [*imansız*] people." The truth of the story—its connection of past, present, and future in this place—was established by means of a grammatical frame that positioned him and his audience in relation to the world. Making places through acts of storytelling involves not only decisions about what events, places, and people to include but also other grammars that render other connections impossible. Yıldırım's version of Eyüp, one in which his audience took on the responsibility of being a neighbor to and in the presence of Halid bin Zeyd, was a place where his vision of Islam was made real in the world.

With its emphasis on self-cultivation, Yıldırım's story echoed the story work of pietistic groups in places like Lebanon and Egypt.[101] His story could be connected to a much broader religious and legal tradition of thinking about the "inward" self.[102] Significantly, however, Yıldırım's 2013 lecture also stressed that the training of one's *nefis* was also the result of being acted upon.[103] To be in the presence (*huzur*) of Halid bin Zeyd involved both the cultivation of these five exemplary qualities and the positioning of the audience in a specific relation of power and authority. This evening of storytelling became an opportunity through which individuals were asked to imagine themselves in intimate connection through Halid bin Zeyd to the Prophet Muhammad in an Istanbul that could not have been without them. In the process, Yıldırım's lecture reminds us that sharing a place requires a common experience of the links that connect that place to other times, places, and people.

## CONCLUSION

Cities are fashioned from the fabric of stories: stories of life, death, friendship, family, nation, love, loss, growth, change, achievement, failure, arrival, departure, memory, tradition, and more. Some of these stories, like fragile scraps of thread scattered in the wind, barely survive the moment of their telling. Others, however, are woven of more durable things: cloth, paper, stone, even bodies. The stories told about Halid bin Zeyd, Companion of the Prophet Muhammad, are exemplary instances of what I call *building stories* in this book: these are stories that weave personal histories with evaluations of the urban landscape; but they are also material projects, both embedded and embodied in a particular time and place even as they establish connections beyond.

Juxtaposing three tellings of Halid bin Zeyd's story, this chapter has offered three linked contributions. First, it has introduced the importance of the Companions to Muslims and Islamic history more generally and outlined the specific contours of Halid bin Zeyd's story. Second—and as the shift from stories to storytelling aims to emphasize—acts of telling and transmitting stories are forms of place making. Storying Halid bin Zeyd functions as one key mode through which people have made Eyüp a place of Islam.

Yet precisely because this story seems to have an almost mythic force, it is crucial to situate acts of storytelling in their spatial and temporal contexts. While much of Halid bin Zeyd's story has remained strikingly consistent, the practices and politics that guide his story's telling have shifted in important ways. Focusing on storytelling in Occupied Istanbul, modernizing Istanbul, and the Istanbul of the Justice and Development Party helps us attend to powerful continuities while also challenging the idea that Eyüp's meaning exists as a single, stable essence.

Finally, this chapter has sought to explore the productive slippage between a "story" and genres like the city letter, *rivayet*, and *siyer*. If geographers' current interest in "story" emerges out of a critique of concepts like "discourse" and "narrative," this chapter points toward an expanded conceptual vocabulary for storytelling. Although historians of the Ottoman Empire have productively explored questions of genre,[104] this chapter suggests one way of bringing "secular" genres like the city letter into conversation with "religious" traditions like *rivayet* and *siyer*.

Of course, there are multiple forms of storytelling that make place in Istanbul. There are the stories of the city's other Companions and its many other saints. There are stories whose telling has made this city Byzantine, Christian, Armenian, Greek, Jewish, and Roma.[105] There are stories that gender the city, making places dangerous or safe.[106] Alongside these "big" stories there are also smaller, everyday forms of storytelling that weave human life with gardens, animals, festivals, music, food, and more. Today, two stories have become especially important for contemporary Istanbul: Istanbul as an "Ottoman" city and Istanbul as a "Muslim" city. Their telling can help to make the city an open place—indeed, a sheltering *mihmandar*—but more often, the telling of this story can also justify an ethnonationalist politics of closure and exclusion. Following Halid bin Zeyd's story provides one way to consider that tension.

# 3

# New Publics, Old Islam

*Eyüp in the 1950s*

Ahmet Hamdi Tanpınar's *The Time Regulation Institute* begins with Hayri İrdal, the book's narrator, introducing himself with a distinctively urban account of his reading practice:

> Those who are acquainted with me know that I don't have a great interest with these reading and writing things. In fact, everything that I've read—if you take out the Jules Verne and Nick Carter stories I read as a child—consists of works like the stories of Tutiname, 1001 Nights, Abu Ali Sina, along with a few history books where I skipped over all the Arabic and Persian words. In the times that followed, just as I glanced at the children's schoolbooks once in a while while unemployed before the founding of our institute, I read the small, serialized sections and articles in the times when I was required to read the newspapers front to back in the cafes of Edirnekapı and Şehzadebaşı where I would sometimes spend my entire day.[1]

The passage is, of course, a work of fiction, but it asks us to think about the messy urban geographies of reading. Books, magazines, and newspapers were picked up, dropped, forgotten, perused, borrowed, purloined, and encountered in a variety of ways. They cost different amounts of money, a fact that shaped uneven levels of access to them. Far from existing within hermetic containers, various genres existed in conversation with each other, particularly on the pages of Istanbul's newspapers. Pulp detective novels sat alongside classic Persian stories and history lessons. As for how people read these stories, their modes of reading could have ranged from the careful to the inattentive. Hayri İrdal's opening description of himself thus helps us imagine reading and writing as an urban practice. These threaded forms of print culture wove the city together.

During the 1950s, Istanbul and its print cultures were dramatically reconfigured by a set of interrelated political, economic, and social transformations. These transformations helped to spark anxious debates about everything from clothing to gender relations to cultural identity to Westernization and beyond. In many cases these debates were also deeply entangled with discussions about Islam. In the process, this new print culture helped to create overlapping publics whose orientation toward Islam could take many forms.

Scholars have provided us with careful accounts of these debates, but their work has largely taken the "nation" as the operative geographical frame. As a result, they have spent less time analyzing how newspapers, books, encyclopedias, and magazines circulated through and were embedded within the material landscapes of the city. Indeed, even as Istanbul was narrated from sites ranging from Eminönü to Beyazit to Şişli to the Golden Horn to Zeytinburnu to Florya to Kadıköy, the many newspapers, pamphlets, magazine articles, and other forms of print culture only rarely provided a map of the city. This suggests that many of Istanbul's residents— or at least those who wrote, edited, and published these stories—shared a tacit imagined geography of Istanbul that "located various social groups [and religious sites] by emplacing their identities and histories in different areas."[2] How and why did these identities and histories come to be placed in the city? How and why did those forms of emplacement change over time?

Eyüp in the 1950s provides a rich site from which to answer those questions. Examining how a range of writers encountered Eyüp during this decade, this chapter shows how Eyüp was enacted as a place of Islam in a moment of flux and transformation. It follows debates between "popular" and "proper" histories; it traces how authors both grappled with vanishing forms of social life and celebrated new projects of urban transformation; and it highlights how Eyüp was described both as a site for others' practice of Islam and as a crucial site for writers' sense of "our" Islam. In the process, it makes two linked arguments.

First, it argues that 1950s print culture should be read not simply in reference to "global" or "national" questions but also in relation to Istanbul's urban geography. In doing so, this chapter engages directly with Gavin Brockett's argument that during this decade "national identity [in Turkey] came to be incorporated within a preexisting repertoire of popular identities, among the most important of which were those associated with Islam."[3] Despite the richness of Brockett's argument, he tells us relatively little about the *places* in and in relation to which these popular identities were lived, experienced, and defined. Shifting the frame of analysis from the nation to the lived topographies of Istanbul—and its places of Islam—provides one way to continue that project. Focusing on Eyüp helps us better understand how debates about history, heritage, tradition, social identity, urban transformation, tourism, modernization, consumer culture, and Islam were worked out in new ways.

Second, this chapter argues that a focus on urban print culture provides a crucial supplement to Talal Asad's formulation of Islam as a "discursive tradition."[4] In a variety of ways, authors who wrote about Eyüp during the 1950s did so to link themselves and their readers to the past and (often) orient them toward the future.

However, this project of transmission and circulation did not occur in a vacuum. It was entangled with the messy realities of urban life, printed in newspapers that blurred boundaries and genres and circulated in many ways. By foregrounding the urban contexts in, from, and through which Eyüp's importance as a place of Islam was articulated and transmitted, this chapter opens a more nuanced geographic account of Islam.

## URBAN ENCOUNTERS WITH THE PAST
## IN 1950S ISTANBUL

The 1950s were a decade of rapid transformation, especially for Istanbul. During this time political shifts, new cultural economies, and social upheaval radically reconfigured what the city looked like. Although many of these dynamics emerged before the 1950s and many would continue well after 1960, "1950s Istanbul" nevertheless provides a useful frame for making sense of these transformations. Before turning to Eyüp and the ways that authors encountered it as a place of Islam, I highlight four especially important dynamics.

The first involved shifting political dynamics in a variety of venues, ranging from national elections to international alliances to local mayoral races. Between Turkey's establishment in 1923 and the 1946 national election, the country had been governed as a one-party state by the Republican People's Party (Cumhuriyet Halk Partisi, or CHP). In 1946, however, an opposition party—the newly established Democrat Party (Demokrat Parti, or DP)—contested the national election. Following the gradual loosening of legal restrictions on the press and political mobilization between 1946 and 1950, the Democrat Party achieved a resounding electoral victory in the May 1950 national election.[5] Celal Bayar replaced İsmet İnönü as president and Adnan Menderes became prime minister. The Democrat Party would win two more general elections in May 1954 and October 1957 but increasingly faced criticism for economic mismanagement and its authoritarianism. On May 27, 1960, a military coup d'etat resulted in the arrest of President Bayar and Prime Minister Menderes and the eventual promulgation of a new constitution.

These political shifts were closely linked to several reforms to the state's governance of Islam. In the run-up to the May 1950 general election, for example, the CHP established two *imam-hatip* schools in January 1949 for the training of authorized religious personnel,[6] reintroduced religious education into the primary school curriculum, and inaugurated a new Faculty of Theology at Ankara University.[7] In March 1950, the government also officially opened to the public a small number of tombs, ending twenty-five years of closure.[8] Following their May 1950 electoral victory, the DP continued and expanded these changes. In June 1950, for example, the language of the call to prayer (*ezan*) was officially changed back to Arabic from Turkish.[9] The DP also benefited from the support of religious networks like those of Said Nursi; those who supported the May 1960 coup cited this relationship and others like it as justification for the military intervention.

These domestic dynamics played out in relation to a second, linked dynamic: a new geopolitical landscape. With the end of World War II, the United States moved quickly to develop new economic and military alliances to combat the perceived threat of the Soviet Union. Turkey's entrance into the North Atlantic Treaty Organization and its participation in the Marshall Plan helped to expand projects of "Westernization" (batılılaşma) and transformed the country's consumer landscapes.[10] Crucially, these projects of Westernization were often linked to a particular kind of "modernization" embodied above all as "hotels and highways."[11]

The 1950s were a decade in which Turkishness and Westernization were woven together in new ways, but they were also one in which the distinction between "Turks" and "Greeks" became much more sharply drawn. As with so many divisions, this distinction had a complicated history. In 1924 a population exchange between Turkey and Greece had resulted in the deportation of Greeks from Anatolia; however, a sizable community of Greeks remained in Istanbul. In September 1955 and during debates over the future of Cyprus, pogroms targeted Istanbul's Greek population and helped to spur that community's exodus from the city.[12]

Third, the decade was also characterized by a rapidly changing social landscape. In quantitative terms, Istanbul's population grew by roughly 8 percent between 1945 and 1950. Over the next five years, it grew by a further 30 percent.[13] The overwhelming majority of these migrants arrived from rural Anatolia, although migration from Yugoslavia, Bulgaria, and other Balkan states was also important. The massive expansion of the city's population generated new debates and anxieties about housing, infrastructure, and urban ways of life.[14] As noted above, Istanbul also became increasingly "Turkish," especially following the 1955 pogrom that targeted the city's Greek-speaking population.[15]

Yet beyond these numbers, this decade also marked a generational shift. Eyüp was a special object of interest for a generation of writers born during the Ottoman Empire but were ambivalent observers of a rapidly changing city. Most of the writers discussed in this chapter were born in the two decades between 1890 and 1910, meaning that even the youngest were adolescents when the Republic was founded in 1923. They learned to read and write using the Ottoman script and would have been teenagers when that script was replaced with a modified Latin script.[16] Similarly, they would have witnessed a city and country reshaped by the economic privations and political expulsions of the 1930s. By the time that social mores, migration, and urban change were reshaping Istanbul and the country beyond in the 1950s, most of these writers would have been between thirty-eight and (in the case of Sermet Muhtar Alus) sixty-three years of age. While many of these writers wrote with one eye on the international context for their work, their lives were also embedded in Istanbul's social topographies.[17] This embeddedness impacted how they came to write about Eyüp and Islam, precisely because the place, its people, and its religious significance were so tightly woven together.

The final dynamic that defined the 1950s was a new cultural economy. Turkey's participation in the Marshall Plan and the decade's economic liberalization greatly expanded the availability of imported consumer goods. American blue jeans, German toys, and other foreign products thus came to be part of a particular social lifestyle. Even for those who were unable to buy these new goods, their presence was still visible in magazines and newspapers. Both as material objects and objects of desire, these new consumer goods came to circulate in complicated ways.

Alongside those consumer goods, the newspaper market expanded on a massive scale. By one measure, the quantity of newsprint produced in Turkey tripled between 1945 and 1955.[18] As the newspaper market expanded metropolitan newspapers competed for readers and advertising dollars. Innovations in color, the use of photographs and cartoons, and the commissioning of serialized romances, mysteries, historical novels, and memoirs all became techniques for newspapers to attract greater readership.[19] Beyond newspapers, two new institutions were also established in the 1950s: the Association of the Conquest (Fetih Derneği, originally established in 1950)[20] and the Istanbul Institute (İstanbul Enstitüsü, established ca. 1955). Through their activities and their publications, these new actors helped to further expand the writing about Istanbul and Islam.[21]

The political, the social, and the cultural came together most visibly in the explosion of "public histories" written during this decade. The founding of the Republic of Turkey in 1923 had been marked by an intentional historiographical project that distanced the new nation from its immediate imperial predecessor. New legal codes, forms of dress, professional institutions, political vocabularies, spatial practices, and urban planning helped to signal a modern country defined in opposition to the Ottoman past. Beginning in the 1940s, however, and especially as the five-hundredth anniversary of the 1453 conquest of Constantinople approached, new debates erupted over how the Ottoman past should be commemorated in a modern Istanbul.[22] Although engagements with the Ottoman past took many forms in 1950s Istanbul, one especially visible vision of the Ottoman past overlapped with an ethnically pure and triumphalist version of Turkish nationalism.[23]

Even beyond 1453, the past emerged as a new site of interest in the public culture of the 1950s. Writers penned regular columns in major newspapers with titles like "According to History," "A Page from the Calendar," "Pages from History," and "Historical Topics." Alongside these daily newspapers, a range of popular history magazines were also published during this decade. These included *Illustrated History Journal, The Treasury of History, The World of History*, and *Life Illustrated*.[24] Beyond history-specific journals, there were also publications from a wide variety of political and cultural backgrounds, including *Yedigün* (which closed in 1951),[25] *Akbaba* (published from 1922 to 1977, with breaks in 1930–31 and 1950–51),[26] and *Büyük Doğu* (edited by Necip Fazıl Kısakürek and variously published and banned between 1943 and 1978).[27]

Another important venue was the magazine published by the Turkish Touring and Automobile Club, a bilingual journal in Turkish and French that addressed a wealthy transnational audience who had begun to look at the country through the automobile.[28] In the background were also exceptional projects like Reşat Ekrem Koçu's *Istanbul Encyclopedia*, first published in 1944, which set out to document the entire city in glorious detail.[29] In short, this was a decade in which writers gained the ability to address their audiences in a new way. This novelty included not simply new columns and publications but also new ways that discussions of religion were embedded within a much larger and messier world.

### TALE OR HISTORY? TELLING POPULAR STORIES

In April 1950 the top story in the Istanbul press was the upcoming national election—the first in which the incumbent Republican People's Party and the Democrat Party would contest the election on relatively even terms. Coverage of the campaign dominated the headlines, with speeches, party lists, accusations, and intrigues all competing for space on the front page. Beyond the election newspapers also brought their readers into a wider world: parliamentary elections in England, a new government cabinet in Greece, fraught diplomatic relations between the Soviet Union and Turkey.

But even amidst these national and international stories, Istanbul itself was also an object of attention. The daily press reported regularly on urban development projects, fires, the city's changing cultural life, and more. To compete in an expanding market, newspapers also commissioned exclusive serials to attract a regular readership. Several of Istanbul's best-known tombs had recently been reopened, so perhaps a customer stopping by a newsstand on the evening of April 8 may have noticed an announcement in bold letters across the top of the evening newspaper *Son Saat (Final Hour)*:

> **Eyub Sultan**. Ziya Şakir has prepared it for you. *Son Saat* once more presents a new work to its readers. EYUB SULTAN. Among the best religious works that you'll read. The best work that Ziya Şakir, benefiting from seventy-three sources, has written.[30]

Over the next two months Şakir would take his readers on a journey across time and place, bringing them from the Prophet Muhammad's flight from Mecca to Medina to the messy industrial present of Istanbul's Golden Horn. Although Eyüp had been an occasional object of interest for writers and journalists during the 1920s, '30s, and '40s, Şakir's serial marked one of the first instances in which Eyüp was turned into a sustained topic for a mass-market readership.

Born in 1883, Ziya Şakir (Soku) was a well-known writer who had been publishing regular columns for newspapers like *Son Posta*, *Tan*, *İkdam*, and *Vatan* since the late 1920s.[31] Although he published on a wide variety of topics, his histories almost always took the form of historical novels, light on archival documents and instead filled with anecdote, narrative, and character.[32] Şakir's work thus fit squarely within the genre of popular histories that exploded during the 1950s.

Şakir's column typically ran on page four, which was the home for most of *Son Saat's* regular serials. His "Eyüp Sultan" thus sat alongside an eclectic mix of topics. There was a serial about Doğan Bey, the Hero of Niğbolu, which told the story of the 1396 Battle of Nicopolis and the Ottoman defeat of an allied Christian army. One column over there was the long-running serial *From the Victory in Izmir to the Assassination in Izmir.* As its title suggests, it told a story that started in September 1922, when forces led by Mustafa Kemal (Atatürk) captured Izmir from Greek forces, and ended in June 1926, when an assassination plot targeting Mustafa Kemal resulted in a clampdown on opposition movements in Turkey.[33] Finally, and immediately adjacent to Ziya Şakir's column, there was *Poisonous Smile,* Zahir Törümküney's novel of intrigue and love. In short, Şakir's column about Eyüp Sultan existed in relation to a set of histories and geographies and topographies.

Şakir's serial about Eyüp Sultan began not with a map of Istanbul nor even a visit to Eyüp but with a novelistic retelling of the story of the Prophet's flight from Mecca. It began by setting the scene: "The weather was scorching hot. Abu Bakr and his daughters were sitting on the low sofas in their home, looking out the window." Şakir's serial drew upon standard tropes: there was the Prophet hiding in a cave to avoid the forces of Abu Jahl, his encounter with Zübeyr, his establishment of a small masjid in Quba, and his eventual arrival in Medina. Şakir then brought Halid bin Zeyd into the story: not wishing to disappoint any of the residents of Medina who wished to host him, the Prophet instead left the choice to his camel, who eventually knelt in front of the home of Halid bin Zeyd.

At least in its broad contours, this story of the Prophet Muhammad's life may have been familiar to the readers of *Son Saat,* but, with its focus on Halid bin Zeyd, the account was novel enough to encourage readers to buy the paper every day. Şakir's language throughout the serial was simple, accessible, and largely consistent with his reputation as a writer of popular histories. As his readers followed along, Şakir listed the many qualities that made Halid bin Zeyd exceptional. Although "not rich," Halid bin Zeyd "possessed a generous heart," spent all his time in the service of the Prophet, and earned the name Host of the Messenger (Mihmandar-ı Resul) on account of the great hospitality he showed the Prophet.[34]

Although Şakir's serial drew on the contemporary genre of the newspaper serial, his story also drew on a second genre: popular stories about the prophets (*kısas-ı enbiya*). This genre, as Brett Wilson has noted, "played a far greater role in the teaching of the Qur'an and the shaping of popular understandings of Islam than Qur'anic translations or commentaries."[35] His serial thus offers one example of how new articulations and understandings of Islam came to circulate during the decade.

Yet Şakir's serial was also a story about place. After relating various stories about the Prophet Muhammad, Halid bin Zeyd's virtues, the importance of Halid bin Zeyd to the Byzantines, and his grave's miraculous rediscovery, Şakir turned to Eyüp itself. He described, for example, how visitors used to crowd the mosque on the first Friday of every *hijri* month: "Those who wanted to realize their wishes would give things like handkerchiefs, scarves, ties, and shirts to the müezzin, who would recite the *salâ* from the minaret. When these müezzin would begin the *salâ*, waving these things in their hands, this great crowd would suddenly begin moving."[36] Everyone, he continued, would ask for help (*istimdat*) from the spirit (*ruhaniyet*) of Halid bin Zeyd. Şakir's serial provides one portrait of a devotional practice channeled through material objects and enabled by the mosque staff themselves. Today such practices have been largely eliminated following a coordinated campaign against "superstitious" practices.[37]

Indeed, Şakir's Eyüp was one in which Islam was woven into a vision of cultural authenticity. As he wrote, "The village that we today call Eyüp Sultan used to be called during those times the Town of Ebâ Eyyüp [Belde-i Ebâ Eyyüp] [*sic*]. In this way a sort of privilege was granted there. . . . There is no doubt that it benefited from his blessed spirit."[38] On account of that spirit, Eyüp was a place that was able to preserve its traditions and sense of identity despite the far-reaching changes that reshaped its contexts. For example, even as the Ottoman Empire transformed during the Tanzimat and Western fashions and modes of living became more fashionable, the residents of Eyüp (Eyüplüler) "preserved their religious and national ancestry [*dini ve milli asaletleri*]," "showed respect and deference in the spiritual presence of Hz. Halid," and "gave no place to pleasures and debauchery [*zevk ve sefahatler*] that morals and the sharia would not approve."[39]

When Şakir's serial was republished as a book in the late 1950s, he expanded on his argument about Eyüp's capacity to preserve its ancestry: "The people of Eyüp changed nothing, from the clothing that they'd been used to for centuries to their simplest manners and customs" and "did not rush to accept the requirements [*icaplar*] of the Tanzimat."[40] In Şakir's account, this essential quality of Eyüp had been lost. Ending his column by describing Eyüp as it appeared in the 1950s, he mourned its transformation into what he called an "exclusively workers' town" (*münhasıran işçi beldesi*). This mode of comparing Eyüp's idealized past to its fallen present would emerge as a potent rhetorical trope for those who took Eyüp as their object.

Şakir's novelized history of Eyüp Sultan, however, drew critiques from writers such as Haluk Şehsuvaroğlu, who insisted on a sharp distinction between "History" (*Tarih*) and "Tales" (*Masal*). Şehsuvaroğlu's career as a writer, like those of many of his peers, overlapped with several other activities, including a successful effort to establish the Naval Museum (Deniz Müzesi) and an honorary position at the Topkapı Palace Museum.[41] He had begun writing public history columns in the late 1940s for the daily newspaper *Akşam*, but in the early 1950s had transitioned to writing for the leading paper, *Cumhuriyet*. In 1953 he had helped to compile a lavishly illustrated newspaper spread entitled "Istanbul through the Centuries" ("Asırlar Boyunca İstanbul").[42] In a column that took its title from the distinction between History and Tales, Şehsuvaroğlu took aim at those "historical novels that have recently been in great demand" because their "writers frequently stray from historical facts and change the truth of events as much as possible."[43]

To write more "historical" work, Şehsuvaroğlu focused on documentary sources: archives, mosque inscriptions, Divan poetry, and Evliya Çelebi above all. Even though he generally avoided commenting on contemporary Istanbul, his writing was often shaped by an implicit comparison. For example, in an article about the mansions (*yalılar*) that had once lined the shores of the Golden Horn, Şehsuvaroğlu noted that "once, Eyüp's tombs and cemeteries had been more orderly [*muntazam*] and its neighborhoods and market more well tended [*bakımlı*]."[44] For him, Eyüp functioned as a place of the past. It was valuable precisely because it seemed to be unchanged while surrounded by a rapidly changing city. This focus on Eyüp was also consistent with a broader complaint about the lack of attention paid to history and especially the Republic's Ottoman inheritance.[45]

Even though Şehsuvaroğlu typically focused on buildings and other inanimate objects, there were exceptions to this rule. A March 1957 column opened with a rueful observation about the relative lack of interest in the lives of those Istanbul residents who had been witness to a century's worth of urban change: "What a shame that these have not yet been recorded, only listened to by those with a curiosity or interest in the old. Where, in fact, in a country where the social history has not been written, the importance of these memories is obvious."[46] In the 1950s discussions were emerging not only about Eyüp and Islam, but also about the ways that the "past" should be defined and located in specific places.

## LOST OR RESTORED? EYÜP AS A PLACE IN BETWEEN

Eyüp's material and social landscapes, however, were rapidly shifting over the course of the 1950s. For many, the landscape's disappearance provoked broader consideration of changing social mores, relationships, and geographies. Consider Sermet Muhtar Alus's essay in *The Treasure of History* (*Tarih Hazinesi*), published in December 1951. Born in 1887, Alus had made his living as a writer by cataloging a city of vanishing things.[47] He began his essay by identifying the three things that made Eyüp famous: "Its kebabs, its cream, and its toys." He proceeded to describe in vivid detail the smells, shapes, textures, and sounds of these objects that once defined Eyüp.

But, in a rhetorical move that became typical for those who wrote about Eyüp, Alus transitioned to a more recent visit that took place after some years away. He began,

> For perhaps ten years I hadn't traveled in that direction, [and] I was shocked [*parmağım ağzımda kaldı*]. In every direction, radios, gramophones, not a trace of the kebab sellers, the cream sellers, the toy makers. Only on one store's wall, a few drums, tambourines, and mortars; in the display case, celluloid babies and balls; soldiers of lead, cars and buses of tin. On all of them, a "Made in Germany" stamp.[48]

The passage condensed a set of tangible material changes embedded into several short blocks in the center of Eyüp. These changes were at once material (from clay, wood, and paper to celluloid and tin), social (because both the shopkeepers and the customers were different), and geopolitical (the "Made in Germany" stamp).

Suggestively, however, Alus's essay about the special qualities of Eyüp had very little to say about the markers of official Islam. Even when Alus entered the Mosque of Eyüp Sultan itself, his attention focused on the social practices woven through the mosque: "There's no mark of the funerals, of the beggars. The pigeons beside the holy tomb have declined in numbers. Of the women who sold corn by the dish and the slumbering storks, only one caught my eye. Its feathers fallen out, its flock flown, even its clattering chatter gone. Looking about, sad and depressed, on a single leg."[49] Alus's essay pointed to the mosque's embeddedness in a set of urban relations that subverted expectations about a purely "religious" experience in Eyüp. Begging in Eyüp was an especially clear example of this. When people would visit the Mosque of Eyüp Sultan to pray for something (for example, good health, a new job, or improved fortunes), they would often leave an offering in return, ranging from distributing charity to beggars to offering food to other visitors to paying for the sacrifice of an animal. This reciprocal relationship between prayer and charity helped to create a situation in which begging was institutionalized in Eyüp.[50] While we can't know precisely why the institution disappeared, it is likely that the tomb's closure and a decrease in the number of visitors led to the disappearance of begging in the way that Alus remembered. This period was also one in which reformers, citizens, and state authorities debated the scale and site for charity and philanthropy.[51]

As for the birds of Eyüp Sultan, scholars have highlighted the central role afforded to birds in Ottoman mosques.[52] Although Alus's essay does not address this topic, one might explore the ecologies of faith once organized through the mosque and its environs: the pilgrims scattering birdseed, the pigeons and storks that once nested in the trees, birdhouses, and graveyards, and the "affective and intellectual possibilities of connecting to the world not as God's deputies . . . but as animals once again in kinship."[53] There are few clues as to why the birds disappeared, although it may have been related to ecological changes linked to Istanbul's industrialization and urbanization. The stork that Alus mentions was a frequent character in contemporary accounts and photographs of Eyüp Sultan.[54] Whatever the case, the departure of both Eyüp's beggars and its birds speaks to the changing nature of the relationships and networks within which the mosque was embedded.

Alus's perspective on Eyüp's transformations was clear. He closed his essay by describing his return to the ferry station, where he would have taken a small *vapur* to return to Istanbul's busier districts. Near the station, he wrote, he overheard a conversation between a group of young men. They spoke of "working out, wrestling, the clubs along the Golden Horn," while one "went on about the ball that would be given that night in Fener, whistling its tangos." Alus's essay provides one

fine-grained observation of a changing Eyüp in the early 1950s, but it also demonstrates how writers used Eyüp as a place from which to tell stories about the
ruptures, tensions, and incongruous encounters that had come to define Istanbul.

The sense of incongruity was similarly palpable in an essay by the writer and
newspaper columnist Nahid Sırrı Örik that was published in May 1954 in *The
Majestic East* (*Büyük Doğu*).[55] Born in 1895, just a few years after Alus, Örik was
similarly part of a generation that had lived through a set of traumatic urban transformations. And, like Alus, Örik also began his essay with an arrival story.

Alighting from the ferry and walking the main street in the direction of the
Mosque of Eyüp Sultan, Örik remarked on the Ottoman-era gravestones pushed
to one side to make room for new roads through Eyüp. "Shouldn't we be protecting
with great care," he mused, "Eyüp's tens of thousands of old graves and countless
tombs?" Passing through the courtyard of the mosque with barely a mention of the
tomb itself, Örik moved inland, toward the then outer district of Taşlıtarla.

His attention was drawn once more to the encounter between the old and the
new. Negotiating his way along the crowded road, he focused on the buildings
on either side: "A few beautiful old houses and quite a number of new apartment
buildings, though one or two already in need of repair . . . So-called modern style
[*güya modern*] apartment buildings that spoil Eyüp's spiritual view [*ruhanî man-
zara*]." Finally, he arrived at a bookstore run by an old acquaintance: "When, seeing
the quantity and variety of French cinema and fashion magazines in the display
window, I expressed my surprise, [the bookshop owner] said that was what he
sold the most. In this old and impoverished Istanbul district, what do these young
women buying these French, English, and German cinema and fashion magazines
and returning to their ruined houses learn from them?"[56] As he returned to the
ferry, Örik broadened his lens: "Just as everything else has taken flight and gone,
Eyüp's meaning—along with that of old Istanbul—has also taken flight and gone
. . . [i]n its place nothing more than a few traces and blotches."[57]

For both Alus and Örik, Eyüp served two linked functions. First, it was a place
of memory. Both men experienced their trip in the 1950s against the backdrop of
their previous visits. The incongruity they perceived was thus both geographical
(about the "foreign" not fitting in Eyüp) and temporal (involving the "now" and
the "then"). More broadly, Eyüp also served as a place where opposites rubbed
up against each other: a whistled tango on a dark street down the road from the
mosque; imported toys on a street named for the toys once made there; cinema
and fashion magazines read in aging houses. Strikingly, however, their essays had
little to say about what we might call "official" Islam. There was no mention of the
Prophet Muhammad, hadith, or even Halid bin Zeyd. Their work thus suggests a
way of thinking about Islam that was woven into the fabric of everyday life and
into a certain urban sociability.

Yet if some writers traced the vanishing of Eyüp's "true" character during the
1950s, other writers looked at the same landscape and told a different story. This

was especially true in 1958 and 1959, as two linked urban projects impacted Eyüp. The first was the urban development spearheaded by Prime Minister Adnan Menderes. New boulevards were an especially important part of these "Menderes Operations."[58] In addition to completely transforming how traffic flowed through the city, these boulevards often created new squares in front of the city's major mosques. The second project was the restoration of many Ottoman-era mosques around Turkey, but particularly in Istanbul.[59] Directed by the General Directorate of Foundations, these restoration projects were often folded into broader debates about the Ottoman past throughout the 1950s.[60]

A two-page spread published in 1958 in *Life* (Hayat) magazine provided one account of how the Menderes Operations and restoration came together in Eyüp.[61] Framed as a narrative of decline and recovery, the article began with nostalgic vision of the past: "Eyüp was once one of Turkey's most developed places [*en mamur yerlerinden*]." However, "with time . . . Eyüp was forgotten" and the mosque's surroundings filled in with wooden shacks (*salaş*) and factories. As a result, "Eyüp, with its factories that spewed smoke and smell, became a work site; with its ruined broken historic works, only a pilgrimage destination. . . . It became a place [*mekanı*] of poor, destitute [*çilekeş*] people."

The author then drew a striking parallel between a devotional practice engaged in by young girls and those down on their luck who would visit Eyüp and the built environment itself: "Some numbers of people have prayed for Eyüp's good fortune and left the faucets open [as young women would do to pray for an auspicious marriage] so that the development project sweeping the entire country has also included Eyüp. . . . The surroundings of the Eyüp Mosque [*sic*] and its tomb [*türbe*] have been opened."[62] This "opening" had a profound impact on the center of Eyüp. A new boulevard linked the Edirne Highway on the ridge above with the network of roads running along the shore of the Golden Horn. In the process, the boulevard's construction led to the destruction of the market immediately in front of the mosque and the reconfiguration of sight lines and transportation networks through the newly built square.

From the point of view of this article—one addressed to the middle-class readers of *Life* who likely lived outside the district—the key goal was rescuing Eyüp from its ostensible disrepair and transforming it into a "district of monuments" (*abideler semti*) that suited its "sanctity" (*kudsiyet*). Making a place for these monuments thus required the creation of new architectural voids.[63] It also required restoration of the buildings themselves, above all the Mosque of Eyüp Sultan, whose restoration was completed in March 1959.[64] A news story in *Life*, for example, celebrated the event by including photos of both the celebration (men eating dates to break their fast during Ramadan) and the building itself (especially the mosque's repainted central dome).[65] Haluk Şehsuvaroğlu also mentioned the event in his regular column "Tarihi Bahisler" (Historical Topics).[66] In keeping with his attitude toward "history," his column was a detailed account of facts pertaining to the building, based on the mosque inscriptions (*kitabe*) and documents in the Topkapı Archives. He closed by situating the mosque and district in relation to the contemporary Menderes Operations.

"Eyüp," he wrote, "received priority consideration [*ayrıca ele alınmış*] during the development operations [*imar hareketleri*]." However, he insisted that these development operations would not make Eyüp "modern" like other parts of the city. "It is without doubt that Eyüp's mystic atmosphere [*mistik hava*] will not be dispersed, and . . . especially that the rococo and Empire traces, mementos of the eighteenth and nineteenth century, will not be destroyed." If the Menderes Operations aimed to make other parts of Istanbul "modern," Şehsuvaroğlu declared that the opposite was true in Eyüp: "Eyüb finds itself made eternal in its spiritual atmosphere [*ruhani havası*]."

The columnist Refi Cevat Ulunay also devoted one of his *Milliyet* columns to the mosque's restoration.[67] His column was more explicitly political. Lauding the government and especially the prime minister, Ulunay wrote, "The effort that they have shown concerning the rescuing of religious buildings, monuments, and tombs from ruin requires [*mucib olmuş*] the thanks of all Muslims." After describing the mosque's restoration in glowing terms, he ended by quoting a brief conversation with Vasfi Egeli, the project's lead architect. Vasfi Bey, he said, deflected any praise for the building's success, saying, "I'm nothing other than a worthless servant [*naçiz hâdim*]."

Although one might assume that urban development projects and restoration projects belong to different worlds, transforming Eyüp into a "district of monuments" was in fact entirely consistent with the project of making a modern city.[68] What was at stake in this project was establishing clear boundaries between the "new" and the "old." Yet as Vasfi Egeli's comment makes clear, this project of development was also not simply a "secular" project but involved complicated feelings of obligation and responsibility to this site of Islam. The journalist Salim Bayar, ending a twelve-part report on Eyüp's redevelopment in the paper *Tercüman*, summed up this hope: "And this tomb [of Eyüp Sultan] will be a source of Islamic comfort [*İslamın bir teselli kaynağı*] until eternity."[69]

## THEIRS OR OURS? PUBLICS OF ISLAM

For writers like Şehsuvaroğlu, Alus, and Örik, Eyüp was a place connected to their sense of self. Narrating Eyüp became a way to stage a particular authorial persona with which the audience was encouraged to identify. Yet Eyüp could also be presented not as a place of "us" but as a place of the "other," assumed to be distant from the modernizing worlds of Istanbul. A two-page spread published in 1954 in *Life Illustrated* (*Resimli Hayat*) shows how Eyüp was presented to a middle-class audience that (likely) did not live in Eyüp. It also asks us to consider how Eyüp, Islam, and religious practice came to be woven into the changing urbanity of 1950s

Istanbul. The juxtaposition of text and image in the article, entitled "A Friday in Eyüpsultan," is notable both for what it showed and what it left out.[70]

The story began with a description of the prayer window (*hacet penceresi*) that looks in from the mosque's inner courtyard onto the tomb itself. The paired photograph showed several women clustered close to the window itself; behind them stood a small boy dressed for his circumcision (*sünnet*) and a young man dressed in uniform. The accompanying text emphasized the crowds that gather at this place and the variety of dress: "The clothing is of all types. . . . Those wearing *çarşaf*, coats, long-sleeved shirts, short-sleeved, no-sleeved, there are even those wearing blue jeans [*blu cin'li*]."[71] Left unspoken was the gendered nature of this observation: all were items of clothing associated with women.

From there the article highlighted several other practices and objects that defined the Mosque of Eyüp Sultan. These included the collecting of forty-one pieces of corn (another practice considered something that women engage in), a brief description of the famous stork Hacı Baba who once lived on the grounds of the mosque, and the "Pigeons' Hilton" built to house the pigeons. The second page added more curiosities for the readers of *Life Illustrated*: a description of a particular tomb linked to young boys' circumcision and the desire for children, identified only as one of the "greats" (*büyükler*); the auntie (*teyze*) selling prayer beads (*tesbih*) to women; the vendor trying to pass off a guinea pig as a rabbit; and the queue waiting to look through the stereoscope at Mecca, Medina, the Kaaba, the capital of America, the beaches of Miami. For five *kuruş*, the author noted, the traveling *sinemacı* would show seven poses. There were—of course—several *çarşaflı* women waiting around, along with lots of children. "The *sinemacı* knows which pictures he's going to show based on the customer's clothing."[72] The tone of the article was mocking. A Friday in Eyüp seemed to be filled with charlatans and cheap cons.

Missing, of course, was the central act of Friday in Eyüp: the Friday prayers. In fact, this two-page spread said nothing about the "orthodox" forms of Islam that one might expect to find in Eyüp. Its vision and description of religion were affectionate but also highlighted "superstitious" behaviors. In the process, the article positioned religion not as a vital and ongoing part of urban life but as a sort of remnant, distant in time and place from the lives of the author and their readership.

In contrast, there were a number of texts in the 1950s that sought to instruct their readers in how to visit Eyüp "correctly." One of the most extensive was Hacı Cemal Öğüt's *The Famous Eyyûb Sultan*, but a small pamphlet prepared in 1958 provides another example. Its front cover showed a photo of the Mosque of Eyüp Sultan taken from the adjacent square. Ironically, the photo could not have been taken only a few years previous, as the photo was taken from the spot where the market complex would have stood.

The title of the pamphlet, printed on the back cover, was *The History and Manner of Visiting Hz. Halid* (*Hazreti Halidin Adabı Ziyareti ve Tarihi*). It was published by a man identified only as M. Akif Bencoşar, a bookseller (*kitapçı*) whose address was listed as the Mosque of Eyüp Sultan itself. A note on the pamphlet's back cover indicated that the pamphlet was itself a selection from an older book, *The Key of Visitation and Its Manners* (*Müftahı Ziyaret ve Adabı*).[73] The end of the pamphlet gives the date of the text as January 26, 1921 (16 Cemaziülevvel 1339), which helps to explain the relatively stilted style of the pamphlet's language, which is rich in Persian and Arabic cognates and markedly different than Şakir's far more readable serial. The pamphlet's existence also speaks to the ongoing work of transmission, the acts of copying and recopying through which understandings and practices of Islam were communicated across time and place.

Those who purchased the short pamphlet during their visit would have found three linked sections. The first provided a brief history of both Halid bin Zeyd and the mosque in which the pamphlet's readers found themselves. It stressed Halid bin Zeyd's excellence, citing the well-known story of the Prophet Muhammad's camel choosing the house of Halid bin Zeyd in Medina, and his position as a beloved Companion of the Prophet. It included a version of Halid bin Zeyd's death during the siege of Constantinople, his burial under a stone inscribed "This is the tomb of Ebu Eyüp" (*Hâzâ kabri Ebi Eyüb*), the destruction of his tombs by the Greeks (*Rumlar, kabri şerifi bozmuşlar*), their rebuilding of the tomb, and its later destruction. Its history closed with a brief story of the discovery of Halid bin Zeyd's tomb by Shaykh Akşemseddin and the endowment and later embellishment of the mosque by Sultan Mehmet the Conqueror and his successors.

The pamphlet then transitioned to a description of how the people of Istanbul would visit Eyüp. It had become, the pamphlet wrote, a tradition of "the righteous of Istanbul's people" (*İstanbul ahalisinin sulehası*) to visit the tomb before engaging in something "auspicious" (*hayırlı*), before enrolling their children in school or celebrating their circumcision, upon finishing a complete reading of the Qur'an (*Hatmi Şerif*), or upon memorizing it. "There are those," it continued, "who, on becoming old and infirm, lament that 'This year I was not able to visit.'"[74] The pamphlet stressed the experience of those who had been alcoholics, addicted to gambling, or womanizers (*sarhoşluk, kumarbazlık, hovardalık*) and—upon visiting this "blessed station" (*mübarek makam*) and repenting and praying to God for forgiveness—had been redeemed.[75]

Finally, the pamphlet presented a series of justifications for why visiting the tomb was religiously appropriate. Its references were eclectic, including Abu 'l-Ḥasan al-Shādhilī (referred to as Şazeli Hazretleri) and Abū l-Mawāhib al-Shādhilī (referred to as Şeyh Ebülmevahib), perhaps indicating that the pamphlet's author was associated with the Shadhiliyya Sufi order.[76] Yet the pamphlet continued by citing a wide range of other religious authorities.[77] The seemingly eclectic nature of the citations suggests that the pamphlet's author was likely a part of an intellectual and religious milieu organized around Sufi orders, but those knowledges circulated between many kinds of people and many kinds of authority. The pamphlet's author ended with a brief note about how one ought to visit the tomb: "Pay attention to the friend that you come with; if you want to give charity, you can, but you can also refrain. In a crowd of visitors, don't rush, be patient and respectful. Let's remember with charitable prayers all our religious brethren who work to protect this blessed place."[78]

Another example of a text addressing its readers as fellow Muslims was Süheyl Ünver's short book *The Tombs of the Companions in Istanbul*.[79] Because of the number of Companions buried there or in adjacent districts, Eyüp was a key place in Ünver's guide. Like the pamphlet's author, Ünver sought to transform how his readers would encounter these tombs. He argued that developing this awareness should be part of the five-hundredth anniversary celebrations. This was because the Companions and holy warriors (*Sahabe ve mücahitler*) had played an important role in the project of making Istanbul both Turkish and a Muslim city (*millileştirme ve Müslümanlaştırma*).[80] Evaluating the state of these tombs after nearly thirty years of closure, he drew a link between the (Muslim) spiritual life of Istanbul's residents and the actual administration of the city: "Just as people cannot live without spirituality [*mâneviyatsız*], cities cannot endure nor be administered without history and spirituality."[81]

In contrast to the gently mocking tone of the spread in *Life Illustrated*, books like Hacı Cemal Öğüt's *The Famous Eyyûb Sultan* and Süheyl Ünver's *The Tombs of the Companions in Istanbul* and pamphlets like *The Key of Visitation and Its Manners* were deeply concerned with religious instruction. In various ways, these texts and those like them sought to "instruct practitioners regarding the correct form and purpose of a given practice."[82] In doing so, readers were asked to "relate conceptually to *a past . . .* and *a future . . .* through *a present*."[83] Rich as Talal Asad's framework is, however, these texts and the broader production of public culture in 1950s Istanbul point the way toward two crucial conceptual insights.

First, these texts were not just concerned with instructing their audiences about proper practice; they were focused on linking those practices to a particular *place*. In other words, discursive traditions are always embedded in and entangled with the messiness of the world. This is not to reduce the "religious" to merely an effect of context; rather, it requires us to think about the complicated ways that writers sought to connect themselves to their audiences and the world around them. This work of connection involved citation practices, the transmission of hadith, the realities of book printing and distribution, the forgetfulness or attention with which people carried these books through the city, and more.

Second, and following on that point, the work of transmission was and remains a material practice, reliant on the capacity of texts to be transcribed, circulated, reproduced, stacked, shelved, and even destroyed. The pamphlet's material qualities—stamped on cheap paper, simply produced, and sold for only forty *kuruş* by M. Akif Bey—shaped the meanings that it carried and how it moved through the city. At the other end of the spectrum, Süheyl Ünver's book relied on a careful practice of reading gravestones and inscriptions (*kitabe*) on mosques and tombs.

In contrast to manuscripts and pamphlets, Ünver's media of transmission were powerfully inert.

## CONCLUSION

Where was Eyüp? Although Eyüp was the frequent subject of articles in the 1950s—articles that were often printed alongside photographs of its central mosque, tomb, and graveyards—readers were never provided with a map. Instead, authors almost always relied on a shared topography of Istanbul, one in which certain identities and histories were linked to different places. However, that topography required work to create and maintain. Istanbul's print cultures played an important role in that project.

The 1950s were a decade of tumult and change during which a generation of writers engaged with Istanbul and its histories in new ways. Eyüp was a crucial place for many of them. They wrote about many topics: its monuments, its urban changes, its social life, and, of course, the Companion buried at its center. What emerged was not a single self-contained place of Islam but instead something composite. There was Ziya Şakir's serialized popular history and Sermet Muhtar Alus's evocative account of a vanished social fabric; there was Haluk Şehsuvaroğlu's insistence on proper documentary history and *Life Illustrated*'s picture of Islam as something that people other than its readers did; and there were new texts that sought to educate and instruct readers in what it meant to be Muslim. Rather than drawing clear distinctions between "secular" and "religious" versions of Eyüp, this chapter has sought to highlight how Eyüp came to be defined at the border between multiple visions. These new publics encountered an old Islam in ways that were contingent, contested, and never a foregone conclusion.[84]

In doing so, this chapter makes two conceptual contributions. First, it asks us to think more expansively about the "labors that go into writing and reading" these stories in order to "see them as elements of [places] in motion rather than static representations."[85] One danger of writing about Eyüp is that we look only at self-identified "Islamic" writers like Necip Fazıl Kısakürek. Instead, this chapter shows us how places of Islam were articulated through many different genres, thus complicating that idea that there was a single "correct" Eyüp. Eyüp circulated through newspapers, pamphlets, magazines, and encyclopedia subscriptions. In moving through the city in diverse ways, these material objects helped to make Eyüp a place in multiple, overlapping ways.

Second, this chapter suggests that we expand how we think about the geographies of Islam during the 1950s. In a 1952 article assessing the visibility of Islam in Turkey, Bernard Lewis argued that many of the new Islamic journals were "somewhat disappointing," written by men who "show all too plainly the scars of thirty years of frustration and isolation."[86] In his view, their visions of Islam were limited by a separation from the experiences of the broader Muslim world.[87] On the one hand, Lewis identified an important rupture between communities in Turkey and networks that once spanned the Ottoman Empire. On the other, however, Lewis missed the way that this geography was also experienced as an *urban* transformation. Even as we continue to explore how Islam and nation were reconfigured during the 1950s, it is also important to think about the uneven topographies that continue to define Istanbul. Working from Eyüp provides one such approach.

# 4

# Fluid Stories

In October 1920 a young man began to keep a journal about his trips to Eyüp.[1] In later decades he would become one of Turkey's best-known cultural historians and an important teacher of traditional arts such as calligraphy, paper marbling, and book binding. In 1920, however, Ahmet Süheyl Ünver was only twenty-two, about to both graduate from medical school and complete his training in calligraphy at the Madrasa of Calligraphy (Medresetü'l-Hattâtîn).[2] The first few pages of his journal consisted of a few pasted-in photographs, a list of Eyüp's Sufi lodges and their appointed meeting days, and an index of his various visits to the district.

But the journal really began on the next page. With great care, Ünver composed a bismillah in careful thuluth script, "In the name of Allah, the Most Gracious, the Most Merciful." A brief signature followed in the style of practiced calligraphers: "*Hurrire* Süheyl" (Süheyl wrote this). This was a page of careful, attentive beginnings.

Following the opening bismillah, Ünver carefully transcribed a long prayer in Arabic from a book entitled *The Virtues of Halid* (*Menakıb-ı Halidiyye*).[3] The prayer addressed Halid bin Zeyd—"Peace be upon you, O Companion of the Messenger of Allah"—and asked for his intercession on behalf of those who visited. At the bottom of the prayer Ünver made a note to himself that the prayer was "to be read on visiting the holy tomb." Beneath the passage he included four stamps of the seal of the tomb's attendant (*türbedar*) and added a final explanation: "The seals which are given in the holy tomb of His Excellency Halid. They dip them in water and then drink the water as an offering [*nezr*, Ar. *nadhr*]."[4]

The fact that Ünver chose to make a note of this specific act suggests how important water was to the act of visiting Halid bin Zeyd's tomb. Although Ünver never precisely identifies the well, it is likely that the water was taken from the tomb itself, offered to visitors by its then-attendants Şemsettin Efendi or his son Refik Özgül.[5] Persons, prayers, and a place brought into relation. This is one enactment of place.

But crucially, this act of place making depended on a material substance: water. Pilgrims visit the tomb of Halid bin Zeyd, offer their prayers, arrange their bodies in gestures of respect, and drink from the water provided by the tomb's attendant. Pilgrims were linked to this place through their encounters with water.[6]

You find water in many places in Eyüp. It flows from the faucets in the inner courtyard of the mosque. It flows from ablution fountains in the mosque's outer courtyard. It flows through wells and cisterns. It flows through old stream-beds, though these are largely lost from view. But water never exists on its own; it requires objects and infrastructures to make it accessible in particular ways. Water is offered, sold, and shared; it leaks, links, springs, and sustains.

Through water, Eyüp is linked to many places and times. There are fluid connections to Istanbul, Ottoman geographies, and the broader world of Islam. Water is the matter of life. As the Qur'an teaches, and as is often inscribed on Ottoman-era fountains, "From water every living thing" (Min al-ma kul shayyin ḥayyin): "Have those who disbelieved not considered that the heavens and the earth were a joined entity, and We separated them and made from water every living thing? Then will they not believe?"[7] In addition to this work of connection, water bears witness to the wonder of creation.[8] As Annemarie Schimmel notes, "Water not only has the power of purifying people externally, but also becomes—as in other religious traditions—a fitting symbol for the purification of hearts. Water is constantly quaking and moving—that is . . . its act of exalting the Lord in unison with all other creatures."[9] Beyond water itself, the Qur'an provides reference to a fluid vocabulary including the sea (bahr), the river (nahir), and springs ('aynan).[10] These forms of water flow through a range of stories, most of all in reference to the creation of the world but also in key encounters such as that between Moses and Khidr.[11]

However, those stories were often shared across and between multiple communities. For example, stories about Khidr both "spanned great distances and became not only an example of cross-cultural contacts, but the very embodiment of both the distances between cultures and the ways in which they intersect."[12] Water—both as a material substance and as something about which stories are told—is woven into histories of cross-cultural and interreligious encounters in Anatolia and the Middle East.[13]

Yet for water to circulate through human worlds, it requires infrastructures: vessels, pipes, fountains, bottles, cups. It requires social relationships to maintain those infrastructures: tomb attendants, municipal workers, friends. For this reason, geographers and others have long been interested in how the relationship between humans and water is mediated by social and technological systems.[14] Elsewhere, scholars of religion and material culture have explored the capacities of "sensational forms . . . relatively fixed modes for invoking and organising access to the transcendental [that offer] structures of repetition to create and sustain links between believers."[15]

FIGURE 6. Visitor drinking from a fountain in the Mosque of Eyüp Sultan, May 2014.

This chapter brings those arguments together by focusing on Eyüp's "fluid stories," a concept that takes inspiration from the etymological link between the word *rivayet* and the qualities of flow, transmission, and connection associated with water. As Mehmet Efendioğlu notes, "The term *rivayet* [Ar. *riwâya*], which has in the dictionary meanings of 'to water, to drink deeply from a spring; to transmit,' is used with the meaning of 'transmitting, through a document, hadith and similar reports [and] attributing them to the one who transmits or undertakes [that act].'"[16] Beyond the etymological link, the concept encourages us to consider water's simultaneous movement through stories about Eyüp and through its material infrastructures. Water's capacity to mediate makes it a key substance for this place of Islam, but this capacity is only religiously appropriate when water's mediating role becomes invisible.[17]

I make two linked arguments. First, water is important to Eyüp because it links multiple places, times, people, and registers.[18] These include links between the tomb of Halid bin Zeyd and the well of Zamzam in Mecca, between the present and centuries-old traditions of healing waters, between people who drink water and those whom they have lost, between states of illness and health, and between the mundane world of human affairs and a world of the divine.

Second, water's capacity to mediate and sustain these links makes it an object of contestation. Because water is "bound in intimate and more distant relations with other persons through shared material habits and habitats,"[19] it plays an important role in creating a community of Muslims. At the same time, because water can be so easily shared, its use (or misuse, as the case may be) generates anxieties about practices that seep through the boundaries between Muslim and non-Muslim, between appropriate and forbidden forms of practice. Rather than argue that there is a fixed "Muslim" or "Islamic" understanding of water, this chapter explores some of the ways that Eyüp's fluid stories help to make this a place of Islam.

I organize the chapter according to the infrastructures that make water available in Eyüp. In doing so, I hope to highlight both relationships shared across multiple sites and the ways that these sites' uses can diverge. Despite being a common substance, water—and the fluid stories it carries—is not a single thing.

## THE WELLS OF ZAMZAM

Among the many priceless objects housed within the tomb of Halid bin Zeyd, there is a small well. Covered with a marble stone (*bilezik taşı*) and still possessed of a wooden pulley to draw water up from the cistern below, this is likely the well whose water was translated into Süheyl Ünver's journal in 1920.[20] Although there are many wells in Istanbul, this is one of the few known for sharing a source with the well of Zamzam in Mecca. Rather than point to the physical impossibility of such a hydrologic relationship, we are better served by taking the claim seriously: how do the waters of Zamzam help us understand the geographies of Islam differently? Precisely because water connects in unexpected ways, it reminds us that even imagined geographies rely on material substances—mediums—to instantiate shared practices, meanings, and the places linked to them.

The most common story of Zamzam runs like this: The Prophet Abraham brought his wife, Hagar, and son, Ismail, to Mecca, where he left them. Near death from thirst, Hagar and Ismail were rescued by the divinely aided discovery of the well of Zamzam.[21] Today the well of Zamzam in Mecca is located within the precincts of the Masjid al-Haram and is still associated with healing properties.[22] As several hadith report, the Prophet stressed the importance of drinking the water of Zamzam not simply in order to slake one's thirst but also as a kind of worship.[23] Yet beyond Mecca itself, there are several sites around the world that have come to be considered as having "zamzam" water, including the Great Mosque of Kairouan in Tunisia and the tomb of Hacı Bektaş in central Anatolia.[24]

It is not clear when the Mosque of Eyüp Sultan came to be associated with the well of Zamzam. However, an inscription commemorating Sultan Ahmed I's rebuilding of the tomb of Halid bin Zeyd in the early seventeenth century suggests that the association between Eyüp Sultan and Mecca was already established by that time. Mehmet Nermi Haskan's history of Eyüp includes several stories (*rivayetler*) that have been transmitted about the well. In one story, the friends of Halid bin Zeyd dug a spring here after burying him, after which the Byzantines turned it into a well. In another story, the daughter of a Byzantine emperor suffering from an affliction of the nerves (*sinir hastalığı*) was cured by washing with the water of this spring after seeing the water in a dream. Because of this spring's healing powers, it came to be known as an *ayazma* (holy spring).[25]

Precisely because *ayazma* are so often associated with Greek Orthodox sites of worship, it might seem strange to speak of *ayazma* in Eyüp. By and large, Eyüp's wells today are rarely identified as *ayazma*. However, Eyüp's hydrologic topography is in some respects an inheritance from the district's Byzantine history. Prior to the Ottoman conquest of Constantinople, this district was known as Cosmidion, after the construction of a church and monastery dedicated to two saints, Cosmas and Damian, known for their power as healers.[26] The monastery was a well-known destination for both residents of Constantinople and visitors to the city.[27]

While it is not precisely clear where the monastery was located, the district of Cosmidion became what is now known as Eyüp. Given the role that water played in the Byzantine traditions associated with Cosmidion, it is highly likely that at least some of these waters were known as *ayazma*, even if they are not called such today. For example, Süheyl Ünver, quoting from Evliya Çelebi, mentioned an *ayazma* known as the Küplüce Ayazma that once sat on a high hill above the road to Kağıthane, surrounded by trees.[28]

Indeed, one could draw Eyüp into a constellation of *ayazma* still found around contemporary Istanbul, including examples found in neighborhoods traditionally associated with Istanbul's Greek-speaking population (Rum), such as Zeytinburnu's Church and Monastery of St. Mary of the Fish (Balıklı Meryem Ana Rum Ortodoks Manastiri)[29] and Ayvansaray's Church of St. Mary of Blachernae (Meryem Ana Kilisesi).[30]

To be clear, this is not to say that the well in the tomb of Halid bin Zeyd is really a "Byzantine" shrine. Such a description mobilizes the chronotope of origins discussed in this book's introduction and tends to reproduce an understanding of places as being only defined by internally coherent and consistent essences. Rather, it should call our attention to the persistence of *ayazma* in Istanbul, and the capacity for this devotional geography to both change and remain.[31]

Ways of knowing did not map neatly onto stable positions of "Christian" and "Muslim." Indeed, foreign, non-Muslim visitors to Eyüp during the nineteenth century similarly mentioned the relationship between the well in the tomb and the "famous well of Zemzem [sic] at Mecca," a belief that "[added] to the sanctity of the spot, and augment[ed] the vigilance with which the approaches [were] guarded."[32] Another English-speaking visitor in the 1830s similarly described the presence of "miraculous water . . . drawn up in silver buckets, and presented to the faithful in vases of the same metal."[33] Those who were healed by the "salutary qualities" of the well would leave "a part of [their] dress as a votiva tabula: and these rags of superstition are seen over holy wells in Turkey, as they are in Africa, Ireland, and other parts of the world."[34] In the case of the latter, the observer mapped Eyüp Sultan onto a broader geography of superstition—Turkey, Africa, Ireland—that coincided with the contours of English imperialism.

FIGURE 7. Zamzam water for sale near Mosque of Eyüp Sultan, May 2013.

Yet knowing the well in the tomb to be associated with Zamzam is not simply an abstract, intellectual relationship. As Ünver's opening note makes clear, this relationship was tangible and embodied. That affective relationship continues to resonate today.

One afternoon in Eyüp in 2013, for example, I was sitting with Serdar, a deeply pious man who often spent time in Eyüp's various *türbe*. Our conversation that day turned to the ritual practice of drinking from the faucets in the mosque. As someone who had once worked in the tomb of Halid bin Zeyd itself, he declared that there was, in fact, a key difference between the water that flowed from the faucets in the courtyard and that available in the tomb itself. The courtyard's water, he said, was simply municipal water, but as for the water that came from the well inside the tomb itself, that was zamzam water.

Serdar was by no means alone in making that connection. Conversations with other interlocutors and a variety of news reports also highlight the relationship between the well in the tomb and the well of Zamzam in Mecca. A restoration project that closed the tomb between 2011 and 2014, rendering the well off-limits to visitors, briefly generated controversy when some worried that the restoration work would disrupt the well's supply of water, mixing it with the system of canals that Istanbul's water agency (İSKİ) had built to manage the district's runoff.[35]

During my fieldwork it was particularly ironic that even though the well inside the tomb had been closed to the public because of the restoration project, visitors to Eyüp Sultan could purchase small bottles of "authentic" zamzam water from vendors in the vicinity of the mosque, who stocked prayer beads, headscarves, Qur'ans, and a range of other religious paraphernalia.[36] The zamzam water had thus come to connect Eyüp to Mecca in a slightly different form. These small bottles were sometimes distributed at some of the more expensive restaurants around the Mosque of Eyüp Sultan during Ramadan. These restaurants' sense of distinction came from their provision of zamzam water to those able to afford their relatively expensive iftar meals.

The zamzam story of Eyüp Sultan encourages us to think about the geographies of Islam differently. Instead of imagining the world of Islam as a "universal" and these local sites "as so many queer particularities that should be either eliminated or protected," we could ask instead how it is that unconnected localities "sometimes [enter] into provisionally commensurable connections."[37] This zamzam geography, to stretch Annemarie Mol and John Law's formulation, is fluid, one whose continuity is secured not by its fixity but by its capacity for gradual change.[38]

## THE FOUNTAINS OF THE INNER COURTYARD

Even though some are never able to drink from the well inside the tomb itself, everyone who visits the Mosque of Eyüp Sultan can drink from the four fountains located in the mosque's inner courtyard. While many major Ottoman-era mosques have a source of water in their courtyard—most often an ablution fountain (*şadırvan*)—the Mosque of Eyüp Sultan is slightly different. Instead of being filled with a central *şadırvan*, its inner courtyard is filled with a small fenced-in plot of earth, from which grows a large poplar tree.

At each of the four corners of the fenced-in plot is a small fountain decorated with the imperial seal (*tuğra*) of Sultan Selim III and a *sikke* associated with the Mevlevi Sufi order.[39] Sometimes referred to as the Fountains of Need (Hacet Çeşmeleri) or Fountains for Marriage Prospects (Kısmet Çeşmeleri), these fountains are frequently used by visitors to the mosque and are woven into the broader patterns of visitation.[40] Some people will visit the four fountains in sequence, while others will drink from only one. Many people use the small metal cups chained beside each spigot, but others cup their hands and bend low to drink. Others bring empty plastic water bottles to take the water home. For a few, the drinking is less important than the act of opening and closing each spigot in turn.

Like the stories of zamzam, these contemporary encounters with water in the Mosque of Eyüp Sultan have a long history. For example, a 1954 article describing Eyüp Sultan as the place where "the troubled find their comfort" points this out.[41] The author—probably male—boards a ferry from central Istanbul to Eyüp. On the ferry the author observes a group of young girls (*genç kızlar*) laughing and joking, discussing dancing, Hollywood artists, and their upcoming social engagements. On disembarking from the ferry the author loses sight of the girls but finds them again in the mosque itself. The girls, now quiet and respectful, pray in the mosque's courtyard before circling the plane tree, opening and closing each of the four faucets in sequence. "Those who open the faucets," the author observed, "will be proposed to" (*açanların kısmeti açılırmış*).[42]

FIGURE 8. Fountains in the inner courtyard of the Mosque of Eyüp Sultan, October 2012.

The waters of these fountains have thus become woven into gendered expectations about fertility and marriage. As with the stories of zamzam, these fountains' relationship to the future predates the twentieth century.[43] The gendered dimension also complicates how we read the sources, as the observers of the practices are almost invariably men; their observations thus become a way to identify gendered forms of difference. As one American observer described the scene in 1913, "[The women] raise their heavy veils and bathe pale, delicate faces in the marble basins, then pause before the grille and stand in silent prayer, outstretched palms upturned for the blessing of Allah."[44] Although this particular observer described these women as an exotic curiosity, there are likely other instances in which proper devotional practice is also linked to judgments about where and how women should move through the mosque and tomb.

Moreover, although discussions of these fountains almost invariably frame this act of drinking water as something unique to the Mosque of Eyüp Sultan (and, by extension, the tomb of Halid bin Zeyd), water and devotional practice are often woven together across Turkey.[45] Similarly, there is also evidence that encounters with the future—such as praying for marriage—similarly persist.[46] In offering these observations, my aim is not to say that what happens in the mosque is exactly what happens at other sites across Turkey today; neither is it to characterize devotional practices today as essentially fixed or unchanged. However, there are suggestive parallels between the devotional relationships with water in Eyüp Sultan and those typically related with more "rural" practices of Islam.[47] To date, many of these dynamics seem to have escaped attention in discussions of Islam in contemporary Istanbul.

## WELLS ON THE MARGINS

Beyond the central mosque, there are several other wells found in Eyüp. These wells are—or were—on the "margins." While their marginal position is sometimes the result of physical location, it has more to do with the kinds of devotional activities that take place beside them. Their ongoing presence suggests forms of enchantment that continue to circulate through Istanbul today.

One of the wells most frequently described is one that was reputed to help people find lost or missing things. Evliya Çelebi's account of Eyüp is the one most frequently drawn upon, and it has been circulated widely in newspaper columns and other publications, both with and without attribution.[48] The well was located somewhere on the large hill that rises behind the Mosque of Eyüp Sultan. In one essay, published in 1941 in the magazine *Yedigün*, the author related this version of Çelebi's story:

> Were one to lose something, they ought to first perform their ablutions and then perform two *rak'as* (Tr. *rekat*) upon the *musalla* beside the well. Then, after reciting a Fatiha and gifting its reward to the Holy Spirit of His Excellency Joseph (blessings upon him), they ought to call into the well's opening, "*Ey sahib-i pîr!* For the love of His Excellency Joseph the Loyal, what happened to my relative or my child or this lost thing of mine?"[49]

The well, Ahmet continued, was supposed to answer. A second version of the story, written by Münevver Alp in the 1960s, includes a similar set of details:

> Those who lose something, who haven't heard for a long time from one missed, who wonder whether a wish will come true used to go to the well of intention [*niyet kuyusu*] in Eyüp Sultan. They'd leave their homes having resolved to go and having performed their ablutions [*niyetli ve abdestli çıkarlar*] and as soon as they entered Eyüp Sultan, they'd visit the *türbe*, and standing in front of the Window of Need wish for true perception [*basiret*] for their heart and eyes. After, they'd reach the wishing well by ascending the narrow and steep path with the cemetery on either side.[50]

On the one hand, we could pass off these references to Evliya Çelebi as mere myth, records of an age long since passed. On the other hand, the repeated references to Çelebi's story suggest that there is something enduring about wells like this one. Moreover, these wells are not unique to Eyüp. The shrine complex of Merkez Efendi in central Istanbul also has a well-known "wishing well" (*dilek kuyusu*) attached to it.[51] These wishing wells and the stories attached to them highlight the capacity of water to link the registers of lost and found, there and here. The importance of these wishing wells across Istanbul prompts us to consider how water provides a sense of orientation in a disorienting city. Finally, these wells also suggest forms of devotional practice that do not map neatly onto a landscape of mosques and other official sites of Islam.

Yet despite the ongoing importance of these sites, they also exist on the margins of "accepted" religious practice today. Most often, practices of visiting wells are castigated as examples of superstition (*hurafe*, Ar. *hurafat*) and novelty (*bidat*, Ar. *bid'ah*). During my fieldwork between 2011 and 2013, I would occasionally become party to conversations about the "wishing well" supposedly located in Eyüp. The existence of any such well was universally denied by the staff who worked in the vicinity of the mosque. "There's nothing like that" (*Öyle bir şey yok*), they would tell people when visitors approached them in the mosque.[52]

On one occasion I was speaking with an acquaintance in the courtyard of the *sıbyan mektebi* where I taught several days a week. A woman entered the courtyard and asked us if we knew where the wishing well and the "door of repentance" (*tövbe kapısı*) were. My acquaintance replied, "You don't need to go anywhere at all, so long as the Surah at-Tawbah is in your heart." "Besides," he added, pointing at the mosque, "you're here, [where] there's a glorious Companion [*koskocaman sahabe var*]." His point was clear: there was no need to go looking for these other superstitious things.

However, there was indeed a well. A short way down the road from the *sıbyan mektebi* and the mosque there sat a small metal box in the courtyard in front of the tomb of Mirimiran Mehmet Ağa. Painted black and secured by a metal padlock, it seemed somewhat incongruous in the otherwise empty courtyard. When I first arrived in Eyüp, its presence had been pointed out to me by Ali, an imam at one of the local mosques who had grown up around the center of Eyüp. There's a well under there, he told me, that people used to drink out of. When we were kids, he added, we even used to pee in there until the municipality came and covered it up.

Although Ali didn't offer the exact date that the well had been covered, it likely followed the municipal electoral victory of the Welfare Party in 1994. As I detail in the next chapter, this project of policing superstitious forms of devotional practice was linked to the restoration of the district's historical religious fabric. Covering the well and thus physically preventing people from drinking its water was connected to an attempt to cleanse the district of inappropriate and unclean things.[53]

Even though the well was covered and locked, it continued to be a site for furtive devotional practice. Small groups—often, though not always, women—would gather around the well in the evenings or at night, and especially during the month of Ramadan. In some cases people simply faced the well while offering their prayers. At other times, however, someone might stand on top of the box itself, turning and turning until they grew dizzy.

People who chose to pray beside the well often attracted negative attention from other passersby. One afternoon in 2013, for example, I was sitting with my

acquaintance Serdar in the tomb of Mirimiran Mehmet Ağa, where he was working as an attendant collecting small donations. A man donated a few liras, and
Serdar handed him a receipt. The man walked out but quickly poked his head back
in, saying, "Just thought you should know, there's a woman out there"—pointing in
the direction of the covered well—"praying" (*namaz kılıyor*).

Serdar jumped up and glanced out the window. The woman had quickly
finished her prayers and was already walking away. He stepped out and called
politely, "*Hanım efendi*, what were you doing? Do you know that there's no benefit
to praying there?"

When he came back inside, I asked him, "Does that happen a lot?"

"Yes," he replied. "There are some people who even still want to light candles,
which we know is absolutely not a part of Islam; that's a part of Christianity, as
you know."[54]

Istanbul has long been a city of shared devotional geographies. Although its
Christian, Jewish, and Muslim communities each claim distinct sacred sites,
there are also places where those boundaries can leak.[55] Eyüp is one such place.
Nineteenth-century non-Muslim visitors often mentioned that the mosque itself
was closed to non-Muslims; to be able to drink from its fountains was a privilege
reserved for Muslims. However, the marginal character of Eyüp's other wells makes
possible other forms of devotional encounter. For some—like Serdar—this leaky
boundary provokes anxiety and the desire to sharply separate between "Christian"
and "Islamic" practices and places.

Yet Serdar's concern also speaks to a broader debate between Muslims over the
appropriateness of mediation. There are a variety of terms that circulate through
these debates, but two especially important terms are *shirk* (Tr. *şirk*) and *tawassul*
(Tr. *tevessül*). The former, commonly translated as "idolatry," is forbidden because
it involves associating God with other divinities.[56] *Tawassul*—typically translated
as "intercession"—is often associated with the capacity of saints or the Prophet
Muhammad to advocate for the community of believers on the Day of Judgment.[57]
Yet both terms share a common interest in mediation. In the case of the former,
idolatry plays out when believers ascribe divinity to the mediating substance, person, or material; in contrast, intercession is permissible because the materiality of
mediation disappears "in the act of conveying something . . . in order to redirect
attention to what is being mediated."[58] From the perspective of *tawassul*, any blessings associated with water are the result of God's grace and nothing more.

These debates about Eyüp's waters and wells signal water's capacity to connect
people with lost objects, distant places, and an unknown future. This capacity
speaks to water's role as a "semiotic form" in Eyüp, a "material manifestation that
makes [an understanding of Islam] available to, interpretable, and, in most cases,
replicable by other people."[59] People can share fluid stories precisely because the
water is material, tangible, in and of the world.

## PROVIDING WATER, MAKING PIETY MATTER

A short distance from the Mosque of Eyüp Sultan is another form of water: the *sebil* of Mihrişah Valide Sultan.[60] *Sebil* can carry a range of meanings in Turkish, including a sense of "road" or "path" that underpins an explanation of one's actions, as in *fî sebilillâh*, on the path of Allah.[61] More often, however, it refers to a specific type of urban institution: a building staffed by an individual (or individuals) who distribute water for free to passersby.[62] The *sebil* played an important role in urban life across the Muslim world, but they became an especially prominent part of cities in the Ottoman Empire in general and Istanbul in particular.

Motivations for building a *sebil* were complex. Political power and patronage were one important part of the story. In Istanbul, these *sebil* were often located in visually or symbolically prominent locations, thus communicating and reinforcing the position of those who endowed them.[63] In the case of the complex of Mihrişah Valide Sultan, it was located at the intersection of two important roads: the main road that followed the Golden Horn back in the direction of central Istanbul and the short road that led between the water and the Mosque of Eyüp Sultan. It thus stood along one of the primary roads that would have channeled visitors to the mosque and served as a backdrop for a new sultan's public investiture. However, more than simply expressing Mihrişah Valide Sultan's power and authority, this *sebil* also provided a shared infrastructure for urban citizenship, one that may have facilitated a common urban experience based on "practices, rituals, and habits."[64]

Yet *sebil* were also devotional acts, an especially noteworthy instance of "ongoing charity" (*sadaka-i câriye*), a term that refers to acts of charity whose benefits continue indefinitely.[65] Suggestively, the word for "ongoing"—*cariye*—is etymologically associated with the flow of a stream, highlighting another way that fluid stories move through both discursive and material worlds. These acts of enduring charity could take diverse forms, including the building of a road or bridge, the planting of fruit trees, the endowment of a school or mosque, or even the raising of a good child.[66]

Today the *sebil* stands dry. The reasons for its closure were complex. The establishment of the Republic of Turkey in 1923 led to the wholesale reorganization of the charitable system that had managed complexes like that of Mihrişah Valide Sultan.[67] In the 1930s and 1940s, Istanbul municipal officials also worried that many of these public water systems were vectors for diseases and bacteria like typhoid fever and *E. coli*.[68] At the same time, *sebil* and other Ottoman-era buildings were defined by some as objects of the past without a place in a modern city.[69] From one point of view, this form of piety no longer flows.

However, there are still ways that the *sebil* persists in Eyüp. Were you to walk the path from the Mosque of Eyüp Sultan to the top of the hill that rises behind it, you would pass a gleaming marble grave about halfway up the hill. The grave is that of Mahmud Esad Coşan, the former leader of the İskenderpaşa Community

FIGURE 9. Detail of *sebil* of Mihrişah Valide Sultan, December 2012.

(*Cemaat*).[70] Coşan passed away in 2001 in Australia, but his body was returned to Istanbul. At any time of day there may be a few people sitting at the edge of the well-maintained plot, reciting a portion of the Qur'an or simply offering a Fatiha for his soul. Most passersby, however, encounter the grave by means of an old man with a trimmed white beard, an easy smile, and a prayer cap on his head.

He calls out, a slight accent shaping his vowels: Water, free of charge, freeeeeee of charge. *Su bedava, bedaaaaaaaaava.* As people slow, he hustles one, two, three small plastic cups of water into their hands. If they protest, saying they could never drink all that water, he smiles and presses one more into their hands. Don't worry, he says, give it to someone else. Thank you, these passersby say. May Allah be content, others respond, *Allah razı olsun.* Regardless of how they phrase it, the spirit is the same: an expression of gratitude for the giving of water.

For the old man, giving water away is a devotional practice, what Christiane Gruber has aptly called an act of "securing good."[71] He is the caretaker for Mahmud Esad Coşan's grave, a duty that deliberately recapitulates older traditions of the *türbedar* (tomb attendant). In addition to distributing water, he tends the flowers planted on the grave and polishes the marble until it is sparkling clean. Distributing water and thus recapitulating the functions of a *sebil*, albeit in a different form, continues to serve as a pious act for this man and for many of those associated with the İskenderpaşa Community.

### GIFTS OF WATER AND CEMETERY ECOLOGIES

Encounters with water provide one means for people to share an experience of and with place. Sometimes, as in the case of the fountains in the Mosque of Eyüp Sultan, drinking the water becomes a means to share in the sacredness woven through Eyüp Sultan; in other cases, as with the wells at Eyüp's margins, sharing water generates anxieties about definitions of "proper" Islam. Yet there is a final, less noticed form through which water is shared: the small troughs or cups carved into the gravestones of Eyüp's cemeteries.[72] Known as both *kuşluk* (derived from *kuş*, bird) and *suluk* (derived from *su*, water), these objects collect rainwater for the animals who live in the cemetery.[73]

Cemeteries are typically thought of as places of human social relations, but as a range of scholars have come to argue, cemeteries also function as key sites for nonhuman ecologies.[74] The cemetery rising from the back of the Mosque of Eyüp Sultan is filled with nonhuman species: there are redbuds and cypresses, rose bushes and trees of heaven, crows and pigeons, dogs, cats, and rodents. Some of these ecologies are maintained through accident and improvisation, but these *kuşluk* and *suluk* signal an intentional effort to care for other species.

Scholars of Istanbul have recently begun to consider the relations between humans and nonhuman species from a variety of perspectives.[75] Christiane Gruber, for example, has looked at Ottoman-era birdhouses attached to mosques as

FIGURE 10. Feeding pigeons near the Mosque of Eyüp Sultan, June 2012.

"articulat[ing] an ethics of engagement with nonhuman others."[76] Similarly, there is a growing body of scholarship on the place of nonhuman species within Islam.[77] Eyüp's cemeteries have been and continue to be an important interface between human worlds and divine, animal, and natural worlds that exist alongside. How is that interface created and sustained? In part, the provision of water might be one way that an ecology of care is sustained.

## CONCLUSION

> *According to the story* [rivayete göre], *some of these waters extend back to the times before Istanbul was captured by the Turks five centuries ago.*
> —AHMET SÜHEYL ÜNVER, "CONCERNING POPULAR KNOWLEDGE OF THE
> HEALING QUALITIES OF SOME OF ISTANBUL'S BITTER AND SWEET WATERS"

Istanbul is a city defined by its multiple densities. Two of the most important are its stories and its waters. Indeed, it is striking how frequently Istanbul's stories mention water, and how any discussion of its waters will make references to the city's stories, as with the epigraph that begins this section. By placing stories and water in conversation, this chapter has followed how water and story combine to make Eyüp a place of Islam. Examining both water's central role in devotional practice in Eyüp and debates over its capacity to sustain connection helps us think about the geographies of Islam in four overlapping ways.

First, water provides a rich point of departure for understanding how places are formed both through embedded practice and symbolic relationships that link those places to elsewhere. We cannot understand the importance of Zamzam to Eyüp, for example, without considering the well of Zamzam in Mecca. Yet water also links places to the past. Some of Eyüp's waters derive their importance from their connection to deeper histories, some of which trace the contours of the district's Byzantine past. Places are not hermetically sealed boxes but "articulated moments . . . where a large proportion of those relations, experiences and understandings are constructed on a far larger scale than what we happen to define for that moment as the place itself."[78] Focusing on water also challenges the assumption that the Mosque of Eyüp Sultan is an essentially "urban" site. Kimberly Hart has usefully called our attention to the persistent urban bias in scholarship on Islam.[79] When we follow water, we see that it brings ostensibly "rural" practices into the city in unexpected ways. Rather than seeing "urban" Islam as the default, we might think in terms of fluid stories to help us imagine the relationship between the urban and the rural differently.

Second, storytelling is a key practice through which people define shared places of Islam. Scholars have done well to consider the role that genre, narrative, and print culture play in these projects and have called our attention to the importance of shared modes of writing, reading, and interpretation.[80] But water might be thought of as a different kind of semiotic form, one that can be shared between many different people in ways distinct from books, manuscripts, or cassette tapes. It is water's capacity to be shared widely that often makes it such an object of contestation and concern.

Third, water is also interesting because it is so deeply interwoven with broader discussions about charity, care, and mutual responsibility. Providing water in Eyüp, whether in the form of Mihrişah Valide Sultan's *sebil* or in the form of an attendant distributing water beside the tomb of Mahmud Esad Coşan or in any number of other ways, is an act that constitutes social relationships.[81] Like any number of other contexts, the place of water has shifted in far-reaching ways over the course of the past century. The development of a municipal water system and the expansion of private water delivery have brought benefits, but they have also transformed how many in Istanbul today interact with water. Perhaps bringing our focus back to water, stories, and Islam will encourage us to think about other forms of enchantment and relationship that might bind people to their city and each other in different ways.

Fourth, Eyüp's fluid stories ask us to think about the multiple ontologies of water. Rather than thinking of water as a single substance—say, two atoms of hydrogen and one atom of oxygen—following water along its various stories and infrastructures asks us to consider both common qualities and the ways that water is encountered differently. Water never exists apart from the infrastructures and objects through which it becomes accessible and ingestible: cups, ewers, beakers, troughs, wells, fountains, springs, and more. Similarly, what water is depends in part on how people know it. Thus Süheyl Ünver's brief essay asks us to consider the different modes—that of the people (*halk*) and that of the hydrologist—through which water was defined, known, and ingested.[82] Ünver's article suggests that these different ways of knowing "healthy waters"—and thus enacting water in this place—were multiple, one perhaps existing alongside each other.

In the second part of the book I turn from these practices of storytelling to a second mode of making Eyüp a place of Islam: building. As readers will notice, many of the themes that I introduced in this section reappear, albeit in slightly different form. Water shows up in the chapter on Ramadan; stories about Halid bin Zeyd continue to matter; and, as we see at the beginning of the next chapter, the story of Eyüp's transformation during the 1990s begins with the case of a curious fountain.

# PART II

# Building (*Bina*)

*And so the great and famous persons who made Byzantium a Muslim city, Constantinople Istanbul, Istanbul İslambol [literally, full of Islam]; the peerless masterpieces and mosques; and thus the eternal seals of Islam and faith; and thus the medals of the nation [milliyet]. These are the works, the memories that make Istanbul ours. The fountains, the mosques, the public fountains founded beside the mosques, the public kitchens [imaret], the madrasas, the libraries. . . . Brought together in these is a balance of this world and the next; they are the faith of Islam embodied in built form [yapı şeklinde]. Not the inescapable looting of the shore, the greed for money that burns the old mansions [yalı], the soulless, faceless apartments rising to the sky . . .*

—ABDÜLBAKI GÖKPINARLI, "EYÜP SULTAN AND ISTANBUL"

*Whosoever builds a mosque for Allah, Allah builds for him a home in Paradise.*

*Man banā lillāhi masjidan banā allāhu lahu baītan fī-l-jannati.*

— HADITH OF THE PROPHET MUHAMMAD, *INSCRIBED ABOVE AN ENTRANCE TO THE MOSQUE OF EYÜP SULTAN*

BUILDINGS MAKE PLACES. They do so in a variety of ways. For example, they provide focal points, places for people to gather and to consider from afar. Buildings—especially monumental ones—also have a politics, often seeking to concretize fluid forms of identity,[1] render communities and populations legible,[2] or orchestrate a spectacle of the state.[3] Their construction, destruction, and redevelopment can help to organize an urban political economy.[4] Buildings can make places by functioning as mnemonic sites, "material vehicles of meaning that either [help] construct a memory of [a past] . . . or [serve] as symbolic markers for commemorations of present national accomplishments and the possibilities of the future."[5] Yet even though buildings often seek to stabilize a specific configuration of history and geography, "the affective materialities of a place . . . may surpass instrumental efforts to make selective pasts speak through them."[6]

Buildings seem to be distinct, well-bounded objects, the boundary between inside and outside marked with walls, doors, thresholds, and windows. For this reason, they often help to mark out legible spaces of the sacred and the profane; in twentieth-century Turkey, they also seem to draw sharp lines between the secular and the religious.

Yet the relationships embodied in built form are neither stable nor homogeneous but embedded in "networks of association that work to keep [them] in place or to pull [them] apart."[7] From this point of view, studying buildings asks us to consider how various building materials link them elsewhere in shifting and unstable ways.[8] Although buildings seem to be grounded in a specific site, they are in fact linked to other places and times through a variety of material and imagined

FIGURE 11. View of the Mosque of Eyüp Sultan from the central square, November 2012. The hadith is inscribed above the entrance.

infrastructures. Buildings make place precisely because they stabilize—sometimes briefly, sometimes for centuries—a set of relationships that exist within them and stretch well beyond them.[9]

Building—translated as *bina*—can refer both to the object (a building) and the practice (to build). As with *rivayet*, I use *bina* in a deliberate expansive sense, as a point of departure to help us think about the "multiplicity that is constitutive of all geographies as they are produced, destroyed, and remade."[10] This approach is especially important because Eyüp's buildings are often encountered as self-evident markers of the past. They are, to quote Abdülbaki Gölpınarlı, "The memories that make Istanbul ours."

We should take these claims seriously and seek to understand how groups and individuals make sense of themselves in relation to this place. On the other hand, however, it is equally important to interrogate the "we" that is defined in relation to this "where." Thinking of places—and thus buildings—as *multiple* helps to remind us that the shape of this world could always be otherwise. Rather than seek to define a "correct" meaning about Eyüp, this section works through buildings to "open [their] various dimensions" and "[give] visibility to the various dimensions" less often considered.[11]

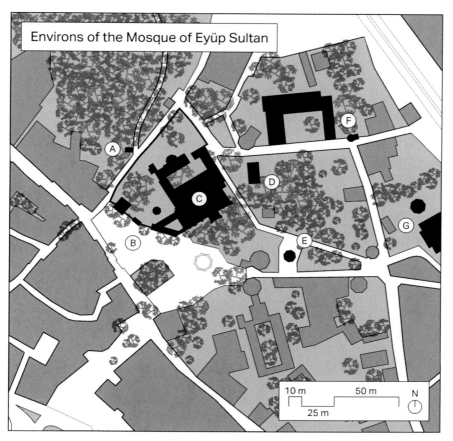

MAP 3. Environs of the Mosque of Eyüp Sultan, showing the Fountain of the Eternal Eyüpsultanlıs (A); the central square (B); the Mosque of Eyüp Sultan (C); the *sıbyan mektebi* (D); the tomb of Mirimiran Paşa (E); the *imaret* and *sebil* of Mihrişah Valide Sultan (F); and the tomb of Sultan Reşad (G).

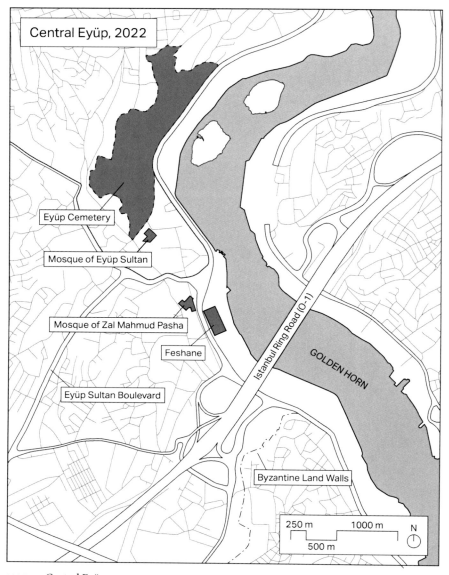

Central Eyüp, 2022

Eyüp Cemetery

Mosque of Eyüp Sultan

Mosque of Zal Mahmud Pasha

Feshane

Eyüp Sultan Boulevard

Istanbul Ring Road (O-1)

GOLDEN HORN

Byzantine Land Walls

250 m          1000 m          N

500 m

MAP 4. Central Eyüp, 2022.

# 5

## Ottoman Topographies

On a warm spring Sunday, visitors from all corners of Istanbul fill Eyüp. Most make a point to visit the Mosque of Eyüp Sultan to pray in front of the tomb of Halid bin Zeyd and—if there's space—many participate in the midday prayers on Saturday. But other people come to Eyüp simply to enjoy the atmosphere, posing for photographs in front of the fountain beside the mosque and walking in small groups through the square. Regardless of whether visitors pass through the mosque itself, many of them make their way up to the top of the hill that begins immediately behind the mosque. There they might stand on the wide platform built by the Istanbul Municipality and can take in a spectacular panorama of Istanbul. Some might pass from there to a nearby café named after the French writer and traveler Pierre Loti, who, the stories say, spent time here at the end of the nineteenth century.

From the center of Eyüp the hilltop is reached in one of two ways: by taking the funicular that ferries visitors above the graves of Eyüp's cemetery or by walking along the original path that begins immediately behind the Mosque of Eyüp Sultan. A fountain stands at the beginning of that path. It is roughly square in shape, its carved white marble rising high above the passersby.

At the top of the fountain, flanked by roundels of the Turkish flag and the Ottoman coat of arms, there is a simple phrase etched into the marble and gilded in gold: "Ebedi Eyüpsultanlılar" (The Eternal Eyüpsultanlıs)." Below, in neatly lettered columns that flank the water spigot, the names of a seemingly arbitrary group of individuals have been inscribed into the marble, along with their dates of birth and death. A moment's reflection and it becomes clear: these are the famous people who are buried here, in a place the fountain calls Eyüpsultan. As someone from the city of Ankara would be called an Ankaralı, someone from Trabzon a Trabzonlu, and someone from Istanbul an İstanbullu, these figures have been marked as natives of Eyüp Sultan.

FIGURE 12. The Fountain of the Eternal Eyüpsultanlıs, June 2012.

At the center of the fountain is a second, smaller inscription. In contrast to the others, this smaller inscription is written in Ottoman Turkish, whose public use was outlawed in 1928, and thus today is illegible to nearly everyone who passes by.

"Is that Arabic?" visitors sometimes ask each other. If their companions know, they will reply, "No, it's Ottoman." Regardless, the illegibility of the script seems to mark the fountain as something older, a reminder of the past. But reading the inscription tells a curious story:

> He built an adorned fountain, may his
>    prayer be answered
> May its proof be Allah, its benevolence Mustafa
> May a drinker drink once more, may it bring
>    them health
> May it be a gift to Eyüp Sultan from Mayor
>    Ahmet Genç.[1]

Below, the inscription adds two dates: May 29, 2002, and 16 Rabi' al-awwal 1423.[2] Amidst a landscape of centuries-old tombs, mosques, and graveyards, this fountain marks a relatively recent figure of the past. How did this fountain come to be

here? Why does it juxtapose markers of the Ottoman past with a decidedly contemporary present? And more broadly, what might this fountain tell us about how
building stories are told in contemporary Istanbul?

The fountain is one product of the broader project that this chapter explores:
how Eyüp became a key place from and through which the Ottoman past was
made. When it comes to buildings, we often think about the past as something that
already exists in the world. We excavate the past, uncover it, discover it, display it,
as though it stands apart from our lives in the present.[3] In contrast, this chapter
argues that the past is always made in specific places and times. Borrowing Nadia
Abu El-Haj's insight, the city must be reconfigured "in particular ways for the
objects of [heritage] to become visible, not simply by transforming absence into
presence, but . . . by creating particular angles of vision through which landscapes
are remade."[4] Thinking in terms of "Ottoman topographies" provides one frame to
help us consider how multiple versions of the past are told through specific places.
The fountain serves as an especially rich point of departure. On the one hand,
its decoration—especially the inscription written in Ottoman Turkish—is deliberately designed to appear in harmony with the Ottoman-era objects that surround
it. On the other hand—and as the inscription itself documents—the fountain is
the product of a far more recent conjunction of people, politics, and the material landscape. Beginning with the 1994 municipal electoral victory of the Welfare
Party, Eyüp was remade as an "authentic" Ottoman neighborhood. This project
was accomplished in two principal ways: the telling of new public histories about
Eyüp, and the systematic restoration and redevelopment of the urban landscape
in Eyüp's central neighborhoods.

The key actor in this project was the local municipality—and two figures in particular, Mayor Ahmet Genç and İrfan Çalışan, the Eyüp Municipality's Director of
Culture and Tourism (*Kültür ve Turizm Müdürü*). But this project was in dialogue
with both residents of and visitors to the district, some of whom supported the
changes and others of whom spoke out against them. The project of making Eyüp
Ottoman was fundamentally a project of establishing new forms of connection
between political institutions, government bodies, district residents (both new
and old), and visitors to Eyüp.

Collectively, these new forms of connection helped to make Eyüp a new kind of
place. Formerly a peripheral district within Istanbul's social geography, Eyüp was
recast and reimagined as Istanbul's religious and cultural center through the recla-
mation of the Ottoman past. Yet as this chapter shows, the reconstruction of Turkey's Ottoman past through the telling of Eyüp's history and the transformation
of Eyüp's landscape created uneven, inconsistent, and even contradictory effects.
These projects enacted new—but not necessarily shared—visions of history and
heritage, economic relationships that rechanneled flows of money and influence,
and conflicts about the district's history and importance.

## MUNICIPAL POLITICS AND MULTIPLE
## OTTOMAN PASTS

On September 12, 1980, following a decade of politically motivated violence, the seeming inability of the country's political parties to govern the country, and an ongoing economic crisis, Turkey's military declared martial law and dissolved the constitution and all political parties. The government was reorganized under the supervision of the newly established National Security Council, which took the lead in liberalizing Turkey's economy, writing a new constitution in 1982, and reorganizing Turkey's system of municipal governance.[5] Prior to the coup, there had been an increasing awareness that municipal institutions (*belediye*) were unable to deliver services like trash, water, asphalt roads, and electricity equally to all municipal residents. The system was at once too centralized (dependent on Ankara for planning and financing) and too dispersed (municipalities mushrooming on the boundaries of urban centers) to function effectively.

The solution was the formation of a two-tier system of municipal governance. Istanbul was declared a "metropolitan municipality" (*büyük belediye*), with smaller "district municipalities" (*ilçe belediyeleri*) nested within it. The goal of the system was to shift authority for planning and development from central authorities to local municipalities that would—in theory—be more responsive to their residents. In 1983 the Eyüp Municipality was one of more than twenty district municipalities created within this new two-tier system.[6]

This shift in governance happened alongside a massive shift in Istanbul's urban economy, involving both the privatization of formerly state-owned enterprises and the systematic relocation of factories from Istanbul's central districts to its peripheries.[7] Although this project involved a range of actors and institutions, one of its central characters was Bedrettin Dalan, the newly elected mayor of the reorganized Istanbul Metropolitan Municipality. In 1985 Dalan authorized the wholesale demolition of the dense fabric of workshops, factories, and warehouses that filled both shores of the Golden Horn in central Istanbul. Almost overnight, both sides of the Golden Horn were bulldozed and expropriated for municipal use. While many of the formerly state-owned factories located along the waterway had already been sold as part of Turkey's economic liberalization between 1980 and 1984, Dalan's urban interventions spelled the end of whatever workshops had survived. Deindustrialization had a massive effect on Eyüp, which to that point had been a largely working-class district. One consequence of this shift was an increased emphasis on developing Eyüp's potential as a tourist destination. As I note below, the new Eyüp Municipality would play an important role in planning its future development.[8]

This municipal-level political and economic transformation intersected with the rise of Necmettin Erbakan and his National Outlook Movement (Milli Görüş Hareketi). First established in the 1970s, this movement initially played a relatively minor role within a political establishment dominated by the conflict between the center-right Justice Party and the center-left Republican People's Party.[9] Erbakan, however, capitalized on the political fragmentation of the 1970s, joining several coalition governments as a junior partner. Following the 1980 coup, Erbakan was initially banned from political life, as were several other leading politicians of the time. Following Erbakan's rehabilitation in 1987, he assumed leadership of the Welfare Party (Refah Partisi).

In the 1994 municipal elections, the Welfare Party was the surprise winner in a split electorate. There were several factors that led to the Welfare Party's unexpected success, including the sudden death of Prime Minister Turgut Özal in 1993, municipal scandals in Istanbul that solidified opposition against the incumbent Social Democratic People's Party, and ongoing political fragmentation. All of this made it possible for Recep Tayyip Erdoğan to become the mayor of the Istanbul Metropolitan Municipality with only 26 percent of the total vote.[10] At the district municipality level, the Welfare Party's vote share was almost the same. Ahmet Genç, a longtime resident of the district, was elected as mayor of the Eyüp Municipality in 1994.

Genç was a *mahalle çocuğu*—a neighborhood kid—who had moved up through the local organization of the Welfare Party. In many ways his election was typical of the Welfare Party's success in promoting locals for political office.[11] But Genç was not actually born in Eyüp; along with his parents, he had migrated to Eyüp in the 1950s from the Black Sea, which made him one of the millions of people who swelled Istanbul's population between the 1950s and the 1990s. These people were part of the large-scale migration to urban centers like Istanbul and Ankara that reshaped cities' landscapes (through the growth of informal *gecekondu* settlements) and their social and political life (through the articulation of contested forms of urban belonging).[12]

In part, the success of the Welfare Party in the 1994 election was predicated upon their claim to represent peripheral neighborhoods that had been "neglected" by an entrenched (and central) political establishment. In one important respect, however, Eyüp differed from peripheral migrant districts such as Ümraniye and Sultanbeyli: Eyüp's built environment—and its identity as a place with its own history—predated the large-scale migration of the 1950s, '60s, and '70s.[13] This provided a different opportunity for local party officials to present themselves not only as representing the desires of an excluded populace but also as rescuing a history materialized in the form of Eyüp's Ottoman-era buildings.

The Welfare Party's 1994 municipal campaign thus mobilized the Ottoman past in a variety of ways. They drew explicit parallels between the 1453 Ottoman conquest of Istanbul and their political campaigns, promising that their victory would be like a second conquest of Istanbul.[14] This enabled two important things: First, they were able to portray themselves as outsiders set on redeeming the fallen city of Istanbul and returning it to its Ottoman Muslim glory. Second, because they framed themselves as "Ottomans," Welfare Party supporters were able to mount an alternative claim for belonging in Istanbul. Even though they were often from migrant families, mobilizing the Ottoman past helped the Welfare Party simultaneously position itself as very new and very old.

The Welfare Party's rethinking of the Ottoman past was the most visible part of a much broader reevaluation of Ottoman identity in the 1980s and 1990s. When the Turkish Republic was founded in 1923, its legitimacy and authority were based in part upon an explicit separation from the Ottoman past. That separation was established in several ways, including a new civil legal code, restrictions on religious dress and worship in public, new forms of architecture and urban planning, new calendars, and a language reform that replaced the modified Arabic script of Ottoman Turkish with the modified Latin script of "modern" Turkish.

One of the first signs of changing official attitudes toward the Ottoman legacy emerged in the 1980s, when the then prime minister Turgut Özal mobilized the Ottoman past to negotiate Turkey's changing international relationships. Emphasizing the Ottoman Empire's experience (and ostensible success) governing different ethnic groups, some came to define the Ottoman past as an exceptional example of pluralism and multiculturalism.[15] Simultaneously, the Ottoman past was also often redefined as a "Turkish" one, suggesting the ways that a distinctly modern definition of Turkish ethnicity was mapped back onto the past.[16] The Ottoman Empire could thus simultaneously function as a peerless example of multiethnic coexistence and a Turkish-Islamic synthesis par excellence.

However, although these two modes sometimes aligned, a series of events in the 1980s and 1990s helped to drive them further apart. First, the rejection of Turkey's application to the European Union in 1989 sparked a shift where some framed the Ottoman Empire not as part of Europe but as an alternative to it.[17] Second, the violence that followed Yugoslavia's dissolution and the perception that Europe's slow response to ethnically and religiously motivated massacres was tacit encouragement of Christian massacres of Muslim populations provided further support for Ottoman imaginaries. Third, Turkey's changing cultural economy made the Ottoman past an attractive landscape. Rather than draw on existing symbols and landscapes of the Kemalist state, these new actors articulated a range of new positions, often drawing on "Ottoman" references to construct a new cultural and social vocabulary. For the Welfare Party and its supporters, the "Ottoman" functioned as an explicit critique of Turkey's Republican legacy.[18]

The entry of the Ottoman (Turkish-Islamic) past into the public sphere coincided with a new attitude about Turkey's Republican history. Much of the secular establishment came to view the first decades of the Republic as a bygone "early Republic."[19] Simultaneously, formerly public "Republican" symbols entered private venues in new ways, part of an affective relationship that Esra Özyürek has described as a "nostalgia for the modern."[20] In short, a new municipal government, the city's deindustrialization, and emerging debates over the meaning of the Ottoman past came together in Eyüp during the 1980s and 1990s.

## MAKING A NEW CENTER THROUGH NEW HISTORIES

In June 2013 I was speaking with a group of young women and men who had grown up in Eyüp. All of us were born in the 1980s, which meant that their child-hoods had taken place amidst the district's transformation, and that they had been teenagers when the Welfare Party came to power in Istanbul and in Eyüp. All three felt positively about the changes that they had witnessed, and Ali used a story from his childhood to explain how Eyüp had changed for the better:

> In 1990, when I was in third grade . . . I remember going to get my teeth looked at in the Çapa Medical Faculty [one of the largest and oldest medical schools in Istanbul, located within the city walls]. I'll never forget this, the doctor asked me, "Where do you live?" "I live in Eyüp," I said. "Allah Allah," the doctor said. "Is there really somewhere like that in Istanbul?" It rubbed me the wrong way because Eyüpsultan, Alibeyköy [the adjacent neighborhood] were always looked down on as slums, bad, filthy neighborhoods [*varoş, kötü, pis semt diye geçiyordu*].

In 2013, by contrast, Eyüp was not that kind of place. "Following the redoing of the Golden Horn," Ali added, "and Eyüpsultan's promotion (*tanıtılması*), people began to say here was a second Kaaba, a second Mecca [*insanlar şöyle bir söz olmaya başladı, burası ikinci Kâbe, ikinci Mekke demeye başladılar*]."

Ali's use of the term *varoş* connects to a broader social geography of Istanbul where Eyüp marked one "urban location of a set of characteristics—poverty, rural origin, Muslim lifestyling, veiling, patriarchy—that function[ed] as an inverting mirror, reflecting back a Turkish modernity characterized by middle-class, urban values and lifestyle, secular clothing, and the autonomous Cartesian individual."[21] Creating a new Ottoman topography involved several parts: a broader reengage-ment with the Ottoman past, a political and cultural critique of Turkey's twentieth century, and the articulation of new forms of Muslim life that connected Turkey to the broader Muslim world.

Ali's story also draws our attention to another equally important consequence of making Eyüp Ottoman: it reconfigured Istanbul's social and cultural geographies, turning a formerly marginal district into a place from which new actors could articulate powerful claims for belonging in Turkey and—more immediately—in Istanbul.[22] Producing that transformation—one neatly captured by Eyüp's shift from being *varoş* to being a religious center comparable to Mecca—was a key goal of defining a new Ottoman topography.

The Eyüp Municipality was the central figure in reshaping Eyüp during this period, but it was embedded within a far more complicated network of central government institutions, local and metropolitan municipalities, and civil soci-ety organizations. These included the Istanbul Metropolitan Municipality and its various offices, the Council for the Preservation of Natural and Cultural Heri-tage (Kültür ve Tabiat Varlıklarını Koruma Kurulu) in Istanbul and Ankara, the

General Directorate of Foundations (Vakıflar Genel Müdürlüğü), and the Prime Minister's Office (Başbakanlık) in Ankara. I turn now, however, to one individual at the center of this project: İrfan Çalışan, the Eyüp Municipality's Director of Culture and Tourism.

In August 1995 Çalışan sat down with Erdal Şimşek, then a reporter from the conservative newspaper *Akit*. In their interview Şimşek turned their conversation to the topic of Pierre Loti. The name referred (and still refers) both to the French writer who visited Istanbul at the end of the nineteenth century and to the café overlooking central Eyüp and the Golden Horn, which was one of the district's best-known tourist destinations. Şimşek began by framing his question in relation to the cultural history of the Republic of Turkey:

> The new regime established in Ankara [in 1923] completely disregarded the riches belonging to our history and our culture and tried to invent new things. It intentionally left Eyüp to die. And it embraced Pierre Loti in Eyüp. . . . How do you evaluate this new system—one built upon a rejection of [its] inheritance [*Redd-i Miras*]—embracing something (Pierre Loti) that still belonged to the Ottomans?[23]

Şimşek's question drew upon a contested topography of heritage that the readers of *Akit* would have been aware of. Eyüp—a place thick with religious meanings—was replaced in the Republican era by the café of Pierre Loti—an "exotic" place associated with a French Orientalist. Although Eyüp retained its "historic" character, that character was produced by absenting Eyüp's religious (and Ottoman) significance.

In his reply, İrfan Bey agreed with Şimşek: Pierre Loti was part of an Ottoman story whose religious core was grounded in Eyüp. However, because the municipality thought of Eyüp "as a whole" (*bir bütün olarak*), İrfan Bey continued, Pierre Loti was not a replacement of an Ottoman story but "a part of [that] whole" (*bir bütünün parçası*). Rather than seeing Pierre Loti as something distinct from a rejected Ottoman identity, İrfan Bey insisted that Loti—both the nineteenth-century writer and the café being redeveloped in the 1990s—had to be understood as being connected to and subsumed under the broader religious whole of Eyüp.

This brief exchange condenses three interrelated parts of the new public history told by the Eyüp Municipality in the late 1990s: a rethinking of the Ottoman legacy that critiqued the twentieth-century project of both Westernization and modernization; the role of conservative religious media in sharing those histories; and the construction of a new physical infrastructure of and for Eyüp's history. In short, the telling of this new public history was embedded within "interlocking institutions and communities of practice out of which artifacts, maps, names, landscapes, architectures, exhibitions, historical visions, and political realities" linked to the Ottoman past came to ground in Eyüp.[24] In the process, Eyüp—or Eyüp Sultan, as most would write—was transformed from a *varoş* place into a "a land of aristocrats" (*aristokrat diyarı*).

Within months of assuming office following the March 1994 elections, the Eyüp Municipality began to articulate a new way of telling Eyüp's history that emphasized two things.[25] First, this new history presented itself as a corrective to previous—that is, more "secular"—ways of understanding the Ottoman past. At the same time, this new way of telling history also stressed Eyüp's essential "Ottoman" identity.[26] Within a city fundamentally shaped by the long intersection of cultures, languages, and religions, Eyüp's importance stemmed not from mixing but from purity, from the district's uniquely Muslim Ottoman character. One of the first articulations of this new history came in the opening pages of a pamphlet produced by the Eyüp Municipality to document their municipal achievements:

> What a shame that throughout the history of the Republic our boorish attitude toward Ottoman history was also reflected in Eyüp and has been able to bring only a few of these elegant works [the wooden mansions and palaces that once lined the shores of the Golden Horn] to the present day.
> The village of Eyüpsultan, created from nothing outside Istanbul's walls, is completely the product of the Ottoman understanding of urbanism. Despite the passage of centuries since the city's founding and especially being wrapped in a veil of neglect for the past seventy years, Eyüpsultan has not changed its character as an authentic example of Ottoman urbanism [*Eyüpsultan Osmanlı şehirciliğinin özgün bir örneği olma vasfını değiştirmemiştir*].[27]

In the Eyüp Municipality's *Third Year Bulletin*, Mayor Genç sharpened his critique of the Kemalist state's rejection of the Ottoman past in favor of "Westernization": "In place of enslaving ourselves to the West [*Batıya köle olup*] for years in the name of Westernization and being imitators, [we have] now, with local administration, taken the step to becoming a leading country."[28]

Mayor Genç criticized the "neglect" of the Ottoman past and the "imitation" of the West in the preface to Mehmet Nermi Haskan's *Eyüp Sultan History*, republished by the Eyüp Municipality:

> However, for the last seventy years, an administration that has not known what to do and has had neither goal nor ideal has shown itself with its talent for degrading the city as with people. . . . Societies should know their histories well [*Toplumlar tarihlerini iyi bilmelidirler*] such that they might claim the values in their possession. Otherwise, they will never know what to do and blindly imitate others.[29]

In critiquing the legacy of Republican reforms and holding up the Ottoman past as the true and authentic ideal of Turkey's cultural identity, the Eyüp Municipality's new public history echoed a wider Islamist critique of the Republic.[30] What made it different, however, was the way that this history was tangibly expressed in Eyüp. The material degradation of Eyüp's tombs, houses, cemeteries, and Sufi lodges was taken as evidence of intentional neglect; following 1994, these buildings' restoration and redevelopment became proof of a new respect for an authentic cultural identity. The Eyüp Municipality grounded its claims for new

FIGURE 13. "A Return to Origins." Photocopy of *Vakit*'s front page, August 1994.

forms of urban, national, and transnational identities in the new public history that it told.

In some respects, the way of telling Eyüp's history that emerged in the 1990s was not new. From the very first decades of the Turkish Republic, a range of writers had contested the rejection of the Ottoman past. Writers like Ahmet Hamdi Tanpınar, Necip Fazıl Kısakürek, and Refik Halit Karay were acutely aware of how the telling of history could function as a potent political and social critique.[31] By the same token, Eyüp's history was not unknown. As chapter 3 described, Eyüp's history was a frequent topic of newspaper serials during the 1950s, with columnists detailing the district's various—and almost always vanished— Ottoman wonders.

What changed in the 1990s were the coordination and the scale of this history telling. For the first time the Eyüp Municipality explicitly positioned itself as the authorized "protector" of Eyüp's history. This account helped establish the local municipality as a key political actor. Newspapers like *Vakit, Milli Gazete, Yeni Şafak, Akit, Yeni Asya,* and *Zaman* played a key role. Marketed to a conservative and religious audience, these newspapers generated a broader public religious awareness about Eyüp and Islam that was neither the "taken for granted" Islam of the Turkish state nor the everyday Islam "embedded in the fabric of social existence and reproduced through communal practice."[32] Instead, these newspaper stories were a mediated heritage that transmitted and transformed everyday understandings of Eyüp(sultan).[33]

In the first two years following the Welfare Party's 1994 municipal victory, Eyüp's transformation was a regular news item in the conservative press. Usually published as full-page spreads that combined text, photographs of Eyüp, and photographs of Mayor Genç and Director Çalışan, newspaper articles closely echoed—if not outright copied—the history told by the municipality in municipal publications. "Eyüp is now a 'Sultan,'" declared one boldface headline in *Milli Gazete* in 1994. An August 1994 article published in *Vakit* declared, "A Return to Origins in Eyüp." Photographs accompanying the article's text juxtaposed the ruins of small mosque in Eyüp with images of workers repairing mosque walls and restoring Ottoman inscriptions. The article began by referencing a prior history of the state using mosques as storehouses and stables as part of Turkey's state-led secularization: "Mosques and historic monuments once used as stables and depots are now embracing their previous identities."[34]

Alongside the newspaper campaign, the Eyüp Municipality also embarked upon an ambitious program of assembling an archive of Eyüp's history and supporting the publication of histories about Eyüp. One of the first books they published was Mehmet Nermi Haskan's *History of Eyüp*, originally published in 1993 by the Turkey Touring and Tourism Administration Foundation and republished in 1995 as the *History of Eyüpsultan*.[35] They also republished Cemal Öğüt's out-of-print and relatively unknown *Eyyûb Sultan*, originally published in 1955.[36]

In addition to republishing (and thus claiming for the municipality) out-of-print volumes, the municipality also organized an annual symposium. Beginning in 1997, a wide variety of individuals presented papers on all manner of topics relating to Eyüp and its history. Despite the breadth of the papers, now published in the twelve volumes of *The Eyüpsultan Symposium with Its History, Culture, and Art (Tarihi, Kültürü ve Sanatıyla Eyüpsultan Sempozyumu)*, only a fraction of papers addressed Eyüp's Republican history.[37] Those that did address Eyüp's more recent history tended to focus on the various restoration projects within the district. On the topic of the district's history in the 1950s, '60s, or '70s, however, there was almost nothing.

Finally, the municipality also opened several new spaces for the consumption of the Ottoman past. As İrfan Bey described in an August 1995 interview, one of the municipality's first goals was gathering documents and knowledge about Eyüp. Finding very little, they set out to acquire whatever materials they could and establish an archive and library under the sponsorship of the Eyüp Municipality that would become the first of its kind among Istanbul's municipalities.[38] In addition to this archive and library, they turned restored Ottoman monuments into public educational centers, a local museum, and municipal offices. Significantly, these spaces were open to a broad range of Eyüp's population. Municipal publications from this period repeatedly stressed the venues' openness to the "people" (*halk*), in contrast to the ostensibly "elite" nature of cultural venues in other districts. The Ottoman past was imagined and presented as an authentic past in which not only the cultural elite but a broad pious public could participate.

When I met with İrfan Bey in his office on the top floor of the Eyüp Municipality in 2013, tall bookshelves overflowing with books about Ottoman history, culture, art, architecture, and poetry lined the walls of his office. Behind his desk was a long credenza topped with an elegantly bound collection of books whose spines spelled *Eyüpsultan Külliyatı (The Collected Works of Eyüp Sultan)*. Included among those books were Mehmet Nermi Haskan's history of Eyüp, Cemal Öğüt's two-volume biography and commentary, and the reprinted proceedings of the Eyüpsultan Symposium. I asked him a general question about how Eyüp had transformed during the 1990s. Expecting that he would list the many changes in Eyüp's material landscape, I was surprised when he opened instead with a discussion of scale:

> It's necessary to evaluate [these changes] at both the micro- and macroscale [*küçük ölçekli ve büyük ölçekli*]. When we say macroscale, how is this center [*merkez*] known as Eyüp accepted within the world of Islam, what kinds of viewpoints are there, what kinds of recognitions are there? . . . How is Eyüp evaluated within the scale of Turkey and how is Eyüp evaluated within the scale of Istanbul? When this is considered in that way—it's only when considered within these scales that the projects undertaken during the 1980s, '90s, and 2000s can be properly understood.[39]

One of the reasons that the Welfare Party and its successors the Virtue Party (Fazilet Partisi) and the currently ruling Justice and Development Party (Adalet ve

Kalkınma Partisi) have been so politically successful is their ability to organize at the local level, mobilizing a form of "vernacular politics" grounded in local cultural and social traditions.[40] At the same time—and as İrfan Bey's emphasis on the "micro- and macroscale" demonstrates—the Welfare Party's understanding of the local (*yerel* or *yerli*) was articulated in relation to the "global." The retelling of Eyüp's history during this period was a scale-making project that connected Eyüp imaginatively and institutionally to other local, national, and global actors.

One site in which those connections were particularly apparent was Mayor Genç's opening address at the annual Eyüpsultan Symposium. In 1998, for example, Mayor Genç drew on the familiar trope of the world as a "global village" to contextualize the importance of the symposium: "Our world, undergoing a very rapid change and transformation, has become a sort of small village. Everyone knows a little about some things, a lot about others. Despite that, we're in a period that is experiencing a great impoverishment of knowledge, far from the real qualities and true topics of 'knowledge.'"[41] As he framed it, the municipality's symposium not only had local significance, but it also contributed to a project of establishing "global" knowledge. Mayor Genç made that connection even more explicitly in his opening address in 2000, saying, "Our own cultural values, acquiring universal dimensions, are obligated to surpass locality [*yerellik*] and become world property."[42]

At one of the last symposia organized while Genç was still mayor, he returned to these familiar themes. After a decade in office, his municipal administration had refined and polished its message. His introduction to the symposium demonstrates that making an Ottoman topography was not just a project of local belonging, national history telling, or even global Islam; instead, it was woven out of all three, both grounded in and helping to reshape Eyüp's connections to the broader world:

> There are three fundamental pillars that make it possible for a society to intervene in history as a subject: religion, culture, and civilization. Religion is the only source of a society's spirit of emergence, existence, and mastery over situations under any circumstance. In this country—despite everything—the thing that has formed society's map of meaning is being Muslim [*Müslümanlık*] and another thing, another doctrine, another project can never replace the local [*yerli*] mentality and attitude that simultaneously surround and render meaningful a person's internal and external world.[43]

Although Eyüp Municipality publications produced in the decade prior to the Welfare Party's 1994 election occasionally alluded to national and global events, they rarely framed local municipal governance in terms broader than Eyüp itself. What changed in 1994 was the emergence of a self-conscious and sustained project of placing Eyüp (rather than Istanbul) on the global map. The project was successful in part because Eyüp was home to the mosque and tomb complex of Eyüp Sultan. Eyüp, the story went, had always been a holy site of global significance, but the Eyüp Municipality took it upon itself to transform Eyüp into a form of "world property."

## RESTORATION AND REDEVELOPMENT

In the lead-up to the March 1994 election, *Eyüp News*, a local newspaper that supported the Welfare Party and edited by Genç himself, published a series of articles that highlighted the dilapidated state of Eyüp's historic built environment. Framing Eyüp's ruinous state as symptomatic of both the current municipality's ineffective governance and the broader antipathy of the secular Kemalist establishment toward any trace of the Ottoman past, these articles promised that an Eyüp under Welfare Party administration would be a very different place.

True to his word, Mayor Genç took immediate steps in April 1994 to transform Eyüp's material landscape. Official municipality publications always included a section on the restoration and reconstruction projects that had been conducted. Making liberal use of "before" and "after" photos, these publications set out to demonstrate the municipality's success. As one headline in the municipality's *Third Year Bulletin* framed the project, "Eyüpsultan has made peace with its history."

If one part of that project was telling new stories about history, the second part involved transforming the buildings linked to them. The Eyüp Municipality played a key role in these transformations, but they were only possible because of coordination between actors and institutions operating at the municipal and national levels. Moreover, Eyüp was not transformed evenly; because of the different legal and economic statuses of different buildings, Eyüp's redevelopment was haphazard and patchwork.

Although the municipality's restoration projects are my focus below, Eyüp's Ottoman topographies were embedded within a context of urban redevelopment and infrastructural expansion. In Eyüp, for example, the Eyüp Municipality worked with the Istanbul Metropolitan Municipality to expand the network of drainage and sewer lines. The administration also set about paving roads with new layers of asphalt, adding parks and gardens throughout the municipality, and introducing better street lighting. In conversations with many longtime residents of central Eyüp, they frequently mentioned the illumination of the Eyüp's central cemetery as one of the significant changes of this period.

The municipality's restoration projects, however, became an object of debate in the Istanbul press. Soon after the unexpected 1994 electoral triumph of the Welfare Party in Istanbul's local elections, the daily newspaper *Cumhuriyet* published a critique by the well-known architect Oktay Ekinci that addressed some of the changes that had begun to take place in Eyüp.[44] Readers of *Cumhuriyet*, a longtime bastion of the laicist, Kemalist, and well-educated political and social establishment, would have been familiar with many of the terms that Ekinci mobilized, words like "religious" (*dinsel*) and "religiosity" (*dinsellik*) and his distinction between "history" (*tarih*) and the "history of Islam" (*İslam tarihi*), because of the heated cultural and political debates precipitated by the emergence of the Welfare Party in the 1990s. They also would have been aware of the central role that Istanbul's material landscapes played in those debates.[45]

These debates were not simply about current and future uses for these land-scapes; they were also about how and why some buildings were used as vehicles for stories about the past.[46] The fact that Ekinci's essay appeared in a national paper with a readership well beyond this one district suggests that these seemingly minor interviews and interventions into the built environment circulated within a much broader reading public. Just as the interviews with municipality officials published in conservative religious newspapers like *Akit* and *Yeni Şafak* addressed a pious readership, Ekinci's article in *Cumhuriyet* was addressed to a readership that generally identified itself as secular.

Referencing the newly elected mayor Ahmet Genç's widely publicized restoration projects, Ekinci phrased a rhetorical question: "Mayor Ahmet Genç's emphasis upon those works 'connected to a religious lifestyle' within such a rich 'mosaic of cultural heritage'—such as his taking ownership of 'türbe and dergah' along with tombstones—while at the same time never mentioning the old Eyüp houses and streets that are at least as valuable and also found in need of protection, might mean what?"[47] A few paragraphs below he answered his own question: "These questions' response doubtless lies both in an understanding of 'historical works' only as related to 'religious culture' and, more importantly, in the protection of the richness of civil architecture creating a situation that openly 'impedes urban rents' [*kentsel rantları*] in our present moment."[48] Ekinci's critique highlighted two issues fundamental to the politics and practice of restoration during the 1990s: First, what sorts of buildings were designated as "historical"? And second, how should the preservation of the built environment be balanced against the desire to maximize the rents generated by those properties? Civil architecture—and Eyüp's historic center in particular—occupied a particularly interesting place within these debates.

Until the 1970s, "historical works" were typically monumental structures like palaces or mosques. Even that understanding generated heated debates about the importance of a mosque: were mosques important as expressions of architectural mastery or as sites of ongoing religious practice? Following the 1968 Venice Charter, in which "civil architecture" came to be designated objects worthy of preservation, the practices and the objects of conservation in Turkey began to change.[49] A new antiquities law in 1973 (Law no. 1710) established the category of the "protected area" (*sit alanı*) to protect monuments within a broader urban context. However, because the practical and policy infrastructures needed to enforce this law were not sufficient, it often proved difficult to establish effective "protected areas."[50]

One of the first of these areas to be established in Istanbul was Eyüp. In 1977, after members of the Council for Immovable Antiquities and Monuments (Gayrimenkul Eski Eserler ve Anıtlar Yüksek Kurulu) reviewed a development plan prepared by the Istanbul Municipality and submitted for their approval, they designated central Eyüp and its surroundings a "protected area."[51] While many of Eyüp's major mosques, tombs, and madrasas had been registered previously, the establishment of the *sit alanı* was important for two reasons: First, it greatly expanded the range of objects designated as "historical" from major mosques, tombs, and monuments to houses, trees, cemeteries, and fountains. Second, and in line with that expanded designation, the object of heritage thus came to be seen not just as a single (usually monumental) object but the urban fabric (*kent dokusu*) itself.[52]

In the aftermath of the 1980 military coup, the network of heritage actors was further complicated. Two new municipal actors—the Metropolitan Municipality and local district municipalities—came to agitate for projects of restoration under their supervision. During the same moment, Turkey's heritage sites were increasingly oriented toward global audiences as "World Heritage" sites, a shift best exemplified by the choice of Turkey's first World Heritage sites, Hagia Sophia and Topkapı Palace. Interestingly, and despite its status as a *sit alanı*, Eyüp was not nominated as a World Heritage site during this period.

Additionally, the formation of a new supervisory body changed the institutional landscape of restoration: the Councils for the Protection of Cultural and Natural Heritage were placed under the supervision of the Ministry for Culture and Tourism. Restoration thus came to be wedded to (and occasionally in tension with) a project of tourism. This was the context in which Ekinci was critiquing the Eyüp Municipality's restoration projects. He worried that the Welfare Party would only protect "religious" heritage on account of their politics while letting "civil" heritage be redeveloped for economic profit.

At the same time there was an alternative answer to Ekinci's question. As one individual who worked for the municipality during that time explained, the different paces of the restoration of religious and civil architectural sites had less to do with a politics of Islam than with the different legal regimes that governed these buildings. In general, mosques, madrasas, and Sufi lodges are property of the Turkish state and administered by the General Directorate of Foundations. Although their restoration required numerous kinds of administrative coordination, it was still simpler than the restoration of civil heritage sites, which could be mired in protracted and messy legal debates over inheritance.

One of the most important sites for these restoration and redevelopment projects was the central square in front of the Mosque of Eyüp Sultan. Since the destruction of the former market in the 1950s, this square had functioned as a major transportation and social hub for the district.[53] Many of the major routes to Istanbul's peripheral districts like Gaziosmanpaşa and Alibeyköy passed through central Eyüp. There were bus stops, taxi stands, auto repair shops, barbers, cafés, and greengrocers. In short, there was a neighborhood ecology that catered to neighborhood residents, many of whom worked in the factories that lined the Golden Horn and lived in the vicinity of the central square. At the same time, the square's urban density posed challenges for the mosque and its surrounding monuments. Pollution, noise, and the automobile traffic passing through Eyüp's center harmed the physical fabric of the mosque and limited the square's use for religious purposes.

FIGURE 14. Buildings adjacent to Eyüp's central square rebuilt during the 1990s based on Nezih Eldem's "Arasta Palace" designs, July 2022.

In fact, planners working in the Eyüp Municipality, including Hülya Yalçın, Gülnur Kadayıfçı, and Hatice Fahrünnisa Kara, had begun developing plans for the square's renovation almost as soon as the municipality was established in 1984. They worked with the widely respected architect and urban planner Nezih Eldem to reimagine the square's function. After eight years of work, their development plan encompassing the entire urban area surrounding the Mosque of Eyüp Sultan was approved in 1993.[54] Several other prominent architects and institutions were also involved in this work.[55] Although the Eyüp Municipality's plan included a range of elements, a core design element was the construction of the "Arasta Palace" (Arasta Kasrı) in the central square.

As Eldem explained in a 1997 presentation, this building would address two needs: it would provide for the functional needs of pilgrims and tourists, offering bathrooms and other opportunities for rest; and it would occupy much of the space of the square, filling in the architectural void—what he called an "embarrassment of development" (*imar ayıbı*)—that was left by road construction in 1957.[56] However, the project required both a substantial financial commitment and extensive coordination between the Istanbul Metropolitan Municipality (responsible for major arterial roads), the General Directorate of Foundations (which managed some of the property in the district's center), and the Councils for the Protection of Cultural and Natural Heritage, among others.

With the election of the Welfare Party in 1994, however, circumstances shifted quickly. The municipality was able to clear out many of the mechanic shops, taxi stands, and cafés that had come to surround the square. They summarized their efforts in 2000:

> Only six years previous, the area immediately across from the Mosque of Eyüp Sultan, among the most important pilgrimage centers of the Islamic world, had been

abandoned to scrap men and repair shops [*hurdacı ve tamirci*]. The historical works and wooden buildings that were found in these environs had been left to disappear. . . . The visitation space [*ziyaret alanı*] of those coming to Eyüp from outside the district had been reduced to only the Mosque of Eyüp Sultan.[57]

Yet redevelopment did not simply remove industrial activity. It also destroyed several businesses with deep roots in the community, something most visible in the struggle over the small Orient Café (Şark Kahvesi). The café was run by Metin Heper, a longtime resident of Eyüp whose family was deeply interwoven into the district's religious and cultural life.[58] Although Heper went to court to challenge the municipality's invocation of eminent domain, he ultimately lost. The building in which his café had been located was bulldozed and replaced with a new two-story complex.

One afternoon in 2013, I was having lunch with a longtime resident of Eyüp in the restaurant that sat above where Metin Heper's Orient Café used to be. "Eyüp is gone," she said, "*Eyüp yok olmuş.*" Her point was that the social relationships that had once constituted the neighborhood for her—relationships often articulated through businesses that used to line the square—no longer existed. Eyüp is more popular today than it has ever been, and the square serves as a key open space for hundreds of thousands of visitors every year. However, the square also serves as a key example of Ekinci's critique: it is a place of commerce. Most of the square's businesses are now oriented toward visitors from outside the district because catering to those visitors helps to pay the square's relatively high rents.

Alongside the square's transformation, debates over the redevelopment of a second site, Feshane, show how questions of urban norms, heritage, and cultural identities played out in the 1990s. Feshane, one of the first factories established by the Ottoman state during the nineteenth century, initially focused on the production of the fez, but it later came to produce a range of textiles. Following the 1923 establishment of the Republic of Turkey, the factory was renamed (the fez having been banned in 1925) and reorganized under the administration of the state industrial holding company Sümerbank. Over the twentieth century the original Ottoman-era building was expanded and rebuilt. By the late 1970s it had become a sprawling complex along the shores of the Golden Horn.[59]

The September 1980 coup set in motion far-reaching shifts. During the economic reforms of the 1980s, many state institutions, including Sümerbank, were privatized. Even if it had been profitable for Feshane to stay open, the policy of removing industrial activity from the Golden Horn to Istanbul's outlying districts policy established by Dalan rendered that impossible. Because the original factory building was a registered landmark, it mostly survived the initial demolitions, but determining its new function posed a problem.

One early plan proposed repurposing the building as the Museum of Textile and Industry, but following the 1989 municipal election Feshane was reimagined as the future site of Istanbul's Museum of Modern Art (Çağdaş Sanat Müzesi).[60] The building was opened to the public in 1993 as the venue of the Second Istanbul

Biennial with the expectation that it would become the city's first modern art museum. The transformation of a former industrial site into an art museum was in keeping with global shifts, but it was framed in a very different light by newspapers associated with the Welfare Party.

In June 1993—nine months before the municipal elections that would bring the Welfare Party to power—*Eyüp Haber* published a front-page photo of flags flying in front of Feshane with the caption, "The flying of all the Zionist and imperialist countries' flags—chief among them Israel and America—in the skies above Feshane and only the Republic of Turkey's flag not being found is attention grabbing." The article accused the biennial of being party to an intentional plot to "erode" the district's spiritual and religious importance. As three high school students were quoted, "Whose culture are you trying to sell to whom?" *Eyüp Haber*'s critique of the modern art biennial—and the proposed modern art museum to follow it—was that "modern art" was foreign to the local grounded forms of belief and social life in Eyüp. It was an imposition from "outside" designed to continue a legacy of Kemalist attempts to secularize and Westernize places like Eyüp.

Political disagreements and the victory of the Welfare Party in the March 1994 elections put an end to the modern art museum, but this created a new problem: an empty building. Despite the building's temporary use as an art gallery, there were still several major structural issues, most notably a location on the shore that left it prone to flooding. In 1998, after four years of disrepair, the Istanbul Metropolitan Municipality began a second restoration project in consultation with the Eyüp Municipality. The complex was reopened in 1999 as a new site for the consumption of a distinct "Ottoman" past. Newspaper articles reviewing the plans described what visitors would find: "Among the interesting sections in the Living Nineteenth Century Market is the historic barber. Gentleman can be shaved in the old style with a straight razor. Inside there's also an old Turk coffeehouse named Kiraathane."[61] Furthermore, all the handicrafts for sale—embossed copper, textiles, and calligraphy—would be produced on-site by local artisans.

In many respects the Istanbul Metropolitan Municipality restoration plans followed those meant to turn the building into a modern art museum. There was, however, one important difference: the main entrance was to face the Golden Horn. When most visitors to Eyüp arrived by water—as was the case until the middle of the twentieth century—the entrance would be the first place that visitors would see.

In Feshane's original configuration, this entrance was topped by the Ottoman coat of arms, a *tuğra* (imperial seal) of the sultan, and two *kitabe* (inscriptions) on either side. With the de-Ottomanification of the Turkish Republic these objects were removed when the factory complex was nationalized and reopened following 1923.[62] In their place, factory directors built a control tower that overlooked the complex. The first restorations undertaken to transform the building into a modern art space did not replace the Ottoman emblems, choosing instead to highlight the building's industrial heritage in ways that echoed the transformation of other repurposed factory spaces such as London's Tate Modern. In contrast, the municipality's restorations in 1998–99 returned the Ottoman insignia, a change in keeping with the broader "recovery" of the Ottoman past under the Welfare Party municipal administration.

Despite the enthusiasm and fanfare with which the complex was reopened, the nostalgic marketplace failed. Less than a year after it opened, news coverage reported that forty of the original fifty stores had closed, citing a combination of high rents and inconsistent customers.[63] The company originally hired to plan events for the complex withdrew from their contract, and in 2000 the site's management was taken over by Beltur, a company owned by the Istanbul Metropolitan Municipality. For the next fifteen years Feshane served as a multipurpose conference venue and fairground, hosting everything from Ramadan festivities and municipal govern-ment functions to regional festivals and religious tourism festivals.

The use of Feshane has continued to generate debate. A March 2013 interview with a tour guide and art historian provides one account. Attila Bey was born in the Aegean city of Izmir but arrived in Istanbul in the 1970s for university. Trained as an art and architectural historian, he had worked in a variety of capacities for several universities and state-run museums. When we spoke, he was also working for a tour company, guiding middle-class secular Turks through Istanbul's historic neighborhoods. Not surprisingly, Eyüp figured prominently in that itinerary.

When asked to explain Eyüp's transformation over the more than three decades in which he'd lived in Istanbul, he began by drawing a general contrast between "Turkish" and "Arabic" culture. Eyüp in general, he said, had been both socially and visually spoiled, transformed by an "Arabic" culture that had replaced and oth-erwise obscured the "Turk" culture that had once existed there. The problem, he continued, was that there were two cultures in Turkey, a top-down elite culture that had never been completely accepted and something that was its complete opposite.

He sighed, "We can't find something in the middle." For him, Feshane's trans-formation—first its failed place as an elite cultural institution (the modern art museum) and its status as fairground—was symptomatic of that inability to find a common ground. "I look at Feshane," he said. "It's either seen as a place for the Istanbul Festival [i.e., the modern art biennial] . . . or it's a garlic festival. . . . Fine, there shouldn't be an opera there, but neither should there be a garlic festival. It should be something more acceptable. Elitist culture can't go everywhere, I understand that . . . but this," he said, referring to the building's current uses, "this isn't culture."[64]

## CONCLUSION

In contrast to the square and Feshane, the fountain with which this chapter opened merited little newspaper coverage. However, and in keeping with a tradi-tion of Ottoman fountains, its inscription helps to date when it was built: May 29, 2002. May 29 is the day on which Fatih Sultan Mehmet conquered Constantinople in 1453, and during the 1990s public reenactments of the Conquest on May 29 were one way that the Welfare Party grounded its present political claims in the Ottoman past in opposition to a ruling "Republican" elite.[65] May 29 continues to be celebrated in Istanbul; the only difference is that the once oppositional character of the Conquest celebrations has now become thoroughly institutionalized in municipal activities. The exact dating of the inscription suggests that the fountain was officially unveiled as part of those celebrations.

A year later, however, the daily newspaper *Milliyet*—likely tipped off by local opposition politicians—published an article about the fountain.[66] In it, Mayor Genç admitted that he was indeed the patron of the fountain but, because he didn't want the inscription to be read, he had asked that it be written in Ottoman. Yet, as the news report explained, the construction of the fountain and family grave complex at the entrance to the cemetery had a complicated legal history.

Because of the Eyüp Cemetery's long history of use, it is very difficult to find an open plot. In 1996 Mayor Genç had purchased a family plot on the back hillside. Meanwhile, the entrance to the cemetery had been occupied by a *mezarcı* (grave maker), a situation common throughout Istanbul. The *mezarcı* owned a quarter of the property, with three-quarters owned by another group of women. The Directorate of Cemeteries (Mezarlıklar Müdürlüğü), attached to the Istanbul Metropolitan Municipality, tried to claim the property. The women sold their share in the property but the *mezarcı* refused, forcing a court case in which he lost his property. At that point Mayor Genç petitioned the Directorate of Cemeteries to exchange his family plot at the back of the cemetery for the location at the front of the cemetery. Upon receiving approval, Mayor Genç erected the fountain beside a family plot. As of summer 2022, the only person buried there was Genç's father, Efraim Genç.

At the beginning of this chapter I opened with three questions that this fountain raises: How did it come to be here? Why is the fountain decorated in the way that it is? And what might this fountain tell us about the politics of the built environment in contemporary Istanbul? The first question is straightforward enough to answer: Mayor Genç leveraged his authority and influence as mayor to petition the Istanbul Directorate of Cemeteries for the right to plot—which resulted in a newspaper article polemically headlined "Ahiret Torpili." *Torpil* are networks of patronage through which official work is accomplished.[67] Here, an *ahiret torpili* refers to those networks that produced a grave site for Mayor Genç and his family. More broadly, building the fountain also required that Mayor Genç coordinate with the municipal water utility (İSKİ) to connect the fountain. As with so many other transformations in Eyüp during this period, the fountain required the conjunction of institutions with diverse interests.

The fountain's decoration was a product of the reemergence of the Ottoman past in late 1990s Istanbul, one part of the debates about the history of the Turkish Republic and the legacy of secularizing and Westernizing reforms that divided "modern" Turkey from its Ottoman past. Even though the fountain was new, it materialized an alternative form of the modern that "challenge[d] the secular-nationalist elites who had occupied positions of administrative authority" for much of Turkey's history.[68] Writing about the same engagements with the Ottoman past in the 1990s, Alev Çınar has pointed out the doubled dimension of history writing: "The national subject that declares itself into being through the writing of history presents itself as having an eternal presence that is validated by its historicity and hoariness; at the same time, it also performs itself as new and modern."[69]

But Çınar's formulation can be further sharpened: what emerged in this moment was not just a new national subject but a new *municipal* one, one that articulated its newness relative to both the distant Ottoman past and its immediate predecessors. Thus the figures commemorated on the fountain were not *İstanbullu*—as one could argue based on the location in the broader city of Istanbul—but *Eyüpsultanlı*. This fountain materialized a new form of place embedded within a shifting set of political, cultural, and economic relationships.

In the process, the district's transformation generated arguments about political and cultural identity. Among some longtime residents, Eyüp's transformations also provoked deep anxieties as the social and economic relationships that once defined the district were swept away. In their place, a new public history stressed Eyüp's Ottoman past even as the traces of the 1950s, '60s, and '70s faded away. But other longtime residents—and many visitors today—praise the transformation. Remembering decades when Eyüp was a *varoş* district on the peripheries of Istanbul, its air thick with the scent of sewage and factory waste, these people praise what Eyüp has become: Istanbul's spiritual center.

Eyüp was remade in the 1990s in large part because the municipality was able to reconfigure the kinds of stories that were told about Eyüp and, by extension, Islam. They articulated new public histories and restored the built environment. In acting, routinizing, and narrating Eyüp's importance, the municipality was able to establish one account of Eyüp as a place of Ottoman Islam.[70] This project had a clear political dimension, as the Welfare Party's "framing" of Eyüp as an essentially Ottoman-Islamic place helped them ground their policies, but it also reminds us that buildings' meanings are never fixed and may yet continue to change.[71]

# 6

# Tourists, Pilgrims, and the Rules of Place

In July 2013 I joined a small group of tourists visiting Eyüp during Ramadan, the Muslim month of fasting. Because it was Ramadan, Eyüp was crowded with people who came to pray in the central Mosque of Eyüp Sultan, attend the municipality's performances, enjoy Eyüp's numerous cafés and restaurants, and take in the district's atmosphere. All the members of our group were citizens of Turkey, Istanbul residents, and able to afford the tour's cost (roughly a hundred dollars). Falling as it did during the month of Ramadan, our tour was advertised as a *sahur* tour, meaning that we would visit Eyüp's monuments at night before finishing with a *sahur* meal at one of Eyüp's local restaurants.[1]

At one point in the tour we passed into the Mosque of Eyüp Sultan. Much of the mosque's inner courtyard had been covered with carpet, and people sat scattered throughout the space. Some were praying in small groups, performing their *teravih namazı*.[2] Others stood facing the tomb of Halid bin Zeyd, their hands cupped in front of them as they prayed. Most people, however, were simply relaxing on the carpets. Our small group followed the guide, listening to his voice over the small earbuds that we had been provided.

We must have made a curious sight, because one man who happened to be in the mosque pulled me aside to ask about our group. "Did you hire the guide yourself?" he asked. "Did you know each other beforehand? How much was it?" I answered the first two questions truthfully: Yes, we had hired our guide, and no, we didn't know each other before we started the tour. I lied about the last question, because I was embarrassed about spending over 150 liras, which seemed almost excessive in a district where many residents made do with monthly incomes of 800 liras or less.[3]

After hearing my answers, the man bid me well and praised what our group was doing. "Helal olsun," he said, "you're gaining knowledge about religion" (*bilgi alıyorsunuz din üzerine*).[4]

FIGURE 15. Passing through the Mosque of Eyüp Sultan on a Ramadan tour, July 2013.

But as we parted, another passing man muttered derisively to his companion, "They're tourists" (*Onlar turist*).

This brief encounter calls our attention to two distinct but interrelated "rules of place" that operate in the Mosque of Eyüp Sultan. The first might be termed "religious" rules, linked to appropriate ways of knowing about Islam and behaving as Muslims. The second might be termed "tourist" rules, linked to a different way of encountering sites of historical, cultural, and artistic value.[5] For those familiar with Istanbul, these two distinct systems are central to the everyday experience of the city's major mosques. On the one hand, mosques like Sultanahmet, Süleymaniye, the New Mosque (Yeni Camii), and most recently the Hagia Sophia are key sites through which Muslims engage with Istanbul as a city with a rich Muslim history.[6] On the other hand, many of these sites are also celebrated as World Heritage sites, a designation that tends to downplay their devotional importance and stress an ostensibly "secular" character. These tensions between these two sets of rules are not unique to Turkey. In sites ranging from the Vatican to the Taj Mahal, from the Shrine of Jalal al-Din Muhammad Rumi in Konya to the missions of San Antonio, Texas, the line between "pilgrim" and "tourist" takes many forms around the world.[7]

Yet the boundaries between religious visitors and tourists are blurred in practice more often than it might seem. While encounters between the different types of visitors sometimes lead to clashes and debates, these different groups can also coexist or simply pass each other by. Rather than assuming that "religious" and "tourist" rules are applied the same way irrespective of geography, this chapter pays attention to the ways that rules of place come to be defined in, from, and for the Mosque of Eyüp Sultan.

Here I take inspiration from scholarship that helps us move beyond static binaries. Lara Deeb and Mona Harb, for example, ask us to consider "moral rubrics," the "different sets of ideals and values that are revealed as well as produced through discourses and actions in [different registers]."[8] Elsewhere, Anna Secor uses the concept of "regimes" to make sense of the "hegemonic rules or norms regarding [everyday life] that characterize particular spaces."[9] These and other terms provide ways to conceptualize the uneven "possibilities of encounter, transformation, and the 'in-between'" that can emerge when different rules come into proximity.[10] Yet I find "rules" important because they capture both lived encounters between the tourist and the religious and the complicated norms, codes, and definitions that define Eyüp as a place of Islam. In a more general sense, the rules of place are at the center of struggles over the meaning and significance of places at multiple scales. The articulation, transmission, and enforcement of these rules play central roles in the making of place.

Although the first man approved of our activities ("You're gaining knowledge about religion"), the second man's derisive comment ("They're tourists") was an implicit judgment that drew upon rules that differentiated between better (that is, religious) and worse (that is, touristic) ways of moving through the mosque. Yet our tour group was also moving through the mosque according to a set of rules other than the "appropriate" rules of place in a mosque. For us, the mosque's historical, cultural, and artistic value didn't rule out its use as a space of worship, but neither did the mosque's status as a site of worship exclude our mode of moving through it.

In the Mosque of Eyüp Sultan, these rules include those that separate the ritual, sacred space of the mosque from the broader fabric of the city; those that establish certain permissible and impermissible acts in certain locations within the mosque; and those that signal visitors' religious identity, the purpose of their visit, and even their place of origin. In short, one might easily speak of the Mosque of Eyüp Sultan having "its" rules of place, in much the same way that places are spoken of as having "their own" histories.[11] One might also see our Ramadan encounter as a competition between two different and fixed sets of rules, one that corresponds to a "religious" lifestyle and one that corresponds to a "secular" life.

It is often tempting to think of the rules of place that apply in the mosque as being essential to the mosque (a product of some internal quality) and as something unchanged (as Eyüp Sultan has always been a sacred place, its current rules of place must have always been). This chapter complicates that assumption by making two linked arguments.

First, although the rules of place in Eyüp Sultan are specific to this mosque, those rules are not rooted in this place. I show that these rules are produced through the interconnections of people, practices, and shared narratives. These rules are both particular to this place and connected to elsewhere. Second, I argue that the rules of place are often incomplete. I focus on three ways in which those rules of place are shown to be flexible and open to other interpretations: when foreigners move through the mosque; when domestic tourists move through the mosque; and when women move through the mosque. These are moments when the commonsense norms and habits that define this mosque encounter people who either don't know those norms, engage with them differently, or are perceived by others as somehow outside the standard rules of place.

### TRANSMITTING THE RULES OF PLACE

As a mosque, Eyüp Sultan shares many of its rules of place with tens of thousands of mosques around the world. Rules that govern how people perform their ablutions before prayer, comport themselves within the mosque, and arrange themselves vis-à-vis others around them form a common texture of faith for Muslims. However, there are also rules specific to Eyüp Sultan, rules that are shaped by the specific conjunction of people, buildings, and objects in this mosque.

The central—and fundamental—architectural space of any mosque is its main prayer space. Prayer spaces almost always share a common set of features. There will be a prayer niche (*mihrab*) that orients people in the direction of Mecca (the *qiblah/kible*). In Friday congregational mosques, there will be a pulpit (*minbar*) along with a preacher's pulpit (*vaiz kursu*). Carpets will cover the floors. Low shelves will be found beside the doors and arranged around the outer edges of the mosque so that visitors might store their shoes during prayer. Although the primary function of this space is the performance of prayer, it can also be used for teaching, reading, thinking, and even sleeping. Although nearly all mosques in Turkey are administered by the Ministry of Religious Affairs, any explicitly political act—such as the distribution of election pamphlets or flyers—is forbidden within the interior of the mosque. The main prayer space of Eyüp Sultan—as with almost all mosques—is also reserved for men. Although women sometimes circulate through the rear section of the main prayer space, the center of the mosque is a strongly gendered space.

The threshold of a mosque thus marks a key zone of transition between an interior space for prayer and the outside world. Although the precise location of a mosque's main door can vary widely, both historic Ottoman mosques and more recently constructed ones usually locate the main entrance along the main axis of the prayer niche. The area immediately outside of this door is known as the *son cemaat yeri*, a place for men who arrive late to the congregational prayer. The *son cemaat yeri* is usually incorporated into a courtyard (*avlu*). In contrast to the interior prayer space of the mosque, the *avlu* can oscillate between being used as an "interior" space for prayer and being used as an "external" space, connected to the broader life of the city. In contrast to the overwhelmingly male character of the mosque's interior, the courtyard—and particularly the courtyard of Eyüp Sultan—is decidedly more mixed, with men and women visiting alongside one another.

Two things make the Mosque of Eyüp Sultan unique among Ottoman-era mosques of Istanbul. First, the tomb of Halid bin Zeyd is built into the mosque itself.[12] Both tombs and mosques are found throughout Istanbul, but they are almost always built separately. In contrast, the tomb of Halid bin Zeyd forms one beautifully tiled wall of the Mosque of Eyüp Sultan. Therefore, the inner courtyard of Eyüp Sultan is used both as an auxiliary prayer space for the mosque proper and as a devotional space for people who come to visit the tomb.

The second thing that makes Eyüp Sultan distinctive is its sequence of courtyards. Until the eighteenth century, most major Ottoman mosques were designed along relatively similar plans: a large interior prayer space, covered with a dome, and a single rectangular courtyard, aligned along an axis marked by the direction of prayer. The current mosque was reconstructed from the ground up at the end of the eighteenth century. In this second form, a new, outer courtyard was added to the structure of the mosque. This outer courtyard included several elements: an ablutions fountain (şadırvan), several small rooms designated for mosque staff; and an entrance to the sultan's loge (now used for the women's section in the mosque). In addition to being architecturally singular within Istanbul, the courtyards are also functionally important. Because of the large number of people who visit the mosque, the outer courtyard has come to be used as an important auxiliary prayer space. Since the renovation of the square adjacent to the mosque in the 1990s, that square has also been used as an auxiliary prayer space.

The unique shape of the Mosque of Eyüp Sultan has several consequences for the rules of place that apply in the mosque. Two are especially important. First, the positioning of the courtyards in relation to the tomb of Halid bin Zeyd means that most of the mosque complex is open to the elements. Entering the mosque—particularly to pray—requires a set of actions that specifically distinguish the interior from the exterior of the mosque (for example, removing one's shoes, women covering their hair and shoulders, performing one's ablutions before prayer, using one's right foot to enter the mosque, uttering a prayer to Allah). Because much of Eyüp Sultan is exterior to the central prayer space, it means that people do not necessarily perform the same actions that they might on entering the mosque's interior.

Second, the blurring of the boundary between the interior and the exterior of the mosque has consequences for the interaction between men and women. The Mosque of Eyüp Sultan is one of the few mosques in Istanbul where women can participate in communal prayers in areas that are visible to the general public. In most cases, women's prayer areas are screened in from view. Because the number

FIGURE 16. Outer courtyard of the Mosque of Eyüp Sultan, showing the ablution fountain (*şadırvan*) and the entrance to the women's section, February 2012.

of women visiting the mosque for communal prayers is so high relative to the space available inside the mosque, mosque authorities have established women's prayer areas at the rear of the outer courtyard and at the rear of the square outside. But if most mosques share a common rule that the performance of prayer by women is to be separate from the performance of prayer by men, Eyüp Sultan represents a modification of that rule.

In addition to the mosque's physical layout, public texts including signs, placards, and posted announcements play an important role in conveying the rules of place.[13] The overwhelming majority of these objects are written in Turkish by the office of the Eyüp district *müftü* (chief religious official). Two permanent placards explain the significance of Halid bin Zeyd. Several signs list a range of appropriate and inappropriate behaviors for those visiting the mosque and tombs. In addition to the tomb of Halid bin Zeyd, the mosque complex is filled with an assortment of other tombs and graves, many of which are also labeled with small signs of varying length. By explaining the "proper" historical and religious significance of the mosque/tomb complex and by communicating a set of rules about "proper" visitation practices, these signs render the mosque complex legible to domestic visitors.

One striking difference between Eyüp Sultan and many of Istanbul's other major mosque monuments is the lack of signage in languages other than Turkish. This contrasts with many of the mosques in the popular tourist areas of Sultanahmet and Süleymaniye. There, the signage almost always includes explanatory text as well as rules (such as dressing in appropriate clothing and not eating) addressed to tourists in different languages. During the years 2011 to 2013, the single instance of a sign in a language other than Turkish in the mosque was a large panel written in Arabic. Donated by King Idris I of Libya in the 1950s, the panel retells the story of Halid bin Zeyd. As Turkey has become an increasingly popular tourist destination for Arabic-speaking visitors over the past decade, the panel has come to be read by an entirely new audience.

It is also important to remember that there is another important kind of public text in the mosque: a wide array of calligraphy in Arabic script. Some of this is Arabic, usually quoting from the Qur'an or from the *hadith* of the Prophet Muhammad. Other passages, however, are written in Ottoman Turkish. The overwhelming majority of visitors today cannot read the inscriptions; despite that, the mere visibility of these inscriptions—even if they are not necessarily legible— marks the mosque complex as a religious space.

The Mosque of Eyüp Sultan is visited by upward of three million people per year, of whom the vast majority are residents of Turkey. Among visitors from Turkey, the majority come for "religious" purposes, and their visits are exceptional events, often coinciding with births, deaths, important exams, weddings, and/or religious holidays. The large number of people who visit the mosque complex— often for the first time—poses a particular challenge for establishing shared rules of place. There are three primary ways that people learn how to configure their bodies according to the rules of place.

Social networks are the most important factor affecting an individual's understanding of the rules of place in Eyüp Sultan. Families continue to be the first and primary source of religious knowledge in contemporary Turkey.[14] When people visit as a family unit, fathers and mothers frequently instruct their children in "appropriate" behaviors, whether by showing them how to hold their hands in prayer, reciting Qur'anic prayers with them, or scolding them if the children are misbehaving. People will also visit with a group of friends, in which case one individual might be more familiar with the mosque than the others. Visitors might also belong to a *tarikat* (Sufi brotherhood) or *cemaat* (Muslim community). Within the space of the mosque, women and men who belong to these groups mark themselves through their dress (ranging from how women tie their headscarves to the sorts of rings that men wear) and their manner of praying (how they hold their hands in supplication).[15]

When people visit the mosque, they can also be acutely aware of the behavior of those around them. Most of the time this awareness is passive, and it resembles the way that people everywhere negotiate crowded situations. Sometimes visitors will imitate the actions of those around them. This is especially true in the immediate vicinity of the Mosque of Eyüp Sultan, where individuals who pray at or concentrate on other (poorly marked or illegible) graves or tombs can attract the attention of passersby. Finally, visitors also critique the actions of those around them. Although these critiques rarely take the form of direct argument or accusation, visitors will frequently share their negative evaluations of other people in the mosque. This explains why our tour group attracted such attention during Ramadan. During a moment in which nearly everybody seemed to be in the mosque for devotional purposes, our group's conduct stood out and generated divergent responses.

Mosque staff and attendants are the third factor shaping visitors' embodied movement through the mosque. Their numbers include tomb attendants, municipal police (*zabita*), plainclothes police officers, and mosque custodial staff. Collectively known as the *görevli* (on duty), they can all intervene in activities they deem inappropriate. For example, custodial staff might ask someone writing their prayer on a wall to stop, or a tomb attendant might interrupt someone's prayer on the grounds that it is "superstitious." Compared to the large number of visitors who pass through Eyüp Sultan every year, the staff presence is relatively small. Nevertheless, their enforcement of the rules of place plays a key role in shaping how the mosque is used.

Although these rules are normative, they are neither unchanging nor always equally applied. Indeed, their very status as normative is the product of ongoing debates about the regulation, requirement, and transformation of the practices that constitute Islam.[16] Below, I turn to three moments in which those rules of place are shown to be flexible and open to other interpretations: when foreigners move through the mosque; when domestic tourists move through the mosque; and when women move through the mosque. These are moments when the commonsense norms and habits that define this mosque encounter people who either don't know those norms, engage with them differently, or are understood by others to be somehow outside of the standard rules of place.

## FOREIGNERS IN THE MOSQUE

Historical Ottoman mosques occupy an interesting field in Istanbul today. On the one hand, they continue to be places of ongoing worship, which are staffed by officially appointed imams, managed by the Ministry of Religious Affairs, and regularly attended by residents and visitors alike. On the other hand, they are also historical sites, identified in guidebooks and tourist itineraries as sites of cultural value. Foreigners' visiting of mosques—and the visiting of non-Muslim foreigners in particular—presents one important challenge to the typical rules of place that apply in a mosque like Eyüp Sultan.

One anecdote, frequently repeated in nineteenth-century Istanbul travelogues, gives one clue to the relationship between foreigners and the rules of place in the Mosque of Eyüp Sultan, and particularly the way that mobility reproduces and transforms the rules of place. In the 19th century, the Mosque of Eyüp Sultan and the tomb of Halid bin Zeyd were off-limits to non-Muslim foreigners. The only way for a non-Muslim to visit the mosque was in disguise. This is because dress marked one of the central means through which ethnic and religious identities were performed in late Ottoman Istanbul. As the story goes, an "infidel" couple donned a "Turkish disguise" (*déguisement turc*) and entered the mosque. As soon as they crossed the mosque's threshold, they were overcome and revealed as Christians.[17] This rule of place no longer applies in the Mosque of Eyüp Sultan, but the anecdote reminds us that non-Muslim foreigners—identifiable by their dress, language, and comportment—were once seen to be violating the rules of place that applied there. The rules of place involve different kinds of mobilities: non-Muslim foreigners are marked as foreign precisely by their mobility through the city (and through the mosque in particular).

Today it is easy to identify non-Muslim foreigners by means of their relationship to the rules of place in Eyüp Sultan. In contrast to Muslim visitors, non-Muslim foreign visitors are generally not familiar with the layout of the mosque and the rules that shape one's movement through it. Likewise, most foreign visitors do not read Turkish. Their ignorance of Turkish renders the mosque's public texts (and the rules they convey) illegible. Foreign visitors do imitate Turkish visitors—most visibly when women cover their head on passing from the square into the outer courtyard—but their mistakes are policed in a different way by mosque staff.

Beginning in the early part of the twentieth century, restrictions on non-Muslim visitation began to change, and foreigners gradually started to visit the Mosque of Eyüp Sultan more freely. While one might assume that foreigners were always liable to be ignorant (and thus potentially in violation of) the rules of place that applied in the mosque, foreigners are sometimes marked as more respectful of the sacredness of a place like Eyüp Sultan. Earlier, for example, we looked at Cemal Öğüt's distinction between domestic and foreign visitors. Öğüt's account articulated what would become a theme common in many of the guides and pamphlets published about Eyüp Sultan in the 1960s and '70s: visitors (from Turkey) were ignorant and did not show the respect appropriate to this place. They key point to draw from Öğüt's account is that *even* foreigners—assumed to be non-Muslims and therefore ignorant of the religious significance of this mosque and tomb—were able to comport themselves in a more appropriate way. Locals and residents refused to change their behavior as they passed from the street (where smoking cigarettes and singing would be appropriate) into the mosque (where such acts were disrespectful). In this case, foreigners provide a useful foil to explain what Muslims should be doing.

Foreigners continue to be a point of reference for many Muslim Turks when they describe what makes the mosque special. I asked Zafer—a young man, pious, and relatively new to Istanbul—about what made Eyüp different from other parts of the city, and he responded by drawing a fascinating comparison between Eyüp

FIGURE 17. Tourists observing Friday prayers in the central square, September 2012.

Sultan and the major historical monuments of Sultanahmet. Here in Eyüp Sultan, he said, "You rarely see underdressed [*çıplak*] people. . . . 'Open' [*açık*] people come but they cover up with something [when they do]. . . . It's not that way in Sultanahmet. [There] someone wearing a miniskirt can go into the mosque there with just a head scarf [*sadece bir baş örtüsüyle*] but that's something I've never encountered here [in Eyüp Sultan]." He continued, "There are clear rules for every place, how a mosque is dressed for, how it is entered. . . . Now, Sultanahmet is a place that should be thought of in the same way, but I think that there are more people who pay attention in Eyüp Sultan."[18]

Zafer's description provides one way to think about the tensions produced by encounters between "non-Muslim" (usually foreign) visitors who don't follow the rules of place and the clear "Muslim" rules of place in Eyüp. Implicit in Zafer's explanation is the topography of tourism in Istanbul. The most touristed district of the city is Sultanahmet. There are two reasons for this. First, three of Istanbul's most important historic monuments—the Hagia Sophia, the Sultanahmet Mosque (also known as the Blue Mosque), and the Topkapı Palace—are located within an easy walk of each other. For tourists with limited time, the district provides an easily accessible snapshot of Istanbul. Second, there is a well-developed infrastructure (good transportation, signage in different languages, the availability of guides, and a dense cluster of hotels) in Sultanahmet that makes it easy for foreign tourists to orient themselves.

In contrast, Eyüp—and here Zafer's use of "Eyüp Sultan" refers to the mosque in particular—is relatively peripheral to the city's primary tourist itineraries. Although the number of restaurants catering to tourists has increased since the late 1990s and new hotels have opened, Eyüp lacks much of the infrastructure that has turned Sultanahmet into a heavily trafficked tourist area.

Zafer's comparison draws our attention not to the numbers of tourists who visit but to the rules of place that they follow. Especially important are the rules that correspond to entering the mosque. All mosques in Istanbul visited by tourists will provide head scarves and ankle-length dresses that visitors—primarily women, but sometimes men as well—can use to cover their bare heads, shoulders, and legs. In many cases, attendants will be stationed at the mosque entrance to make sure that foreign visitors are dressed appropriately. However, because of the number of people who visit Sultanahmet, it is sometimes difficult for attendants to stop every foreign tourist, hence Zafer's observation about someone entering the mosque "wearing a miniskirt."

The "foreignness" of tourists is not a fixed, physical quality. Rather, it is signaled through embodied practices and objects that tourists use. These include the use of cameras, speaking in languages other than Turkish, traveling in groups, participating in religious practices like prayer, and choices about dress. Because Sultanahmet is usually visited as part of a "heritage" itinerary that links the Topkapı Palace, the Sultanahmet Mosque, and—until its 2020 reclassification as a mosque—the Hagia Sophia, tourists often encounter Islam as something looked at rather than lived in.[19] In Eyüp, by contrast, non-Muslim tourists often visit precisely to experience a "living" Islam. This brings its own tensions with it, but it helps to explain why "foreignness" plays out differently in Eyüp. Despite the relative absence of staff monitoring their behavior, tourists seem to follow a different set of rules in this place.

In Zafer's telling, every mosque should have the same rules: they should be entered in a certain way, and one should dress in a certain way. Ideally, he believed, the rules would be the same everywhere, but he noted that these rules of place are more frequently observed in Eyüp Sultan. His observation points to a broader insight: buildings are defined by their rules, but those rules are also always in dialogue with places and the people who move through them. How and for whom these rules operate can take multiple forms.

## IS HERITAGE "FOREIGN"?

One striking shift of the past two decades has been the increasing number of Muslim tourists visiting Turkey. Many of these tourists are from the Arabic-speaking Middle East, including the Persian Gulf, Saudi Arabia, and Egypt, but there are also tourists from Indonesia, Malaysia, Pakistan, and the United Kingdom.[20] These tourists share many of the same itineraries as other foreign tourists (such as visiting the Topkapı Palace, climbing the Galata Tower, and visiting the Grand Bazaar), but they differ in their understanding of the rules of place that apply in Eyüp Sultan. The key difference lies in their relationship to the mosque: non-Muslim foreign tourists move through the Mosque of Eyüp Sultan as a devotional space for other people; Muslim foreign tourists move through the mosque as their own devotional space. While foreign Muslim tourists often find much of the mosque's signage illegible (because they don't speak or read Turkish), their knowledge of the embodied practices of piety make their adherence to the rules of place quite different. If nothing else, the increasingly visible presence of foreign Muslim tourists has helped to decouple a long-standing association between being foreign and being non-Muslim.

In November 2011, for example, a small group of men from Pakistan were reading the inscription donated by King Idris I. I was reminded suddenly that nearly all the mosque's signage is in Turkish, something that sets the mosque apart from many of the other historic mosques like Sultanahmet and Süleymaniye. They turned to a group of people standing beside them. "Turkiya?" they asked. "No," their neighbors answered, "España."

More than anything, the presence of foreign tourists in the mosque demonstrates that "foreignness" is produced in part by violating the "proper" rules of place. At the beginning of the twentieth century, foreigners' different habits of dress, language, and worship helped to mark them as "foreign." A century later, some of those habits have changed: many "foreigners" are now visiting from majority Muslim countries, and many forms of dress are less visibly marked as "Turk" and "foreign." At the same time, many Turks have also shifted their relationship to the mosque, encountering it not necessarily as worshippers but as heritage tourists.

Since the 1990s, a second shift has reconfigured assumptions about what it means to be a tourist in Eyüp Sultan: the emergence of domestically oriented "heritage tourism," a term I use to refer to a subset of the Turkish tourism industry that caters to individuals explicitly interesting in learning about "their" history. This was the motivation that guided the 2013 *sahur* tour with which I opened this chapter. While on that tour I spoke with one of the other participants—a middle-aged Istanbul resident—about why he joined tours like this. He explained, "We go to Europe, and we see all their churches and museums, but we don't do the same in our own country. A couple of years ago, we realized we didn't know Istanbul. So we started to do these tours, and bit by bit we've started to learn Istanbul."

These tours offer a fascinating opportunity to think about the encounter between two different kinds of rules: those that apply to religious visitors to Eyüp Sultan, and those that apply to "tourists." While often in tension, these two types of rules are not necessarily mutually exclusive. As I showed above, foreign tourists often visit mosques alongside domestic worshippers. Domestic tourists in mosques, however, raise a different sort of issue, because they challenge the assumed equivalence of "Turk" and "Muslim."

The visibility of domestic tour companies catering to domestic tourists who want to visit sites of the Ottoman past is a relatively recent phenomenon, dating back to the 1990s. While this sector's growth has many causes, four stand out. First, the Ottoman past was reconfigured as an attractive and cosmopolitan destination.[21] Although major monuments like mosques and palaces had always been important tour destinations, the 1990s were marked by a popularization of the Ottoman past. Second, beginning in the 1990s but especially since the 2000s, there have been massive investments in tourist facilities and restoration projects.[22] Third, the rise in living standards in Turkey has enabled the growth of leisure activities like tourism. Domestic tourism is one part of an expanded landscape of popular consumption. Being able to go on boutique tours like these is part of the complicated cultural politics of tourism in Turkey today, a politics that turns on questions of public access and social distinction.[23] Finally, there has also been a shift in the cultural politics of distinction that characterize Turkey's relationship to Europe. Whereas being "cultured" once involved visiting Europe's museums, it can now include domestic tourism organized around the splendors of the Ottoman past.

The tour company I joined was one of the first to be established in Istanbul. They have been in business for roughly the past twenty years and currently offer a varied range of tours, including Istanbul-focused tours, domestic tours, and international tours to locations ranging from Cuba and the Great Wall of China to Central Europe and India. In the two tours I joined, their clientele seemed to be relatively wealthy and well-educated Istanbul residents. Consequently, the rules of place observed by this tourist agency linked expectations about class, cultural outlook, and a particular form of tourist mobility. The ethnographic encounters below are drawn from those two tours.

Our tours followed an itinerary similar to the one traced by "foreign" tourists: we began at the café of Pierre Loti, walked down through the cemetery, visited the Mosque of Eyüp Sultan, and then passed through a variety of other heritage sites, including the public kitchen (*imaret*) of Mihrişah Sultan and the tomb of Sultan Reşad (Mehmed V). While everyone who comes to Eyüp—religious visitor or tourist—visits the Mosque of Eyüp Sultan, "religious" visitors generally do not visit sites like the *imaret* of Mihrişah Sultan or the tomb of Sultan Reşad, marking one key difference between the itineraries of "religious" visitors and heritage tourists.

While many domestic heritage tourists share a common understanding of the rules of place with "foreign" tourists, there is one key difference: their relationship to those sites, one that oscillates between "other" and "ours." This is why the man's description of going to Europe to see "churches and museums" but not making the same investment in "our country" is so interesting. Despite visitors engaging with this history as "ours," the everyday sharing of history (as when different groups of Turks visit and move through Eyüp Sultan) is often far more complicated. The imagined community suggested by "our Ottoman past" frequently dissolves into debates about political, ethnic, social, and religious identity. Indeed, many of these boutique heritage tourists overlap with foreign tourists who rarely engage with the people and ongoing life that fills many monumental spaces in Istanbul.

On a December morning in 2012, our small group met in front of the Atatürk Culture Center in Taksim. We were twelve in total: two older couples, perhaps retired, two friends traveling together, four of us on our own, a representative from the tour company, and our guide. We boarded our small bus, where we were given portable broadcasting sets and headphones. The day before, I had received a text message from the tour operator: "Note: We request that our female guests bring a head covering [*baş örtüsü*] with them." Implicit in the note was an assumption that the tour participants did not wear *tesettür*, the head covering that frequently marks women's piety. As I noticed when our group gathered, none of the women, in fact, did.

While our bus made its way through light morning traffic from Taksim to Eyüp, our guide explained the importance of the district. He began—as most of my pious interlocutors in Eyüp did—with the figure of Eyüp Sultan, the standard-bearer (*bayraktar*) of the Prophet. However, I noticed that his phrasing differed in one small but important way from many of my devout interlocutors in Eyüp. Whereas they would almost always say "our Prophet" (*Hz. Peygamberimiz*), our guide dropped the possessive, saying only "the Prophet" (*Hz. Peygamber*).

The shift between "the Prophet" and "our Prophet" corresponds to two different ways that people engage with the religious importance of Eyüp. Those who use "our Prophet" are trying to evoke a mutual religious community in which connection to the Prophet Muhammad functions as one of the primary markers of belonging. On this trip, our guide's use of "the Prophet" instead of "our Prophet" was not a rejection of belief or religious identity. Rather, it marked one attempt to bracket off the use of Islam as a common axis of identity.

Indeed, these tours have a complicated relationship to the public forms of religiosity found in Eyüp today. The tours that I participated in always visited the Mosque of Eyüp Sultan, but we never stopped to pray formally. This isn't to say that participants were opposed to religion in their lives. As one woman explained to me as we toured Eyüp together, she used to come regularly to the mosque to perform two *rekat*.[24] "I'm Muslim," she said, "so coming here is a sort of relationship; it's good for one's soul." But our tours were never timed to coincide with the large communal prayers that now take place in Eyüp, particularly on Fridays and weekends. While there may have been a logistical benefit to this (the mosque was less crowded), it also avoided a very visible contrast between the communal performance of prayer and tourists' modes of moving through the mosque

The mosque complex of Eyüp Sultan is frequently crowded with visitors. Observing people's adherence to the "normative" rules of place is a quick and relatively easy way for visitors to classify the people around them. Practices like taking photographs, listening to guides, not praying at the tomb of Halid bin Zeyd, and moving in groups quickly mark visitors as "tourists."

Yet when I returned on a second tour during Ramadan, I realized that tourist practices, especially when those who practice them are identified as Turkish, become even more charged. Ramadan is marked by an intensification of religious observance in Eyüp. Although the exact form of the celebrations varies from year to year, the Eyüp Municipality constructs a variety of temporary structures and organizes a range of activities open to the public. Eyüp's restaurants shift their hours and menus to cater to visitors seeking *iftar* and *sahur* meals (the two meals that mark, respectively, the end and the beginning of the fast). The number of people visiting Eyüp also increases. These visits almost always involve a visit to the mosque complex, where people will either pray in front of the tomb of Halid bin Zeyd or participate in one of the communal prayers (either the evening prayer following *iftar*, the supererogatory *teravih* prayers, or the dawn prayer immediately before the fast begins). Most importantly, the rules of place become sharpened, with the lines between observance and nonobservance becoming more defined during Ramadan.

Amidst that heightened observance, our tour group must have made a curious sight. It was nighttime, a period in which tours were rarely organized, and it was Ramadan, a period of more visible observance during which the rules of place were more defined. We were following our guide, shepherded along by a representative from the tour company. As we entered the mosque, our guide explained the significance of Lale Mustafa Paşa, a seventeenth-century grand vizier whose tomb abutted the tomb of Halid bin Zeyd. He called our attention to the baroque details of the mosque, the fountains constructed by Sultan Selim III that were adorned with Mevlevi headgear. From the way that our group arranged itself relative to these objects and our tour guide, it was clear that our visit was not guided by a set of religious norms, in contrast to that of nearly everyone else in the mosque. And yet our group was speaking in Turkish, which placed us alongside nearly everyone else in the mosque.

To be a tourist in Eyüp Sultan is to not follow the "normal" rules of place. However, responses to an encounter between religious and tourist rules could take many forms, as this chapter's opening vignette made clear. One man approved of what we were doing: although we weren't praying as a group or conducting ourselves in the typical way, we were learning about religion in our own way. But the second man's dismissive comment—"They're tourists"—was a reminder that the practice of tourism can be seen as less valuable than the practice of worship in the Mosque of Eyüp Sultan.

The increased number of visitors associated with Ramadan also results in a second tension, one produced by the interaction between men and women. I now turn to a series of moments and responses in which the visibility of women in the mosque complex of Eyüp Sultan has produced tensions related to the "proper" rules of place.

## WOMEN IN THE MOSQUE

One of the unique features of Eyüp Sultan is the relatively large presence of women. In part, this presence stems from the location of the tomb of Halid bin Zeyd. While both men and women practice tomb visitation to varying degrees around Istanbul, visiting tombs is frequently described as women's devotional work.[25] Because a greater number of women visit the Mosque of Eyüp Sultan relative to other mosques in Istanbul, their participation in communal prayers raises questions about the "standard" rules of place that ought to govern the space of the mosque. Two rules are particularly important: the first governs the physical proximity between men and women immediately before and during prayer times; and the second concerns the visibility of women. While men often encounter these as "problems," that evaluation is necessarily gendered in nature.[26]

The most crowded night in the Mosque of Eyüp Sultan is the Night of Power (Kadir Gecesi), the night on which the Qur'an was first revealed to the Prophet Muhammad. As it falls during the last week of Ramadan, the night is the devotional high point of the month of fasting. Even people who do not fast for the month of Ramadan (or even observe it in any other way) will seek out a mosque on the Night of Power. The huge crowds that appear in Eyüp present a special difficulty because of the way that crowds render "appropriate" gender divisions nearly impossible.

The day before Kadir Gecesi in 2012, I had been advised to avoid the mosque. "You won't even be able to take a step [from the crowds]," a policeman had warned me. He was right: by the time of the *teravih* prayers, the entire square in front of the mosque was filled with people trying to find a space in which to pray. I overheard two men from Ankara complaining about the scene. They were dismayed by what they found and complained about the proximity of men and women, who were praying "right beside one another" (*yanyanına*). This proximity posed special challenges for men who follow the Shafi'i *madhab*.[27] According to the strictures of that *madhab*, any physical contact between a man and a woman violates a man's state of purity before prayer. If it happens, a man has to perform his ritual ablutions a second time for his prayers to be deemed acceptable and religiously appropriate.[28]

There simply isn't enough space to accommodate all the people who want to pray in Eyüp Sultan during Ramadan. Although the municipality works to arrange the square as an auxiliary prayer space, that still does not meet everyone's needs. The women's section is always more crowded than the men's prayer section, to say nothing of the facilities for performing one's ablutions. When I was observing morning prayers in 2012 and 2013, some women positioned themselves immediately in front of the mosque's forward door. They could easily hear the

FIGURE 18. Signs in the Mosque of Eyüp Sultan, June 2013. From left to right, the signs warn women about appropriate dress, present the life of Halid bin Zeyd, and warn visitors about religiously inappropriate practices.

imam—and so follow the congregation in prayer—but their location sparked heated arguments. From where they prayed, the women were both in front of men and in front of the line marked by the imam inside the mosque.

In addition to the physical proximity of men and women in the mosque, women are also more visible in mixed gender spaces. One of the most notable examples of this visibility is women's performance of communal prayers in the square outside the mosque, where they can be seen by passersby. Although there are designated women's sections in nearly every mosque in Istanbul—both historic ones and those of more recent construction—it is rare that women's participation in prayers as part of the congregation (*cemaat*) is visible to the general public. One of my interlocutors, a young woman named Seher, also expressed her ambivalence with women's performance of communal prayers in the square. "It's not appropriate" (*uygun değildir*), she said.

Sharper debates emerge over how women dress within the mosque complex itself. In January 2013 I noticed a new sign that had been posted in visible locations within the mosque. It was addressed directly to the "esteemed women visitors [*ziyaretçi*]" to Eyüp Sultan: "Visitors [*misafir*] ... conducting their pilgrimage [*ziyaret*] in accordance with Allah's commands is a religious commandment [*dini bir esas*]. For this reason, women visitors' entering of mosques (The House of Allah) and courtyards *bareheaded* and with tight and sleeveless blouses and tight *pants* and *short skirts* is not appropriate. Please, *let's pay attention*. Let's be of assistance to the staff."[29] The phrasing of the sign was noteworthy in several respects. First, it lumped the interior of the mosque with the exterior courtyards. One of the key rules of place that applies to women in mosques is the covering of one's head. However, whether the courtyard of a mosque is part of that interior space remains an open question. While I observed many women—otherwise uncovered—who would tie a simple scarf around their head as they passed from the square into the outer courtyards of the mosque, I also saw many women who didn't.

This visibility continues to be a debated topic. One online comment about Eyüp Sultan, posted by a male visitor in early 2015, raised a similar critique about the visibility of women. He wrote, "The spiritual [*manevi*] atmosphere there is being destroyed! I was there the first day of *bayram*! Both the interior and courtyard of the mosque had been turned into a podium! Women, [with] their butts and heads uncovered [*göt başı her yeri açık*], were displaying themselves everywhere!"

## CONCLUSION

This chapter has made two arguments. First, the rules of place in Eyüp Sultan are conveyed in three primary ways: through the building itself; through the public texts posted throughout the complex; and through the management and control of bodies as they move through the mosque complex. Rather than understand those rules as connected only to Eyüp Sultan, I tried to show how the configuration of rules in this place are the product of interconnections that link this mosque to other places and histories.

Second, I argued that the rules of place are fragile and incomplete. Rather than "filling" the mosque (in the way that water fills a glass), these rules are tangled threads that snare some people but not others. Looking at three kinds of movement through the mosque complex—that of foreigners, heritage tourists, and women—I tried to show some of the ways that different subjects encountered the rules of place. To not follow the "rules" in Eyüp Sultan is to be foreign. Rather than an inherent (and unchanging) quality of visitors, "foreignness" is a condition produced by an inability to follow (or outright ignorance of) the rules. In the case of heritage tourists, I explored some of the ways that people from Turkey visit the mosque not as a space for their religious worship but as a heritage site. Despite the mosque being imagined as part of a shared "Ottoman" heritage, the experience of heritage tourists moving through Eyüp Sultan is sometimes in tension with the everyday devotional practices that typically fill the mosque. Finally, I turned to the presence of women in the mosque, arguing that the proximity between men and women in the mosque complex and the visibility of women provoked particular (male) anxieties about piety and sacredness.

There are four brief points that I want to draw from this analysis of the rules of place in Eyüp Sultan. First, it suggests that we should complicate our understanding of the geographies of the religious and secular that constitute Istanbul today. That geography can be conceptualized in terms of "districts"—one district is conservative, another liberal, one religious, another secular. Building on Berna Turam's critique of the "neighborhood wars" rubric, this chapter focuses instead on the small relations through which people negotiate the place of Islam.[30] Such an analysis is especially important in what we might assume to be the paradigmatic "sacred" space of the city: the mosque. Careful attention to the transmission and contestation of the rules of place directs our attention not only to the contested boundaries of the religious and secular but also to the places in which they overlap.

Second, the different ways that people follow (or don't follow) the rules of place open up a discussion of what Lara Deeb has termed "authentication," the "[establishment of] the true or correct meaning, understanding, or methods of various religious and social practices and beliefs."[31] Extending Deeb's account, we might also focus not solely on the authentication of practices but also on the authentication of places. A feeling of authenticity requires ongoing forms of work and labor.[32] But authenticating places also requires the articulation and definition of connections that link a place to elsewhere. Defining, articulating, and enforcing those rules of place is an important part of this project.

Third, rules of place are the products of different mobilities.[33] This is true in at least two senses. First, the rules of place constrain forms of mobility. Second, the rules of place that apply in Eyüp Sultan are also produced by the different movement of people, narratives, and objects into and out of the mosque. Debates about superstition and saint worship, for example, are shared between different mosques and tomb complexes, but they must also be brought there. Thought of in this way, we might also think about mobilities not only across space but also across time. Many of Eyüp Sultan's rules of place are constituted by reference to an authoritative past, although the definition of that past remains an ongoing subject of debate.[34] The ongoing nature of that debate also reminds us that Eyüp Sultan's rules also have their own history. The rules of place are "bound up with the *histories* which are told of them, *how* those histories are told, and which history turns out to be dominant."[35]

Finally, thinking in terms of the rules of place provides a useful complement to recent debates that conceptualize buildings not as fixed objects but as ongoing processes, variously made and unmade.[36] One of the key advantages of this approach is that it prompts us to understand the coherence of buildings—such as the Mosque of Eyüp Sultan—not as an inherent quality but as the product of contested everyday practices of inhabitation, movement, and consumption.[37] This chapter has tried to show that buildings—their physical layout, the public texts posted on them, and the people who work in them—are not simply the backdrop for social life but important agents in shaping the rules of place.

7

# Sharing Place

## *Ramadan in Eyüp*

After iftar one night in August 2013, I sat on the balcony of a friend's home with another guest, a man named Nedim Bey.[1] We had spent the earlier part of the evening talking about the district's history, one he knew well from his youth in the neighborhood and his close involvement in its politics. We looked out in the direction of Eyüp's central square; even though our view of the domes and minarets of the Mosque of Eyüp Sultan was obscured by the four-story concrete apartment buildings that filled most of the district's center, its loudspeakers were audible in the humid evening. Our conversation returned to the nature of Ramadan in Eyüp, a month characterized by large crowds, television programs, restaurants overflowing with people, public performances, and, above all, an intensified religious atmosphere.

That year, one of the most visible markers of the month's arrival was the temporary structure erected in Eyüp's central square, immediately in front of the mosque. Fashioned of fiberglass, paint, and fabric, this structure was designed to look like the arcades (*revaklar*) that once surrounded the Kaaba in Mecca.[2] During the day, it provided a welcome respite from the heat, a place to read and reflect, and it was used as a venue for performances and lectures. At night, it became an area for prayer, providing extra space for the large number of visitors who visited the mosque during Ramadan. Nedim Bey, however, criticized both the arcades and the other public events that took place in Eyüp: "You're bringing a cheap imitation [*çakma*] Kaaba.... If you're going to do something, be honorable and respectable [*şerefli ve namuslu*] about it. If you're going to have a recitation of the Qur'an, follow it with an explanation in clear Turkish so that everybody can understand. If nothing else, let those who come derive a little bit of enlightenment [*hiç olmazsa gelenler feyiz alsınlar*]."

The arcades had been built by the Eyüp Municipality. Depending on one's perspective, the municipality's highly visible role in organizing Ramadan-themed events served as either evidence of the municipality's success or, as Nedim Bey argued, as a clear marker of its failure. But Nedim Bey's negative evaluation was not just a question of local politics. His characterization of the "cheap imitation Kaaba" was implicitly positioned in relation to the real Kaaba in Mecca. He drew a distinction between external markers of religion like the arcades or a public recitation of the Qur'an and an internal world of understanding and "enlightenment." In short, his critique was one part of a much broader question this chapter examines: What should be the place of Islam in public life?

In response to that question, this chapter explores how individuals and institutions made Eyüp a place for Ramadan in 2012 and 2013. For some, the phrase "a *place* for Ramadan" might seem counterintuitive. Ramadan, after all, is usually defined as a *time*, a month of fasting. However, I argue that focusing exclusively on the temporal dimensions of Ramadan—its daily fast, its heightened acts of religious observance, its month-long duration—sheds light on only one dimension of the month's meanings.[3] Just as the observance of Ramadan requires a set of temporal markers, so too its observance demands a set of practices that ground forms of being Muslim in the world. Extending Birgit Meyer's formulation, making Eyüp a place of Ramadan requires various material formations that create common subjects, communities, and temporalities.[4]

The arcades erected by the Eyüp Municipality in 2013 were one example of these acts of place making. They helped to transform Eyüp's central square in a way that brought a new form of order and made possible a novel set of social practices. In the process, the municipality sought not just to transform the district but also to shape the people who moved within it. Given its relative power and authority over public spaces, the municipality had an especially important role in this process, but it was not the only actor at work. Restaurant owners served meals for those who could afford them, religious organizations distributed fliers and free books to passersby, and media personalities offered their own perspectives on Ramadan's importance. Meanwhile, visitors and residents alike moved through Eyüp, engaging in their own acts of place making that were sometimes congruent with the municipality's efforts, sometimes in tension with them, and sometimes ignored those efforts entirely.

This chapter also highlights the importance of material things, objects, and practices in mediating the relationships that define Ramadan. During this month, material objects and practices—ranging from the arcades built by the municipality to the food shared by people at the breaking of the fast—become "sensational forms" through which Ramadan is experienced collectively.[5] However, because these material objects and practices are available to be shared, they also become sites of contestation and debate. Ramadan thus becomes a month in which those shared objects and practices can also spark deep divisions between people and places.

To develop this argument, this chapter narrates a series of encounters that took place during Ramadan in 2012 and 2013.[6] The narrative is deliberately nonchronological to draw attention both to continuities (including debates about public spectacle and consumption) and to shifts (such as the municipality's decision to organize more elaborate celebrations in 2013 than in 2012). This helps to expose not only the temporalities internal to Ramadan but also those that link Ramadan to a much broader world. These are the temporalities of municipal elections, urban protests, political transformation, and lived experience, to name only a few.

## THE MUNICIPAL POLITICS OF RAMADAN, JULY 2013

On a normal day during my fieldwork, I would trace a familiar route: arriving in Eyüp by ferry or bus, I would begin at the pier or the bus stop adjacent to the shore road. Working my way toward the dome of the mosque, I would pass through the narrow streets of Eyüp's center, past the walled-off cemeteries and the restored Ottoman-era tombs, before entering the main square in front of the mosque itself. If the weather was pleasant, there would usually be small groups of people gathered around the splashing fountain, taking photographs or feeding pigeons. On sunny days, the square, paved in white marble, would shine brightly.

The upper section of the square was roughly rectangular in shape. During the week it was often vacant, with visitors and residents perhaps sitting on the benches around its perimeter. On Fridays and weekends, however, this section of the square was transformed into an overflow prayer space for the large number of people who came for communal prayers. Before prayer times municipal crews would wash the marble pavement, set up portable wooden fences, and spread out rugs for prayer. Their work was facilitated by small architectural details built into the square itself: the paving stones were aligned with the direction of prayer, and a small brass line at the end of the section marked the position of the imam conducting prayers inside the mosque.

In early July 2013, a few days before the beginning of Ramadan, I found a very different square. A jumble of fiberglass columns stood in the square, half-assembled and occupying the space where overflow prayer usually happened. As I stood there taking photographs to document the construction, an older man on his way to visit the mosque asked me, "Do you know what these are going to be?" I shrugged my shoulders and responded by quoting a small sign that I had seen taped to one of the columns. "Some arcades are going to be built," I said, "like the ones they have in Mecca." Without looking at the columns again, the man bid me a good day and passed into the mosque itself.

FIGURE 19. The completed arcades beside the Mosque of Eyüp Sultan, July 2013.

A few days after the beginning of Ramadan, the large square had assumed the form it would have for the entire month. The new arcades filled the upper half of the square. Painted to resemble white marble, their columns were linked with arches textured to look like stone; at the center of each arch was a roundel inscribed with "Allah." Fabric was draped over the entire structure, and municipal crews would later install misting fans from the columns. Carpets were placed under the arches, and cushions and small bookshelves were organized throughout the space.

The other major element defining the Ramadan festivities was the large stage built in the square's lower section over what was normally a splashing fountain. The fountain had been turned off to allow the building of the stage. The stage was flanked by two video screens that could be used to broadcast either feeds from inside the mosque itself or the live television shows that were installed on two raised platforms in the square. At the top of the stage, a panel displayed the municipality's Ramadan slogan again: "In Eyüp Ramadan Has a Special Beauty." At the very center of the panel was the municipality's logo. In case visitors to the square had not already noticed the municipality's role in sponsoring these events, two vertical panels to either side of the stage also carried the municipality's name.

Istanbul's district municipalities (*ilçe belediyeleri*) play a key role in making Ramadan visible. They do so strategically, both to advertise themselves and to generate rents. Crucially, however, the thirty-seven district municipalities make Ramadan visible in different ways. Municipalities controlled by the CHP (Cumhuriyet

FIGURE 20. Platform built for live television broadcasts next to the Mosque of Eyüp Sultan, July 2013.

Halk Partisi, or Republican People's Party), a party traditionally associated with a public commitment to "secular" celebrations, tend to mark the arrival of Ramadan in relatively small ways. Posted signs may welcome the month, but districts like Beşiktaş and Kadıköy do not usually sponsor large Ramadan events. In contrast, municipalities controlled by the AKP (Adalet ve Kalkınma Partisi, or Justice and Development Party), as Eyüp was in 2012 and 2013, almost always organize highly visible events for a broad public. Consequently, Istanbul's district-level political geography plays an important part in generating an uneven geography of observance.

At the same time, not all AKP-controlled municipalities celebrate Ramadan in the same way. Municipalities' capacity to stage expensive Ramadan events is constrained by the financial resources available to the municipality, the wealth of the private business interests affiliated with the municipality, the uneven flows of visitors to different Istanbul districts, and the potential rents that can be generated from Ramadan events. Finally, even though municipality-level politics impacts how and why these Ramadan events emerge, there are other ways that visitors to and residents of Eyüp make sense of the geographies of Ramadan.

These Ramadan festivities were noteworthy for several reasons, including their size and the visibility of the municipality's name, but I was especially curious about the fact that the events in 2013 far outstripped those of 2012. In 2012 the municipality had not transformed the square in any permanent way for Ramadan: there was no stage with nightly performances, no platforms for live TV broadcasts, and no arcades modeled on the Kaaba in Mecca. To learn why, I spoke with Kenan Bey, an employee at the local municipality.

It was quiet in the municipality building when I visited in 2013. A lot of the contractors and other businesses take most of the month off, Kenan Bey explained, so the staff was mostly engaged with small tasks here and there. I asked him about the square, and he began by placing the square's transformation in context. "It's an investment [*yatırım*] for the election next year," he noted. "But as you know, the municipality did other things last year [as well]; they did the neighborhood [*mahalle*] iftars and the Haliç Activity Area, but they didn't do anything special for the square."

The rhythm of municipal elections thus marked one temporal background against which Ramadan was observed. These elections generally take place in March every five years.[7] In March 2009, a relatively unknown figure named Ismail Kavuncu had been nominated by the AKP in Eyüp.[8] Kavuncu's 2009 victory may have been the result of his own political savvy, but my conversations suggested that he also benefited from the AKP's strength in the municipality.

I encountered divided opinions about Kavuncu during my fieldwork between 2011 and 2013. Some praised his industriousness and relative modesty after the fifteen-year tenure of his predecessor, Ahmet Genç. Others criticized his lack of connection to Eyüp and the changes that took place between Genç's mayorship and his. He was also dismissed as a *cemaatçı*, a term used derisively to described people associated with the Gülen movement.[9]

Although I had no almost direct contact with people closely involved in the Gülen movement, many of my interlocutors suggested that the movement had been well established in Eyüp even before 2009.[10] However, Mayor Kavuncu's election had helped to make the movement's presence more obvious. Several properties previously used by the municipality for municipal purposes were transformed into restaurants and cafés. There were also rumors that the Eyüp Municipality's building would be transformed into a hotel under the ownership of a prominent figure associated with Gülen.

Ramadan in 2013 played out in relation to two distinct but interrelated temporal trajectories. First, and as Kenan Bey highlighted, there was the temporality of municipal elections. Whereas the Ramadan events of 2012 were relatively modest, Ramadan programming in 2013 was explicitly used by Mayor Kavuncu to advertise himself and the party in advance of the March 2014 elections. The second trajectory that became visible only in hindsight involved the Gülen movement itself. In December 2013 the indictment of several high-ranking government officials on corruption charges sparked one of the first open struggles between the Gülen movement and others within the AKP.[11] Not surprisingly given Kavuncu's association with the Gülen movement, central party leadership did not nominate him to run for a second term in March 2014.

Kenan Bey continued, "A couple of television programs talked about doing something [in 2012], but that didn't happen either, that's just the way it was. . . . There were a number of people who complained . . . last year, so we put together this project, and this is what happened this year." Kenan Bey did not explain what the "complaints" were, but, having spent a great deal of time in Eyüp the previous Ramadan, I knew that they may have been about one of two linked issues: The first involved the general lack of public events in the square. Ahmet Genç, Eyüp's mayor from 1994 to 2009, had made public celebrations during Ramadan a central part of the municipality's work; in contrast, Ismail Kavuncu's Ramadan celebrations seemed rather modest in scope. The second issue may have been related to the large number of people who took to organizing picnics in the square to break their fast. Indeed, many who complimented the municipality's efforts in 2013 often compared the square to 2012, when it had been filled with this practice of picnic iftar.

Although the municipality's transformation of the square in 2013 was different from the previous year, there were other municipality projects that remained the same. One of the most visible of these projects was the row of "Ottoman houses" (*Osmanlı evleri*) erected on Feshane Boulevard, a short walk from the center of Eyüp and parallel to the four-lane shore road that connected Eyüp to Istanbul's central districts. Built of simple plywood and lumber and painted in a variety of pastel colors, some of these houses also included the overhanging *cumba* balcony that is widely used as a marker of the "traditional" Turkish house.[12]

A few days before the beginning of Ramadan in 2013, nylon scrims advertised either the Eyüp Municipality and its Ramadan slogan or the company ESBAŞ, or Eyüp Belediyesi Anonim Şirketi (Eyüp Municipality Corporation). Established in 1992 as a public-private partnership in the midst of the privatization of a range of public services, the company had come to play a key role in the delivery of municipal services and the generation of significant economic benefits for the private individuals who worked with these partnerships.[13] This collaboration benefits the municipality because it reduces the financial burden of paying for services like street cleaning and trash pickup and generates profits through the use of various venues owned by the municipality. It benefits the corporation's private partners by allowing them to capitalize on "public" properties without transferring the ownership of those properties.

These Ramadan "houses" were one example of that mutually beneficial relationship. The houses were built directly on one of the pedestrianized boulevards of Eyüp. Restaurant owners and small entrepreneurs from outside Eyüp were willing to pay several thousand liras to rent the temporary structures for the month with the expectation that they would be able to turn a profit by selling meals, souvenirs, photographs, candy, and other sundries to the dense Ramadan crowds. The municipality was also able to generate money from a space that—without the houses—would have simply been a pedestrian boulevard.

## ENCOUNTERING THE ARCADES: AMBIENCE, OPENNESS, ORGANIZATION

### *Appreciating the Arcades, July–August 2013*

Even though the arcades and the stage were prominently marked with the Eyüp Municipality's logo in 2013, individuals' responses to the arcades did not necessarily center the role of the municipality. Positive evaluations of the Ramadan events were rarely phrased in terms of explicit support for the local municipality. Instead, they highlighted qualities like the square's ambience, value as a domestic space, openness, and order. The relative invisibility of the municipality, even as its logo was prominently displayed nearly everywhere in the square, points to the complex way that "political" activities fade into the background of the broader city, both to the benefit of the municipality and to its detriment. Reactions to the arcades also highlighted the different audiences for these arcades, with a repeated distinction being drawn between those from Eyüp and those who came from "outside."

I came to appreciate the benefits the complex provided. I would remove my shoes at the edge of the carpets and sit with my back against one of the fiberglass columns. If there was a lecture, I would half listen as I closed my eyes and rested in the shared space, tired from fasting during the heat of the long summer days. As I spent time under the arcades during Ramadan, I realized that the value of the complex was in part derived from the way that it provided a place of comfort, one cooled by misters mounted to the arches, shaded by a fabric roof, and well provisioned with cushions and low desks for reading the Qur'an or simply reclining in the middle of the square. Its audience during the middle of the day tended to skew older, mostly men and women who seemed to be retirees. Mothers would sometimes shepherd their children to the lectures and performances during the day. One day I spoke with an older Eyüp resident as we sat next to each other under the awnings. "For the people of Eyüp it's OK," he said, shrugging as he spoke, "but for those who come from outside, it's a wonderful ambience [*güzel bir ambiyans*]."

On another afternoon I spoke with one mother about the square's events. She also lived near the center of Eyüp, and her children were frequent participants in the English classes that I taught nearby. She liked the complex and the events, she explained, because they provided an outlet during the day for her children's energy, particularly because she was fasting and they weren't. By carpeting the square, installing misters and an awning, and organizing lectures during the day, the Eyüp Municipality had succeeded in transforming the square into a different kind of public space, one that felt more domestic and associated with the interior spaces of the home.

In addition to providing a pleasing ambience and a semidomestic space for some families, the square was also distinguished by what some described as its "openness." Even though the municipality-sponsored programming was largely

FIGURE 21. The arcades on a typical Ramadan day, July 2013.

oriented toward ostensibly religious activities, such as recitations of the Qur'an, lectures about Islamic ethics, and plays about the early history of Islam, one acquaintance explained that the public forms of Islam in Eyüp were different from those in other religious districts in the city. When we crossed paths in the square, Selim Bey was helping to coordinate the activities sponsored by the municipality. Behind us on stage, a group of men were performing *ilahis* (religious hymns) in front of a small audience scattered among the plastic seats that faced the stage. Selim Bey worked for the Eyüp Municipality, and our conversation picked up with a comment he had made a few days previously, when we had interviewed each other about our respective experiences in and observations about Eyüp.

"See," he said, "this is what I was talking about. There are all sorts of people here, women with headscarves, without scarves, in short skirts, in pants; there are people of all shapes, sorts, and sizes. You don't find this in Fatih, for example."

"Why?" I asked. "Is it stricter [*tutucu*] there?"

"Yes, exactly," he replied. "It's not as mixed [*karışık*] as this."

Selim was referencing a widely shared social geography of Istanbul, one in which the city was divided into zones depending on their religious character.[14] Within that geography, districts like Taksim, Kadıköy, Nişantaşı, and Beşiktaş are usually described as more secular.[15] In those districts there are relatively few public markers of Muslim religious practice; mosques are often hidden between apartment buildings, the call to prayer is often less audible, and religiously marked forms of dress and bodily comportment are less prominent.[16] For people seeking these markers of a public Muslim identity, these districts can sometimes be alienating. In contrast, districts like Eyüp, Fatih, and Üsküdar are often described as more religious in character. Whereas secular districts of Istanbul are defined by the relative invisibility of public Muslim practices, these districts derive their religious identity from the public forms of Muslim religious practice, including prominent mosques, highly audible calls to prayer, and certain practices of dress, grooming, and social encounter.

Selim Bey, however, complicated that binary geography of secular and religious by calling attention to the differences between Fatih and Eyüp. He singled out women's dress as a key marker of Eyüp's diversity, noting that in Eyüp women both did and did not wear headscarves; some wore dresses, he noted, while others wore pants. While it is possible for men to blend in as they move through different districts of the city, women's dress is frequently used as a marker of piety and functions as one metric to evaluate how religiously conservative a district might be. In "conservative" districts, most women wear headscarves and long coats. Those who do not still usually wear long pants and blouses that cover their arms. The reverse holds true for "liberal" districts: most women—during the summer, at least—will wear T-shirts, skirts, or shorts. In both cases, women whose dress does not match the character of the district will attract attention, ranging from sidelong sneers to public critique.

In Selim's eyes, Eyüp was special because both conservative and liberal forms of dress coexisted within its central square. The municipality sponsored religious programming, but of a type that was accessible and attractive to a broad public, a public that Selim identified primarily based on people's dress. In the process, he implicitly suggested that there was value in noting the differences not just between religious and secular districts but also between different kinds of religious districts. As Selim Bey looked out on the audience, he saw a diverse crowd that could exist anywhere in the city. I looked out on the audience with him and asked, "Do you think people are happy? Are they enjoying all these performances?"

"Oh yes," he said. "Everyone is really happy with this. There are *ney* performances, Qur'an recitation, and *sema*. It's important that we organize these sorts of things."[17] The "sorts of things" associated with Ramadan included a range of events. Some, such as the recitation of the Qur'an, were events directly linked to a set of explicit religious proscriptions. Others, such as the *ney* performances and *sema*, were part of the broader cultural field within which Islam is practiced in Turkey today.[18] There are often heated disagreements between different groups and individuals about how one's Muslim-ness should be practiced in public. In its choices about what speakers to invite, what performances to sponsor, and what publications to distribute, the Eyüp Municipality played one part in creating a public Islam. Selim Bey's praise of Eyüp's "openness," in contrast to the more conservative (*tutucu*) character of a district like Fatih, was in part shaped by the institution for which he worked.

Selim Bey's positive evaluation of the square highlighted another opinion that many of my interlocutors echoed in 2013: the square's organization and order. During a separate conversation with Salih Bey, a shopkeeper on a small street near the central square, he told me that although he prayed regularly and was fasting in observance of Ramadan, he tended to avoid the Mosque of Eyüp Sultan in favor of the smaller neighborhood mosques in the area. When I asked why, he explained that space in Eyüp Sultan should be reserved for those who visited from a greater distance than he. I followed up by asking for his perspective on the activities in the square. He paused a moment before answering, "It's a good thing, because last year it was disorganized [*düzensiz*]. This year it's more organized [*daha düzenli*] . . . they've done a much better job. This is what people should see when they come to visit Eyüp."

Salih Bey's positive evaluation echoed many conversations I had with other residents during Ramadan in 2013. For example, on another afternoon I crossed paths with Ziya, a young man with whom I'd had several discussions about Islam, his own piety, and his opinion about what constituted appropriate public religious behavior. Knowing that he passed through the square frequently, I asked him about the square's changed appearance. He focused immediately on how this year the Ramadan complex prevented the square's use as a picnic area, as it had been in 2012. "It's good," he noted, "better than last year. Last year people came and spread out their meals [*sofra*]; it wasn't appropriate, something that shouldn't have happened [*uygun değildi, olmaması gereken bir şey*]."

### Picnic Iftar and a Disordered Square, July 2012

Although Ramadan is experienced as a month of heightened religious observance, it is also experienced against the memory of the Ramadans that have come before. In 2013, many people referred either directly or indirectly to the way that the square had been used in 2012. That year, the municipality did not build any structures in the square. Their only obvious concession to Ramadan was placing a series of portable fences around the perimeter of the overflow prayer space and adding a set of portable awnings in the space that could be opened to shade visitors.

At the beginning of the month, small groups of families began to bring their food and picnic supplies to the square to share their iftar immediately in front of the mosque. Starting in the late afternoon, people would arrive with plastic rugs, portable propane stoves, bottles of water and soda, and containers of food that they had prepared at home. When the call to prayer sounded from the minarets of Eyüp Sultan, people were able to break their fast at the very heart of the district's religious life. By the end of the month, the square had become crowded with small groups of people who filled most of its space.

While this practice of sharing one's iftar in the square in 2012 made the center of Eyüp accessible to people who might not otherwise have been able to visit the expensive restaurants that surrounded the square, this practice of picnic iftar also presented a major challenge to one of the square's most important functions during Ramadan: its use as a supplemental prayer space when the mosque fills up, as usually happens on weekends and major religious holidays. Because prayer spaces are supposed to be kept clean and distinct from the "outside," the use of the square as a prayer space typically requires a cleaning crew and a gradual process of demarcating the prayer space from the neighborhood's urban fabric. That process was made vastly more difficult by people's *sofra* scattered throughout the square. Cleaning crews and municipal police often were forced to chivy families away from the prayer spaces as an impatient congregation tried to make their way to pray.

The tensions were not simply between the people who shared their iftar in the square and the municipality, the institution responsible for officially regulating the public square. Tensions also emerged between different groups of people about the appropriateness of this open-air iftar. One afternoon in August 2012, I had stopped in for a shave at the shop of Sefat Amca, a longtime resident of the district. Many of his customers were themselves people with long histories of connection to Eyüp. On this day, one of his customers came in complaining about the practice of iftar in the square during Ramadan. "It's as though people think that it's a blessing [*sevap*] to eat in front of the mosque; it's a sin [*günah*]! Pardon me, but they're sleeping like cows, the congregation can't even pray [*Affedersin, inek gibi uyuyorlar, cemaat namaz kılamıyor bile*]."

The customer's complaint drew on a much broader critique linked to discussions about religious knowledge, social class, and public norms. At the center of this critique was the distinction drawn between "blessings" and "sins." These blessings are conferred upon a person or upon those that they love by engaging in specific practices. These practices could include anything from reciting prayers, visiting shrines, and distributing food to—in this case—eating meals in front of the mosque. However, precisely because practices can take many forms, the distinction between "correct" and "incorrect" practices is crucial. Were one to seek blessings by engaging in religiously inappropriate practice, it would in fact be considered a sin. Hence the distinction between blessings and sin resonates with a complex debate about correct religious practice in contemporary Turkey, a debate shaped by claims to authority but also social class and urban norms. The customer's immediate segue into a comparison with "cows" points to precisely that overlap. People may often correlate a lack of religious knowledge—a lack that would lead people to confuse "blessings" and "sins"—with a lower socioeconomic status. This is an equation that many who are considered relatively "poor" work to challenge through their own pursuit of knowledge about Eyüp, Halid bin Zeyd, and Eyüp Sultan. Here, I seek to highlight the way that the critique of iftar in the square blurs the distinction between a lack of religious knowledge and a class-based critique.

## SHARING RAMADAN, UNEVENLY

Throughout the month of Ramadan, many of Istanbul's larger mosques hang strands of lights between their minarets that spell out various phrases. Known as *mahya*, these lights are one of the most visible forms of shared observance during the month. These phrases always make a claim, at once aspirational and normative, about what Ramadan is and how it (and, by extension, Islam) should be lived. Passing between Üsküdar and Eyüp as I did, I would often glance at the *mahya* hung from the mosques near the shore in Üsküdar and Eminönü. One night in 2012, I noticed the phrase "Ramadan Is Sharing" (*Ramazan Paylaşmaktır*).

Sharing emerges as a key theme during the month; people share in a variety of ways and in a variety of places. The square in front of the Mosque of Eyüp Sultan was one key site for this sharing. Sometimes, as in 2012, the sharing of activities like picnic iftar generated critique. Other times, as in 2013, the municipality helped to create a welcoming environment for people from outside Eyüp to come and share in the district's distinctiveness. But debates over the square's use and appearance during Ramadan did not simply turn on tensions over shared spaces and public norms; they also emerged around the contested boundary between practices associated with worship (*ibadet*) and those associated with entertainment (*eğlence*) and personal benefit (*menfaat*).

Although Ramadan is a month in which many people become more attentive to religious observance, it is also a month that creates tremendous economic value, as the municipality's "Ottoman houses" make clear. The municipality rents out temporary houses to entrepreneurs from outside Eyüp; restaurant and café owners in Eyüp spill out into the streets as they expand their capacity for guests; and even businesses not necessarily associated with food service will rent out their storefronts to Ramadan entrepreneurs. Some residents in Eyüp suggested to me that business owners can make as much during Ramadan as they do the rest of the year combined.

### Criticizing Iftar, July 2012

Sharing Ramadan was thus not nearly as simple as being in the same square together. A week into Ramadan in 2012, after the crowds of the first weekend had subsided and Eyüp residents had returned to the rhythms of the workweek, I gathered with a small group of friends to share iftar. One of us, a doctor, began to tell a story about another iftar to which he'd been invited a few days previous, on the first Saturday of the month. "It was at one of the expensive restaurants adjacent to the square," he said, "and I went with a friend of mine." Although he didn't name the specific restaurant, all the "expensive restaurants" in the vicinity of the square shared a set of characteristics.

First, they were housed in either renovated wooden mansions or in the buildings constructed during the district's redevelopment in the 1990s. Second, although these restaurants were adjacent to the square, they were also clearly demarcated from it: their dining areas were behind walls or doors, or they were upstairs. Finally, these restaurants advertised their menus as being simultaneously traditional and sumptuous. As one promotional brochure advertised, "Welcome Ramadan, the Sultan of the Eleven Months, in Eyüp. . . . Alongside traditional tastes, variety after variety of iftar appetizers, soups, olive oil mezzes, varieties of sherbets, soft drinks, and unlimited tea, your iftar table turns into a banquet. Iftar tables, colored by the melodies of live Sufi music, gain another meaning within the historical fabric." They promised a kind of intimacy within the "historical," "traditional," and religious atmosphere of the district's center without the crowds of people who visited the district during Ramadan.

The doctor continued by describing the sheer quantity of food that was served to break their fast. "The portions were enormous," he said. "There wasn't any way that we were going to be able to finish it. I could only eat half, my friend could only eat half, and we had to take the rest and push it to the side. Can you imagine this? It's a sin [günah]." From there our conversations spiraled into a discussion of the tension between being modest and publicly displaying one's wealth. They could put half the food on the plate, the doctor added, and charge less money, and everybody would be better off. Debates about public displays of wealth are neither unique to Istanbul nor specific to the contemporary moment. Over the past two decades, however, these debates about public consumption have intersected with new debates about religious practice in public. Critiques of lavish iftar have been at the center of these debates.[19]

### Ramadan Is Not What It Used to Be, July 2012

On another afternoon during Ramadan I ran into an acquaintance named Cavit Bey. Knowing that I was interested in meeting more people in the district, he took me to visit a small barbershop a short walk from the central square run by two men, Ömer Amca and İzzet Amca. Although I was fasting, Cavit Bey wasn't. As we walked into the small shop, he asked, "Ömer Amca, can you give me a shave without breaking your fast?" He asked not out of ignorance but out of politeness. People's observance of Ramadan, like their observance of Islam, can take many forms in Istanbul. While negotiating those everyday differences can be tense, Cavit Bey's polite question offered an alternative and far less tense negotiation.[20] Ömer Amca motioned him into the chair and, as Ömer Amca lathered up Cavit's face, they began to talk about Ramadan and how Ramadan used to be.

Ömer Amca began to tell a story about when he was younger and working as a barber in Balat, the neighborhood just inside the city walls that used to be one of the centers of Istanbul Greek Christian and Jewish life. Now in his seventies, Ömer Amca remembered a different Balat in a very different Istanbul. Even though his neighbors back then weren't Muslim, he explained, during Ramadan "not a single

FIGURE 22. Banner advertising iftar and sahur at a restored Ottoman-era mansion in central Eyüp, July 2013. The prices were substantially higher than those at places advertised to the general public.

person would smoke beside [him], drink anything, go after any soft drinks. They all respected that we were fasting. But now," he continued, "the other day, I was here and some group of people came in from out of town, their license plates said they were from Samsun. They set up in front of the barbershop and were just eating and drinking and carrying on." He added, in a phrase I came to hear repeated throughout Ramadan: "Ramadan is a month of worship [*ibadet ayı*], not a month of entertainment [*eğlence ayı değil*]. In this poor country, why is there a need for this much entertainment?" As he was being shaved, Cavit summed up the conversation: "Ramadan used to be more unpretentious [*daha sade idi*]."

*Not Worship but Personal Benefit, July 2013*

Even though the municipality brought a new level of order and organization to the square in 2013, a conversation with Kadir Bey in the same year highlighted the continued tension surrounding the square's orientation toward business. Like Salih Bey, Kadir Bey was another longtime resident of Eyüp and owned a small shop a little way from the central square. He also prayed regularly and was fasting for Ramadan. Yet when we talked about the uses of the square and the changes between 2012 and 2013, he was dismissive of the municipality's efforts. "The square isn't being used for worship [*ibadet*]," he said. "It's become an open restaurant, not the sort of thing you should find in a house of worship [*ibadethane*]."

FIGURE 23. "Ramadan is not a month of enjoyment but of worship." Banner hung from local Felicity Party office, August 2013.

I murmured my agreement and repeated one of the phrases that I had frequently heard as a critique of Ramadan's public spectacles in Istanbul: "Ramadan's not a month of enjoyment," I said, "it's a month of worship" (*eğlence ayı değil, ibadet ayıdır*). Kadir Bey nodded his agreement and added a second point: "Wherever there's personal benefit [*menfaatın olduğu yerde*], Allah's approval is absent [*Allah'ın rızası olmaz*]." At stake in Kadir Bey's critique of the square was the relationship between success in this world and true success in the afterlife. *İbadet* is an act that reminds Muslims of their smallness before God. When people seek personal benefit (*menfaat*) in this world, they neglect what should be the true goal, which is "Allah's approval." Insofar as the square became a place of profit, that profit seeking replaced the practice of worship. The municipality occupied a complicated position within this debate. On the one hand—and as Said Bey, Ziya, and many others noted approvingly—the municipality had brought a needed level of organization and coordination to the square in 2013. The square was, for them, a more comfortable and well-managed place than it had been in 2012. But on the other hand, the municipality was both financially and symbolically invested in attracting business to Eyüp during Ramadan and benefiting from business activity during the month.

The debates over Ramadan in 2013 were also set against the background of Istanbul's changing urban norms and forms. These changes shaped the trajectory of my fieldwork between 2011 and 2013 and provided a key point of reference for conversations about appropriate urban behavior, profit, and the use of public space. Especially in the aftermath of the 2002 electoral victory of the AKP, Istanbul had been transformed in far-reaching ways. These involved both spatial transformations like new malls, housing developments, and the expropriation and redevelopment of specific districts of the city,[21] and social transformations that provided new opportunities and challenges in the rapidly changing city.[22] My conversations in 2013 tapped into a set of broadly circulating vocabularies about these shifts. These conversations were further sharpened by the temporal and spatial proximity of the Gezi Park Protests, which ended only weeks before the beginning of Ramadan.[23] Although Eyüp's religious atmosphere was in many ways distinct from the events in Taksim Square, the protests served as both an implicit and explicit point of reference in some of my conversations.

## CONTESTED MARKERS OF WORSHIP, JULY 2013

One afternoon in 2013, as I was sitting in the square taking advantage of the misters during the July heat, I saw Sema Hanım exiting from the mosque. Now retired, she was a well-known resident of the district, and she exchanged greetings with many of the shopkeepers as we walked back to her home. As a longtime resident of Eyüp, she was very attuned to its changes over time and the ways that these changes had emerged in relation to a set of changing everyday practices. She told me a story of a recent time that she had gone to pray in the mosque. While she was praying, another woman approached her and told her that her arms were not covered enough and that her prayers would not be accepted. Sema Hanım pointed to the joint of her hand and her wrist to show me how far her sleeves had extended. The other woman insisted, Sema Hanım continued, until she agreed to add two half sleeves that would fully cover the backs of her palms. "Our people are getting too fundamentalist" (*halkımız yobazlaşıyor*), she complained. She described her own practice of worship as something that was not marked by a set of external signals but as something that emerged from an internal commitment: "I try to worship in a way that comes from inside me" (*içimden geldiği gibi ibadet etmeye çalışıyorum*).

She transitioned to a discussion of how people today had ceased to treat each other with the respect that they once did. "Our people have become arrogant" (*halkımız küstahlaştı*). When I asked her why, she said that she didn't know the reason, but she shared a story that illustrated her point. She had been in the square, she said, and had seen a group of people sitting on one of the benches, where they were eating sunflower seeds and throwing the shells on the ground. When I scolded them, she added, they looked at me like I was crazy. In her telling, "becoming fundamentalist" and "becoming arrogant" were closely linked. The former involved an obsessive attention to external markers of piety while the latter signaled a disregard for any sort of shared experience of the city.

That night Sema Hanım invited me for iftar, when we would be joined by several other people, including Filiz Hanım and Nedim Bey. Filiz Hanım was even more deeply rooted in Eyüp, as her grandfather had worked at one of the first Ottoman factories and her father was a local official. Our conversations were frequently inflected by her deep sense of Eyüp's lived history. Nedim Bey had been born in the district but moved away later; his joining us for iftar that night was thus also an opportunity to maintain a set of social relationships that had been spread out across the city. As we sat down to iftar that night, I asked them about their sense of the events taking place in the square of Eyüp Sultan. Both were critical. Filiz Hanım explained, "Eyüp's mystical atmosphere has been ruined [*ulvi atmosferi mahvolmuş*]." Both Filiz Hanım and Nedim Bey agreed that the problem with the municipality's events was that they had drawn so many people to the district that the act of contemplation—ostensibly at the center of one's individual responsibilities during Ramadan—had become impossible. The crowds, everyone agreed, hadn't always been like this. Eyüp wasn't this crowded ten years ago, Sema Hanım added, saying that it had only become so in the past decade.

Our conversation that night marked one example of the way that people make a place for Ramadan through stories that link them to multiple temporal and geographical references. Their collective critique compared Eyüp in 2013 to decades of lived experience in the district, family connections to the district's Ottoman past, and the more recent reference point of "ten years ago." Their critique also implicitly referenced the district's changing connection to the broader city: without the sponsorship of the municipality, Eyüp might never have become this crowded.

After we finished dinner, Nedim Bey expanded on this critique. As we sat on the balcony and looked out in the direction of the Mosque of Eyüp Sultan, he added the judgment with which I opened the chapter: "You're bringing a cheap imitation Kaaba [*çakma Kabe*]. . . . If nothing else, let those who come derive a little bit of enlightenment [*hiç olmazsa gelenler feyiz alsınlar*]." The arcades that stood immediately in front of the Mosque of Eyüp Sultan were modeled upon the arcades that surround the Kaaba in Mecca. Nedim Bey linked the "cheap imitation" municipality events with a recitation of the Qur'an that was unintelligible to most listeners. In critiquing the recitation of the Qur'an without an accompanying Turkish translation, Nedim Bey was not arguing against a form of Islam in public; rather, he was critiquing a recitation of the Qur'an that substituted for understanding it. By calling for an explanation in Turkish, Nedim Bey imagined a situation in which visitors might at least be able to derive a benefit from their visit in the form of "enlightenment."

As he continued, his critique broadened out from the square to the district's transformation. Because Eyüp had become such a destination for visitors during Ramadan, traffic and parking had become significant problems for residents. "As it is now," he continued, "visitors come to the neighborhood, then park in the first open space they can find and then leave their car. People can't get into and out of their houses. It's a shame, an embarrassment; there's no value in their pilgrimage [*ziyaret*] because they're infringing on someone else's rights [*hakkını yiyorlar*]."

Nedim Bey's discussion pivoted on one of the tensions at the center of this chapter's argument: how should individual beliefs, practices, and understandings of Islam be negotiated in relation to the shared space of the city? Recall Ömer Amca's critique of the people who drove to Eyüp from outside the district, parked in front of his barbershop, and set about eating and drinking without considering where they had parked. To satisfy one's individual needs—even if, like pilgrimage, they are ostensibly "religious" in nature—in a way that negatively impacts others violated something fundamental about social relationships in Eyüp. During my two years of fieldwork, this critique of others "infringing on one's rights" was repeated by many different individuals as a judgment on the transformations that they saw in Eyüp. Crucially, rights can function both as something absolute (derived from God) and something relational (always contingent upon the social contexts within which one is embedded).

## CONNECTED BY A DREAM, JULY 2012

In a month characterized by exceptional attention to one's religious obligations, the nightly ritual of iftar is one of the most intense moments of connection, a moment when you become acutely conscious not only of your own experience of drink and food after a complete day of fasting but also of the fact that this intimate act is shared by people all around you. It is at once personal and expansive, a moment in time that links you to a broader geography of belief. To this point, this chapter has focused on some of the public debates over how Ramadan should be observed within the city. These debates hinge on competing understandings of what a well-ordered public looks like, the ways that people should and should not profit from the religious activity of Ramadan, and the appropriateness of consumption. I turn now to a different Ramadan encounter to highlight one way that this place can be shared without participating in those debates at all.

It was near the end of Ramadan in 2012, in the middle of July's long days heavy with heat and humidity. I took the ferry from Üsküdar to Eminönü at about 6 p.m., so there was still quite some time before iftar. The bus platforms were crowded in Eminönü, people waiting three rows deep for a bus home after work or shopping. When I finally got on a bus for Eyüp and found a seat, the woman beside me fell asleep on my shoulder, both of us lost in the press of people trying to get home. I got off the bus at the ferry station in Eyüp and walked by the park where people—mostly men—were sitting on the park benches. It was the middle of the week, so the park wasn't as crowded as it was on the weekends. When I made it to the municipality's free iftar, located on a small street behind the mosque, I was surprised to find it nearly full. I heard small arguments between people about saving empty seats for the friends and relatives; a cluster of municipal police stood to the side. I cut through the mosque, where people were asleep on the rugs or simply sitting in the shade of the courtyard, waiting for the last hour before the breaking of the fast.

I made my way into the central square and sat down on the curb in front of the ice cream shop. An older man sat to my left. Tanned and wearing a flat-brimmed cap, he was from somewhere else, somewhere not Istanbul; his Turkish was accented with the heavier consonants of Anatolia. He shared a plastic-wrapped piece of bread from his bag, one of the small rolls distributed by the Istanbul People's Bakery (İstanbul Halk Ekmekleri). The man sitting on my right offered an *ayran* for me to drink. I didn't have anything to offer and found myself ashamed by their generosity. I murmured the only thing I could, *Allah razı olsun, teşekkürler.* May God be pleased, thank you.

I began to speak with the second man. In his fifties, Nazım Bey was from the mountains between Ankara and Kastamonu, but he was born and raised in Zeytinburnu. He lived in Bahçelievler now, on the spreading margins of the city. "When did you first come here?" I asked him. He must have been twelve, he said, so it had been a long time. So why tonight? I asked.

"Last night," he answered, "I had a dream that told me to go to Eyüp Sultan and drink the water there to break my fast. When I woke up this morning, I thought about it a little; there was nobody else in the house, everybody else had gone back to the village to visit relatives, and it seemed like the right thing to do. And so I came here, and now we've met and are talking— that's about it." He showed me the bottle of water in his bag with which he would break the fast.

"If you buy it down the street," he added, "they're only seventy-five *kuruş*. They're selling the same size here in the square for two liras." He dumped out the entire bottle and then left for a moment to enter the mosque, where he refilled his bottle from the fountains in the courtyard. When the call to prayer came, we broke our fast there together: small bread rolls, *ayran*, water from the faucets in the mosque. All around us in the square, families had spread their meals out; there was a powerful sense of sharing in a collective act.

## CONCLUSION

One of the most remarkable aspects of Ramadan is the profound shift in one's relationship to the world. The experience of fasting for the entire day and breaking one's fast at the same moment that thousands, even millions, of other people engage in the same act produces a powerful sense of belonging that spans place and time.

This chapter has shown some of the ways that marking Ramadan as a distinct temporal experience also involves making a particular kind of place for Ramadan, one that is continually remade through relationships between people and the city in which they live. It told the stories of the two Ramadans that were at the center of my fieldwork in 2012 and 2013, periods in which different people and institutions articulated the importance of this time and place in shifting and sometimes contradictory ways. It showed how the construction of the arcades in 2013 was a material transformation that aimed to simultaneously control and channel how Eyüp's central square was used as a site for public worship. The arcades' construction and the debates that they generated were not simply about a set of religious concerns; they were also connected to the broader politics of the city, a politics that were in a state of rapid transformation in June and July 2013. But the arcades' appearance also tied into a more expansive set of debates about the entertainments of Ramadan and the often-blurred line between worship and entertainment, faith and public spectacle. Welcoming the month of Ramadan involved a set of temporal and geographical transformations that were inextricable from the ongoing rhythms and routines of the city, the country, and the world beyond.

At the beginning of Ramadan, signs in Istanbul's public places frequently declare, "Welcome, O month of Ramadan" (*Hoş geldin, ya şehr-i Ramazan*). "*Hoş geldin,*" which is used to welcome guests who arrive from somewhere else, reminds us that the temporal and the geographical are linked, whether consciously or not, when we think about Ramadan. One of the ironies of the observance of Ramadan in Eyüp is precisely this tension between a religious obligation incumbent upon all practicing Muslims and the way that certain modes of religious consumption—in particular, the breaking of the fast—come to separate and divide groups of people. This in turn raises tensions between concepts of worship and entertainment, as well as of order, control, and public space.

"Who is Eyüp Sultan for during Ramadan?" I asked many people during Ramadan in 2012 and 2013. I came to realize that even though the Mosque of Eyüp Sultan is at the center of the district, many people who live in the district stay away from its crowds and spectacle. That thought came to mind during the last week of Ramadan in 2013, on a night when the district was even more crowded than usual. I shouldered my way through the press of people in the mosque's central courtyard and remembered what an acquaintance on the mosque's staff had said: this mosque "isn't enough for us" (*yetmiyor bize*).

Public Ramadan celebrations in districts like Eyüp serve as a key instrument of municipal politics. Their organization speaks to a particular configuration of politics and piety that has emerged over the past two decades. However, it would be a mistake to say that the politics of Ramadan are associated only with the ruling Justice and Development Party. Making a place for Ramadan—an act that brings people, objects, and buildings into multiple forms of alignment—asks us to consider something bigger: How different groups of people might come together to define a common place.

# Conclusion

## *Common Places and Hospitality in a Changing World*

*Yetişmez mi bu şehrin halkına bu nimet-i bâri*
*Habib-i Ekrem'in yârî Ebû Eyyûb el-Ensârî.*

*Won't this blessing of God suffice for the people of this city,*
*the friend of the most generous Prophet, Ebu Eyyub el-Ensari.*

There is a small, framed piece of calligraphy that hangs from the wall near the *mihrab* in the Mosque of Eyüp Sultan. "Won't this blessing of God suffice," it asks, "for the people of this city?" The blessing of God is, of course, Halid bin Zeyd Ebû Eyyûb el-Ensârî. The phrasing of the question tells us two things: first, that Halid bin Zeyd *should* suffice for the people of Istanbul; but second, that he doesn't always, because if he did, we would never need to ask this question.

Halid bin Zeyd is often described as Istanbul's "spiritual conqueror," a description easily enrolled into a politics of religious triumphalism. Such a description is, for many, central to the definition of this place. But there is a second aspect to the story of Halid bin Zeyd—one suggested by this inscription—his hospitality. He was the *mihmandar*, the person who hosted the Prophet Muhammad in Medina and whose spirit of hospitality is tied to this place.

In this conclusion I briefly restate the key arguments and conclusions of the book, describe some of the ongoing changes playing out in Eyüp, and reflect on the limits and possibilities of a cultural geography of Islam. I close, however, by speculating a little more on how Eyüp might help us think about hospitality in a changing world.

FIGURE 24. Visitors to the Mosque of Eyüp Sultan speaking with a photographer, March 2012.

## KEY ARGUMENTS AND CONCLUSIONS

The broad argument that guides this book is that thinking in terms of place provides a novel and nuanced way for understanding *where* Islam is; defining *what* Islam is—whether that happens in academic texts, among communities of Muslims, or anywhere else—is inextricable from that definition of *where*. Understanding these places of Islam as multiple helps us follow how different connections link people, places, objects, and times in shifting and overlapping ways. Examining geographies of connection—in contrast to the container geographies that tend to underpin many of our discussions of space—shows us that sharing a place is neither a simple function of location nor some innate cultural, ethnic, or religious force. Sharing a place of Islam is to share a set of connections to the past and the future and forms of affiliation that often exceed the legible boundaries provided by the map.

Places are made through human activity, but, crucially, they come to acquire a kind of agency and status that situate them outside the solely human. In my account, the project of making place involves the articulation of multiple forms of connection, variously imagined, symbolic, immaterial, material, thick, thin, fragile, durable, mobile, and powerfully rooted. The book's organization into two sections sought to call attention to two distinct forms of place making that are, in fact, woven together: storytelling and building.

At first glance, stories seem to be imagined, mutable, ephemeral, often a matter of perspective, while buildings seem to be concrete, rooted, durable, incontrovertibly *there*. But as I hope to have shown, taking these forms of place making together affords a new approach for thinking about Islam, particularly in the context of contemporary Turkey. Structuring the book by concentrating on these forms of place making (i.e., rather approaching the topic chronologically) also helps highlight echoes and shared experiences that might not otherwise be visible.

This is especially important for discussions of the historicity of Islam in Republican Turkey. For some, being Muslim—often, though not necessarily, linked to being Turkish—becomes a way to ground one's unchanged identity in opposition to the "West." One of the reasons Eyüp has been so important to these claims is because it provides both a story and a material landscape that is seemingly unchanged. For some, this ostensibly fixed Muslim geography helps to ground an internally consistent Muslim identity.

One way that such claims could be critiqued is by conceptualizing them as "invented traditions," fabricated to serve the needs of political Islam during the 1990s or to fit with the postmodern world in which Istanbul residents now find themselves. Yet to call Eyüp and its meanings an invented tradition serves to flatten its complex historicities. Some encounter Eyüp and find a connection to the Prophet Muhammad; some encounter a link to the Byzantine past; some see Sultan Mehmed the Conqueror; some remember the neighborhood of their childhood in the 1950s; still others trace an Eyüp of the 1980s. These encounters with multiple pasts are channeled by means of social, political, and religious relationships and networks. The problem of simply calling these woven braids of time and place "invented traditions" is that it obscures that complexity. Thinking in terms of place thus provides one approach to negotiate the long-running debate between stability and change, continuity and rupture that has played out in studies of Islam in Turkey. If there are powerful forms of continuity at work, it thus challenges us to examine how the meanings of a place like Eyüp are reproduced and transmitted over time to create a shared geography of tradition.

This approach also expands how we come to think about the meaningfulness of Islam. For a variety of reasons, Islam in contemporary Turkey has been studied largely in relation to discourses of modernity, secularization, and the political institutions linked to those discourses. While such an approach is of course valuable and important, it can limit how we understand the meanings of Islam. Being Muslim is not simply about one's relationship to the state or modernity; it can also involve how one encounters the meanings of the city. Thinking in terms of place thus maps out one approach for expanding how we come to think about the meanings of Islam. Yet these meanings continue to shift.

## A CHANGING EYÜP(SULTAN)

This book has set out to explore the tensions—sometimes productive, sometimes destructive—between continuity and change in Eyüp. One thing that makes Eyüp exceptional is its striking continuities: in its meaning, in the ways that people visit, in parts of its built environment. Nevertheless, the district's political and urban landscapes have shifted in dramatic ways since I first began this research.

When I began my fieldwork in 2011, the network of individuals, associations, and businesses affiliated with Fethullah Gülen formed an ever-present background to many of my conversations. At the time, the mayor of the Eyüp Municipality was a man named İsmail Kavuncu. Elected to the position in 2009, Kavuncu had little organic connection to Eyüp. In contrast to his predecessor, Ahmet Genç—who had grown up in Eyüp and risen through the local party networks—Kavuncu seemed to secure his nomination as the result of political connections at the national party level. Nevertheless, some residents were optimistic about the apparent energy, modesty, and probity with which he approached his position. Others dismissively labeled him a *cemaatçı* —a term used to identify people affiliated with Gülen's network.

It should be noted that Gülen's network was active in Eyüp well before 2009. The newspaper *Zaman*, the primary print medium for the movement, frequently published articles about Eyüp's religious importance in the 1990s. The movement's ubiquitous presence in the Eyüp Municipality between 2011 and 2013 was another ign of its prominence within municipal politics. It is likely that people associated h Gülen also invested in Eyüp's redevelopment during the 1990s and the first de of the 2000s, most visibly in some of Eyüp's hotels and restaurants, as they id elsewhere. Although I never participated in one, I was also aware that reading groups operated in Eyüp.

wing the 1994 municipal election, the Eyüp Municipality worked to d repurpose several historic properties in the center of the district. Most operties were registered as property belonging to pious foundations Ar., *waqf*), and this legal designation had helped to prevent their t. Following their restoration, many of these properties were

-c-
tion
s cur-
politics.
hanged in
vay line was
rom Eminönü
thin the city and
e road built in the
s near the Mosque of
e from the water. Dur-
rce critique from promi-
. It remains to be seen if and
iship between Eyüp's historic

ie large building that sits along the
s from its original function as a fac-
ring the final decades of the Ottoman
ie factory became the hub for a sprawl-
aftermath of the area's deindustrialization,
in object of some debate. Variously imagined
istry, the site for the Museum of Modern Art,
an-crafts bazaar, the building served primarily as
ils, and fairs between 2011 and 2014. More recently,
closed for restorations. Recent news reports suggest
opened in 2022 under the administration of the Istanbul
ity as the Museum of Sufism.[3]
redevelopment projects (*kentsel dönüşüm*) continue to
üpsultan Municipality neighborhoods. The local municipal-
to lead a large-scale historic preservation project in the center
projects also remind us that Eyüp's transformations have hap-
y different scales, ranging from individual property owners to the
ipality to the Metropolitan Municipality to national-level institutions.[4]
graphy is thus much more complicated than a top-down political project.
her area of study—one not addressed in this book—would be considering
s political and urban changes within a different framework: in what ways
he activities of religious networks intersect with urban life? There is a long

transformed
municipal cafés. During
of these sites had been transfor
were even rumors that the buildi
formed into a new hotel following
every instance, rumors and gossip seem
were associated with the Gülen moveme
ioned as a sort of open secret, neither
or Kavuncu's association with
le to leverage political

uggles

place they selected Deniz Köken, another longtime party member with similarly deep connections to the district and local party leadership.

The March 2019 municipal election was one of the closest elections in recent history, with Köken narrowly edging out Emel Bilenoğlu, the Republican People's Party candidate. At the level of the Istanbul Metropolitan Municipality, however, residents of the Eyüpsultan Municipality voted differently in the June 2019 electoral runoff, with almost 54 percent voting for Ekrem İmamoğlu, the opposition candidate. While Eyüp's municipal politics merit closer attention, even this cursory description points to both the complexity and the dynamism of local [...]

Alongside municipal politics, Eyüp's built environment has also [...] far-reaching ways over the past decade. Most notably, a new tram[way] opened on January 1, 2021. The line runs along the Golden Horn [...] to Alibeyköy and will likely help to shift patterns of movement w[...] perhaps alleviate some of the automobile traffic along the sho[...] 1980s. However, the tramway—built onto piers where it pass[...] Eyüp Sultan—will also further separate Eyüp's historic co[...] ing the 1990s, the shore road's construction sparked fi[...] nent architects like Turgut Cansever and Nezih Eldem [...] how this tramway line will reconfigure the relatio[...] core and the Golden Horn.

Similarly unknown is the future of Feshane, t[...] shores of the Golden Horn and takes it name [...] tory producing fezzes and other textiles du[...] Empire. During the twentieth century, t[...] ing textile production complex. In the [...] however, Feshane's function became [...] as the Museum of Textile and Ind[...] and a site for an authentic Ottom[...] a venue for conferences, festiv[...] the building was once more [...] that the building will be re[...] Metropolitan Municipal[...]

*Meanwhile, urban[...]* emerge in many E[...] ity is also seeking [...] of Eyüp. These [...] pened at ma[...] local muni[...] Their geo[...]

And [...] Eyü[...] do[...]

news [...]
"Eyüpsultan [...]
further contribute to o[...]
ertheless, party leaders declin[...]

history of religious networks like the Gülen network, the Association for the Dissemination of Knowledge (İlim Yayma Cemiyeti), and various Naqshbandi groups establishing bookstores, cafés, media centers, and dormitories in cities across Turkey. In Eyüp, some of these groups also worked with municipal and national leaders to lease historic properties, thereby accruing a form of cultural capital in addition to consolidating their economic activities.

While these groups are diverse in their background and composition, they often seem to share the quality of appealing to first- and second-generation migrants to Istanbul. In contrast, there are several other Sufi orders, such as the Mevlevi, the Kadiri, and the Cerrahi, with deep roots in Istanbul's urban fabric. Are there meaningful differences between these older religious networks and more recent arrivals? The challenge, I think, is to take seriously how these groups narrate their traditions without flattening the lived complexity of their worlds and motivations.

How, why, and for whom these projects will play out remains uncertain, but these projects also speak to a key part of this book's argument: Eyüp is not and has never been a static, unchanging place. Its material landscapes, social relationships, and cultural significance have always been in flux. Eyüp continues to be a fascinating site for research because it asks us to consider the tensions between ongoing change and powerful continuities in its religious significance.

## A CULTURAL GEOGRAPHY OF ISLAM?

*People foolishly imagine that the broad generalities of social phenomena afford an excellent opportunity to penetrate further into the human soul; they ought, on the contrary, to realise that it is by plumbing the depths of a single personality that they might have a chance of understanding those phenomena.*
—MARCEL PROUST, *IN SEARCH OF LOST TIME*

Beyond describing how Eyüp—and thus its geography of Islam—has changed over the course of the past century, I've also tried to sketch out one model of what a cultural geography of Islam might look like. Here, I briefly reflect on the limits of that project and offer several reasons why—despite its limits—a cultural geography of Islam is even more urgent today.

In many respects, my methodological and conceptual approach is defined by a narrowing of the scope of inquiry, a situating of myself in a particular place while simultaneously trying to follow how that place is connected—imaginatively, materially, practically—elsewhere.[5] For me, working and thinking in terms of place has provided an especially rich and productive way to do so. In the process I've also tried to be more precise about the geographical terms that I use, especially concepts of *space, place,* and *landscape*. Particularly as the "spatial turn" continues to become increasingly interdisciplinary and our theoretical vocabulary expands, this book is an argument for spending more time understanding how and why other disciplines—and geography in particular—have come to conceptualize their objects of study.[6] Thinking in terms of place is less an attempt to reduce Islam to a single "master concept" and more a call to take place and place making as a point of departure.[7] Places can be made, transformed, and shared in many ways. This multiplicity both prompts us to examine how particular places come to be so durable and reminds us that places could be otherwise.

That said, I find at least three limitations to this argument. In the spirit of a provisional ending and with a desire to build future conversations, I find it useful to engage with those limitations openly. The first limitation involves the methodological gaps and failings in my own work. I opened the book with a brief discussion of my position as researcher, a move familiar to anthropologists, sociologists, and geographers, though less common among political scientists and historians.[8] While we are accustomed to opening with a brief reflexive assessment of our own positions, I am often struck by the way that those reflexive considerations tend to drop from view once we begin our "real" argument. We thus lose sight of the iterative process—the failures, the coincidences, the distractions, and the disciplines—through which our arguments were developed. In the case of this book, I am acutely aware of the failures in my own field notes; my accidental erasure of dozens of interviews before I'd transcribed them; my frustration at the imbalance between my participant observation (a lot) and deep, searching interviews (very few). I am also aware of the value of time: how the possibility of returning to the interviews, texts, images, and buildings that weave their way through this book has changed how I think about Islam in small but important ways. A cultural geography of Islam, as I approach it in this book, pushes us to be more humble—more situated—in the ways that we think about how meanings and places are made through shifting connection.[9]

Such methodological considerations are especially important in relation to discussions of Islam in Turkey. At least as they make their way into English, analyses of Islam in Turkey—this book included—often find themselves forced to respond to a set of categories and frameworks that have dominated the field. These include the methodological nationalism that tends to define the field of Turkish studies; the long-running debate about secularism in Turkey; and the tendency to focus on the state in our discussions of the politics of Islam. How might we expand where and for whom we speak about Islam? Such a project might be more attentive to different disciplinary traditions and their respective blind spots. It also might push us to move beyond tactical appropriations of other disciplines to a richer engagement with their respective traditions.

The second limitation of this argument involves the question of its representativeness. After all, this book focuses on a specific district of Istanbul; more precisely, two or three neighborhoods around the Mosque of Eyüp Sultan. One could walk from edge to edge of this field in forty minutes. What hope does such a site provide for a discussion of a cultural geography of Islam? In answer, I reply: What does it mean to be representative? And *where* does knowledge become representative? One way to think about "representative" knowledge is that it is knowledge no longer linked to places—it can travel in particular ways.[10] But what are lost in discussions of "representativeness" are the practices through which that argument has been decontextualized in the first place. The great virtue of a cultural geography of Islam is that it does not claim representativeness; *a* cultural geography of Islam in, of, and from Eyüp is not *the* cultural geography of Islam. It is one of many possible worlds. Working in terms of place helps me better understand *how is this where made, and how might it be made otherwise?*

The final limitation I find in my argument involves what might be termed the "context of context."[11] In other words, my focus on the connections through which people make places could be critiqued on the grounds that it obscures a discussion of the forces, structures, and systems that really matter. Some might ask about this book: But where is capitalism and neoliberalism? Where is the state? What about the roles of *tarikat, cemaat,* and other religious institutions? Such questions are valuable and important, and I hope that other scholars will take them up. But what is lost when we focus only on those questions is—in many respects—an individual experience in and of the world.[12]

As I approach it in this book, meaning—both of Islam and Istanbul—is generated not in relation to static categories or containers but through shifting relations and connections. The possibility of making connections is necessarily shaped by dynamics often well outside human control, but how, why, and for *where* people make those connections is neither solely nor simply reducible to the operation of structures, systems, or material conditions. How people learn to share places and the meanings associated with them turns out to be neither straightforward nor as simple as we first might imagine.

A cultural geography of Islam could challenge us to think more creatively and expansively about the forms of connection that our interlocutors use, be they human, animal, natural, manuscript, monument, or otherwise. It could push us to be more attentive to the temporalities and geographies that exist in the world, thus reframing many of our received normative categories.[13] Perhaps most importantly, a cultural geography of Islam could help us to be open to many forms of meaning but also insist on the possibility of a shared form of being in the world. This form of shared place making needs to be defined not by projects of exclusion (we have enough of those in the world already) but by an expanded capacity for hospitality. What might it mean to hold open the idea of shared place in the world without insisting on a single possible form?

Such a project speaks to Asu Aksoy's call to protect Istanbul's "worldliness" by "nurtur[ing] and sustain[ing] this civic imagination of the city and of its possibilities."[14] For this project to have any hope of success, I think, it needs to take seriously traditions of Islam that are deeply embedded in the imagination of this city. This is not to adopt a naïve view of Islam where we are incapable of critique. Adapting

Kabir Tambar's astute formulation, we need forms of inquiry that attend to the costs of defining who and what belongs where and to the limits of what is sayable within those geographies.[15] This is not to trace the same oppositions between "secular" politics and "religious" politics but to call for an engagement with Islam in Istanbul that is open. To borrow Annemarie Mol's formulation, "Open endings do not imply immobilization."[16]

## A STORY ABOUT HOSPITALITY

In July 2018, I returned to Eyüp for the first time in over four years. I had come back for several reasons: to reconnect with friends and interlocutors, to fumble through the beginning of a new research project, and, of course, to wander the streets of Istanbul. While I was gone, the Eyüpsultan Municipality had opened a new research center. As far as I'm aware, it's the first instance of a municipality opening a locally focused research center. The Eyüp Sultan Research Center (Eyüp Sultan Araştırma Merkezi) provided a browsing library, a room with several computers for researchers, several small offices, and a small seminar room on the top floor for invited guests. The center is located in the former offices of the district governor (kaymakam), a reminder that the geography of government offices often builds on older histories and mostly invisible relationships.

In any event, they very generously invited me to speak one evening about a small part of my project, the notebook prepared by Süheyl Ünver that I described in chapter 4. But before I began my lecture, a friend from Eyüp pulled me aside. "Look," he said, "before you talk about Ünver, talk a little bit more about yourself, about how you found yourself here and the people you've met. You know, about Eyüp Sultan, about Halid bin Zeyd, about his hospitality [misafirperverliği]."

By the time that you read this book, it will have been more than decade since I first arrived in Eyüp to begin research. I was in every way a misafir, a mihman, a visitor and guest in a place I knew very little about. Although there were certainly moments of exclusion and suspicion, there were also frequent moments of welcome and friendship. If, in some small way, I'm no longer the same visitor in this place I have come to know, that change is due at least in part to those who have welcomed me there along the way. May this book also have welcomed you.

## PREFACE

1. These names come from Şener Türkmenoğlu, *Eyüp: Bir Semte Gönül Vermek* (Istanbul: ABC Yayın Grubu, 2005), 328.

2. "Companions" are people who interacted with the Prophet Muhammad during his lifetime. They form a crucial part of the history of Islam. M. Muranyi, "Sahâba," in *The Encyclopaedia of Islam*, ed. C. E. Bosworth et al. (Leiden: Brill, 1995).

3. Annemarie Mol, *The Body Multiple: Ontology in Medical Practice* (Durham, NC: Duke University Press, 2003), 29–48.

4. Annemarie Mol, "Ontological Politics. A Word and Some Questions," *Sociological Review* 47, no. 1 (1999).

5. Shahid Amin, *Conquest and Community: The Afterlife of Warrior Saint Ghazi Miyan* (Chicago: University of Chicago Press, 2016), xviii.

6. Orhan Pamuk, *İstanbul: Hatıralar ve Şehir* (Istanbul: Yapı Kredi Yayınları, 2003), 331.

7. Sevgi Parlak, "Mihrişah Valide Sultan Külliyesi," in *TDV İslam Ansiklopedisi* (Istanbul: Türkiye Diyanet Vakfı, 2005).

8. During the final decades of the Ottoman Empire, education was provided through one of two systems: a religious system linking the *sıbyan mektebi* and *medrese* and a civil system culminating in military or administrative schooling. In March 1924, the Law for the Unification of Education (Tevhid-i Tedrisat) reorganized that educational model, leading to the closure of schools like this *sıbyan mektebi*. See Asım Arı, "Tevhid-i Tedrisat ve Laik Eğitim," *G.Ü. Gazi Eğitim Fakültesi Dergisi* 22, no. 2 (2002): 183–85.

9. The İlim Yayma Cemiyeti was founded in 1951 to support a variety of educational activities, particularly those oriented toward religious education. See Mustafa Bilge and Hamza Akbulut, "İlim Yayma Cemiyeti," in *TDV İslam Ansiklopedisi* (Istanbul: Türkiye Diyanet Vakfı, 2016). Although I observed many activities linked to the teachings of Bediüzzaman

Said Nursi, the society insists that its activities are separate from any religious group (*cemaat* or *tarikat*). See Anadolu Ajansı, "İlim Yayma Cemiyeti: Hiçbir Cemaat Ya Da Tarikatla Bağımız Yok," *Risale Haber*, September 7, 2019, www.risalehaber.com/ilim-yayma-cemiyeti -hicbir-cemaat-ya-da-tarikatla-bagimiz-yok-360550h.htm.

10. Generally, the district was typically labeled "Eyûb" in maps produced during the nineteenth and twentieth centuries. Similarly, records of the legal court (*kadı sicilleri*) responsible for this region during the Ottoman Empire typically referred to the area as "Eyüb." During the twentieth century some writers would occasionally name the district "Eyüp Sultan," but its usage was inconsistent.

11. This tension between secular and religious identities is most often visible in districts like Taksim or Beyoğlu. See, for example, Ayfer Bartu, "Who Owns the Old Quarters? Rewriting Histories in a Global Era," in *Istanbul: Between the Global and the Local*, ed. Çağlar Keyder (Lanham, MD: Rowman & Littlefield, 1999); Alev Çınar, "National History as a Contested Site: The Conquest of Istanbul and Islamist Negotiations of the Nation," *Comparative Studies in Society and History* 43, no. 2 (2001). However, Berna Turam's work in Nişantaşı astutely points out the multiple forms of encounter between the "secular" and the "religious." Berna Turam, "The Primacy of Space in Politics: Bargaining Rights, Freedom and Power in an Istanbul Neighborhood," *International Journal of Urban and Regional Research* 37, no. 2 (2013), https://doi.org/10.1111/1468-2427.12003.

## INTRODUCTION

1. Yi-Fu Tuan, *Space and Place: The Perspective of Experience* (Minneapolis: University of Minnesota Press, 1977); Edward S. Casey, *Getting Back into Place: Toward a Renewed Understanding of the Place-World*, 2nd ed. (Bloomington: Indiana University Press, 2009).

2. Tim Cresswell provides a useful introduction to debates about "place" in *Place: A Short Introduction* (Malden: Blackwell Publishers, 2004).

3. William Mazzarella, "Culture, Globalization, Mediation," *Annual Review of Anthropology* 33 (2004): 356.

4. For a compelling demonstration of this, see Anand Vivek Taneja, *Jinnealogy: Time, Islam, and Ecological Thought in the Medieval Ruins of Delhi* (Stanford, CA: Stanford University Press, 2017); Amira Mittermaier, "Dreams from Elsewhere: Muslim Subjectivities beyond the Trope of Self-Cultivation," *Journal of the Royal Anthropological Institute* 18, no. 2 (2012).

5. Emilio Spadola, "On Mediation and Magnetism: Or, Why Destroy Saint Shrines?," in *Muslim Pilgrimage in the Modern World*, ed. Babak Rahimi and Peyman Eshaghi (Chapel Hill: University of North Carolina Press, 2019).

6. Doreen Massey, "Places and Their Pasts," *History Workshop Journal* 39 (1995). But this is also a point that Shahzad Bashir raises, pointing out that "Islamic history" is wedded to a model of chronology "pegged to a straight timeline." Shahzad Bashir, "On Islamic Time: Rethinking Chronology in the Historiography of Muslim Societies," *History and Theory* 53, no. 4 (2014): 520.

7. This topic addresses a much larger debate that has taken many different forms. Here, at least, I take for granted that most people in Turkey, were they asked about the nature of God's revelation (*vahiy*), would answer that it is unchanging and unchanged.

The unchanged nature of the Qur'an is sometimes used as a point of debate with people assumed to be Christian.

8. Donald Preziosi, "Introduction: The Mechanisms of Urban Meaning," in *The Ottoman City and Its Parts: Urban Structure and Social Order*, ed. Irene A. Bierman, Rifa'at Ali Abou-El-Haj, and Donald Preziosi (New Rochelle, NY: A.D. Caratzas, 1991), 5. I was reminded of this reference in Çiğdem Kafescioğlu, *Constantinopolis/Istanbul: Cultural Encounter, Imperial Vision, and the Construction of the Ottoman Capital* (University Park: Pennsylvania State University Press, 2009), 51.

9. Doreen Massey, *Space, Place, and Gender* (Minneapolis: University of Minnesota Press, 1994), 154.

10. This phrasing draws on arguments presented in John Law, "Objects and Spaces," *Theory, Culture, and Society* 19, no. 5/6 (2002); John Law and Annemarie Mol, "Situating Technoscience: An Inquiry into Spatialities," *Environment and Planning D: Society and Space* 19, no. 5 (2001), https://doi.org/10.1068/d243t.

11. My thinking about relational place is indebted to the work of Doreen Massey. See her *For Space* (London: SAGE Publications, 2005). For a valuable extension and discussion of Massey, see Joseph Pierce, Deborah G. Martin, and James T. Murphy, "Relational Place-making: The Networked Politics of Place," *Transactions of the Institute of British Geographers* 36, no. 1 (2010).

12. The phrase "texted past" comes from the work of Greg Dening, quoted in Rian Thum, *The Sacred Routes of Uyghur History* (Cambridge, MA: Harvard University Press, 2014), 2. I note a much richer body of scholarship on a wide range of different genres. Among many examples, I have benefited from discussions in Nancy Khalek, "Dreams of Hagia Sophia: The Muslim Siege of Constantinople in 674 CE, Abû Ayyûb al-Ansârî, and the Medieval Islamic Imagination," in *The Islamic Scholarly Tradition: Studies in History, Law, and Thought in Honor of Professor Michael Allan Cook*, ed. Asad Q. Ahmad, Behnam Sadeghi, and Michael Bonner (Leiden: Brill, 2011); John Renard, *Friends of God: Islamic Images of Piety, Commitment, and Servanthood* (Berkeley: University of California Press, 2008); Enseng Ho, *The Graves of Tarim: Genealogy and Mobility across the Indian Ocean* (Berkeley: University of California Press, 2006).

13. My interest in "building stories" and "places of Islam" echoes recent discussions of "saintly spheres." See Daphna Ephrat, Ethel Sara Wolper, and Paulo G. Pinto, "Introduction: History and Anthropology of Sainthood and Space in Islamic Contexts," in *Saintly Spheres and Islamic Landscapes*, ed. Daphna Ephrat, Ethel Sara Wolper, and Paulo G. Pinto (Leidin: Brill, 2020).

14. Matthew S. Hull, *Government of Paper: The Materiality of Bureaucracy in Urban Pakistan* (Berkeley: University of California Press, 2012), 13.

15. Emilie Cameron, *Far Off Metal River: Inuit Lands, Settler Stories, and the Making of the Contemporary Arctic* (Vancouver: UBC Press, 2015), 24.

16. Zayde Antrim, *Routes and Realms: The Power of Place in the Early Islamic World* (Oxford: Oxford University Press, 2012).

17. Law, "Objects and Spaces," 92.

18. See, for example, Dick Houtman and Birgit Meyer, eds., *Things: Religion and the Question of Materiality* (New York: Fordham University Press, 2012); David Chidester, *Religion: Material Dynamics* (Berkeley: University of California Press, 2018); David Morgan,

*The Thing about Religion: An Introduction to the Material Study of Religions* (Chapel Hill: University of North Carolina Press, 2021).

19. See the essays collected in Sally M. Promey, ed., *Sensational Religion: Sensory Cultures in Material Practice* (New Haven, CT: Yale University Press, 2014).

20. Birgit Meyer, "Mediation and Immediacy: Sensational Forms, Semiotic Ideologies and the Question of the Medium," *Social Anthropology* 19, no. 1 (2011): 27.

21. Brian Larkin, "Islamic Renewal, Radio, and the Surface of Things," in *Aesthetic Formations: Media, Religion, and the Senses*, ed. Birgit Meyer (New York: Palgrave Macmillan, 2009), 118.

22. The idea of the chronotope comes from the work of Mikhail Bakhtin. There is an expansive literature mobilizing this concept. Three recent examples are Rana Issa and Einar Wigen, "Levantine Chronotopes: Prisms for Entangled Histories," *Contemporary Levant* 5, no. 1 (2020), https://doi.org/10.1080/20581831.2019.1710666; Jeremy F. Walton, *Muslim Civil Society and the Politics of Religious Freedom in Turkey* (Oxford: Oxford University Press, 2017); Shahzad Bashir, "The Living Dead of Tabriz: Explorations in Chronotopic Imagination," *History of Religions* 59, no. 3 (2020).

23. In the case of Eyüp, this plays out as follows: at the center of Eyüp is Halid bin Zeyd; at the center of Ottoman Istanbul is Eyüp.

24. There are affinities between this argument and Cemal Kafadar's critique of the "lid model of historiography." Cemal Kafadar, *Between Two Worlds: The Construction of the Ottoman State* (Berkeley: University of California Press, 1995).

25. Massey, "Places and Their Pasts," 191.

26. This argument is made most forcefully in the work of Talal Asad. Brian Silverstein's discussion of Islam develops this specifically in thinking about the Ottoman Empire and the Republic of Turkey. Talal Asad, *Genealogies of Religion: Discipline and Reasons of Power in Christianity* (Baltimore, MD: Johns Hopkins University Press, 1993); Brian Silverstein, *Islam and Modernity in Turkey* (New York: Palgrave Macmillan, 2011).

27. Consider Edward Said's insistence on "beginnings" instead of "origins." Edward Said, *Beginnings: Intention and Method* (New York: Columbia University Press, 1985).

28. Kafescioğlu, *Constantinopolis/Istanbul*, 49.

29. Bashir, "On Islamic Time," 530.

30. Dale F. Eickelman, "The Study of Islam in Local Contexts," *Contributions to Asian Studies* 17, no. 1 (1982): 11.

31. Talal Asad, *The Idea of an Anthropology of Islam*, Occasional Paper Series (Washington, DC: Center for Contemporary Arab Studies, Georgetown University, 1986), 14. Suggestively, he argues this is not "finding the right scale but . . . formulating the right concepts." Asad's dismissal of scale is not unique. Scale—and geography more generally—is not incidental to concepts but in fact needs to be thought of as inextricably part of their articulation.

32. Shahab Ahmed, *What Is Islam? The Importance of Being Islamic* (Princeton, NJ: Princeton University Press, 2017), 148.

33. Key reference points include miriam cooke and Bruce Lawrence, eds., *Muslim Networks from Hajj to Hip Hop* (Chapel Hill: University of North Carolina Press, 2005); Ho, *The Graves of Tarim*; Lâle Can, *Spiritual Subjects: Central Asian Pilgrims and the Ottoman Hajj at the End of Empire* (Stanford, CA: Stanford University Press, 2020); James Gelvin and Nile Green, eds., *Global Muslims in the Age of Steam and Print* (Berkeley: University of California Press, 2013).

34. Cemil Aydin, *The Idea of the Muslim World: A Global Intellectual History* (Cambridge, MA: Harvard University Press, 2017); Peter Mandaville, *Transnational Muslim Politics: Reimagining the Umma* (London: Routledge, 2001).

35. Nile Green, "Migrant Sufis and Sacred Space in South Asian Islam," *Contemporary South Asia* 12, no. 4 (2003): 494, http://dx.doi.org/10.1080/0958493042000212678; Nile Green, *Bombay Islam: The Religious Economy of the West Indian Ocean* (Cambridge: Cambridge University Press, 2011), 10.

36. Armando Salvatore, *The Sociology of Islam: Knowledge, Power and Civility* (Malden, MA: Wiley Blackwell, 2016), 10.

37. Samuli Schielke and Georg Stauth, "Introduction," in *Dimensions of Locality: Muslim Saints, Their Place and Space*, ed. Georg Stauth and Samuli Schielke (New Brunswick, NJ: Transaction Publishers, 2008), 13–14.

38. Michael Curry, "On Space and Spatial Practice in Contemporary Geography," in *Concepts in Human Geography*, ed. Carville Earle, Martin S. Kenzer, and Kent Mathewson (Lanham, MD: Rowman & Littlefield, 1996), 5.

39. Anna Tsing, *Friction: An Ethnography of Global Connection* (Princeton, NJ: Princeton University Press, 2005), 7–9.

40. As I was preparing the final revisions on this manuscript, I encountered Kalyani Menon's remarkable ethnography of Muslim place making in old Delhi. Although we draw on slightly different references, there is considerable affinity between this book's arguments and her focus on the "multiplicity, rather than coherence" of Delhi's religious and spatial practices. Kalyani Menon, *Making Place for Muslims in Contemporary India* (Ithaca, NY: Cornell University Press, 2022), 21.

41. Asad, *The Idea of an Anthropology of Islam*, 15.

42. Brian Silverstein, "Disciplines of Presence in Modern Turkey: Discourse, Companionship, and the Mass Mediation of Islamic Practice," *Cultural Anthropology* 23, no. 1 (2008): 143.

43. Lara Deeb, *An Enchanted Modern: Gender and Public Piety in Shi'i Lebanon* (Princeton, NJ: Princeton University Press, 2006), 6, 16.

44. Gregory Starrett, "The Political Economy of Religious Commodities in Cairo," *American Anthropologist* 97, no. 1 (1995); Samuli Schielke, "Being Good in Ramadan: Ambivalence, Fragmentation, and the Moral Self in the Lives of Young Egyptians," *Journal of the Royal Anthropological Institute* 15, no. S1 (2009); Samuli Schielke, "Ambivalent Commitments: Troubles of Morality, Religiosity and Aspiration among Young Egyptians," *Journal of Religion in Africa* 39, no. 2 (2009).

45. Amira Mittermaier, *Dreams That Matter: Egyptian Landscapes of the Imagination* (Berkeley: University of California Press, 2011); Mittermaier, "Dreams from Elsewhere"; Amira Mittermaier, "How to Do Things with Examples: Sufis, Dreams, and Anthropology," *Journal of the Royal Anthropological Institute* 21, no. S1 (2015).

46. Deeb, *An Enchanted Modern*; Lara Deeb and Mona Harb, *Leisurely Islam: Negotiating Geography and Morality in Shi'ite South Beirut* (Princeton, NJ: Princeton University Press, 2013).

47. Nicolas Howe, *Landscapes of the Secular: Law, Religion, and American Sacred Space* (Chicago: University of Chicago Press, 2016); Justin Wilford, *Sacred Subdivisions: The Postsuburban Transformation of American Evangelicalism* (New York: New York University Press, 2012).

48. Banu Gökarıksel, "Beyond the Officially Sacred: Religion, Secularism, and the Body in the Production of Subjectivity," *Social & Cultural Geography* 10, no. 6 (2009); Banu Gökarıksel, "The Intimate Politics of Secularism and the Headscarf: The Mall, the Neighborhood, and the Public Square in Istanbul," *Gender, Place and Culture* 19, no. 1 (2012): Deeb and Harb, *Leisurely Islam*; Ghazi-Walid Falah and Caroline Nagel, *Geographies of Muslim Women: Gender, Religion, and Space* (New York: The Guilford Press, 2005).

49. See, for example, Vincent Artman's discussion of the interaction between Kyrgyz identity and understandings of Islam. Vincent M. Artman, "Nation, Religion, and Theology: What Do We Mean When We Say 'Being Kyrgyz Means Being Muslim?'," *Central Asian Affairs* 5, no. 3 (2018), https://doi.org/10.1163/22142290–00503001.

50. Michael Curry, "Toward a Geography of a World without Maps: Lessons from Ptolemy and Postal Codes," *Annals of the Association of American Geographers* 95, no. 3 (2005); Timur Hammond, "The Middle East without Space?," *International Journal of Middle East Studies* 49, no. 2 (2017).

51. My key reference point is the work of Doreen Massey, *Space, Place, and Gender*, 154. I am also inspired by discussions of topology and actor-network theory, although they do not always mobilize "place" as a key concept. See, for example, Kevin Hetherington, "Museum Topology and the Will to Connect," *Journal of Material Culture* 2, no. 2 (1997); Anna Secor, "2012 Urban Geography Plenary Lecture Topological City," *Urban Geography* 34, no. 4 (2013), https://doi.org/10.1080/02723638.2013.778698.

52. Bruno Latour, "On Actor-Network Theory: A Few Clarifications," *Soziale Welt* 47, no. 4 (1996): 372.

53. Latour, "On Actor-Network Theory," 371.

54. Ho, *The Graves of Tarim*.

55. Salvatore, *The Sociology of Islam*.

56. Can, *Spiritual Subjects*, 25.

57. Key references include Lily Kong, "Mapping 'New' Geographies of Religion: Politics and Poetics in Modernity," *Progress in Human Geography* 25, no. 2 (2001); Elizabeth Olson, Peter E. Hopkins, and Lily Kong, "Introduction—Religion and Place: Landscape, Politics, and Piety," in *Religion and Place: Landscape, Politics, and Piety*, ed. Peter E. Hopkins, Elizabeth Olson, and Lily Kong (London: Springer, 2013); Justin K. H. Tse, "Grounded Theologies: 'Religion' and the 'Secular' in Human Geography," *Progress in Human Geography* 38, no. 2 (2014), https://doi.org/10.1177/0309132512475105; Ethan Yorgason and Veronica della Dora, "Geography, Religion, and Emerging Paradigms: Problematizing the Dialogue," *Social & Cultural Geography* 10, no. 6 (2009); Adrian Ivakhiv, "Toward a Geography of 'Religion': Mapping the Distribution of an Unstable Signifier," *Annals of the Association of American Geographers* 96, no. 1 (2006).

58. Kim Knott, "Religion, Space, and Place: The Spatial Turn in Research on Religion," *Religion and Society* 1, no. 1 (2010), https://doi.org/10.3167/arrs.2010.010103, is an outstanding review. Selected references include David Chidester and Edward Tabor Linenthal, *American Sacred Space* (Bloomington: Indiana University Press, 1995); Jonathan Z. Smith, *To Take Place: Toward Theory in Ritual* (Chicago: University of Chicago Press, 1992); Jonathan Z. Smith, "Religion, Religions, Religious," in *Critical Terms for Religious Studies*, ed. Mark C. Taylor (Chicago: University of Chicago Press, 1998).

59. Key references include Caitlin DeSilvey, "Observed Decay: Telling Stories with Mutable Things," *Journal of Material Culture* 11, no. 3 (2006); Tim Edensor, "Waste Matter: The

Debris of Industrial Ruins and the Disordering of the Material World," *Journal of Material Culture* 10, no. 3 (2005); Tim Edensor, "Vital Urban Materiality and Its Multiple Absences: The Building Stone of Central Manchester," *cultural geographies* 20, no. 4 (2012). On assemblage, see Elizabeth Angell, Timur Hammond, and Danielle van Dobben Schoon, "Assembling Istanbul: Buildings and Bodies in a World City: Introduction," *City* 18, no. 6 (2014); Timur Hammond, "Matters of the Mosque: Changing Configurations of Buildings and Belief in an Istanbul District," *City* 18, no. 6 (2014).

60. For examples, see Banu Gökarıksel and Anna Secor, "Islamic-ness in the Life of a Commodity: Veiling-Fashion in Turkey," *Transactions of the Institute of British Geographers* 35, no. 3 (2010): 329; Wilford, *Sacred Subdivisions*; Orlando Woods, "Converting Houses into Churches: The Mobility, Fission, and Sacred Networks of Evangelical House Churches in Sri Lanka," *Environment and Planning D: Society and Space* 31, no. 6 (2013), https://doi.org/10.1068/d7912.

61. Elizabeth Olson et al., "Retheorizing the Postsecular Present: Embodiment, Spatial Transcendence, and Challenges to Authenticity among Young Christians in Glasgow, Scotland," *Annals of the Association of American Geographers* 103, no. 6 (2013): 1424.

62. Veronica della Dora, "Infrasecular Geographies," *Progress in Human Geography* 42, no. 1 (2016): 45, https://doi.org/10.1177/0309132516666190.

63. Although see Gökarıksel and Secor, "Islamic-ness in the Life of a Commodity."

64. Amy Mills and Banu Gökarıksel, "Provincializing Geographies of Religion: Muslim Identities Beyond the 'West,'" *Geography Compass* 8, no. 12 (2014).

65. See, for example, Michael E. Bonine, "The Morphogenesis of Iranian Cities," *Annals of the Association of American Geographers* 69, no. 2 (1979); Michael E. Bonine, "The Sacred Direction and City Structure: A Preliminary Analysis of the Islamic Cities of Morocco," *Muqarnas* 7, no. 1 (1990); Michael E. Bonine, "Waqf and Its Influence on the Built Environment in the Medina of the Islamic Middle Eastern City," in *Urban Space in the Middle Ages and the Early Modern Age*, ed. Albrecht Classen (Berlin: Walter de Gruyter, 2009); Sarah Moser, "Islamic Cities," in *The Wiley Blackwell Encyclopedia of Urban and Regional Studies*, ed. Anthony Orum (New York: John Wiley & Sons, 2019); Natalie Koch, Anar Valiyev, and Khairul Hazmi Zaini, "Mosques as Monuments: An Inter-Asian Perspective on Monumentality and Religious Landscapes," *cultural geographies* (2017); Paul Wheatley, *The Places Where Men Pray Together: Cities in Islamic Lands, Seventh through the Tenth Centuries* (Chicago: University of Chicago Press, 2001). For a partial review of this scholarship, see Timur Hammond, "Heritage and the Middle East: Cities, Power, and Memory," *Geography Compass* 14, no. 2 (2020), https://doi.org/10.1111/gec3.12477.

66. See, e.g., Sibel Bozdoğan, *Modernism and Nation Building: Turkish Architectural Culture in the Early Republic* (Seattle: University of Washington Press, 2001); Esra Akcan, *Architecture in Translation: Germany, Turkey, & the Modern House* (Durham, NC: Duke University Press, 2012); Zeynep Kezer, *Building Modern Turkey: State, Space, and Ideology in the Early Republic* (Pittsburgh, PA: University of Pittsburgh Press, 2015).

67. See, e.g., Michael Meeker, "Once There Was, Once There Wasn't: National Monuments and Interpersonal Exchange," in *Rethinking Modernity and National Identity in Turkey*, ed. Reşat Kasaba and Sibel Bozdoğan (Seattle: University of Washington Press, 1997); Bülent Batuman, *New Islamist Architecture and Urbanism: Negotiating Nation and Islam through Built Environment in Turkey* (New York: Routledge, 2018); Alev Çınar, *Modernity, Islam, and Secularism in Turkey: Bodies, Places, and Time* (Minneapolis: University of

Minnesota Press, 2005); Walton, *Muslim Civil Society and the Politics of Religious Freedom in Turkey*; Christopher Houston, "The Brewing of Islamist Modernity: Tea Gardens and Public Space in Istanbul," *Theory, Culture, and Society* 18, no. 6 (2001).

68. See, e.g., Heiko Henkel, "The Location of Islam: Inhabiting Istanbul in a Muslim Way," *American Ethnologist* 34, no. 1 (2007); Jenny B. White, *Islamist Mobilization in Turkey: A Study in Vernacular Politics*, Studies in Modernity and National Identity (Seattle: University of Washington Press, 2002); Çağlar Keyder, "A Brief History of Modern Istanbul," in *The Cambridge History of Turkey*, ed. Reşat Kasaba (Cambridge: Cambridge University Press, 2008); Anna Secor, "Toward a Feminist Counter-Geopolitics: Gender, Space and Islamist Politics in Istanbul," *Space and Polity* 5, no. 3 (2001).

69. This argument draws upon an exceptional body of scholarship. In addition to work cited elsewhere, see Claudia Liebelt, "Grooming Istanbul: Intimate Encounters and Concerns in Turkish Beauty Salons," *Journal of Middle East Women's Studies* 12, no. 2 (2016); Berna Turam, "Ordinary Muslims: Power and Space in Everyday Life," *International Journal of Middle East Studies* 43, no. 1 (2011); Turam, "The Primacy of Space in Politics"; Nazlı Alimen, *Faith and Fashion in Turkey: Consumption, Politics and Islamic Identities* (London: I.B. Tauris, 2018); Gökarıksel, "The Intimate Politics of Secularism and the Headscarf"; Banu Gökarıksel and Anna Secor, "Post-Secular Geographies and the Problem of Pluralism: Religion and Everyday life in Istanbul, Turkey," *Political Geography* 46, no. 1 (2015); Ayşe Çavdar, "Building, Marketing and Living in an Islamic Gated Community: Novel Configurations of Class and Religion in Istanbul," *International Journal of Urban and Regional Research* 40, no. 3 (2016), https://doi.org/10.1111/1468-2427.12364.

70. Reşat Kasaba and Sibel Bozdoğan, eds., *Rethinking Modernity and National Identity in Turkey* (Seattle: University of Washington Press, 1997).

71. Hale Yılmaz, *Becoming Turkish: Nationalist Reforms and Cultural Negotiations in Early Republican Turkey, 1923–1945* (Syracuse, NY: Syracuse University Press, 2013); Hakan Kaynar, *Projesiz Modernleşme: Cumhuriyet Istanbulu'ndan Gündelik Fragmanlar* (Istanbul: Istanbul Araştırmaları Enstitüsü, 2012).

72. Ayşe Öncü, "Packaging Islam: Cultural Politics on the Landscape of Turkish Commercial Television," *Public Culture* 8, no. 1 (1995).

73. Markus Dressler, *Writing Religion: The Making of Turkish Alevi Islam* (Oxford: Oxford University Press, 2013); Walton, *Muslim Civil Society and the Politics of Religious Freedom in Turkey*; Behlül Özkan, *From the Abode of Islam to the Turkish Vatan: The Making of a National Homeland in Turkey* (New Haven, CT: Yale University Press, 2012).

74. Esra Özyürek, *Nostalgia for the Modern: State Secularism and Everday Politics in Turkey* (Durham, NC: Duke University Press, 2006); Amy Mills, *Streets of Memory: Landscape, Tolerance, and National Identity in Istanbul* (Athens: University of Georgia Press, 2010); Kabir Tambar, *The Reckoning of Pluralism: Political Belonging and the Demands of History in Turkey* (Stanford, CA: Stanford University Press, 2014).

75. Houston, "The Brewing of Islamist Modernity"; Çınar, *Modernity, Islam, and Secularism in Turkey*; Batuman, *New Islamist Architecture and Urbanism*.

76. Karen Till's conceptualization of "geo-ethnography" has been a source of inspiration. Karen E. Till, *The New Berlin: Memory, Politics, Place* (Minneapolis: University of Minnesota Press, 2005).

77. Amy Mills calls this a practice of neighboring. Amy Mills, "Gender and *Mahalle* (Neighborhood) Space in Istanbul," *Gender, Place and Culture* 14, no. 3 (2007).

78. Timur Hammond, "Papering, Arranging, and Depositing: Learning from Working with an Istanbul Archive," *Area* 52, no. 1 (2020), https://doi.org/10.1111/area.12578.

79. Lara Putnam, "The Transnational and the Text-Searchable: Digitized Sources and the Shadows They Cast," *American Historical Review* 121, no. 2 (2016): 401. I draw on Putnam's work in Hammond, "Papering, Arranging, and Depositing."

80. Taymiya Zaman, "An Islam of One's Own," *Comparative Studies of South Asia, Africa and the Middle East* 40, no. 1 (2020): 218.

81. See the preface, note 2, for more on the Companions.

## 1. SITES AND HISTORIES

1. Several encyclopedia entries provide a starting point for further research. They include Hatice Fahrünnisa Kara, "Eyüp," in *Dünden Bugüne İstanbul Ansiklopedisi* (Istanbul: Türkiye Ekonomik ve Toplumsal Tarih Vakfı, 1993); Tülay Artan, "Eyüp," in *TDV İslam Ansiklopedisi* (Istanbul: Türkiye Diyanet Vakfı, 1995); Çiğdem Kafescioğlu, "Eyüp," in *Encyclopedia of Islam, Three*, ed. Kate Fleet et al. (Leiden: Brill, 2016). The Eyüpsultan Symposia, organized by the Eyüpsultan Municipality, are another valuable source. Two surveys of the proceedings from those symposia are Gündegül Parlar, "Eyüp Index," in *Eyüp Sultan Symposia I–VIII: Selected Articles* (Istanbul: Eyüp Belediyesi, 2005); Gündegül Parlar, "Eyüpsultan Sempozyumları Üzerine Tematik Bir Değerlendirme," in *Tarihi, Kültürü ve Sanatıyla Eyüpsultan Sempozyumu IX: Tebliğler* (Istanbul: Eyüp Belediyesi Kültür ve Turizm Müdürlüğü, 2006).

2. Mahmut Mesut Koman, *Eyüp Sultan, Loti Kahvesi, Çevresi (Le Café de Pierre Loti à Eyüp)* (Istanbul: Güler Basımevi, 1966).

3. The name Karyağdı is a reference to a Bektaşi *tekke*, now ruined, located near the top of the hill. A *tekke* is a building or lodge used as a gathering place for a specific Sufi order. On the history of this specific lodge, see Nicolas Vatin and Thierry Zarcone, "İstanbul'da bir Bektaşi Tekkesi: Karyağdı (Eyüp) Tekkesi," *Türk Kültürü ve Hacı Bektaş Veli Araştırma Dergisi* 11 (1999). İdris-i Bitlis is a reference to the sixteenth-century writer and Ottoman state official who built a small palace and fountain at the top of the hill and is buried nearby.

4. On Constantine, see Jonathan Harris, *Constantinople: Capital of Byzantium*, 2nd ed. (London: Bloomsbury Academic, 2017), 23. Prior to the Ottoman conquest, the city was also captured in 1205 by Latin Crusaders, who ruled the city until 1261. See Harris, *Constantinople*, 149–66.

5. Artan, "Eyüp," 1.

6. Robert Bartlett, *Why Can the Dead Do Such Great Things? Saints and Worshippers from the Martyrs to the Reformation* (Princeton, NJ: Princeton University Press, 2015), 41–43.

7. Nuray Ozaslan, "From the Shrine of Cosmidion to the Shrine of Eyup Ensari," *Greek, Roman and Byzantine Studies* 40, no. 4 (1999): 389.

8. Kafescioğlu, *Constantinopolis/Istanbul*.

9. Kafadar, *Between Two Worlds*.

10. See, for example, Ethel Sara Wolper, "Khidr and the Politics of Place: Creating Landscapes of Continuity," in *Muslims and Others in Sacred Space*, ed. Margaret Cormack (Oxford: Oxford University Press, 2013); Karen Barkey, "Religious Pluralism, Shared Sacred Sites, and the Ottoman Empire," in *Choreographies of Shared Sacred Sites: Religion, Politics,*

*and Conflict Resolution*, ed. Elazar Barkan and Karen Barkey (New York: Columbia University Press, 2015).

11. Khalek, "Dreams of Hagia Sophia"; Feray Coşkun, "Sanctifying Ottoman Istanbul: The Shrine of Abū Ayyūb al-Anṣārī" (Ph.D. diss., Freie Universitaet, 2015).

12. In Turkish, it is typically transcribed as "Istanbul (Konstantiniyye) mutlaka fethedilecektir. Onu fetheden komutan ne güzel komutan; O ordu ne güzel ordudur." In Arabic, it is typically written as "La-tuftaḥanna al-qusṭanṭīnīyyatu fa-la-niʾma al-amīru amīruhā wa-la-niʾma al-jaīshu dhālaka al-jaīshu." The provenance of this hadith is sometimes debated, although scholarship in Turkish typically argues that the hadith is valid. See, for example, İsmail Lütfi Çakan, "Fetih Hadisi ve Akşemseddin'in Fetihteki Yeri," paper presented at the Akşemseddin Sempozyumu Bildirileri, 1990, 155–57; Mehmet Ali Kulat, "İstanbul'un Fethini Müjdeleyen Hadisin Değerlendirilmesi," *Diyanet İlmi Dergi* 37, no. 2 (2001).

13. Halil İnalcık, "Istanbul: An Islamic City," *Journal of Islamic Studies* 1, no. 1 (1990).

14. Kafescioğlu, *Constantinopolis/Istanbul*, 46.

15. Kafescioğlu, *Constantinopolis/Istanbul*, 47.

16. Hatice Fahrünnisa Kara, "İstanbul Metropoliten Alan Gelişme Sürecinde Bir Dini, Kültürel Sosyal Yerleşim Merkezi—Eyüp" (PhD diss., İstanbul Teknik Üniversitesi, 1994).

17. A *kadı* was roughly equivalent to a judge. On Eyüp's *kadı* court, the work of Tulay Artan provides a starting place. Tülay Artan, ed., *18. Yüzyıl Kadı Sicilleri Işığında Eyüp'te Sosyal Yaşam* (Istanbul: Tarih Vakfı Yurt Yayınları, 1998). See also Suraiya Faroqhi, "Migration into Eighteenth-Century 'Greater Istanbul' as Reflected in the Kadi Registers of Eyüp," *Turcica: Revue d'Etudes Turques* 30 (1998): 163–83. A useful introduction, noting that an alternative name for Eyüp's *kadı* court was the *havâss-ı refia*, is provided in Mehmet İpşirli, "İstanbul Kadılığı," in *TDV İslam Ansiklopedisi* (Istanbul: Türkiye Diyanet Vakfı, 2001). The research center İSAM is also continuing to publish transcriptions of the court records.

18. Nicolas Vatin, "Aux Origens du Pèlerinage à Eyüp des Sultans Ottomans," *Turcica: Revue d'Etudes Turques* 27 (1995); Cemal Kafadar, "Eyüp'te Kılıç Kuşanma Törenleri," in *Eyüp: Dün/Bugün: Sempozyum, 11–12 Aralık 1993*, ed. Tülay Artan (Istanbul: Tarih Vakfı Yurt Yayınları, 1994); Mehmet Zeki Pakalın, "Kılıç Alayı," in *Osmanlı Tarih Deyimleri ve Terimleri Sözlüğü* (Istanbul: Milli Eğitim Basımevi, 1983); Necdet Sakaoğlu, "Kılıç Alayları," in *Dünden Bugüne İstanbul Ansiklopedisi* (Istanbul: Türkiye Ekonomik ve Toplumsal Tarih Vakfı, 1993); M. Baha Tanman, "Kılıç Kuşanma Törenlerinin Eyüp Sultan Külliyesi ile Yakın Çavresine Yansıması," in *Tarihi, Kültürü ve Sanatıyla Eyüpsultan Sempozyumu II Tebliğler*, ed. Osman Sak (Istanbul: 1998); F. W. Hasluck, "Studies in Turkish History and Folk-Legend," *Annual of the British School at Athens* 19 (1912/1913).

19. Gulru Necipoğlu, "Dynastic Imprints on the Cityscape: The Collective Message of Imperial Funerary Mosque Complexes in Istanbul," in *Cimetières et Traditions Funéraires dans la Monde Islamique*, ed. Jean-Louis Bacque-Grammont and Aksel Tibet (Ankara: Türk Tarih Kurumu, 1996).

20. Ebru Boyar and Kate Fleet, *A Social History of Ottoman Istanbul* (Cambridge: Cambridge University Press, 2010), 62–63.

21. Mehmet Nermi Haskan provides a detailed inventory of these sites in *Eyüp Tarihi*, 2 vols. (Istanbul: Türk Turing Turizm İşletmeciliği Vakfı, 1993).

22. Sevgi Parlak, "Sokollu Mehmed Paşa Külliyesi," in *TDV İslam Ansiklopedisi* (Istanbul: Türkiye Diyanet Vakfı, 2009).

23. İsmail Orman, "Zal Mahmut Paşa Külliyesi," in *TDV İslam Ansiklopedisi* (Istanbul: Türkiye Diyanet Vakfı, 2013).

24. Semavi Eyice, "Beşir Ağa Külliyesi," in *TDV İslam Ansiklopedisi* (Istanbul: Türkiye Diyanet Vakfı, 1992), 2–3; İsmail E. Erünsal, "Beşir Ağa Kütüphanesi," in *TDV İslam Ansiklopedisi* (Istanbul: Türkiye Diyanet Vakfı, 1992).

25. Sevgi Parlak, "Şah Sultan Külliyesi," in *TDV İslam Ansiklopedisi* (Istanbul: Türkiye Diyanet Vakfı, 2010).

26. Semavi Eyice, "Eyüp Sultan Külliyesi," in *TDV İslam Ansiklopedisi* (Istanbul: Türkiye Diyanet Vakfı, 1995).

27. Jean-Louis Bacque-Grammont, "Eyüp Mezarlıklarının İncelenmesi Üzerine Düşünceler," in *Eyüp: Dün/Bugün*, ed. Tülay Artan (Istanbul: Tarih Vakfı Yurt Yayınları, 1994). See also Nidayi Sevim, *Medeniyetimizin Sessiz Tanıkları: Eyüp Sultan'da Osmanlı Mezar Taşları ve Ebedi Eyüp Sultan'lılar* (Istanbul: Mephisto Yayınları, 2007).

28. For more on the Sufi lodges, see the essays by Raymond Lifchez and Baha Tanman in Raymond Lifchez, ed., *The Dervish Lodge: Architecture, Art, and Sufism in Ottoman Turkey*, Comparative Studies on Muslim Societies (Berkeley: University of California Press, 1992).

29. Eyüp's toy makers were a centuries-long presence. The last toy maker closed shop in the late 1990s. İskender Özsoy, "Son Eyüp Oyuncakçısı," *Popüler Tarih*, June 2001, 76–79.

30. See, for example, the discussion of Eyüp's cream shops in Reşat Ekrem Koçu, "Eyyubsultan Kaymağı, Kaymakçı Dükkanları," in *İstanbul Ansiklopedisi* (Istanbul: Koçu Yayınları, 1971).

31. Reşat Ekrem Koçu, "Eyyubsultanda Fulya Tarlası, Bağı," in *İstanbul Ansiklopedisi* (Istanbul: Koçu Yayınları, 1971). The entry is based on notes provided by Ahmet Ağın, a longtime resident of Eyüp and a former teacher.

32. Tulay Artan makes this point, noting complexes built by Şah Sultan (daughter of Sultan Selim I); Hançerli Sultan; a different Şah Sultan (daughter of Selim II); and Kaya Sultan. Tülay Artan, "Eyüp'ün Bir Diğer Çehresi: Sayfiye ve Sahilsaraylar," in *Eyüp: Dün/ Bugün*, ed. Tülay Artan (Istanbul: Tarih Vakfı Yurt Yayınları, 1993).

33. For example, the property on which Hançerli Sultan's palace was located became the site of the İplikhane, completed in 1827. Semavi Eyice, "Haliç," in *TDV İslam Ansiklopedisi* (Istanbul: Türkiye Diyanet Vakfı, 1997), 268–69. The destruction of these mansions also created an opportunity for other types of buildings, such as the Bahariye Mevlevi Sufi lodge built on the site of the former Bahariye Palace (Bahariye Kasrı). M. Baha Tanman, "Musiki Tarihimizde Onemli Yeri Olan Bahariye Mevlevihanesi'nin Tarihçesi ve Sosyokültürel Çevresi," *Darülelhan Mecmuası* 8 (2017): 14.

34. Parlak, "Mihrişah Valide Sultan Külliyesi."

35. Ünver Rüstem, *Ottoman Baroque: The Architectural Refashioning of Eighteenth-Century Istanbul* (Princeton, NJ: Princeton University Press, 2018).

36. M. Erdem Kabadayı, "Working in a Fez Factory in Istanbul in the Late Nineteenth Century: Division of Labour and Networks of Migration Formed along Ethno-Religious Lines," *International Review of Social History* 54, no. S17 (2009).

37. İsmail Orman, "Mehmed Reşad Türbesi," in *TDV İslam Ansiklopedisi* (Ankara: Türkiye Diyanet Vakfı, 2003).

38. See, for example, Kezer, *Building Modern Turkey*.

39. Reşat Ekrem Koçu, "Defterdar Mensucat Fabrikası," in *İstanbul Ansiklopedisi* (Istanbul: Koçu Yayınları, 1966); Önder Küçükerman, *Feshane, Defterdar Fabrikasi: Türk Giyim Sanayii Tarihindeki Ünlü Fabrika* (Ankara: Sümerbank, 1988).

40. For accounts of Istanbul's modernization, see Murat Gül, *The Emergence of Modern Istanbul: Transformation and Modernisation of a City* (London: Tauris Academic Studies, 2009); Keyder, "A Brief History of Modern Istanbul"; Ipek Akpınar, "The Rebuilding of İstanbul Revisited: Foreign Planners in the Early Republican Years," *New Perspectives on Turkey* 50 (2014); Ipek Akpınar, ed., *Osmanlı Başkentinden Küreselleşen İstanbul'a: Mimarlık ve Kent, 1910–2010* (Istanbul: Osmanlı Bankası Arşiv ve Araştırma Merkezi, 2010); Cana Bilsel and Pierre Pinon, eds., *From the Imperial Capital to the Republican Modern City: Henri Prost's Planning of Istanbul (1936–1951)* (Istanbul: Istanbul Research Institute, 2010).

41. This history is covered in Timur Hammond, "Mediums of Belief: Muslim Place Making in 20th Century Turkey" (Ph.D. diss., University of California, Los Angeles, 2016), 57–68.

42. For example, a November 1957 report signed by Hans Högg, Vasfi Egeli, Cevat Erbel, and Necdet Ceyhan includes a map setting aside much of central Eyüp as a protected area. Eyüp Eski Eserler ve Tarihi Abideler Sahasi İmar Planı İzah Raporu, SALT Research, Ali Saim Ülgen Archive, TASUDOC0766.

43. Şener Türkmenoğlu has extensively documented these social textures. See Türkmenoğlu, *Eyüp: Bir Semte Gönül Vermek*; Şener Türkmenoğlu, *Son Yüzyılın Hikayesi Eyüp: Yaşayanların Dilinden* (Istanbul: Yayın Dünyamız Yayınları, 2018).

44. Although he does not focus on Eyüp, Christopher Houston provides background on these struggles. See Christopher Houston, *Istanbul, City of the Fearless: Urban Activism, Coup d'Etat, and Memory in Turkey* (Berkeley: University of California Press, 2020).

PART I. STORYTELLING

1. Divya P. Tolia-Kelly, "Locating Processes of Identification: Studying the Precipitates of Re-Memory through Artefacts in the British Asian Home," *Transactions of the Institute of British Geographers* 29 (2004): 314.

2. Curry, "Toward a Geography of a World without Maps," 683–84.

3. To cite two very different examples, consider Robert J. Shiller, *Narrative Economics: How Stories Go Viral and Drive Major Economic Events* (Princeton, NJ: Princeton University Press, 2020), and Katherine McKittrick, *Dear Science and Other Stories* (Durham, NC: Duke University Press, 2021).

4. For example, Trevor J. Barnes and James S. Duncan, eds., *Writing Worlds: Discourse, Text, and Metaphor in the Representation of Landscape* (London: Routledge, 1992).

5. Emilie Cameron, "New Geographies of Story and Storytelling," *Progress in Human Geography* 36, no. 5 (2012): 575.

6. Cameron, *Far Off Metal River*, 24.

7. Till, *The New Berlin*, 8.

8. DeSilvey, "Observed Decay"; Gareth Hoskins, "Materialising Memory at Angel Island Immigration Station, San Francisco," *Environment and Planning A: Economy and Space* 39, no. 2 (2007), https://doi.org/10.1068/a38174.

9. Ben Kafka, "Paperwork: The State of the Discipline," *Book History* 12, no. 1 (2009).

10. See, for example, Farzin Vejdani, *Making history in Iran: Education, Nationalism, and Print Culture* (Stanford, CA: Stanford University Press, 2015); Ziad Fahmy, *Ordinary Egyptians: Creating the Modern Nation through Popular Culture* (Stanford, CA: Stanford University Press, 2011).

11. "Rivayet," *Türk Dil Kurumu Sözlükleri.*

12. Stefan Leder, "Riwâya," in *Encyclopedia of Islam, Second Edition*, ed. P. Bearman et al. (Amsterdam: Brill, 2012), http://dx.doi.org.libezproxy2.syr.edu/10.1163/1573–3912_is lam_COM_0927; Mehmet Efendioğlu, "Rivayet," in *TDV Islam Ansiklopedisi* (2008).

13. Parsing out the relationships between these different genres is beyond the scope of this book. My point here is to stress that geographers tend to operate within a relatively limited range of genres and languages. Working from Turkish provides one opportunity to provincialize our conceptual vocabularies.

## 2. STORYING THE *SAHABE*

1. Key references include Hüseyin Algül, "Ebû Eyyûb el-Ensârî," in *TDV İslam Anskik-lopedisi* (Istanbul: Türkiye Diyanet Vakfı, 1994); E. Levi-Provençal, J. H. Mordtmann, and Cl. Huart, "Abū Ayyūb Khālid b. Zayd b. Kulayb al-Nadjdjārī al-Anṣārī," in *Encyclopedia of Islam, Second Edition*, ed. P. Bearman et al. (Leiden: Brill, 2012); Michael Lecker, "Abū Ayyūb al-Anṣārī," in *Encyclopedia of Islam, Three*, ed. Kate Fleet et al. (Leiden: Brill, 2013).

2. On the importance of the Companions, see, for example, Nancy Khalek, "Medieval Biographical Literature and the Companions of Muḥammad," *Der Islam* 91, no. 2 (2014), https://doi.org/10.1515/islam-2014–0012, www.degruyter.com/view/j/islam.2014.91.issue-2 /islam-2014–0012/islam-2014–0012.xml; Muranyi, "Sahâba"; Mehmet Efendioğlu, "Sahabe," in *TDV İslam Ansiklopedisi* (Istanbul: Türkiye Diyanet Vakfı, 2008).

3. The cause of his death varies from account to account.

4. Coşkun, "Sanctifying Ottoman Istanbul," 35–37.

5. Algül, "Ebû Eyyûb el-Ensârî," 124.

6. Khalek, "Dreams of Hagia Sophia."

7. İnalcık, "Istanbul."

8. This insight has been key to a range of recent scholarship. For one discussion of how materiality impacted the circulation of religious knowledge in the seventeenth century, see Nir Shafir, "The Road from Damascus: Circulation and the Redefinition of Islam in the Ottoman Empire, 1620–1720" (PhD diss., University of California, Los Angeles, 2016).

9. Cameron, "New Geographies of Story and Storytelling," 579.

10. Khalek, "Dreams of Hagia Sophia"; Kafescioğlu, *Constantinopolis/Istanbul*, 45–52; Kafescioğlu, "Eyüp"; Coşkun, "Sanctifying Ottoman Istanbul"; Feray Coşkun, "Osmanlı İstanbulu'nda Müstesnâ bir Ziyâretgâh: Eyüp Sultân Türbesi," in *Osmanlı İstanbulu*, ed. Feridun Emecen, Ali Akyıldız, and Emrah Safa Gürkan (Istanbul: Istanbul 29 Mayıs Üniversitesi, 2015).

11. Rian Thum, "What Is Islamic History?," *History and Theory* 58, no. 4 (2019): 19, https://doi.org/10.1111/hith.12133.

12. Yahya Kemal Beyatlı (1884—1958) was one of the most important literary and cultural figures of early twentieth-century Istanbul. See M. Orhan Okay, "Beyatlı, Yahya Kemal," in *TDV İslam Ansiklopedisi* (Istanbul, 1992). Yahya Kemal's essay was published on

May 5, 1922. It is reprinted (with the wrong date) in Yahya Kemal Beyatlı, *Aziz İstanbul* (Istanbul: İstanbul Fethi Cemiyeti, 2010).

13. For other surveys of this period, see Erdağ Göknar, "Reading Occupied Istanbul: Turkish Subject-Formation from Historical Trauma to Literary Trope," *Culture, Theory and Critique* 55, no. 3 (2014); Christine Philliou, *Turkey: A Past Against History* (Berkeley: University of California Press, 2021), 90–122.

14. Deeb, *An Enchanted Modern*.

15. Yahya Kemal Beyatlı, "Bir Rüya'da Gördüğümüz Eyüp," in *Aziz İstanbul* (Istanbul: İstanbul Fethi Cemiyeti, 2010), 106.

16. Nur Bilge Criss, *Istanbul under Allied Occupation: 1918–1923* (Leiden: Brill, 1999).

17. Amy Mills, "The Cultural Geopolitics of Ethnic Nationalism: Turkish Urbanism in Occupied Istanbul (1918–1923)," *Annals of the American Association of Geographers* 107, no. 5 (2017), https://doi.org/10.1080/24694452.2017.1298433.

18. Mostafa Minawi's forthcoming *Losing Istanbul: Arab-Ottoman Imperialists and the End of Empire* (Stanford University Press, 2023) will also likely speak to these discussions.

19. See, for example, Lâle Can's *Spiritual Subjects*, a discussion of Hajj pilgrims from Central Asia who passed through Istanbul.

20. G. Carole Woodall, "'Awakening a Horrible Monster': Negotiating the Jazz Public in 1920s Istanbul," *Comparative Studies of South Asia, Africa and the Middle East* 30, no. 3 (2011), https://doi.org/10.1215/1089201x-2010-035.

21. Selim Deringil, "The Invention of Tradition as Public Image in the Late Ottoman Empire, 1808 to 1908," *Comparative Studies in Society and History* 35, no. 1 (2009), https://doi.org/10.1017/s0010417500018247.

22. Gelvin and Green, eds., *Global Muslims in the Age of Steam and Print*.

23. Aydin, *The Idea of the Muslim World*.

24. Zainab Bahrani, Zeynep Çelik, and Edhem Eldem, eds., *Scramble for the Past: A Story of Archaeology in the Ottoman Empire, 1785–1914* (Istanbul: SALT, 2011).

25. Ahmet Ersoy, "Architecture and the Search for Ottoman Origins in the Tanzimat Period," *Muqarnas* 24 (2007).

26. One example of this engagement was the establishment of groups like the Association of the Lovers of Istanbul (Istanbul Muhibleri Cemiyeti). Vesile Gül Cephanecigil and Günkut Akın, "Geç Osmanlı ve Erken Cumhuriyet Dönemi Türkiyesinde Milliyetçilik ve Mimarlık Tarihi," *İTÜ Dergisi/A* 9, no. 2 (2010): 34.

27. Zeynep Çelik, *The Remaking of Istanbul: Portrait of an Ottoman City in the Nineteenth Century* (Seattle: University of Washington Press, 1986).

28. Yiğit Akın, *When the War Came Home: The Ottomans' Great War and the Devastation of an Empire* (Stanford, CA: Stanford University Press, 2018).

29. Okay, "Beyatlı, Yahya Kemal," 36.

30. Yahya Kemal Beyatlı, *Siyasi ve Edebi Portreler* (Istanbul: Yahya Kemal Enstitüsü, 1968), 52.

31. The paper was published by Velid Ebüzziya. Although Ebüzziya supported the National Movement, he fell afoul of Ankara authorities in 1922 for his defense of the caliphate and was later arrested for allegedly causing the Shaykh Said rebellion. Ziyad Ebüzziya, "Ebüzziya, Velid," in *TDV İslam Ansiklopedisi* (Istanbul, 1994).

32. In July 1908, military officers based in Macedonia declared themselves in rebellion against the Ottoman state, then led by Sultan Abdülhamid II. In late July, the sultan agreed

to reconvene parliament and restore the constitution. On the continuities and changes in official censorship, see İpek K. Yosmaoğlu, "Chasing the Printed Word: Press Censorship in the Ottoman Empire, 1876–1913," *Turkish Studies Association Journal* 27, no. 1/2 (2003): 31–47.

33. For a brief discussion of this genre, see Florian Riedler, "Public People. Temporary Labor Migrants in Nineteenth Century Istanbul," in *Public Istanbul: Spaces and Spheres of the Urban*, ed. Frank Eckardt and Kathrin Wildner (Bielefeld: transcript Verlag, 2008), 244.

34. Mills, "The Cultural Geopolitics of Ethnic Nationalism," 1181.

35. The Battle of Sakarya (where the defeat of Greek forces helped turn the tide of the war) took place in August and September 1921. The Great Offensive (Büyük Taaruz) would be launched in August 1922. Kemal's essays thus fall within that period of stalemate.

36. New sultans would be girded with a dynastic sword that linked them to political and religious traditions. For example, Sultan Reşad donned the sword of the Caliph Umar in a ceremony led by a Mevlevi shaykh and adorned with a variety of objects to previous sultans. Özcan, "Kılıç Alayı," 409.

37. Kemal was not alone in this project. The work of Ruşen Eşref Ünaydın, who also wrote a Ramadan essay about Eyüp, is another important reference point. See Nuri Sağlam, "Ruşen Eşref Ünaydın," in *TDV İslam Ansiklopedisi* (2012); Beşir Ayvazoğlu, "Mehmed Rauf 'Eyüp Yolunda,'" in *12. Uluslararası Eyüp Sultan Sempozyumu: Tebliğler* (2016); Necat Birinci, "Ruşen Eşref'in Yazılarında İstanbul Sevgisi," *Kubbealtı Akademi Mecmuası* 12, no. 1 (1983).

38. The phrase "envelope of space-time" is borrowed from Massey, "Places and Their Pasts." This analysis of the spatiotemporal structure of the essay takes inspiration from Shahzad Bashir's discussions of the chronotopes in his recent article, "The Living Dead of Tabriz."

39. Beyatlı, "Bir Rüya'da Gördüğümüz Eyüp," 106–7.

40. Two recent dissertations examine these debates in detail: Ceren Abi, "Digging Deeper: Cultural Property in the Ottoman Empire During the Great War and Allied Occupation 1914–1923" (PhD diss., University of California, Los Angeles, 2019); Firuzan Melike Sümertaş, "From Antiquarianism to Urban Archaeology: Transformation of Research on 'Old' Istanbul throughout the Nineteenth Century" (PhD diss., Boğaziçi University, 2021).

41. M. Brett Wilson, "The Twilight of Ottoman Sufism: Antiquity, Immorality, and Nation in Yakup Kadri Karaosmanoğlu's Nur Baba," *International Journal of Middle East Studies* 49, no. 2 (2017): 235–36, https://doi.org/10.1017/s0020743817000034.

42. For a useful discussion of similar debates playing across the Mediterranean and Levant, see Anne-Laure Dupont and Catherine Mayeur-Jaouen, "Monde nouveau, voix nouvelles: Etats, sociétés, islam dans l'entre-deux-guerres," *Revue des mondes musulmans et de la Méditerranée* 95–98 (2002), https://doi.org/10.4000/remmm.224, http://journals.openedition.org/remmm/224.

43. For a detailed account of Musa Kazım Efendi's life and thought, see Bayram Ali Çetinkaya, "Musa Kazım Efendi'nin Dini, Siyasi ve Felsefi Düşüncesi," *C. Ü. İlahiyat Fakültesi Dergisi* 9, no. 2 (2007). For a useful introduction to Ahmed Naim, see İsmail Lütfi Çakan, "Babanzâde Ahmed Naim," in *TDV İslam Ansiklopedisi* (Istanbul: Türkiye Diyanet Vakfı, 1991).

44. İsmail Kara, *Din ile Modernleşme Arasında: Çağdaş Türk Düşüncesinin Meseleri* (Istanbul: Dergah Yayınları, 2003), 277–82.

45. On Ahmet Ağaoğlu's life and thought, see Nuri Yüce, "Ağaoğlu, Ahmet," in *TDV İslam Ansiklopedisi* (Istanbul: Türkiye Diyanet Vakfı, 1998).

46. Quoted in Kara, *Din ile Modernleşme Arasında*, 38.

47. "Badr, Battle of," in *The Oxford Dictionary of Islam*, ed. John Esposito (London: Oxford University Press, 2003).

48. Halil Pasha was removed from office and arrested immediately following the conquest of Constantinople and was later executed. Aktepe, "Çandarlı Halil Paşa," 213. As Cemal Kafadar has shown, debates over the role of the Çandarlı family have a long tradition in Ottoman historiography. Kafadar, *Between Two Worlds*, 109–14.

49. Beyatlı, "Bir Rüya'da Gördüğümüz Eyüp," 110.

50. Aydin, *The Idea of the Muslim World*, 125.

51. Cemal Öğüt, *Eyyûb Sultan: Hz. Hâlid Ebu Eyyûb el-Ensârî* (Istanbul: Eyüp Belediyesi Kültür Yayınları, 2012), 47.

52. This book was originally published in two volumes by the Ahmet Sait Publishing House in 1955 (volume 1) and 1957 (volume 2). The Eyüp Municipality has republished at least two editions: Cemal Öğüt, *Eyyûb Sultan: Hz. Hâlid Ebu Eyyûb el-Ensârî* (Istanbul: Eyüp Belediyesi, 2005); Öğüt, *Eyyûb Sultan* (see the preceding note). Citations below draw on the 2012 edition.

53. With the exception of the establishment of the Ministry of Religious Affairs, all of these changes are listed in İsmail Kara, *Cumhuriyet Türkiye'sinde Bir Mesele Olarak İslam 1* (Istanbul Dergah Yayınları, 2016), 31–32. On the removal of the *tuğra*, see Hakan T. Karateke, "Interpreting Monuments: Charitable Buildings, Monuments, and the Construction of Collective Memory in the Ottoman Empire," *Wiener Zeitschrift für die Kunde des Morgenlandes* 91 (2001).

54. For example, figures associated with the Mevlevi lodge in Bahariye such as Sadettin Heper became well known as musicians and composers. Nuri Özcan, "Sadettin Heper," in *TDV İslam Anskiklopedisi* (Istanbul: Türkiye Diyanet Vakfı, 1998).

55. E.g., the growth of the movement associated with the religious scholar Said Nursi. Şerif Mardin, *Religion and Social Change in Modern Turkey: The Case of Bediuzzaman Said Nursi* (Albany: State University of New York, 1989).

56. For a detailed history of the ministry's formation, see İştar B. Gözaydın, *Diyanet: Türkiye Cumhuriyeti'nde Dinin Tanzimi* (Istanbul: İletişim Yayınları, 2009).

57. Cana Bilsel, "Henri Prost's Planning Works in Istanbul (1936–1951): Transforming the Structure of a City through Master Plans and Urban Operations," in *From the Imperial Capital to the Republican Modern City: Henri Prost's Planning of Istanbul (1936–1951)*, ed. Cana Bilsel and Pierre Pinon (Istanbul: Istanbul Research Institute, 2010); Bilsel and Pinon, *From the Imperial Capital to the Republican Modern City*; Akpınar, "The Rebuilding of İstanbul Revisited."

58. On international institutions and rural-urban migration, see Erik Zürcher, *Turkey: A Modern History*, 3rd ed. (London: I.B. Tauris, 2004), 215–27.

59. A useful overview of the cultural, professional, and political context can be found in Sibel Bozdoğan, "Turkey's Postwar Modernism: A Retrospective Overview of Architecture, Urbanism and Politics in the 1950s," in *Mid-Century Modernism in Turkey: Architecture across Cultures in the 1950s and 1960s*, ed. Meltem Ö. Gürel (London: Routledge, 2015).

60. Many of these transformations are covered in Kezer, *Building Modern Turkey*.

61. A. Kıvanç Esen, "Tek Parti Dönemi Cami Kapatma/Satma Uygulamaları," *Tarih ve Toplum Yeni Yaklaşımlar* 13 (2011).

62. This point is made especially well in Dinç, "677 Sayılı Kanun, Türbeleri 'Millileştirme' ve Yıkıcı Sonuçları."

63. This and the following biography are based on Vehbi Vakkasoğlu, "Öğüt, Cemal," in *TDV İslam Ansiklopedisi* (Istanbul: Türkiye Diyanet Vakfı, 2007), https://islamansiklopedisi .org.tr/ogut-cemal.

64. The müezzin (*mu'adh·dhin*) delivers the call to prayer and helps to maintain the mosque; the *vaiz* (*wā 'iz*) delivers a regular lecture to an audience on appointed days during the week, but particularly on Friday before congregational prayers; the imam is responsible for leading communal prayers and for delivering the *hutbe* (*hutbah*), or Friday address.

65. A selection of these lectures is accessible in manuscript form. Hacı Cemal Öğüt, "Defter-i Mev'ıza (Vaaz Defteri I-II)," Marmara University, Rare Works Collection [12512], http://dspace.marmara.edu.tr/handle/11424/41988.

66. This comes from M. Murtaza Özeren, "Kimler Hacı Cemal Öğüt'ün Talebesi Olmamış Ki," *Dünya Bizim*, March 21, 2016, www.dunyabizim.com/portre/kimler-haci-cemal -ogut-un-talebesi-olmamis-ki-h23518.html.

67. This count is based on the list provided Vakkasoğlu, "Öğüt, Cemal."

68. Dale F. Eickelman, "Qur'anic Commentary, Public Space, and Religious Intellectuals in the Writings of Said Nursi," *Muslim World* 89, no. 3–4 (1999): 261.

69. Öğüt, *Eyyûb Sultan*, 72–73.

70. Öğüt, *Eyyûb Sultan*, 49.

71. Although Öğüt's project played out in the 1950s, it complements Brian Silverstein's observations about Islamic traditions in 1990s Turkey. Brian Silverstein, "Islamist Critique in Modern Turkey: Hermeneutics, Tradition, Genealogy," *Comparative Studies in Society and History* 47, no. 1 (2005).

72. Öğüt, *Eyyûb Sultan*, 165.

73. Öğüt, *Eyyûb Sultan*, 49.

74. Öğüt, *Eyyûb Sultan*, 50.

75. Talal Asad, "Thinking about Religion through Wittgenstein," *Critical Times* 3, no. 3 (2020): 409.

76. This echoes Fabio Vicini's thoughtful discussion of the role of reading and meditative contemplation within Nur communities, *Reading Islam: Life and Politics of Brotherhood in Modern Turkey* (Leiden: Brill, 2019), 97–131.

77. Joel Blecher, *Said the Prophet of God: Hadith Commentary across a Millennium* (Berkeley: University of California Press, 2018).

78. Efendioğlu, "Rivayet"; Leder, "Riwâya."

79. Öğüt, *Eyyûb Sultan*, 211.

80. Curry, "Toward a Geography of a World without Maps," 683–84.

81. Blecher, *Said the Prophet of God*, 171.

82. Öğüt, *Eyyûb Sultan*, 210. Öğüt criticizes popular accounts of Halid bin Zeyd that describe him as a military commander or the Prophet's standard-bearer (*alemdar, sancaktar*). Here and elsewhere he insists that these epithets refer to Halid bin Zeyd's role on the Day of Judgment, when he will stand before the people of Islam.

83. Blecher, *Said the Prophet of God*, 169.

84. On Nursi in the 1950s, see John Obert Voll, "Renewal and Reformation in the Mid-Twentieth Century: Bediuzzaman Said Nursi and Religion in the 1950s," in *Globalization, Ethics and Islam*, ed. Ian Markham and Ibrahim Özdemir (New York: Ashgate Publishing, 2005). On Kısakürek, see Burhanettin Duran and Cemil Aydin, "Competing Occidentalisms of Modern Islamist Thought: Necip Fazıl Kısakürek and Nurettin Topçu on Christianity, the West and Modernity," *Muslim World* 103, no. 4 (2013); Michelangelo Guida, "Nurettin Topçu and Necip Fazıl Kısakürek: Stories of 'Conversion' and Activism in Republican Turkey," *Journal for Islamic Studies* 34, no. 1 (2014). On Ayverdi, see İlker Aytürk and Laurent Mignon, "Paradoxes of a Cold War Sufi Woman: Sâmiha Ayverdi between Islam, Nationalism, and Modernity," *New Perspectives on Turkey* 49 (2013); Feyza Burak Adli, "Trajectories of Modern Sufism: An Ethnohistorical Study of the Rifai Order and Social Change in Turkey" (PhD diss., Boston University, 2020).

85. The use of "foundation" here is distinct from its Islamic legal usage. On its changing meanings, see Gizem Zencirci, "From Property to Civil Society: The Historical Transformation of *Vakıfs* in Modern Turkey (1923–2013)," *International Journal of Middle East Studies* 47, no. 3 (2015).

86. On *i'lâ-yi kelimetullah*, see Metin Yurdagür, "İ'lâ-yi Kelimetullah," in *TDV İslâm Ansiklopedisi* (Istanbul: Türkiye Diyanet Vakfı, 2000).

87. *Nefis* is difficult to translate because it has so many meanings. In general it can be translated as "self" or "person," but it is also defined as the seat and site of blameworthy characteristics or desires. It is often contrasted with the *ruh*, an opposition roughly between *nefis* (body) versus *ruh* (soul). Our acts of piety are oriented toward training our bodies—in Turkish, *nefsimizi terbiye etmek*. See, for example, Süleyman Uludağ, "Nefis," in *TDV İslâm Ansiklopedisi* (Istanbul: Türkiye Diyanet Vakfı, 2006). A more detailed philosophical history of the term can be found in E. E. Calverly, "Nafs," in *Encyclopedia of Islam, Second Edition*, ed. P. Bearman et al. (Leiden: Brill, 2012).

88. It's from that recording that I draw most of my quotes of his speech, although this passage has been paraphrased to try to render the spirit of his address in a slightly condensed form. See www.siyertv.com/istanbul-istanbulun-fatihi-hz-ebu-eyyub-el-ensari/.

89. Öncü, "Packaging Islam"; Gökarıksel, "The Intimate Politics of Secularism and the Headscarf"; Gökarıksel and Secor, "Islamic-ness in the Life of a Commodity"; Alimen, *Faith and Fashion in Turkey*; Houston, "The Brewing of Islamist Modernity"; Hikmet Kocamaner, "Strengthening the Family through Television: Islamic Broadcasting, Secularism, and the Politics of Responsibility in Turkey," *Anthropological Quarterly* 90, no. 3 (2017), https://doi.org/10.1353/anq.2017.0040.

90. Walton, *Muslim Civil Society and the Politics of Religious Freedom in Turkey*; Berna Turam, *Between Islam and the State: The Politics of Engagement* (Stanford, CA: Stanford University Press, 2007).

91. Tambar, *The Reckoning of Pluralism*.

92. Silverstein, *Islam and Modernity in Turkey*.

93. See www.siyervakfi.org/hakkimizda/.

94. See www.siyervakfi.org/hakkimizda/.

95. Deeb, *An Enchanted Modern*.

96. "Siyar," in *The Oxford Dictionary of Islam*, ed. John Esposito (Oxford: Oxford University Press, 2003).

97. For an earlier version of this religious challenge to Republican histories, see Esra Özyürek, "Public Memory as Political Battleground: Islamist Subversions of Republican Nostalgia," in *The Politics of Public Memory in Turkey*, ed. Esra Özyürek (Syracuse, NY: Syracuse University Press, 2007).

98. See, e.g., Tanil Bora, "Istanbul of the Conqueror: The 'Alternative Global City' Dreams of Political Islam," in *Istanbul: Between the Global and the Local*, ed. Çaglar Keyder (Lanham, MD: Rowman & Littlefield, 1999).

99. Compare Amy Mills, "The Place of Locality for Identity in the Nation: Minority Narratives of Cosmopolitan Istanbul," *International Journal of Middle East Studies* 40, no. 3 (2008).

100. See Uludağ, "Nefis." This characterization is also consistent with Yıldırım's other writing. Muhammed Emin Yıldırım, *İnsanî İlişkilerde İlahî Ölçü* (Istanbul: Siyer Yayınları, 2004).

101. Deeb, *An Enchanted Modern*; Saba Mahmood, *The Politics of Piety: The Islamic Revival and the Feminist Subject* (Princeton, NJ: Princeton University Press, 2005).

102. Mittermaier, *Dreams That Matter*, 182–83.

103. Mittermaier, "Dreams from Elsewhere."

104. See, e.g., Dana Sajdi, *The Barber of Damascus: Nouveau Literacy in the Eighteenth-Century Ottoman Levant* (Stanford, CA: Stanford University Press, 2013).

105. See, e.g., Christoph Herzog and Richard Wittman, eds., *Istanbul-Kushta-Constantinople: Narratives of Identity in the Ottoman Capital, 1830–1930* (London: Routledge, 2019).

106. Issues of gender are closely woven into the experience of the Mosque of Eyüp Sultan. However, the partial nature of my fieldwork and archival sources largely excludes those questions.

## 3. NEW PUBLICS, OLD ISLAM

1. Ahmet Hamdi Tanpınar, *Saatleri Ayarlama Enstitüsü* (Istanbul: Dergah Yayınları, 2017), 7.

2. Mills, "The Cultural Geopolitics of Ethnic Nationalism," 1184.

3. Gavin Brockett, *How Happy to Call Oneself a Turk: Provincial Newspapers and the Negotiation of a Muslim National Identity* (Austin: University of Texas Press, 2011), 3.

4. Asad, *The Idea of an Anthropology of Islam*, 14.

5. Zürcher, *Turkey: A Modern History*, 206–18.

6. Halis Ayhan, "İmam-Hatip Lisesi," in *TDV İslam Ansiklopedisi* (Istanbul: Türkiye Diyanet Vakfı, 2000), 191.

7. Bernard Lewis, "Islamic Revival in Turkey," *International Affairs* 28, no. 1 (1952): 41.

8. Significantly, Halid bin Zeyd's tomb was not on the original list of tombs with "historic value." It was only following the DP's electoral victory that the tomb was added to the list. See Gökçen Beyinli Dinç, "677 Sayılı Kanun, Türbeleri 'Millileştirme' ve Yıkıcı Sonuçları: Geç Osmanlı'dan Cumhuriyet'e Türbedarlık," *Cihannüma* 3, no. 2 (2017): 158–59. On the broader politics of this shift, see Gökçen Beyinli Dinç, "Reframing Turkey, Istanbul and National Identity: Ottoman History, 'Chosen People' and the Opening of Shrines in 1950," *Nations and Nationalism* 28, no. 4 (2022): 1428–43.

9. On the shift from Arabic to Turkish in 1932, see Umut Azak, "Secularism in Turkey as a Nationalist Search for Vernacular Islam: The Ban on the Call to Prayer in Arabic (1932–1950)," *Revue des mondes musulmans et de la Méditerranée* 124 (2008), https://doi .org/10.4000/remmm.6025. On its shift back to Arabic, see also İsmail Kara, *Cumhuriyet Türkiye'sinde Bir Mesele Olarak İslam 2* (Istanbul: Dergah Yayınları, 2016), 37.

10. Some of these transformations are discussed in Meltem Ö. Gürel, ed., *Mid-Century Modernism in Turkey: Architecture across Cultures in the 1950s and 1960s* (London: Routledge, 2015). Sarah-Neel Smith provides a sophisticated account of how art was entangled with these dynamics in *Metrics of Modernity: Art and Development in Postwar Turkey* (Berkeley: University of California Press, 2022).

11. Begüm Adalet, *Hotels and Highways: The Construction of Modernization Theory in Cold War Turkey* (Stanford, CA: Stanford University Press, 2018).

12. Dilek Güven, "Riots against the Non-Muslims of Turkey: 6/7 September 1955 in the Context of Demographic Engineering," *European Journal of Turkish Studies* 12 (2011), https://doi.org/10.4000/ejts.4538; Tuna Kuyucu, "Ethno-Religious 'Unmixing' of 'Turkey': 6–7 September Riots as a Case in Turkish Nationalism," *Nations and Nationalism* 11, no. 3 (2005).

13. These figures are based on statistics provided by the Istanbul Metropolitan Municipality. *Sayılarla İstanbul* (Istanbul: İstanbul Büyükşehir Belediyesi, 2000).

14. İpek Türeli, *Istanbul, Open City: Exhibiting Anxieties of Urban Modernity* (New York: Routledge, 2018); Tahire Erman, "Becoming 'Urban' or Remaining 'Rural': The Views of Turkish Rural-to-Urban Migrants on the 'Integration' Question," *International Journal of Middle East Studies* 30, no. 4 (1998).

15. Speros Vryonis, *The Mechanism of Catastrophe: The Turkish Pogrom of September 6–7, 1955, and the Destruction of the Greek Community of Istanbul* (New York: Greekworks .com, 2005).

16. Geoffrey Lewis, *The Turkish Language Reform: A Catastrophic Success* (Oxford: Oxford University Press, 1999); Nergis Ertürk, *Grammatology and Literary Modernity in Turkey* (New York: Oxford University Press, 2011).

17. Although I do not reference Sezai Karakoç's work in this chapter, Cemil Aydin and Burhanettin Duran's discussion of Karakoç's work demonstrates the wider point. "Arnold J. Toynbee and Islamism in Cold War–Era Turkey: Civilizationism in the Writings of Sezai Karakoç," *Comparative Studies of South Asia, Africa and the Middle East* 35, no. 2 (2015), https://doi.org/10.1215/1089201x-3139084.

18. Brockett, *How Happy to Call Oneself a Turk*, 89.

19. Brockett, *How Happy to Call Oneself a Turk*, 99.

20. Çağlar Derya Tağmat, "Fetih Derneği ve İstanbul'un Fetihin 500. Yılı," *Tarih Kültür ve Sanat Araştırmaları Dergisi* 3, no. 4 (2014).

21. For a more focused discussion of Islamist political organizing between 1945 and 1960 and its relationship to print culture, see Menderes Çinar and Ipek Gencel Sezgin, "Islamist Political Engagement in the Early Years of Multi-Party Politics in Turkey: 1945–60," *Turkish Studies* 14, no. 2 (2013): 330–32, https://doi.org/10.1080/14683849.2013.802921.

22. Gavin Brockett, "When Ottomans Become Turks: Commemorating the Conquest of Constantinople and Its Contribution to World History," *American Historical Review* 119, no. 2 (2014); Nicholas Danforth, *The Remaking of Republican Turkey: Memory and Modernity Since the Fall of the Ottoman Empire* (London: Cambridge University Press,

2021), 107–18. For a bibliography summarizing much of the work published about the conquest, see Müjgan Cumbur, "İstanbul'un 500üncü Fetih Yıldönümü Dolayısiyle Tertiplenen Sergilere, Yapılan Kültür, San'at ve Neşriyat Hareketlerine Dair," *Vakıflar Dergisi* 4 (1958).

23. Rüstem Ertuğ Altınay, "The Queer Archivist as Political Dissident: Rereading the Ottoman Empire in the Works of Reşad Ekrem Koçu," *Radical History Review* 122 (2015).

24. *Resimli Tarih Mecmuası* was published by Server İskit; *Tarih Hazinesi* was published by İbrahim Hakkı Konyalı; *Tarih Dünyası* was published by Niyazi Ahmet Banoğlu; Şevket Rado and Yılmaz Özyuna published *Life Illustrated*, which was published under a changing series of names, including *Hayat, Resimli Hayat*, and *Hayat Tarih Mecmuası*. This list is based on the Turkish-language Wikipedia entry for "Türkiye'de yayımlanmış tarih dergileri."

25. Camilla Trud Nereid, "Domesticating Modernity: The Turkish Magazine *Yedigün*, 1933–9," *Journal of Contemporary History* 47, no. 3 (2012), https://doi.org/10.1177/0022009412441651.

26. There is limited English-language scholarship on *Akbaba*. In Turkish, see Necati Tonga, "Türk Edebiyatı Tarihinde Mühim Bir Mecmua: Akbaba (1922–1977)," *Turkish Studies: International Periodical for the Languages, Literature and History of Turkish or Turkic* 3, no. 2 (2008); Hasip Saygılı and Elif Konar, "Türkiye'nin 1950'li Yıllarına Mizah Gözüğyle Bakmak: Akbaba Dergisi (1952–1960)," *Akademik Tarih ve Düşünce Dergisi* 8, no. 2 (2021).

27. Burhanettin Duran and Cemil Aydın, in "Competing Occidentalisms of Modern Islamist Thought," analyze the work of Necip Fazıl but largely extract it from the urban context of the 1950s.

28. The Turkish Touring and Automobile Club was originally founded in 1923 as part of the new Republic's project of "modernity," but it continued to publish articles throughout the 1950s.

29. Semavi Eyice, "İstanbul Ansiklopedisi," in *TDV İslam Ansiklopedisi* (Istanbul: Türkiye Diyanet Vakfı, 2001); Altınay, "The Queer Archivist as Political Dissident."

30. Şakir's serial began on April 8, 1950. Halid bin Zeyd's tomb was reopened on September 1, 1950. For a detailed discussion, see Beyinli Dinç, "Reframing Turkey," 1431–38.

31. Arzu Özyön, "Ziya Şakir (Soku)'nun Selçuk Saraylarında Ömer Hayyam'ın Hayat ve Maceraları Adlı Romanının Tarihsel Roman Olarak İncelenmesi," *Turkish Studies—International Periodical for the Languages, Literature and History of Turkish or Turkic* 9, no. 3 (2014): 1137.

32. A November 1945 column by Mahmut Yesari gently satirized Ziya Şakir (alongside many other writers) for his propensity to write these historical novels. That said, more recent comments have stressed his importance as an oral historian. See Ayda Üstündağ, *Dedem Ziya Şakir* (Istanbul: Akıl Fikir Yayınları, 2011).

33. Zürcher, *Turkey: A Modern History*, 174. The serial's author was only identified as "Kandemir" but it was likely written by the journalist and writer Feridun Kandemir.

34. Ziya Şakir, *Eyüp Sultan ve Haliç* (Istanbul: Akıl Fikir Yayınları, 2011), 46–47.

35. M. Brett Wilson, *Translating the Qur'an in an Age of Nationalism: Print Culture and Modern Islam in Turkey* (London: Oxford University Press, 2014), 85.

36. Ziya Şakir, *Son Saat*, May 25, 1950. *Hijri* refers to the Islamic, lunar-based calendar. The *sala* (*salâ*) is a specific prayer common in Turkey. Its performance is also associated with a musical tradition. See Nuri Özcan, "Salâ," in *TDV İslam Ansiklopedisi* (Istanbul: Türkiye Diyanet Vakfı, 2009).

37. Hammond, "Matters of the Mosque," 683–86.

38. Ziya Şakir, *Son Saat*, May 27, 1950.

39. Ziya Şakir, *Son Saat*. May 29, 1950. The Tanzimat involved a series of far-reaching legal, cultural, and political reforms between 1839 and 1878. In Şakir's account, it is also closely linked to a project of Westernization. For one recent discussion of the Tanzimat and its conceptual history, see Alp Eren Topal, "Political Reforms as Religious Revival: Conceptual Foundations of *Tanzimat*," *Oriente Moderno* 101, no. 2 (2021), https://doi.org /10.1163/22138617-12340261.

40. Şakir, *Eyüp Sultan ve Haliç*, 135.

41. Osman Nebioğlu, "Kaybettiğimiz Değerler," in an unknown newspaper, December 26, 1963 (Marmara University, Taha Toros Archive, http://hdl.handle.net/11424/131836).

42. Danforth, *The Remaking of Republican Turkey*, 114.

43. Haluk Şehsuvaroğlu, "Tarihi Bahisler: Tarih ve Masal," *Cumhuriyet*, n.d. (Marmara University, Taha Toros Archive, 001583548010).

44. Haluk Şehsuvaroğlu, "Tarihten Sahifeler: Eyüb Yalıları," n.d. (Marmara University, Taha Toros Archive, 001500546006).

45. See, for example, Haluk Şehsuvaroğlu, "Tarihi Bahisler: Medeniyetimize Dair," *Cumhuriyet*, n.d. (SALT Research, TASUDOCP0548), and Haluk Şehsuvaroğlu, "Tarih ve Bugün: Millî kıymetlerimize dair," *Cumhuriyet*, n.d. (SALT Research, TASUDOCP0418).

46. Haluk Sehsuvaroglu, "Tarihten Sahifeler: Aramızda eski İstanbulluların Eyübe dair anlattıkları," March 7, 1957 (Marmara University, Taha Toros Archive, 001500542006)

47. Alim Kahraman, "Alus, Sermet Muhtar," in *TDV İslam Ansiklopedisi* (Istanbul: Türkiye Diyanet Vakfı, 2016); Gisela Prochazka-Eisl, "Alus, Sermet Muhtar," in *Encyclopedia of Islam, Three*, ed. Kate Fleet et al. (Leiden: Brill, 2016).

48. Sermet Muhtar Alus, "Eyüp Oyuncakları," *Tarih Hazinesi*, December, 1951, https:// archives.saltresearch.org/handle/123456789/24485.

49. Alus, "Eyüp Oyuncakları."

50. Süheyl Ünver similarly speaks about this situation in his 1953 pamphlet "İstanbul'da Sahabe Kabirleri." A. Süheyl Ünver, "İstanbul'da Sahâbe Kabirleri," in *İstanbul Risaleleri* (Istanbul: Istanbul Büyükşehir Belediyesi Kültür İşleri Daire Başkanlığı, 1993), 258.

51. Kathryn Libal, "'The Child Question': The Politics of Child Welfare in Early Republican Turkey," in *Poverty and Charity in Middle Eastern Contexts*, ed. Michael Bonner, Mine Ener, and Amy Singer (Albany: SUNY Press, 2003), 256–57.

52. Christiane Gruber, "Like Hearts of Birds: Ottoman Avian Microarchitecture in the Eighteenth Century," *Journal18*, no. 11 (2021), www.journal18.org/5689.

53. Taneja, *Jinnealogy*, 225. Taneja's work focuses on the Delhi shrine complex of Firoz Shah Kotla, and there are important differences between the devotional cultures attached to that place and those woven through Eyüp Sultan. Nevertheless, his work highlights the relative absence of nonhuman worlds in discussions of Islam in Istanbul.

54. A Google search for "Ara Güler leylek" or "Ara Güler stork" will pull up the image.

55. Nahid Sırrı Örik, "Eyüp Sultan," *Büyük Doğu* 2, May 14, 1954, p. 12. Republished in Nahid Sırrı Örik, *İstanbul Yazıları*, ed. Bahriye Çeri (Ankara: Türk Tarih Kurumu Basımevi, 2011), 154–57.

56. Örik, *İstanbul Yazıları*.

57. Örik, *İstanbul Yazıları*.

58. Gül, *The Emergence of Modern Istanbul.*

59. One hundred fifty monuments were ordered restored in 1957. See the order signed by President Celal Bayar on April 13, 1957 (T.C./BCA 30.018.1.2/146.22.16).

60. See also the discussion in Hammond, "Mediums of Belief," 68–94.

61. Avni Aktuç, "Eyüpsultan," *Hayat*, April 11, 1958. The text is divided into two sections, and it is not clear whether Aktuç was the author of both.

62. Aktuç, "Eyüpsultan," 8.

63. In many respects, this project would be echoed by restoration projects of the 1980s. My reference to architectural voids draws on Zeynep Çelik's observation that Baron Haussman's urban demolitions remained an important reference point for Istanbul's planners. Çelik, "Urban Preservation as Theme Park," 84.

64. This project was supervised by Chief Architect Vasfi Egeli, but another key participant was the architect Ali Saim Ülgen. For an introduction to Ülgen's importance and archive, see Zeynep Ahunbay, "Genç Cumhuriyetin Koruma Alanındaki Öncülerinden Yüksek Mimar Ali Saim Ülgen (1913–1963)," SALT Research, June 5, 2015, http://blog.salton line.org/post/120786511984/asu-zeynepahunbay.

65. "Eyüp Camii Gene Açık," *Hayat*, n.d. (SALT Research, FFT185011).

66. Haluk Şehsuvaroğlu, "Tarihi Bahisler: Eyüp Camii'ne Dair," *Cumhuriyet*, March 30, 1959 (SALT Research, FFT185007).

67. Refi Cevat Ulunay, "Takvimden Bir Yaprak: Eyyub Camii," *Milliyet*, March 14, 1959 (SALT Research, FFT185005).

68. Gavin Moulton provides a superb account of Egeli's role in designing the Şişli Mosque as simultaneously modern and classic. Gavin Moulton, "Mid-Century Sinan: Vasfi Egeli and the Turkish Republic's First Mosque," *Yıllık: Annual of Istanbul Studies* 3 (2021).

69. Salim Bayar, "Yeni Plana Göre Eyüp Yemyeşil bir Site Oluyor," *Tercüman* (Istanbul), 1958 (likely late November or early December). The series is collected in the files of Ali Saim Ülgen and digitized by SALT Research.

70. Kapsız, "Eyüpsultanda Cuma," *Resimli Hayat* (Istanbul), September 29, 1954. *Çarşaf* is a loose-fitting style of women's dress similar to styles such as the burqa or chador.

71. Kapsız, "Eyüpsultanda Cuma," 48.

72. Kapsız, "Eyüpsultanda Cuma," 48. Here, a *sinemacı* refers to one who shows films (*sinema*).

73. I have not found any other reference to this book. It may have been a manuscript or a published book.

74. M. Akif Bencoşar, *Eyüp Sultan* (Istanbul: Ercan Matbaası, 1958), 11.

75. Bencoşar, *Eyüp Sultan*, 11.

76. On the Shadhiliyya order, see P. Lory, "Shadhiliyya," in *Encyclopedia of Islam, Second Edition*, ed. P. Bearman et al. (Leiden: Brill, 2012); Ahmet Murat Özel, "Şâzeliyye," in *TDV İslam Ansiklopedisi* (Istanbul: Türkiye Diyanet Vakfı, 2010).

77. These included Imam al-Ghazali (the prominent eleventh-century philosopher and jurist), Fahri Razi Hz. (possibly a reference to Fahreddin er-Razi, the twelfth-century scholar), Abdülkadir Geylani (the twelfth-century founder of the Qadiriyya Sufi order), and Imam Nuri Hz. (unknown, but possibly Abdülahad Nuri, a seventeenth-century shaykh affiliated with the Halvetiyye order and buried in Eyüp).

78. Bencoşar, *Eyüp Sultan*, 14.

79. Ünver, "İstanbul'da Sahâbe Kabirleri." A cultural historian, Ünver played a crucial role in training later generations in the traditional Turkish arts, including calligraphy, paper marbling, and book binding. The standard reference for his biography is Ahmed Güner Sayar, *A. Süheyl Ünver: Hayatı, Şahsiyeti ve Eserleri* (Istanbul: Eren, 1994).

80. Ünver, "İstanbul'da Sahâbe Kabirleri," 223. A direct translation of *millileştirme* would be "making *milli*," by which Ünver means to say "making it Turk."

81. Ünver, "İstanbul'da Sahâbe Kabirleri," 224.

82. Asad, *The Idea of an Anthropology of Islam*, 14.

83. Asad, *The Idea of an Anthropology of Islam*, 14.

84. These encounters might be read against what İpek Türeli has described as anxieties about Istanbul as an "open" city. See Türeli, *Istanbul, Open City*.

85. Bashir, "The Living Dead of Tabriz," 169.

86. Lewis, "Islamic Revival in Turkey," 44.

87. I found reference to Lewis's article in Danforth, *The Remaking of Republican Turkey*, 188.

## 4. FLUID STORIES

1. Ahmet Süheyl Ünver, *Hazret-i Eyûb el-Ensârî ve civarı hatıratı*, Notebook no. 267 (Süleymaniye Manuscripts Library [Süleymaniye Yazma Eser Kütüphanesi], Istanbul). For an expanded discussion of this notebook, see Timur Hammond, "Conjunctions of Islam: Rethinking the Geographies of Art and Piety through the Notebooks of Ahmet Süheyl Ünver." *cultural geographies* (2022). https://doi.org/10.1177/14744740221120248.

2. On the Madrasa of Calligraphy, see M. Uğur Derman, "Medresetü'l-Hattâtîn," in *TDV İslam Ansiklopedisi* (Ankara: Türkiye Diyanet Vakfı, 2003).

3. Published in two separate editions in the late nineteenth century, this book was frequently referenced by other authors, including Hacı Cemal Öğüt. See Hafız Mehmed Emin, *El-Âsar ül-Mecidiye fi l-Menakıb il-Halidiye* (Istanbul: Mahmud Bey Matbaası, 1314 [1896/97]). My choice to translate *menakıb* (Ar. *manâqib*) as "virtues" is based on Charles Pellat's discussion in "Manakib," in *Encyclopedia of Islam, Second Edition*, ed. P. Bearman et al. (Leiden: Brill, 2012). For a Turkish-language survey of the genre, see Haşim Şahin, "Menâkıbnâme," in *TDV İslam Ansiklopedisi* (Ankara: Türkiye Diyanet Vakfı, 2004).

4. The association between seals, health, and water was not unique to the tomb of Halid bin Zeyd. For one discussion of seals and their healing powers, see Christiane Gruber, "A Pious Cure-All: The Ottoman Illustrated Prayer Manual in the Lilly Library," in *The Islamic Manuscript Tradition: Ten Centuries of Book Arts in Indiana University Collections*, ed. Christiane Gruber (Bloomington: Indiana University Press, 2010), 117. On *nadhr*, see J. Pedersen, "Nadhr," in *Encyclopedia of Islam, Second Edition*, ed. P. Bearman et al. (Leiden: Brill, 2012). These offerings or vows are also called *adak* in Turkish. Ahmet Murat Özel, "Adak," in *TDV İslam Ansiklopedisi* (Istanbul: Türkiye Diyanet Vakfı, 1988).

5. These names are provided by Şener Türkmenoğlu. Based on her interview with a long-time Eyüp resident, Gökçen Beyinli Dinç also mentions two men named Ahmet Efendi and Recep Efendi who continued to serve as *türbedar* even after the position's formal abrogation in 1925. Beyinli Dinç, "677 Sayılı Kanun, Türbeleri 'Millileştirme' ve Yıkıcı Sonuçları," 121.

6. This practice echoes examples found across the world of Islam. See Finbarr B. Flood, "Bodies and Becoming: Mimesis, Mediation, and the Ingestion of the Sacred in Christianity

and Islam," in *Sensational Religion: Sensory Cultures in Material Practice*, ed. Sally M. Promey (New Haven, CT: Yale University Press, 2014); Gruber, "A Pious Cure-All."

7. Surah al-Anbiya', verse 30, Saheeh International Translation. Suggestively, the verb for "to make" (*ja-'ayn-nûn*) also carries the meaning of "to place" elsewhere in the Qur'an.

8. Water can also signal God's punishment. See Carole Hillenbrand, "Gardens beneath Which Rivers Flow: The Significance of Water in Classical Islamic Culture," in *Rivers of Paradise: Water in Islamic Art and Culture*, ed. Sheila S. Blair and Jonathan M. Bloom (New Haven, CT: Yale University Press, 2009).

9. Annemarie Schimmel, *Deciphering the Signs of God: A Phenomenological Approach to Islam* (Albany: State University of New York Press, 1994), 6.

10. Although it is not present in the Qur'an, we could also add *ḥawḍ* (cistern) to this list. See Andrew Rippin, "Ḥawḍ," in *Encyclopedia of Islam, Three*, ed. Kate Fleet et al. (Leiden: Brill, 2013).

11. Surah al-Kahf, verses 60–65.

12. Ethel Sara Wolper, "Khiḍr and the Changing Frontiers of the Medieval World," *Medieval Encounters* 17, no. 1–2 (2011): 121, https://doi.org/10.1163/157006711x561730.

13. Frederick William Hasluck and Margaret Masson Hardie Hasluck, *Christianity and Islam under the Sultans*, 2 vols. (London: Clarendon Press, 1929).

14. See, for example, Karen Bakker, "Water: Political, Biopolitical, Material," *Social Studies of Science* 42, no. 4 (2012), https://doi.org/10.1177/0306312712441396; Jessica Barnes, *Cultivating the Nile: The Everyday Politics of Water in Egypt* (Durham, NC: Duke University Press, 2014).

15. Meyer, "Mediation and Immediacy," 29.

16. Efendioğlu, "Rivayet."

17. This phrasing is adapted from Patrick Eisenlohr's formulation in "The Anthropology of Media and the Question of Ethnic and Religious Pluralism," *Social Anthropology* 19, no. 1 (2011): 42–44.

18. Although I don't follow her cosmological approach, Carol Delaney's work explores the interrelationships between human and nonhuman worlds. Carol Delaney, *The Seed and the Soil: Gender and Cosmology in Turkish Village Society* (Berkeley: University of California Press, 1991).

19. Sally M. Promey, "Religion, Sensation, and Materiality: An Introduction," in *Sensational Religion: Sensory Cultures in Material Practice*, ed. Sally M. Promey (New Haven, CT: Yale University Press, 2014), 4.

20. Access to the tomb was restricted during my in-person fieldwork, and I have never seen the well in person. These details borrow from "Eyüp Sultan ve Zemzem Kuyusu," *Hürriyet*, 2009, www.hurriyet.com.tr/gundem/eyup-sultan-ve-zemzem-kuyusu-12327054.

21. For different versions of this story, see Jacqueline Chabbi, "Zamzam," in *Encyclopedia of Islam, Second Edition*, ed. P. Bearman et al. (Leiden: Brill, 2012). Zayde Antrim also discusses this story in *Routes and Realms*, 45.

22. Mustafa Sabri Küçükaşçı, "Zemzem," in *TDV İslam Ansiklopedisi* (Istanbul: Türkiye Diyanet Vakfı, 2013). On its healing properties, see Ahmad Ghabin, "The Well of Zamzam: A Pilgrimage Site and Curative Water in Islam," in *Sacred Waters: A Cross-Cultural Compendium of Hallowed Springs and Holy Wells*, ed. Celeste Ray (New York: Routledge, 2020).

23. Küçükaşçı, "Zemzem," 245.

24. See Chabbi, "Zamzam"; Mehmet Ali Yolcu, "Kutsalın Yeniden Üretimi: Kutsal Su İnançları ve Hacıbektaş Zemzem Çeşmesi," 21. *Yüzyılda Eğitim ve Toplum Eğitim Bilimleri ve Sosyal Araştırmalar Dergisi* 3, no. 8 (2014).

25. Mehmet Nermi Haskan, *Eyüp Sultan Tarihi*, 2 vols. (Istanbul: Eyüp Belediyesi Kültür Yayınları, 2009), 440. Nuray Özaslan also provides a rich discussion of this district's Byzantine history in "From the Shrine of Cosmidion to the Shrine of Eyup Ensari." I am grateful to Feray Coşkun for her discussion of Özaslan's work in Coşkun, "Sanctifying Ottoman Istanbul," 17.

26. Timothy S. Miller, "Hospital Dreams in Byzantium," in *Dreams, Healing, and Medicine in Greece: From Antiquity to the Present*, ed. Steven M. Oberhelman (Burlington, VT: Ashgate, 2013), 200–201.

27. George Majeska, "Russian Pilgrims in Constantinople," *Dumbarton Oaks Papers* 56 (2002), https://doi.org/10.2307/1291857.

28. A. Süheyl Ünver, "İstanbulun Bazı Acı ve Tatlı Sularının Halkça Maruf Şifa Hassaları Hakkında," *Türk Tıb Tarihi Arkivi* 5, no. 18 (1940): 92. According to Çelebi, the waters were especially valuable for people suffering from malaria (*humma-yı rub'*). Ünver's essay also draws upon *Mehâhü'l-miyâh*, a book about Istanbul's water written by Mehmed Hafîd Efendi and published in 1797 that does not appear to have been discussed in English-language scholarship. Abdülkadir Özcan, "Hafîd Efendi," in *TDV İslam Ansiklopedisi* (Istanbul: Türkiye Diyanet Vakfı, 1997).

29. Dionigi Albera and Benoit Fliche cite a late nineteenth-century account of this church being visited by Muslims as well, reminding us that just as Christian communities have often visited Muslim shrines in Istanbul, there are also instances where Muslims have visited Christian shrines. Dionigi Albera and Benoiît Fliche, "Muslim Devotional Practices in Christian Shrines: The Case of Istanbul," in *Sharing Sacred Spaces in the Mediterranean*, ed. Dionigi Albera and Maria Couroucli (Bloomington: Indiana University Press, 2012), 94.

30. Christiane Gruber, "The Prophet as a Sacred Spring: Late Ottoman *Hilye* Bottles," in *The Presence of the Prophet in Early Modern and Contemporary Islam*, ed. Denis Gril, Stefan Reichmuth, and Dilek Sarmis (Leiden: Brill, 2021), 565–77; Önder Kaya, "İstanbul'da Ayazma Kültürü ve Balıklı Ayazması," *Z Dergisi*, 2020, www.zdergisi.istanbul/makale /istanbulda-ayazma-kulturu-ve-balikli-ayazmasi-92; Demet Kılınç Çimen, "Halk İnanışları Açısından İstanbul'daki Kilise ve Ayazmalar" (MA thesis, Ankara Üniversitesi, 2010).

31. This point is made in Jean-François Pérouse, "Les non musulmans à Istanbul aujourd'hui: Une présence en creux? Le cas de l'arrondissement de Fatih," *Revue des mondes musulmans et de la Méditerranée* 107–10 (2005).

32. Charles White, *Three Years in Constantinople; or, Domestic Manners of the Turks in 1844*, vol. 3 (London: Henry Colburn, Publisher, 1846), 347. Also cited in Coşkun, "Sanctifying Ottoman Istanbul," 144.

33. James Ellsworth De Kay, *Sketches of Turkey in 1831 and 1832* (New York: J. & J. Harper, 1833), 222.

34. Thomas Allom and Robert Walsh, *Constantinople and the Scenery of the Seven Churches of Asia* (London: Peter Jackson, Late Fisher, Son, & Co., 1840), 49–50.

35. "Eyüp Sultan Türbesi'nde Şifalı Suda Skandal Sızıntı," *Sabah* (Istanbul), May 26, 2011.

36. Christiane Gruber, "Bereket Bargains: Islamic Amulets in Today's 'New Turkey,'" in *Islamicate Occult Sciences in Theory and Practice*, ed. Liana Saif et al. (Leiden: Brill, 2020).

37. Latour, "On Actor-Network Theory," 370.

38. Law and Mol, "Situating Technoscience," 614.

39. A *sikke* is a tall, felted wool hat traditionally associated with the Mevlevi Sufi order.

40. Haskan, *Eyüp Sultan Tarihi*, 74.

41. "Dertlilerin Teselli Bulduğu Yer: Eyüb Sultan," June 2, 1954.

42. "Dertlilerin Teselli Bulduğu Yer."

43. Coşkun, "Sanctifying Ottoman Istanbul," 179.

44. Sydney Adamson, "The Mosque of Eyoub," *Harper's Magazine*, 1913, 32.

45. Erdal Aday, "Kütahya Ile Türbe ve Yatırları Etrafında Oluşan İnanç ve Uygulamalar" (PhD diss., Balıkesir University, 2013).

46. Aslıhan Haznedaroğlu, "Kısmet İçin Rüyaya Yatmak: Alata Kolotisi Hakkında," *Kültür Araştırmaları Dergisi* 10 (2021), https://doi.org/10.46250/kulturder.950733.

47. Kimberly Hart's ethnography of rural piety presents numerous examples of how water flows through social and religious life. *And Then We Work for God: Rural Islam in Western Turkey* (Stanford, CA: Stanford University Press, 2013).

48. Evliya Çelebi was a writer and traveler who lived in the early seventeenth century. His travelogue includes extensive descriptions of Istanbul. Feray Coşkun references a version of his story in Coşkun, "Osmanlı İstanbulu'nda Müstesnâ bir Ziyâretgâh," 564.

49. Niyazi Ahmet, "Eyüp," *Yedigün*, February 17, 1941. Here "Joseph the Loyal" refers to the Prophet Joseph. There is no explanation as to why Joseph's name should be invoked, but it may stem from a story about Joseph being thrown into a well by his siblings.

50. Quoted in Ayşe Pekin, "İstanbul'un Kutsal Semti: Eyüp," *Skylife*, December 1992, 92. *Basiret* is a term derived from Sufi thought referring to the capacity to perceive the truth of the world. Süleyman Uludağ, "Basiret," in *TDV İslam Ansiklopedisi* (Istanbul: Türkiye Diyanet Vakfı, 1992).

51. Ayşe Duvarcı, "Su ile Bakılan Fallar," in *Geleneksel Türk Sanatında ve Edebiyatımızda Su*, ed. Nurettin Demir (Ankara: Ankara Büyükşehir Belediyesi, 2013).

52. Field notes, June 2012.

53. Hammond, "Matters of the Mosque," 683–86.

54. Field notes, March 2013.

55. Each of these three categories masks considerable differences within them. For example, Greek Orthodox Christians do not necessarily share sacred topographies with Armenian Christians or Roman Catholics; similarly, Sunni Muslim devotional geographies are often distinct from Alevi communities. Social class, educational background, ethnic identity, and place of birth can also inflect how different individuals learn the city's sacred places.

56. Daniel Gimaret, "Shirk," in *Encyclopaedia of Islam, Second Edition*, ed. P. Berman et al. (Leiden: Brill, 1960). The term can also be translated as "polytheism," a translation that highlights the shared critique across the Abrahamic religions of taking any other god but God.

57. Richard McGregor, "Grave Visitation/Worship," in *Encyclopaedia of Islam, Three*, ed. Kate Fleet et al. (Leiden: Brill, 2016). As McGregor notes, this capacity is also referred to by the term *shafāʿa* (Tr. *şefaat*). As discussed in chapter 2, this is often identified as one of the virtues of Halid bin Zeyd. See also Flood, "Bodies and Becoming," 469.

58. Eisenlohr, "The Anthropology of Media," 44.

59. Webb Keane, "The Evidence of the Senses and the Materiality of Religion," *Journal of the Royal Anthropological Institute* 14, no. s1 (2008): S114.

60. This building is part of the broader complex endowed by Mihrişah Valide Sultan in the late eighteenth century and constructed between 1792 and 1796. Parlak, "Mihrişah Valide Sultan Külliyesi." This complex's construction roughly coincides with the wholesale reconstruction of the Mosque of Eyüp Sultan between 1798 and 1800. Eyice, "Eyüp Sultan Külliyesi."

61. Nur Urfalıoğlu, "Sebil," in *TDV İslam Ansiklopedisi* (Istanbul: Türkiye Diyanet Vakfı, 2009).

62. Doris Behrens-Abouseif, "Sabīl," in *Encyclopedia of Islam, Second Edition*, ed. P. Bearman et al. (Leiden: Brill, 2012).

63. Shirine Hamadeh, "Splash and Spectacle: The Obsession with Fountains in Eighteenth-Century Istanbul," *Muqarnas* 19 (2002): 125.

64. Engin Isin and Ebru Üstündağ, "Wills, Deeds, Acts: Women's Civic Gift-Giving in Ottoman Istanbul," *Gender, Place and Culture* 15, no. 5 (2008): 520.

65. Ali Duman, "Sadaka," in *TDV İslam Ansiklopedisi* (Istanbul: Türkiye Diyanet Vakfı, 2008), 384.

66. For example, the *sıbyan mektebi* endowed by Mihrişah Valide Sultan, where I taught English classes during my fieldwork, was also an example of "ongoing charity."

67. The *waqf* (Tr. *vakıf*) system was a crucial institution across the world of Islam. For an overview of its importance to urban form, see Randi Deguilhem, "The Waqf in the City," in *The City in the Islamic World*, ed. Salma Jayyusi et al. (Leiden: Brill, 2008). For broad histories of the institution, see Murat Çizakça, *A History of Philanthropic Foundations: The Islamic World from the Seventh Century to the Present* (Istanbul: Boğaziçi University Press, 2000); Nazif Öztürk, *Türk Yenileşme Tarihi Çevresinde Vakıf* (Ankara: Türkiye Diyanet Vakfı, 1995). For a discussion of *waqf* and their role in forms of public charity, see, for example, Amy Singer, *Charity in Islamic Societies* (Cambridge: Cambridge University Press, 2008).

68. Noyan Dinçkal, "Reluctant Modernization: The Cultural Dynamics of Water Supply in Istanbul, 1885–1950," *Technology and Culture* 49, no. 3 (2008): 696–98.

69. For a brief discussion of this narrative, see Hatice Aynur, "İstanbul'da Kadınların Yaptırdığı Çeşmeler Üzerine—Istanbul Fountains Commissioned by Women—Les Fontaines d'Istanbul Commandées par des Femmes" (Voyvoda Caddesi Toplantıları 2005–2006, Istanbul, 2006).

70. This community identifies itself as part of the Khalidiye-Naqshbandi tradition. See www.iskenderpasa.com/08722033-A143-4AEE-A1D6-0A38235F4480.aspx. The community played a formative role in the politics of Turkey during the 1970s and 1980s in particular. See Fulya Atacan, "Explaining Religious Politics at the Crossroad: AKP-SP," *Turkish Studies* 6, no. 2 (2007): 191, https://doi.org/10.1080/14683840500119510.

71. Christiane Gruber, "The Arts of Protection and Healing in Islam: Water Infused with Blessing," *Ajam Media Collective*, 2021.

72. I am grateful to Christiane Gruber for this observation.

73. I learned of the term *kuşluk* from Aysel Uslu, "An Ecological Approach for the Evaluation of an Abandoned Cemetery as a Green Area: The Case of Ankara/Karakusunlar Cemetery," *African Journal of Agricultural Research* 5, no. 10 (2010): 1043, https://doi.org/10.5897/AJAR09.200.

74. See, for example, Matthew Gandy's discussion of an urban cemetery in London, "Queer Ecology: Nature, Sexuality, and Heterotopic Alliances," *Environment and Planning D: Society and Space* 30, no. 4 (2012), https://doi.org/10.1068/d10511. Elsewhere, Thierry Zarcone traces the invention of "ecology" to the zoologist and artist Ernest Haeckel; he notes that Haeckel's discussion of monism was originally translated into Turkish as *vahdet-i vücud* (Ar. *wahdat al-wujūd*), suggesting an interesting convergence between traditions of Islamic thought and the natural sciences. Thierry Zarcone, "Stone People, Tree People and Animal People in Turkic Asia and Eastern Europe," *Diogenes* 52, no. 3 (2016): 44, https://doi.org/10.1177/0392192105055168.

75. See, for example, *Dört Ayaklı Belediye: İstanbul'un Sokak Köpekleri*, ed. Istanbul Araştırmaları Enstitüsü (Istanbul: İstanbul Araştırmaları Enstitüsü, 2016); Kim Fortuny, "Islam, Westernization, and Posthumanist Place: The Case of the Istanbul Street Dog," *Interdisciplinary Studies in Literature and Environment* 21, no. 2 (2014), https://doi.org/10.1093/isle/isu049; Kimberly Hart, "Istanbul's Intangible Cultural Heritage as Embodied by Street Animals," *History and Anthropology* 30, no. 4 (2019), https://doi.org/10.1080/02757206.2019.1610404.

76. Gruber, "Like Hearts of Birds."

77. For example, Mohammed Hocine Benkheira, Catherine Mayeur-Jaouen, and Jacqueline Sublet, *L'Animal en Islam* (Paris: Les Indes Savantes, 2005); Sarra Tlili, *Animals in the Qur'an* (Cambridge: Cambridge University Press, 2012); Anand Vivek Taneja, "Saintly Animals: The Shifting Moral and Ecological Landscapes of North India," *Comparative Studies of South Asia, Africa and the Middle East* 35, no. 2 (2015); Taneja, *Jinnealogy*, 182–92.

78. Massey, *Space, Place, and Gender*, 154.

79. Hart, *And Then We Work for God*, 7–9.

80. Vicini, *Reading Islam*.

81. For a remarkable discussion of the relationship between water, Islam, and social relationships in a Moroccan oasis, see Jamie Fico, "Watering the Desert, Draining the Oasis: Navigating Drought, Development and Irrigation Politics in the Draa Valley, Morocco" (MA thesis, Syracuse University, 2022).

82. Ünver, "İstanbulun Bazı Acı ve Tatlı Sularının Halkça Maruf Şifa Hassaları Hakkında."

## PART II. BUILDING (*BINA*)

1. David Atkinson and Denis Cosgrove, "Urban Rhetoric and Embodied Identities: City, Nation, and Empire at the Vittorio Emanuele II Monument in Rome, 1870–1945," *Annals of the Association of American Geographers* 88, no. 1 (1998).

2. James C. Scott, *Seeing Like a State: How Certain Schemes to Improve the Human Condition Have Failed* (New Haven, CT: Yale University Press, 1998).

3. Natalie Koch, *The Geopolitics of Spectacle: Space, Synechdoche, and the New Capitals of Asia* (Ithaca, NY: Cornell University Press, 2018).

4. See, for example, David Harvey, "The Urban Process under Capitalism," *International Journal of Urban and Regional Research* 2, no. 1–4 (1978).

5. Takashi Fujitani, *Splendid Monarchy: Power and Pageantry in Modern Japan* (Berkeley: University of California Press, 1996), 11; Karen E. Till, "Places of Memory," in *A Companion to Political Geography*, ed. John Agnew, Katharyne Mitchell, and Gerard Toal (Malden, MA: Blackwell Publishers, 2003).

6. Karen E. Till, "Memory Studies," *History Workshop Journal* 62, no. 1 (2006): 330.

7. Jane M. Jacobs, "A Geography of Big Things," *Cultural Geographies* 13, no. 1 (2006): 4.

8. Tim Edensor, "Entangled Agencies, Material Networks and Repair in a Building Assemblage: The Mutable Stone of St Ann's Church, Manchester," *Transactions of the Institute of British Geographers* 36, no. 2 (2011): Caitlin DeSilvey, *Curated Decay: Heritage beyond Saving* (Minneapolis: University of Minnesota Press, 2017).

9. Doreen Massey, *Power-Geometries and the Politics of Space-Time* (Heidelburg, Germany: University of Heidelberg, 1999), 22.

10. Gaston R. Gordillo, *Rubble: The Afterlife of Destruction* (Durham, NC: Duke University Press, 2014), 2.

11. Mol, *The Body Multiple: Ontology in Medical Practice*, 184.

## 5. OTTOMAN TOPOGRAPHIES

1. Müzeyyen bir çeşme kıldı duası müstecab olsun/Delili Hazret-i Allah, şefiği Mustafa olsun/Bir içen bir daha içsin, içene şifa olsun/Reis Ahmet Genç'ten Eyüp Sultan'a hediye olsun.

2. Rabî' al-awwal (Tr. *Rabiulevvel*) is one of the twelve months of the *hijri* calendar.

3. Ömür Harmanşah makes a similar point in critiquing the assumption that archaeology studied objective truths "*beyond* or *underneath* the material contaminations of the recent past." Ömür Harmanşah, *Place, Memory, and Healing: An Archaeology of Anatolian Rock Monuments* (New York: Routledge, 2015), 4.

4. Nadia Abu El-Haj, *Facts on the Ground: Archaeological Practice and Territorial Self-Fashioning in Israeli Society* (Chicago: University of Chicago Press, 2001), 131.

5. See, for example, Jean-François Pérouse, "Gouverner Istanbul aujourd'hui," *Rives méditerranéennes* 2 (1999), https://doi.org/10.4000/rives.152.

6. This new system of metropolitan governance also created a situation in which local municipalities were competing to attract investment and capital, similar to global shifts from "managerialism" to "entrepreneurialism." David Harvey, "From Managerialism to Entrepreneurialism: The Transformation of Urban Governance in Late Capitalism," *Geografiska Annaler, Series B: Human Geography* 71, no. 1 (1989).

7. Çaglar Keyder and Ayşe Öncü, "Globalization of a Third-World Metropolis: Istanbul in the 1980s," *Review* 17, no. 3 (1994).

8. The local municipality's planning projects are discussed in Hatice Fahrünnisa Kara, "Eyüpsultan Tarihi Yerleşme Dokusunda Planlama Süreci ve Planlama—Uygulama İlişkileri," in *1. Eyüpsultan Sempozyumu: Tebliğler* (Istanbul: Eyüpsultan Belediyesi, 1997).

9. On Erbakan and the Milli Görüş movement, see Jenny B. White, "Milli Görüş," in *Islamic Movements of Europe: Public Religion and Islamophobia in the Modern World*, ed. Frank Peter and Rafael Ortega (London: I.B. Tauris, 2014); Tanil Bora, *Cereyanlar: Türkiye'de Siyasî İdeolojiler* (Istanbul: İletişim, 2021), 469–74.

10. For comparison, the second- and third-place parties finished with vote shares of 20.3 percent and 19.6 percent.

11. M. Hakan Yavuz, "Political Islam and the Welfare (Refah) Party in Turkey," *Comparative Politics* 30, no. 1 (1997): 77.

12. See, for example, Erman, "Becoming 'Urban' or Remaining 'Rural'"; Anna Secor, "'There Is an Istanbul That Belongs to Me': Citizenship, Space and Identity in the City," *Annals of the Association of American Geographers* 94 (2004).

13. Ümraniye and Sultanbeyli are two districts on the Anatolian side. Ümraniye's transformations are documented in White, *Islamist Mobilization in Turkey*. Sultanbeyli is discussed in Cihan Tuğal, "The Appeal of Islamic Politics: Ritual and Dialogue in a Poor District of Turkey," *Sociological Quarterly* 47 (2006), and Cihan Tuğal, *Passive Revolution: Absorbing the Islamic Challenge to Capitalism* (Stanford, CA: Stanford University Press, 2009).

14. Bora, "Istanbul of the Conqueror"; Çınar, "National History as a Contested Site."

15. Lerna K. Yanık, "Constructing Turkish 'Exceptionalism': Discourses of Liminality and Hybridity in Post–Cold War Turkish Foreign Policy," *Political Geography* 30, no. 2 (2011): 5–8; Yilmaz Çolak, "Ottomanism vs. Kemalism: Collective Memory and Cultural

Pluralism in 1990s Turkey," *Middle Eastern Studies* 42, no. 4 (2006); Mills, "The Place of Locality for Identity in the Nation."

16. M. Hakan Yavuz, "Turkish Identity and Foreign Policy in Flux: The Rise of Neo-Ottomanism," *Critique: Critical Middle Eastern Studies* 7, no. 12 (1998): 23.

17. Turkey had first applied for membership in 1967, but it was their 1987 application that was rejected in 1989, ostensibly on the grounds of Europe's concern about Turkey's authoritarian political system and economic underdevelopment. However, some EU countries rejected Turkey's membership on explicitly religio-cultural grounds. The rapid expansion of the EU to former Warsaw Pact countries in 1997 served as further confirmation of some Turkish skeptics' view of the EU as a crypto-Christian project. Yavuz, "Turkish Identity and Foreign Policy in Flux," 35–37.

18. Özyürek, "Public Memory as Political Battleground."

19. Bülent Batuman, "'Early Republican Ankara': Struggle over Historical Representation and the Politics of Urban Historiography," *Journal of Urban History* 37, no. 5 (2011).

20. Özyürek, *Nostalgia for the Modern.*

21. White, *Islamist Mobilization in Turkey,* 59.

22. Anna Secor and Christopher Houston both analyze how the built environment socially and spatially marginalizes Kurdish migrants. The situation here was slightly different insofar as the people who felt marginalized were primarily pious and conservative. Secor, "There Is an Istanbul That Belongs to Me"; Christopher Houston, "Provocations of the Built Environment: Animating Cities in Turkey as *Kemalist,*" *Political Geography* 24, no. 1 (2005).

23. Erdal Şimşek, "Eyüp Belediyesi Kültür ve Turizm Müdürü İrfan Çalışır ile . . . Aristokrat Diyarı: Eyüp," *Akit,* August 28, 1995. *Redd-i miras* is a legal term that applies to situations when heirs disclaim or reject their inheritance.

24. Abu El-Haj, *Facts on the Ground,* 7.

25. Annegret Roelcke has recently addressed this project of history telling. See Annegret Roelcke, "Pre-AKP Urban Rehabilitation Projects for Istanbul's Eyüp Quarter," in *Türkeiforschung im deutschsprachigen Raum* (Wiesbaden: Springer VS, 2020), 208, 13–17.

26. One of the first ways they did this was by renaming the municipality the Eyüpsultan Municipality. They were sued for this name change and later required to change the name back to the Eyüp Municipality.

27. Quoted in *1. Yıl Bülteni* (Istanbul: Eyüpsultan Belediyesi, 1995), 4; *2. Yıl Bülteni* (Istanbul: Eyüpsultan Belediyesi, 1996), 8–9.

28. *3. Yıl Bülteni* (Istanbul: Eyüpsultan Belediyesi, 1997), 6.

29. Ahmet Genç, "Sunuş," in *1. Eyüpsultan Sempozyumu: Tebliğler* (Istanbul: Eyüpsultan Belediyesi, 1997).

30. Özyürek, "Public Memory as Political Battleground."

31. See, for example, Christine Philliou, "When the Clock Strikes Twelve: The Inception of an Ottoman Past in Early Republican Turkey," *Comparative Studies of South Asia, Africa and the Middle East* 31, no. 1 (2011); Philliou, *Turkey: A Past Against History.*

32. Öncü, "Packaging Islam," 69.

33. Jordan Sand, *Tokyo Vernacular: Common Spaces, Local Histories, Found Objects* (Berkeley: University of California Press, 2013), 5.

34. Vuslat Aygün, "Eyüp'te Öze Dönüş" *Vakit* (Istanbul), August 31, 1994. See also Fatima Demircioğlu, "İstanbul'un Manevi Semti Eyüpsultan," *Yeni Şafak,* May 17, 1995.

35. Haskan, *Eyüp Tarihi*. The municipality has published several editions of this history (albeit with a changed name). I cite Haskan, *Eyüp Sultan Tarihi*.

36. Cemal Öğüt, *Eyyüb Sultan* (Istanbul: Eyüp Belediyesi, 1997).

37. Annegret Roelcke expands on the different modes through which Eyüp's Ottoman and Republican histories have been mobilized. Annegret Roelcke, "Two Tales of a Neighborhood: Eyüp as a Stage for the Ottoman Conquest and the Turkish War of Independence," in *Urban Neighbourhood Formations: Boundaries, Narrations, and Intimacies* (London: Routledge, 2020).

38. Şimşek, "Eyüp Belediyesi Kültür ve Turizm Müdürü İrfan Çalışır ile . . . Aristokrat Diyarı: Eyüp."

39. Interview, March 28, 2013. During our first conversation İrfan Bey asked me where I had found the seminar books. He was quite satisfied when I told him that I had found some in libraries in the United States

40. White, *Islamist Mobilization in Turkey*.

41. Ahmet Genç, "Takdim," in *Tarihi, Kültürü ve Sanatıyla Eyüpsultan Sempozyumu II. Tebliğler*, ed. Osman Sak (Istanbul: Eyüp Belediyesi, 1998), 7.

42. Ahmet Genç, "Takdim," in *Tarihi, Kültürü ve Sanatıyla Eyüpsultan Sempozyumu III. Tebliğler 28–30 Mayıs 1999*, ed. Osman Sak (Istanbul: Eyüp Belediyesi, 2000), 7.

43. Ahmet Genç, "Büyük Medeniyetimizin Eyüp'teki İzdüşmeleri," in *Tarihi, Kültürü ve Sanatıyla Eyüpsultan Sempozyumu IX. Tebliğler* (Istanbul: Eyüp Belediyesi, 2005), 9.

44. Ekinci, who died in 2013, was a practicing architect and a former president of the Chamber of Architects (Mimarlar Odası). Eyüp's built environment had been an occasional topic of his newspaper columns even before 1994.

45. Bartu, "Who Owns the Old Quarters?"

46. Amy Mills, "Reading Narratives in City Landscapes: Cultural Identity in Istanbul," *Geographical Review* 95, no. 3 (2006).

47. Oktay Ekinci, "Eyüp'te Tarih, Kültür ve 'Dinsellik'" (History, Culture, and 'Religiosity' in Eyüp), *Cumhuriyet* (Istanbul), 1994. It was likely published in August 1994 because it makes direct reference to Mayor Genç's August 5, 1994, interview.

48. Ekinci, "Eyüp'te Tarih, Kültür ve 'Dinsellik.'"

49. İpek Türeli, "Heritagisation of the 'Ottoman/Turkish House' in the 1970s: Istanbul-Based Actors, Associations and their Networks," *European Journal of Turkish Studies* 19 (2014).

50. İclal Dinçer et al., *İstanbul'da Tarihi ve Doğal Miras Değerleri: Potansiyeller, Riskler ve Koruma Sorunları* (Istanbul: Bilgi Universitesi Yayınları, 2011), 25.

51. Dinçer et al., *İstanbul'da Tarihi ve Doğal Miras Değerleri*, 28. See also İclal Dinçer, "The Impact of Neoliberal Policies on Historic Urban Space: Areas of Urban Renewal in Istanbul," *International Planning Studies* 16, no. 1 (2011): 46.

52. One example of this shifting approach was a report prepared and published with the support of the Aga Khan Award for Architecture. See Melih Kamil et al., "The Eyüp Conservation Area," in *Conservation as Cultural Survival*, ed. Renata Holod (Philadelphia, PA: The Agha Khan Award for Architecture, 1980).

53. The destruction of the market and the broader context of 1950s urban transformation is covered in Hammond, "Mediums of Belief," 43–93.

54. Hülya Yalçın, "Eyüpsultan'da Nezih Eldem'in İzleri," *Mimarlık* 407 (2019): 40.

55. The History Foundation (Tarih Vakfı) houses a detailed architectural survey prepared under the supervision of Orhan Silier and Doğan Kuban. This work overlapped

with a 1993 symposium organized by the History Foundation, published in Tülay Artan, ed., *Eyüp: Dün/Bugün: Sempozyum, 11–12 Aralık 1993* (Istanbul: Tarih Vakfı Yurt Yayınları, 1994). Other examples of plans for restoring Eyüp include Kamil et al., "The Eyüp Conservation Area," and Cengiz Bektaş's 1987 plan for the creation of a toy workshop in Eyüp (SALT Research, Cengiz Bektaş Archive, TCBPTOD002).

56. Nezih Eldem, "Eyüp Sultan Camii ve Yakın Çevresi," in *Tarihi, Kültürü ve Sanatıyla Eyüpsultan Sempozyumu II. Tebliğler*, ed. Osman Sak (Istanbul: Eyüp Belediyesi, 1998), 52.

57. *Eyüp'te Altı Yıl* (Istanbul: Eyüp Belediyesi, 2000), 41.

58. His brother Sadettin Heper was a well-known composer and musician. See Özcan, "Sadettin Heper." His father had been one of the chief stewards of the Mosque of Eyüp Sultan and the family home was located immediately behind the mosque. See Türkmenoğlu, *Eyüp "Bir semte gönül vermek,"* 164–65.

59. Koçu, "Defterdar Mensucat Fabrikası"; Küçükerman, *Feshane, Defterdar Fabrikası*.

60. SALT Research has digitized many documents relating to these efforts, particularly papers donated by Tomur Atagök and Vasıf Kortun.

61. *Hurriyet*, September 22, 1999. See also Zehra Güngör, "Kapalıçarşı'ya rakip geliyor," *Milliyet*, April 30, 1999; *Hurriyet*, June 8, 1999; and *Hurriyet*, October 1, 1999. The complex is described as "Europe's largest culture and arts center" in Savaş Özbey, "İstanbul'u Dinliyorum," *Hurriyet*, October 7, 1999.

62. Karateke, "Interpreting Monuments," 183–99.

63. "51 dükkandan 40'ı kapandı," *Hurriyet*, January 31, 2000. Because of Turkey's rapid inflation at the time, rent had been fixed in dollars rather than liras, leading to major problems when the number of visitors to the market dropped off outside major festival periods.

64. Interview, March 6, 2013.

65. Bora, "Istanbul of the Conqueror."

66. Mehmet Demirkaya, "Ahiret Torpili," *Milliyet* (Istanbul), August 24, 2003.

67. Yael Navaro-Yashin, *The Make-Believe Space: Affective Geography in a Postwar Polity* (Durham, NC: Duke University Press, 2012), 84.

68. Tambar, *The Reckoning of Pluralism*, 16.

69. Çınar, "National History as a Contested Site," 367.

70. Curry, "Toward a Geography of a World without Maps."

71. Deborah G. Martin, "'Place-Framing' as Place making: Constituting a Neighborhood for Organizing and Activism," *Annals of the Association of American Geographers* 93, no. 3 (2003).

## 6. TOURISTS, PILGRIMS, AND THE RULES OF PLACE

1. *Sahur* is the predawn meal before the fast begins during the month of Ramadan.

2. These are supererogatory prayers specific to the month of Ramadan. They are especially observed within Turkey.

3. In July 2013 the exchange rate was roughly $1 to 1.50 liras.

4. *Helal olsun* literally means "Let it be *halal*" (i.e., religiously appropriate, the opposite of *haram*), but the phrase is used in a more general sense to praise someone else's actions in the sense of "well done" or "good for you."

5. Cf. Tim Edensor, "Performing Tourism, Staging Tourism: (Re)Producing Tourist Space and Practice," *Tourist Studies* 1, no. 1 (2001); Tim Edensor, "Mundane Mobilities, Performances and Spaces of Tourism," *Social & Cultural Geography* 8, no. 2 (2007).

6. See Henkel, "The Location of Islam." The Hagia Sophia, also known as the Aya Sofya, was transformed from a museum back into a congregational mosque in 2020. On the debate, see Edhem Eldem, "The Reconversion of the Hagia Sophia into a Mosque: A Historian's Perspective," *Journal of the Ottoman and Turkish Studies Association* 8, no. 1 (2021).

7. See, for example, Marry Lee Nolan and Sidney Nolan, "Religious Sites as Tourism Attractions in Europe," *Annals of Tourism Research* 19, no. 1 (1992); Tim Edensor, *Tourists at the Taj: Performance and Meaning at a Symbolic Site* (London: Routledge, 1998); Rose Aslan, "The Museumification of Rumi's Tomb: Deconstructing Sacred Space at the Mevlana Museum," *Journal of Religious Tourism and Pilgrimage* 2, no. 2 (2014); Thomas Bremer, *Blessed with Tourists: The Borderlands of Religion and Tourism in San Antonio* (Chapel Hill: University of North Carolina Press, 2004).

8. Deeb and Harb, *Leisurely Islam*, 19.

9. Anna Secor, "The Veil and Urban Space in Istanbul: Women's Dress, Mobility, and Islamic Knowledge," *Gender, Place and Culture* 1, no. 9 (2002): 19.

10. Gökarıksel, "The Intimate Politics of Secularism and the Headscarf," 2.

11. Massey, "Places and Their Pasts."

12. The building's history is considerably more complicated. Çiğdem Kafescioğlu provides a detailed discussion of its transformations. Kafescioğlu, *Constantinopolis/Istanbul*, 48–51. Semavi Eyice also provides a detailed description of the complex in "Eyüp Sultan Külliyesi."

13. Irene A. Bierman, *Writing Signs: The Fatimid Public Text* (Berkeley: University of California Press, 1998).

14. Aysun Özkan, "Türbe Ziyaretlerinin Psiko-Sosyolojik Boyutu (Eyüp Sultan Türbesi Örneği)" (M.A. thesis, T.C. Marmara Üniversitesi, 2009), 56–66.

15. Alimen, *Faith and Fashion in Turkey*; Fabio Vicini, "'Do Not Cross Your Legs': Islamic Sociability, Reciprocity and Brotherhood in Turkey," *La Ricerca Folklorica* 69, no. 1 (2014).

16. Asad, *The Idea of an Anthropology of Islam*, 15–16.

17. Henry Carnoy and Jean Nicolaïdès, *Folklore de Constantinople* (Paris: Emile Lechevalier, Libraire, 1894), 157.

18. Interview, June 2013.

19. My discussion is based on fieldwork primarily conducted between 2011 and 2013. The 2020 decision to change the status of the Hagia Sophia from museum to mosque and the ongoing growth of international tourism from Muslim-majority countries have likely shifted the rules of place that operate in Sultanahmet.

20. As with many other parts of Turkey, Eyüp has also become home for a substantial population of people from Syria fleeing its civil war. As of 2020 there were just over twenty thousand Syrians registered as living in the district of Eyüpsultan. See "İstanbul'da en çok Suriyeli hangi ilçede? İşte sayılar," *Sözcü*, February 26, 2020, www.sozcu.com.tr/2020/gundem/istanbulda-en-cok-suriyeli-hangi-ilcede-iste-sayilar-5646012/.

21. Key references include Mills, "The Place of Locality for Identity in the Nation"; Ayşe Öncü, "The Politics of Istanbul's Ottoman Heritage in the Era of Globalism," in *Space, Culture and Power: New Identities in Globalizing Cities*, ed. Petra Weyland and Ayşe Öncü (London: Zed Books, 1997); Jeremy F. Walton, "Practices of Neo-Ottomanism: Making Space and Place Virtuous in Istanbul," in *Orienting Istanbul: Cultural Capital of Europe?*, ed. Deniz Göktürk, Levent Soysal, and İpek Türeli (New York: Routledge, 2010).

22. Zeynep Çelik, "Urban Preservation as Theme Park: The Case of Soğukçeşme Street," in *Streets: Critical Perspectives on Public Space*, ed. Zeynep Çelik, Diane Favro, and Richard Ingersoll (Berkeley: University of California Press, 1994).

23. Houston, "The Brewing of Islamist Modernity."

24. A *rekat* (Ar. rak'a) is a sequence of prayer that results in someone placing their forehead on the ground in secde (Ar. *sujûd*). Two *rekat* is a form of prayer known as *şükür namazı* (prayer of thanks).

25. F. Gökçen Beyinli Dinç, "The Religious and National 'Others' of the State: People, Superstitions and the Nationalization of Islam in Turkey (1925–1970)" (Ph.D. diss., Humboldt University, 2016).

26. There is a broad literature exploring the relationships between gender, architecture, and space/place. See, for example, Tutin Aryanti, "Breaking the Wall, Preserving the Barrier: Gender, Space, and Power in Contemporary Mosque Architecture in Yogyakarta, Indonesia" (PhD diss., University of Illinois at Urbana-Champaign, 2013); Shampa Mazumdar and Sanjoy Mazumdar, "In Mosques and Shrines: Women's Agency in Public Sacred Space," *Journal of Ritual Studies* 16, no. 2 (2002).

27. A *madhab* is a school of Islamic law and teaching. Within the Sunni tradition, there are four: Maliki, Hanbali, Hanafi, and Shafi'i. The primary legal tradition in Turkey today is Hanafi, but many people with roots in eastern Anatolia have been raised within Shafi'i communities. I encountered this teaching informally in conversation with interlocutors.

28. I suspect—although did not establish—that this holds true for women as well if they make contact with men.

29. Emphasis in the original.

30. Turam, "The Primacy of Space in Politics," 411.

31. Deeb, *An Enchanted Modern*, 20.

32. Cf. Dydia DeLyser, "Authenticity on the Ground: Engaging the Past in a California Ghost Town," *Annals of the Association of American Geographers* 89, no. 4 (1999).

33. Paulo G. Pinto, "Pilgrimage, Commodities, and Religious Objectification: The Making of Transnational Shiism between Iran and Syria," *Comparative Studies of South Asia, Africa and the Middle East* 27, no. 1 (2007), https://doi.org/10.1215/1089201x-2006-047.

34. Talal Asad, *Formations of the Secular: Christianity, Islam, Modernity* (Stanford, CA: Stanford University Press, 2003), 222; Deeb, *An Enchanted Modern*.

35. Massey, "Places and Their Pasts," 186 (emphasis in the original).

36. Jacobs, "A Geography of Big Things"; Gillian Rose, Monica Degen, and Begum Basdas, "More on 'Big Things': Building Events and Feelings," *Transactions of the Institute of British Geographers* 35, no. 3 (2010).

37. Loretta Lees, "Towards A Critical Geography of Architecture: The Case of an Ersatz Colosseum," *Cultural Geographies* 8, no. 1 (January 1, 2001): 55, https://doi.org/10.1177/096746080100800103, http://cgj.sagepub.com/cgi/content/abstract/8/1/51.

## 7. SHARING PLACE

1. Iftar is the meal eaten at sundown to break the fast during Ramadan.

2. The arcades surrounding the Kaaba in Mecca were built by the Ottoman Empire in the late sixteenth century; their destruction in 2011 by Saudi Arabian authorities was criticized in the Turkish press at the time. Murat Bardakçı, "Kâbe'nin Revakları," *Habertürk*, November 9, 2011, www.haberturk.com/yazarlar/murat-bardakci/686625-kabenin-revaklari.

3. Scholars have examined the temporal dimensions of Ramadan in a variety of ways. See, for example, Walter Armbrust, "The Riddle of Ramadan," in *Everyday Life in the Muslim Middle East*, ed. Donna Lee Bowen and Evelyn A. Early (Bloomington: Indiana University

Press, 2002); Adam Mestyan, "Upgrade? Power and Sound during Ramadan and 'Id al-Fitr in the Nineteenth-Century Ottoman Arab Provinces," *Comparative Studies of South Asia, Africa and the Middle East* 37, no. 2 (2017), https://doi.org/10.1215/1089201x-4132893; Schielke, "Being Good in Ramadan."

4. Birgit Meyer, "Introduction: From Imagined Communities to Aesthetic Formations: Religious Mediations, Sensational Forms, and Styles of Binding," in *Aesthetic Formations: Media, Religion, and the Senses*, ed. Birgit Meyer (New York: Palgrave Macmillan, 2009), 7.

5. Meyer, "Mediation and Immediacy," 29.

6. According to the official Islamic calendar in Turkey, the month of Ramadan spanned from July 20 to August 18 in 2012, and from July 9 to August 7 in 2013.

7. This schedule has been in place since March 1984, when the first municipal elections were organized following the 1980 military coup and the country's system of municipal governance was completely reorganized.

8. Although local party organizations can be consulted about their preferred nominee, Kavuncu's nomination seemed to be the result of a decision made at higher levels of the party that was then transmitted to the district municipality level. It is probable that his arrival in 2009 was linked to the growing power of Fethullah Gülen's movement in local politics.

9. A full evaluation of the Gülen Movement's activities in Eyüp, both before Kavuncu's 2009 election and following the 2016 coup attempt, is outside the scope of this chapter.

10. The growth of the Gülen Movement in Eyüp parallels its wider role in the rise of the AKP between 2002 and 2013. For more on the movement, see Joshua D. Hendrick, *Gülen: The Ambiguous Politics of Market Islam in Turkey and the World* (New York: New York University Press, 2013).

11. Caroline Tee, "The Gülen Movement and the AK Party: The Rise and Fall of a Turkish Islamist Alliance," in *Turkey's July 15th Coup: What Happened and Why*, ed. M. Hakan Yavuz and Bayram Balcı (Salt Lake City: University of Utah Press, 2018).

12. Carel Bertram, *Imagining the Turkish House: Collective Visions of Home* (Austin: University of Texas Press, 2008), 191–205.

13. Gürbüz Özdemir, "Belediye İktisadi Teşebbüslerinin Özelleştirilmesi," *Sayıştay Dergisi* 71 (2008).

14. Henkel, "The Location of Islam."

15. Turam, "The Primacy of Space in Politics"; Gökarıksel, "The Intimate Politics of Secularism and the Headscarf"; Secor, "The Veil and Urban Space in Istanbul."

16. Whether the 2021 opening of the Taksim Mosque has changed these geographies remains open to question.

17. The *ney* is a type of flute often associated with traditional Turkish music and religious uses. The *sema* is a type of dance associated with Sufi traditions in Turkey, especially those of the Mevlevi order.

18. Banu Şenay, "The Fall and Rise of the Ney: From the Sufi Lodge to the World Stage," *Ethnomusicology Forum* 23, no. 3 (2014).

19. There is an instructive comparison to the iftar meals known as *yeryüzü sofraları* that were organized by the Anti-Capitalist Muslims during the 2013 Gezi Park Protests. See, for example, Cengiz Haksöz, "Eating in Gezi, Devoured by Gezi: Food and Resistance in Istanbul Gezi Park Protests," in *Another Brick in the Barricade: The Gezi Resistance and Its Aftermath*, ed. Güneş Koç and Harun Aksu (Bremen: Wiener Verlag für Sozialforschung, 2015), 65–68.

20. This small encounter speaks to recent discussions of religion and everyday life in Istanbul. Banu Gökarıksel and Anna Secor, "Post-Secular Geographies and the Problem of Pluralism: Religion and Everyday Life in Istanbul, Turkey," *Political Geography* 46, no. 1 (2015): 21–30.

21. Tuna Kuyucu and Özlem Ünsal, "'Urban Transformation' as State-Led Property Transfer: An Analysis of Two Cases of Urban Renewal in Istanbul," *Urban Studies* 47, no. 7 (2010); Ayfer Bartu and Biray Kolluoğlu, "Emerging Spaces of Neoliberalism: A Gated Town and a Public Housing Project in Istanbul," *New Perspectives on Turkey* 39 (2008); Gökarıksel, "The Intimate Politics of Secularism and the Headscarf"; Ozan Karaman, "Urban Neoliberalism with Islamic Characteristics," *Urban Studies* 50, no. 16 (2013); Angell, Hammond, and van Dobben Schoon, "Assembling Istanbul"; Ayfer Bartu Candan and Cenk Özbay, eds., *Yeni İstanbul Çalışmaları: Sınırlar, Mücadeler, Açılımlar* (Istanbul: Metis Yayınevi, 2014).

22. See, for example, Gökarıksel and Secor, "Islamic-ness in the Life of a Commodity"; Banu Gökarıksel and Anna Secor, "'Even I Was Tempted': The Moral Ambivalence and Ethical Practice of Veiling-Fashion in Turkey," *Annals of the Association of American Geographers* 102, no. 4 (2012); Deniz Göktürk, Levent Soysal, and İpek Türeli, eds., *Orienting Istanbul: Cultural Capital of Europe?* (New York: Routledge, 2010); Mills, *Streets of Memory;* Turam, "The Primacy of Space in Politics"; Berna Turam, *Gaining Freedoms: Claiming Space in Istanbul and Berlin* (Stanford, CA: Stanford University Press, 2015).

23. The events in Gezi Park erupted in late May 2013. Initially organized around a local defense of the park from bulldozers, it quickly transformed into one of the largest protests in Turkey's history. The park and Taksim Square were cleared of protestors in mid-June. Ramadan began on the night of July 9, 2013. The literature on the protests is expansive and wide-ranging. See, for example, Anthony Alessandrini, Nazan Üstündağ, and Emrah Yildiz, eds., *"Resistance Everywhere": The Gezi Protests and Dissident Visions of Turkey* (Washington, DC: Tadween Publishing, 2014); Umut Özkırımlı, ed., *The Making of a Protest Movement in Turkey: #Occupygezi* (New York: Palgrave Macmillan, 2014); Isabel David and Kumru F. Toktamış, eds., *"Everywhere Taksim": Sowing the Seeds for a New Turkey at Gezi* (Amsterdam: Amsterdam University Press, 2015); Kaan Ağartan, "Review Article: Politics of the Square: Remembering Gezi Park Protests Five Years Later," *New Perspectives on Turkey* 58 (2018).

## CONCLUSION

I am grateful to Nidayi Sevim for helping me with the translation of the epigraph.

1. Annegret Roelcke discusses changes between Kavuncu and Aydın's respective "branding" of Eyüpsultan. Annegret Roelcke, "Constructing the Capital of Peace: Changing Branding Strategies for Istanbul's Eyüp Quarter," *Middle East—Topics & Arguments* 12 (2019), https://doi.org/10.17192/meta.2019.12.7931.

2. İHA, "Torba Yasadan Bu Da Çıktı: Artık Eyüp Sultan Diyeceksiniz," *Cumhuriyet,* October 20, 2017, www.cumhuriyet.com.tr/haber/torba-yasadan-bu-da-cikti-artik-eyup-sultan-diyeceksiniz-848881.

3. DHA, "Müze Olacak Feshane'nin Restorasyonunun Yüzde 60'ı Tamamlandı," *Cumhuriyet,* July 24, 2021, www.cumhuriyet.com.tr/haber/muze-olacak-feshanenin-restorasyonunun-yuzde-60i-tamamlandi-1854854.

4. A recent short article describes some of the changes on Kızılmescit Boulevard, a central street a short walk from the Mosque of Eyüp Sultan. Meltem Bali, "Kentsel Yenileme ve Soylulaştırma Eşiğinde Bir Sokağın Tanzimi: Eyüp Sultan Kızılmescit Sokak," *Journal of Environmental and Natural Studies* 2, no. 3 (2020).

5. Compare Carlo Ginzburg's observation: "By narrowing the scope of our inquiry, we hope to understand more." Carlo Ginzburg, "Latitude, Slaves, the Bible: An Experiment in Microhistory," *Critical Inquiry* 31, no. 3 (2005): 665. The epigraph to this section also appears in the article on p. 683.

6. Amy Mills and Timur Hammond, "The Interdisciplinary Spatial Turn and the Discipline of Geography in Middle East Studies," in *Middle East Studies for the New Millennium: Infrastructures of Knowledge*, ed. Seteney Shami and Cynthia Miller-Idriss (New York: New York University Press, 2016).

7. Cf., Helga Leitner, Eric Sheppard, and Kristin M. Sziarto, "The Spatialities of Contentious Politics," *Transactions of the Institute of British Geographers* 33, no. 1 (2008): 158.

8. Although for exceptions see Antoinette Burton, "Introduction: Archive Fever, Archive Stories," in *Archive Stories: Facts, Fictions, and the Writing of History*, ed. Antoinette Burton (Durham, NC: Duke University Press, 2005); Ebru Aykut, Nurçin İleri, and Fatih Artvinli, eds., *Tarihçilerden Başka Bir Hikâye* (Istanbul: Can Yayınları, 2019).

9. Donna Haraway, "Situated Knowledges: The Science Question in Feminism and the Privilege of Partial Perspective," in *Simians, Cyborgs, and Women: The Reinvention of Nature*, ed. Donna Haraway (New York: Routledge, 1991).

10. For versions of this critique, see Timothy Mitchell, "Deterritorialization and the Crisis of Social Science," in *Localizing Knowledge in a Globalizing World: Recasting the Area Studies Debate*, ed. Ali Mirsepassi, Amrita Basu, and Frederick Weaver (Syracuse, NY: Syracuse University Press, 2003); John Agnew and James S. Duncan, eds., *The Power of Place: Bringing Together Geographical and Sociological Imaginations* (Boston: Unwin Hyman, 1989).

11. The argument below is guided in part by Colin McFarlane's discussion of assemblage and context. Colin McFarlane, "On Context," *City* 15, no. 3–4 (2011).

12. Although we work within slightly different conceptual traditions, Christopher Houston makes this point clearly in developing a critique of "mainstream" social science approaches. Houston, *Istanbul, City of the Fearless*.

13. Bashir, "On Islamic Time."

14. Asu Aksoy, "Riding the Storm: 'New Istanbul,'" *City* 16, no. 1–2 (2012): 94; Asu Aksoy, "Istanbul's Worldliness," in *Public Istanbul: Spaces and Spheres of the Urban*, ed. Frank Eckardt and Kathrin Wildner (Bielefeld: transcript Verlag, 2008), 218.

15. Tambar, *The Reckoning of Pluralism*, 175.

16. Mol, *The Body Multiple*, 184.

# BIBLIOGRAPHY

*1. Yıl Bülteni.* Edited by Zekeriya Yıldız. Istanbul: Eyüpsultan Belediyesi, 1995.

*2. Yıl Bülteni.* Edited by Zekeriya Yıldız. Istanbul: Eyüpsultan Belediyesi, 1996.

*3. Yıl Bülteni.* Edited by Zekeriya Yıldız. Istanbul: Eyüpsultan Belediyesi, 1997.

Abi, Ceren. "Digging Deeper: Cultural Property in the Ottoman Empire During the Great War and Allied Occupation 1914–1923." PhD diss., University of California, Los Angeles, 2019.

Abu El-Haj, Nadia. *Facts on the Ground: Archaeological Practice and Territorial Self-Fashioning in Israeli Society.* Chicago: University of Chicago Press, 2001.

Adalet, Begüm. *Hotels and Highways: The Construction of Modernization Theory in Cold War Turkey.* Stanford, CA: Stanford University Press, 2018.

Adamson, Sydney. "The Mosque of Eyoub." *Harper's Magazine*, June 1913, 28–40.

Aday, Erdal. "Kütahya Ile Türbe ve Yatırları Etrafında Oluşan İnanç ve Uygulamalar." PhD diss., Balıkesir University, 2013.

Ağartan, Kaan. "Review Article: Politics of the Square: Remembering Gezi Park Protests Five Years Later." *New Perspectives on Turkey* 58 (2018): 201–17.

Agnew, John, and James S. Duncan, eds. *The Power of Place: Bringing Together Geographical and Sociological Imaginations.* Boston: Unwin Hyman, 1989.

Ahmed, Shahab. *What Is Islam? The Importance of Being Islamic.* Princeton, NJ: Princeton University Press, 2017.

Ahmet, Niyazi. "Eyüp." *Yedigün*, February 17, 1941.

Ahunbay, Zeynep. "Genç Cumhuriyetin Koruma Alanındaki Öncülerinden Yüksek Mimar Ali Saim Ülgen (1913–1963)." SALT Research, June 5, 2015. http://blog.saltonline.org /post/120786511984/asu-zeynepahunbay.

Ajansı, Anadolu. "İlim Yayma Cemiyeti: Hiçbir Cemaat Ya Da Tarikatla Bağımız Yok." *Risale Haber*, September 7, 2019. www.risalehaber.com/ilim-yayma-cemiyeti-hicbir-cemaat -ya-da-tarikatla-bagimiz-yok-360550h.htm.

Akcan, Esra. *Architecture in Translation: Germany, Turkey, & the Modern House.* Durham, NC: Duke University Press, 2012.

Akın, Yiğit. *When the War Came Home: The Ottomans' Great War and the Devastation of an Empire.* Stanford, CA: Stanford University Press, 2018.

Akpınar, Ipek, ed. *Osmanlı Başkentinden Küreselleşen İstanbul'a: Mimarlık ve Kent, 1910–2010.* Istanbul: Osmanlı Bankası Arşiv ve Araştırma Merkezi, 2010.

———. "The Rebuilding of İstanbul Revisited: Foreign Planners in the Early Republican Years." *New Perspectives on Turkey* 50 (2014): 59–92.

Aksoy, Asu. "Istanbul's Worldliness." In *Public Istanbul: Spaces and Spheres of the Urban,* edited by Frank Eckardt and Kathrin Wildner, 215–32. Bielefeld: transcript Verlag, 2008.

———. "Riding the Storm: 'New Istanbul.'" *City* 16, no. 1–2 (2012): 93–111.

Aktepe, Münir. "Çandarlı Halil Paşa." In *TDV İslam Ansiklopedisi,* 212–13. Istanbul: Türkiye Diyanet Vakfı, 1993.

Aktuç, Avni. "Eyüpsultan." *Hayat,* April 11, 1958, 8–9.

Albera, Dionigi, and Benoît Fliche. "Muslim Devotional Practices in Christian Shrines: The Case of Istanbul." In *Sharing Sacred Spaces in the Mediterranean,* edited by Dionigi Albera and Maria Couroucli, 94–117. Bloomington: Indiana University Press, 2012.

Alessandrini, Anthony, Nazan Üstündağ, and Emrah Yildiz, eds. *"Resistance Everywhere": The Gezi Protests and Dissident Visions of Turkey.* Washington, DC: Tadween Publishing, 2014.

Algül, Hüseyin. "Ebû Eyyûb El-Ensârî." In *TDV İslam Ansiklopedisi,* 123–25. Istanbul: Türkiye Diyanet Vakfı, 1994.

Alimen, Nazlı. *Faith and Fashion in Turkey: Consumption, Politics and Islamic Identities.* London: I.B. Tauris, 2018.

Allom, Thomas, and Robert Walsh. *Constantinople and the Scenery of the Seven Churches of Asia.* London: Peter Jackson, Late Fisher, Son, & Co., 1840.

Altınay, Rüstem Ertuğ. "The Queer Archivist as Political Dissident: Rereading the Ottoman Empire in the Works of Reşad Ekrem Koçu." *Radical History Review* 122 (2015): 89–102.

Alus, Sermet Muhtar. "Eyüp Oyuncakları." *Tarih Hazinesi,* December, 1951, 701–2. https://archives.saltresearch.org/handle/123456789/24485.

Amin, Shahid. *Conquest and Community: The Afterlife of Warrior Saint Ghazi Miyan.* Chicago: University of Chicago Press, 2016.

Angell, Elizabeth, Timur Hammond, and Danielle van Dobben Schoon. "Assembling Istanbul: Buildings and Bodies in a World City: Introduction." *City* 18, no. 6 (2014): 644–54.

Antrim, Zayde. *Routes and Realms: The Power of Place in the Early Islamic World.* Oxford: Oxford University Press, 2012.

Arı, Asım. "Tevhid-i Tedrisat ve Laik Eğitim." *G.Ü. Gazi Eğitim Fakültesi Dergisi* 22, no. 2 (2002): 181–92.

Armbrust, Walter. "The Riddle of Ramadan." In *Everyday Life in the Muslim Middle East,* edited by Donna Lee Bowen and Evelyn A. Early, 335–48. Bloomington: Indiana University Press, 2002.

Artan, Tülay, ed. *18. Yüzyıl Kadı Sicilleri Işığında Eyüp'te Sosyal Yaşam.* Istanbul: Tarih Vakfı Yurt Yayınları, 1998.

———. "Eyüp." In *TDV İslam Ansiklopedisi,* 1–6. Istanbul: Türkiye Diyanet Vakfı, 1995.

———, ed. *Eyüp: Dün/Bugün: Sempozyum, 11–12 Aralık 1993.* Istanbul: Tarih Vakfı Yurt Yayınları, 1994.

———. "Eyüp'ün Bir Diğer Çehresi: Sayfiye ve Sahilsaraylar." In *Eyüp: Dün/Bugün*, edited by Tülay Artan, 106–14. Istanbul: Tarih Vakfı Yurt Yayınları, 1993.

Artman, Vincent M. "Nation, Religion, and Theology: What Do We Mean When We Say 'Being Kyrgyz Means Being Muslim?'" *Central Asian Affairs* 5, no. 3 (2018): 191–212. https://doi.org/10.1163/22142290-00503001.

Aryanti, Tutin. "Breaking the Wall, Preserving the Barrier: Gender, Space, and Power in Contemporary Mosque Architecture in Yogyakarta, Indonesia." PhD diss., University of Illinois at Urbana-Champaign, 2013.

Asad, Talal. *Formations of the Secular: Christianity, Islam, Modernity*. Stanford, CA: Stanford University Press, 2003.

———. *Genealogies of Religion: Discipline and Reasons of Power in Christianity*. Baltimore, MD: Johns Hopkins University Press, 1993.

———. *The Idea of an Anthropology of Islam*. Occasional Paper Series. Washington, DC: Center for Contemporary Arab Studies, Georgetown University, 1986.

———. "Thinking about Religion through Wittgenstein." *Critical Times* 3, no. 3 (2020): 403–42.

Aslan, Rose. "The Museumification of Rumi's Tomb: Deconstructing Sacred Space at the Mevlana Museum." *Journal of Religious Tourism and Pilgrimage* 2, no. 2 (2014): 1–16.

Atacan, Fulya. "Explaining Religious Politics at the Crossroad: AKP-SP." *Turkish Studies* 6, no. 2 (2007): 187–99. https://doi.org/10.1080/14683840500119510.

Atkinson, David, and Denis Cosgrove. "Urban Rhetoric and Embodied Identities: City, Nation, and Empire at the Vittorio Emanuele II Monument in Rome, 1870–1945." *Annals of the Association of American Geographers* 88, no. 1 (1998): 28–49.

Aydin, Cemil. *The Idea of the Muslim World: A Global Intellectual History*. Cambridge, MA: Harvard University Press, 2017.

Aydin, Cemil, and Burhanettin Duran. "Arnold J. Toynbee and Islamism in Cold War–Era Turkey: Civilizationism in the Writings of Sezai Karakoç." *Comparative Studies of South Asia, Africa and the Middle East* 35, no. 2 (2015): 310–23. https://doi.org/10.1215/1089201x-3139084.

Aygün, Vuslat. "Eyüp'te Öze Dönüş." *Vakit* (Istanbul), August 31, 1994.

Ayhan, Halis. "İmam-Hatip Lisesi." In *TDV İslam Ansiklopedisi*, 191–94. Istanbul: Türkiye Diyanet Vakfı, 2000.

Aykut, Ebru, Nurçin İleri, and Fatih Artvinli, eds. *Tarihçilerden Başka Bir Hikâye*. Istanbul: Can Yayınları, 2019.

Aynur, Hatice. "İstanbul'da Kadınların Yaptırdığı Çeşmeler Üzerine—Istanbul Fountains Commissioned by Women—Les Fontaines d'Istanbul Commandées par des Femmes." Voyvoda Caddesi Toplantıları 2005–2006, Istanbul, 2006.

Aytürk, İlker, and Laurent Mignon. "Paradoxes of a Cold War Sufi Woman: Sâmiha Ayverdi between Islam, Nationalism, and Modernity." *New Perspectives on Turkey* 49 (2013): 57–89.

Ayvansarayî Hüseyin Efendi. *Hadikatü'l-Cevami: İstanbul Camileri ve Diğer Dini-Sivil Mimari Yapılar [The Garden of the Mosques]*. Istanbul: İşaret Yayınları, 2001.

Ayvazoğlu, Beşir. "Mehmed Rauf 'Eyüp Yolunda.'" In *12. Uluslararası Eyüp Sultan Sempozyumu: Tebliğler*, 100–109, 2016.

Azak, Umut. "Secularism in Turkey as a Nationalist Search for Vernacular Islam: The Ban on the Call to Prayer in Arabic (1932–1950)." *Revue des mondes musulmans et de la Méditerranée* 124 (2008): 161–79. https://doi.org/10.4000/remmm.6025.

Bacque-Grammont, Jean-Louis. "Eyüp Mezarlıklarının İncelenmesi Üzerine Düşünceler." In *Eyüp: Dün/Bugün*, edited by Tülay Artan, 62–105. Istanbul: Tarih Vakfı Yurt Yayınları, 1994.

"Badr, Battle of." In *The Oxford Dictionary of Islam*, edited by John Esposito. London: Oxford University Press, 2003.

Bahrani, Zainab, Zeynep Çelik, and Edhem Eldem, eds. *Scramble for the Past: A Story of Archaeology in the Ottoman Empire, 1785–1914*. Istanbul: SALT, 2011.

Bakker, Karen. "Water: Political, Biopolitical, Material." *Social Studies of Science* 42, no. 4 (2012): 616–23. https://doi.org/10.1177/0306312712441396.

Bali, Meltem. "Kentsel Yenileme ve Soylulaştırma Eşiğinde Bir Sokağın Tanzimi: Eyüp Sultan Kızılmescit Sokak." *Journal of Environmental and Natural Studies* 2, no. 3 (2020): 116–32.

Bardakçı, Murat. "Kâbe'nin Revakları." *Habertürk*, November 9, 2011. www.haberturk.com /yazarlar/murat-bardakci/686625-kabenin-revaklari.

Barkey, Karen. "Religious Pluralism, Shared Sacred Sites, and the Ottoman Empire." In *Choreographies of Shared Sacred Sites: Religion, Politics, and Conflict Resolution*, edited by Elazar Barkan and Karen Barkey, 33–68. New York: Columbia University Press, 2015.

Barnes, Jessica. *Cultivating the Nile: The Everyday Politics of Water in Egypt*. Durham, NC: Duke University Press, 2014.

Barnes, Trevor J., and James S. Duncan, eds. *Writing Worlds: Discourse, Text, and Metaphor in the Representation of Landscape*. London: Routledge, 1992.

Bartlett, Robert. *Why Can the Dead Do Such Great Things? Saints and Worshippers from the Martyrs to the Reformation*. Princeton, NJ: Princeton University Press, 2015.

Bartu, Ayfer. "Who Owns the Old Quarters? Rewriting Histories in a Global Era." In *Istanbul: Between the Global and the Local*, edited by Çağlar Keyder, 31–45. Lanham, MD: Rowman & Littlefield, 1999.

Bartu, Ayfer, and Biray Kolluoğlu. "Emerging Spaces of Neoliberalism: A Gated Town and a Public Housing Project in Istanbul." *New Perspectives on Turkey* 39 (2008): 5–46.

Bartu Candan, Ayfer, and Cenk Özbay, eds. *Yeni İstanbul Çalışmaları: Sınırlar, Mücadeler, Açılımlar*. Istanbul: Metis Yayınevi, 2014.

Bashir, Shahzad. "The Living Dead of Tabriz: Explorations in Chronotopic Imagination." *History of Religions* 59, no. 3 (2020): 169–92.

———. "On Islamic Time: Rethinking Chronology in the Historiography of Muslim Societies." *History and Theory* 53, no. 4 (2014): 519–44.

Batuman, Bülent. "'Early Republican Ankara': Struggle over Historical Representation and the Politics of Urban Historiography." *Journal of Urban History* 37, no. 5 (2011): 661–79.

———. *New Islamist Architecture and Urbanism: Negotiating Nation and Islam through Built Environment in Turkey*. New York: Routledge, 2018.

Bayar, Salim. "Yeni Plana Göre Eyüp Yemyeşil Bir Site Oluyor." *Tercüman* (Istanbul), 1958.

Behrens-Abouseif, Doris. "Sabîl." In *Encyclopedia of Islam, Second Edition*, edited by P. Bearman, Th. Bianquis, C. E. Bosworth, E. van Donzel, and W. P. Heinrichs. Leiden: Brill, 2012.

Bencoşar, M. Akif. *Eyüp Sultan*. Istanbul: Ercan Matbaası, 1958.

Benkheira, Mohammed Hocine, Catherine Mayeur-Jaouen, and Jacqueline Sublet. *L'Animal en Islam*. Paris: Les Indes Savantes, 2005.

Bertram, Carel. *Imagining the Turkish House: Collective Visions of Home*. Austin: University of Texas Press, 2008.

Beyatlı, Yahya Kemal. *Aziz İstanbul*. Istanbul: İstanbul Fethi Cemiyeti, 2010.

———. "Bir Rüya'da Gördüğümüz Eyüp." In *Aziz İstanbul*, 106–10. Istanbul: İstanbul Fethi Cemiyeti, 2010.

———. "Bir Rüya'da Gördüğümüz Eyüp." *Tevhid-i Efkâr*, May 5, 1922.

———. *Siyasi ve Edebi Portreler*. Istanbul: Yahya Kemal Enstitüsü, 1968.

Beyinli Dinç, Gökçen. "677 Sayılı Kanun, Türbeleri 'Millileştirme' ve Yıkıcı Sonuçları: Geç Osmanlı'dan Cumhuriyet'e Türbedarlık." *Cihannüma* 3, no. 2 (2017): 113–37.

———. "Reframing Turkey, Istanbul and National Identity: Ottoman History, 'Chosen People' and the Opening of Shrines in 1950." *Nations and Nationalism* 28, no. 4 (2022): 1428–43. https://doi.org/10.1111/nana.12824.

———. "The Religious and National 'Others' of the State: People, Superstitions and the Nationalization of Islam in Turkey (1925–1970)." PhD diss., Humboldt University, 2016.

Bierman, Irene A. *Writing Signs: The Fatimid Public Text*. Berkeley: University of California Press, 1998.

Bilge, Mustafa, and Hamza Akbulut. "İlim Yayma Cemiyeti." In *TDV İslam Ansiklopedisi*, 637–38. Istanbul: Türkiye Diyanet Vakfı, 2016.

Bilsel, Cana. "Henri Prost's Planning Works in Istanbul (1936–1951): Transforming the Structure of a City through Master Plans and Urban Operations." In *From the Imperial Capital to the Republican Modern City: Henri Prost's Planning of Istanbul (1936–1951)*, edited by Cana Bilsel and Pierre Pinon, 101–65. Istanbul: Istanbul Research Institute, 2010.

Bilsel, Cana, and Pierre Pinon, eds. *From the Imperial Capital to the Republican Modern City: Henri Prost's Planning of Istanbul (1936–1951)*. Istanbul: Istanbul Research Institute, 2010.

Birinci, Necat. "Ruşen Eşref'in Yazılarında İstanbul Sevgisi." *Kubbealtı Akademi Mecmuası* 12, no. 1 (1983): 23–46.

Blecher, Joel. *Said the Prophet of God: Hadith Commentary across a Millennium*. Berkeley: University of California Press, 2018.

Bonine, Michael E. "The Morphogenesis of Iranian Cities." *Annals of the Association of American Geographers* 69, no. 2 (1979): 208–24.

———. "The Sacred Direction and City Structure: A Preliminary Analysis of the Islamic Cities of Morocco." *Muqarnas* 7, no. 1 (1990): 50–72.

———. "Waqf and Its Influence on the Built Environment in the Medina of the Islamic Middle Eastern City." In *Urban Space in the Middle Ages and the Early Modern Age*, edited by Albrecht Classen, 615–44. Berlin: Walter de Gruyter, 2009.

Bora, Tanıl. *Cereyanlar: Türkiye'de Siyasî İdeolojiler*. Istanbul: İletişim, 2021.

———. "Istanbul of the Conqueror: The 'Alternative Global City' Dreams of Political Islam." In *Istanbul: Between the Global and the Local*, edited by Çaglar Keyder, 47–58. Lanham, MD: Rowman & Littlefield, 1999.

Boyar, Ebru, and Kate Fleet. *A Social History of Ottoman Istanbul*. Cambridge: Cambridge University Press, 2010.

Bozdoğan, Sibel. *Modernism and Nation Building: Turkish Architectural Culture in the Early Republic*. Seattle: University of Washington Press, 2001.

———. "Turkey's Postwar Modernism: A Retrospective Overview of Architecture, Urbanism and Politics in the 1950s." In *Mid-Century Modernism in Turkey: Architecture across Cultures in the 1950s and 1960s*, edited by Meltem Ö. Gürel, 9–25. London: Routledge, 2015.

Bremer, Thomas. *Blessed with Tourists: The Borderlands of Religion and Tourism in San Antonio*. Chapel Hill: University of North Carolina Press, 2004.

Brockett, Gavin. *How Happy to Call Oneself a Turk: Provincial Newspapers and the Negotiation of a Muslim National Identity*. Austin: University of Texas Press, 2011.

———. "When Ottomans Become Turks: Commemorating the Conquest of Constantinople and Its Contribution to World History." *American Historical Review* 119, no. 2 (2014): 399–443.

Burak Adli, Feyza. "Trajectories of Modern Sufism: An Ethnohistorical Study of the Rifai Order and Social Change in Turkey." PhD diss., Boston University, 2020.

Burton, Antoinette. "Introduction: Archive Fever, Archive Stories." In *Archive Stories: Facts, Fictions, and the Writing of History*, edited by Antoinette Burton, 1–24. Durham, NC: Duke University Press, 2005.

Çakan, İsmail Lütfi. "Babanzâde Ahmed Naim." In *TDV İslam Ansiklopedisi*, 375–76. Istanbul: Türkiye Diyanet Vakfı, 1991.

———. "Fetih Hadisi ve Akşemseddin'in Fetihteki Yeri." Paper presented at the Akşemseddin Sempozyumu Bildirileri, 1990.

Calverly, E. E. "Nafs." In *Encyclopedia of Islam, Second Edition*, edited by P. Bearman, Th. Bianquis, C. E. Bosworth, E. van Donzel, and W. P. Heinrichs. Leiden: Brill, 2012.

Cameron, Emilie. *Far Off Metal River: Inuit Lands, Settler Stories, and the Making of the Contemporary Arctic*. Vancouver: UBC Press, 2015.

———. "New Geographies of Story and Storytelling." *Progress in Human Geography* 36, no. 5 (2012): 573–92.

Can, Lâle. *Spiritual Subjects: Central Asian Pilgrims and the Ottoman Hajj at the End of Empire*. Stanford, CA: Stanford University Press, 2020.

Carnoy, Henry, and Jean Nicolaidès. *Folklore de Constantinople*. Paris: Emile Lechevalier, Libraire, 1894.

Casey, Edward S. *Getting Back into Place: Toward a Renewed Understanding of the Place-World*. 2nd ed. Bloomington: Indiana University Press, 2009.

Çavdar, Ayşe. "Building, Marketing and Living in an Islamic Gated Community: Novel Configurations of Class and Religion in Istanbul." *International Journal of Urban and Regional Research* 40, no. 3 (2016): 507–23. https://doi.org/10.1111/1468-2427.12364.

Çelik, Zeynep. *The Remaking of Istanbul: Portrait of an Ottoman City in the Nineteenth Century*. Seattle: University of Washington Press, 1986.

———. "Urban Preservation as Theme Park: The Case of Soğukçeşme Street." In *Streets: Critical Perspectives on Public Space*, edited by Zeynep Çelik, Diane Favro, and Richard Ingersoll, 83–94. Berkeley: University of California Press, 1994.

Cephanecigil, Vesile Gül, and Günkut Akın. "Geç Osmanlı ve Erken Cumhuriyet Dönemi Türkiyesinde Milliyetçilik ve Mimarlık Tarihi." *İTÜ Dergisi/A* 9, no. 2 (2010): 29–40.

Çetinkaya, Bayram Ali. "Musa Kazım Efendi'nin Dini, Siyasi ve Felsefi Düşüncesi." *C.Ü. İlahiyat Fakültesi Dergisi* 9, no. 2 (2007): 75–141.

Chabbi, Jacqueline. "Zamzam." In *Encyclopedia of Islam, Second Edition*, edited by P. Bearman, Th. Bianquis, C. E. Bosworth, E. van Donzel and W. P. Heinrichs. Leiden: Brill, 2012.

Chidester, David. *Religion: Material Dynamics*. Berkeley: University of California Press, 2018.

Chidester, David, and Edward Tabor Linenthal. *American Sacred Space*. Bloomington: Indiana University Press, 1995.

Çimen, Demet Kılınç. "Halk Inanışları Açısından İstanbul'daki Kilise ve Ayazmalar." MA thesis, Ankara Üniversitesi, 2010.

Çınar, Alev. *Modernity, Islam, and Secularism in Turkey: Bodies, Places, and Time*. Minneapolis: University of Minnesota Press, 2005.

———. "National History as a Contested Site: The Conquest of Istanbul and Islamist Negotiations of the Nation." *Comparative Studies in Society and History* 43, no. 2 (2001): 364–91.

Çinar, Menderes, and Ipek Gencel Sezgin. "Islamist Political Engagement in the Early Years of Multi-Party Politics in Turkey: 1945–60." *Turkish Studies* 14, no. 2 (2013): 329–45. https://doi.org/10.1080/14683849.2013.802921.

Çizakça, Murat. *A History of Philanthropic Foundations: The Islamic World from the Seventh Century to the Present*. Istanbul: Boğaziçi University Press, 2000.

Çolak, Yilmaz. "Ottomanism vs. Kemalism: Collective Memory and Cultural Pluralism in 1990s Turkey." *Middle Eastern Studies* 42, no. 4 (2006): 587–602.

cooke, miriam, and Bruce Lawrence, eds. *Muslim Networks from Hajj to Hip Hop*. Chapel Hill: University of North Carolina Press, 2005.

Coşkun, Feray. "Osmanlı İstanbulu'nda Müstesnâ bir Ziyâretgâh: Eyüp Sultân Türbesi." In *Osmanlı İstanbulu*, edited by Feridun Emecen, Ali Akyıldız, and Emrah Safa Gürkan, 547–65. Istanbul: Istanbul 29 Mayıs Üniversitesi, 2015.

———. "Sanctifying Ottoman Istanbul: The Shrine of Abū Ayyūb Al-Anṣārī." PhD diss., Freie Universitaet, 2015.

Cresswell, Tim. *Place: A Short Introduction*. Malden: Blackwell Publishers, 2004.

Criss, Nur Bilge. *Istanbul under Allied Occupation: 1918–1923*. Leiden: Brill, 1999.

Cumbur, Müjgan. "İstanbul'un 500üncü Fetih Yıldönümü Dolayısiyle Tertiplenen Sergilere, Yapılan Kültür, San'at ve Neşriyat Hareketlerine Dair." *Vakıflar Dergisi* 4 (1958): 265–81.

Curry, Michael. "On Space and Spatial Practice in Contemporary Geography." In *Concepts in Human Geography*, edited by Carville Earle, Martin S. Kenzer, and Kent Mathewson, 3–32. Lanham, MD: Rowman & Littlefield, 1996.

———. "Toward a Geography of a World without Maps: Lessons from Ptolemy and Postal Codes." *Annals of the Association of American Geographers* 95, no. 3 (2005): 680–91.

Danforth, Nicholas. *The Remaking of Republican Turkey: Memory and Modernity since the Fall of the Ottoman Empire*. London: Cambridge University Press, 2021.

David, Isabel, and Kumru F. Toktamış, eds. *"Everywhere Taksim": Sowing the Seeds for a New Turkey at Gezi*. Amsterdam: Amsterdam University Press, 2015.

Deeb, Lara. *An Enchanted Modern: Gender and Public Piety in Shi'i Lebanon*. Princeton, NJ: Princeton University Press, 2006.

Deeb, Lara, and Mona Harb. *Leisurely Islam: Negotiating Geography and Morality in Shi'ite South Beirut*. Princeton, NJ: Princeton University Press, 2013.

Deguilhem, Randi. "The Waqf in the City." In *The City in the Islamic World*, edited by Salma Jayyusi, Renata Holod, Attilio Petruccioli, and Andre Raymond, 923–50. Leiden: Brill, 2008.

Delaney, Carol. *The Seed and the Soil: Gender and Cosmology in Turkish Village Society*. Berkeley: University of California Press, 1991.

Della Dora, Veronica. "Infrasecular Geographies." *Progress in Human Geography* 42, no. 1 (2016): 44–71. https://doi.org/10.1177/0309132516666190.

DeLyser, Dydia. "Authenticity on the Ground: Engaging the Past in a California Ghost Town." *Annals of the Association of American Geographers* 89, no. 4 (1999): 602–32.

Demircioğlu, Fatima. "İstanbul'un Manevi Semti Eyüpsultan." *Yeni Şafak*, May 17, 1995.

Demirkaya, Mehmet. "Ahiret Torpili." *Milliyet* (Istanbul), August 24, 2003, 1.

Deringil, Selim. "The Invention of Tradition as Public Image in the Late Ottoman Empire, 1808 to 1908." *Comparative Studies in Society and History* 35, no. 1 (2009): 3–29. https://doi.org/10.1017/s0010417500018247.

Derman, M. Uğur. "Medresetü'l-Hattâtîn." In *TDV İslam Ansiklopedisi*, 341–42. Ankara: Türkiye Diyanet Vakfı, 2003.

"Dertlilerin Teselli Bulduğu Yer: Eyüb Sultan." June 2, 1954.

DeSilvey, Caitlin. *Curated Decay: Heritage beyond Saving*. Minneapolis: University of Minnesota Press, 2017.

———. "Observed Decay: Telling Stories with Mutable Things." *Journal of Material Culture* 11, no. 3 (2006): 318–38.

Dinçer, İclal. "The Impact of Neoliberal Policies on Historic Urban Space: Areas of Urban Renewal in Istanbul." *International Planning Studies* 16, no. 1 (2011): 43–60.

Dinçer, İclal, Zeynep Enlil, Yiğit Evren, and Senem Kozaman Som. *İstanbul'da Tarihi ve Doğal Miras Değerleri: Potansiyeller, Riskler ve Koruma Sorunları*. Istanbul: Bilgi Üniversitesi Yayınları, 2011.

Dinçkal, Noyan. "Reluctant Modernization: The Cultural Dynamics of Water Supply in Istanbul, 1885–1950." *Technology and Culture* 49, no. 3 (2008): 675–700.

*Dört Ayaklı Belediye: İstanbul'un Sokak Köpekleri*. Edited by Istanbul Araştırmaları Enstitüsü. Istanbul: İstanbul Araştırmaları Enstitüsü, 2016.

Dressler, Markus. *Writing Religion: The Making of Turkish Alevi Islam*. Oxford: Oxford University Press, 2013.

Duman, Ali. "Sadaka." In *TDV İslam Ansiklopedisi*, 383–84. Istanbul: Türkiye Diyanet Vakfı, 2008.

Dupont, Anne-Laure, and Catherine Mayeur-Jaouen. "Monde nouveau, voix nouvelles: Etats, sociétés, islam dans l'entre-deux-guerres." *Revue des mondes musulmans et de la Méditerranée* 95–98 (2002): 9–39. https://doi.org/10.4000/remmm.224. http://journals.openedition.org/remmm/224.

Duran, Burhanettin, and Cemil Aydin. "Competing Occidentalisms of Modern Islamist Thought: Necip Fazıl Kısakürek and Nurettin Topçu on Christianity, the West and Modernity." *Muslim World* 103, no. 4 (2013): 479–500.

Duvarcı, Ayşe. "Su ile Bakılan Fallar." In *Geleneksel Türk Sanatında ve Edebiyatımızda Su*, edited by Nurettin Demir, 165–68. Ankara: Ankara Büyükşehir Belediyesi, 2013.

Ebüzziya, Ziyad. "Ebüzziya, Velid." In *TDV İslam Ansiklopedisi*, 371–73. Istanbul: Türkiye Diyanet Vakfı, 1994.

Edensor, Tim. "Entangled Agencies, Material Networks and Repair in a Building Assemblage: The Mutable Stone of St Ann's Church, Manchester." *Transactions of the Institute of British Geographers* 36, no. 2 (2011): 238–52.

———. "Mundane Mobilities, Performances and Spaces of Tourism." *Social & Cultural Geography* 8, no. 2 (2007): 199–215.

———. "Performing Tourism, Staging Tourism: (Re)Producing Tourist Space and Practice." *Tourist Studies* 1, no. 1 (2001): 59–81.

———. *Tourists at the Taj: Performance and Meaning at a Symbolic Site.* London: Routledge, 1998.

———. "Vital Urban Materiality and Its Multiple Absences: The Building Stone of Central Manchester." *cultural geographies* 20, no. 4 (2012): 447–65.

———. "Waste Matter: The Debris of Industrial Ruins and the Disordering of the Material World." *Journal of Material Culture* 10, no. 3 (2005): 311–32.

Efendioğlu, Mehmet. "Rivayet." In *TDV İslam Ansiklopedisi*, 135–37. Istanbul: Türkiye Diyanet Vakfı, 2008.

———. "Sahabe." In *TDV İslam Ansiklopedisi*, 491–500. Istanbul: Türkiye Diyanet Vakfı, 2008.

Eickelman, Dale F. "Qur'anic Commentary, Public Space, and Religious Intellectuals in the Writings of Said Nursi." *Muslim World* 89, no. 3–4 (1999): 260–69.

———. "The Study of Islam in Local Contexts." *Contributions to Asian Studies* 17, no. 1 (1982): 1–16.

Eisenlohr, Patrick. "The Anthropology of Media and the Question of Ethnic and Religious Pluralism." *Social Anthropology* 19, no. 1 (2011): 40–55.

Ekinci, Oktay. "Eyüp'te Tarih, Kültür ve 'Dinsellik' [History, Culture, and 'Religiosity' in Eyüp']." *Cumhuriyet* (Istanbul), 1994.

Eldem, Edhem. "The Reconversion of the Hagia Sophia into a Mosque: A Historian's Perspective." *Journal of the Ottoman and Turkish Studies Association* 8, no. 1 (2021): 243–60.

Eldem, Nezih. "Eyüp Sultan Camii ve Yakın Çevresi." In *Tarihi, Kültürü ve Sanatıyla Eyüpsultan Sempozyumu II. Tebliğler*, edited by Osman Sak, 51–53. Istanbul: Eyüp Belediyesi, 1998.

Ellsworth De Kay, James. *Sketches of Turkey in 1831 and 1832.* New York: J. & J. Harper, 1833.

Ephrat, Daphna, Ethel Sara Wolper, and Paulo G. Pinto. "Introduction: History and Anthropology of Sainthood and Space in Islamic Contexts." In *Saintly Spheres and Islamic Landscapes*, edited by Daphna Ephrat, Ethel Sara Wolper, and Paulo G. Pinto, 1–31. Leidin: Brill, 2020.

Erman, Tahire. "Becoming 'Urban' or Remaining 'Rural': The Views of Turkish Rural-to-Urban Migrants on the 'Integration' Question." *International Journal of Middle East Studies* 30, no. 4 (1998): 541–61.

Ersoy, Ahmet. "Architecture and the Search for Ottoman Origins in the Tanzimat Period." *Muqarnas* 24 (2007): 117–39.

Ertürk, Nergis. *Grammatology and Literary Modernity in Turkey.* New York: Oxford University Press, 2011.

Erünsal, İsmail E. "Beşir Ağa Kütüphanesi." In *TDV İslam Ansiklopedisi*, 4. Istanbul: Türkiye Diyanet Vakfı, 1992.

Esen, A. Kıvanç. "Tek Parti Dönemi Cami Kapatma/Satma Uygulamaları." *Tarih ve Toplum Yeni Yaklaşımlar* 13 (2011): 91–158.

Eyice, Semavi. "Beşir Ağa Külliyesi." In *TDV İslam Ansiklopedisi*, 1–3. Istanbul: Türkiye Diyanet Vakfı, 1992.

———. "Eyüp Sultan Külliyesi." In *İslam Ansiklopedisi*, 9–12. Istanbul: Türkiye Diyanet Vakfı, 1995.

———. "Haliç." In *TDV İslam Ansiklopedisi*, 264–80. Istanbul: Türkiye Diyanet Vakfı, 1997.

———. "İstanbul Ansiklopedisi." In *TDV İslam Ansiklopedisi*, 303–4. Istanbul: Türkiye Diyanet Vakfı, 2001.

"Eyüp Sultan Türbesi'nde Şifalı Suda Skandal Sızıntı." *Sabah* (Istanbul), May 26, 2011.

"Eyüp Sultan ve Zemzem Kuyusu." *Hürriyet*, 2009. www.hurriyet.com.tr/gundem/eyup -sultan-ve-zemzem-kuyusu-12327054.

*Eyüp'te Altı Yıl*. Istanbul: Eyüp Belediyesi, 2000.

Fahmy, Ziad. *Ordinary Egyptians: Creating the Modern Nation through Popular Culture*. Stanford, CA: Stanford University Press, 2011.

Falah, Ghazi-Walid, and Caroline Nagel. *Geographies of Muslim Women: Gender, Religion, and Space*. New York: The Guilford Press, 2005.

Faroqhi, Suraiya. "Migration into Eighteenth-Century 'Greater Istanbul' as Reflected in the Kadi Registers of Eyüp." *Turcica: Revue d'Etudes Turques* 30 (1998): 163–83.

Fico, Jamie. "Watering the Desert, Draining the Oasis: Navigating Drought, Development and Irrigation Politics in the Draa Valley, Morocco." MA thesis, Syracuse University, 2022.

Flood, Finbarr B. "Bodies and Becoming: Mimesis, Mediation, and the Ingestion of the Sacred in Christianity and Islam." In *Sensational Religion: Sensory Cultures in Material Practice*, edited by Sally M. Promey, 459–93. New Haven, CT: Yale University Press, 2014.

Fortuny, Kim. "Islam, Westernization, and Posthumanist Place: The Case of the Istanbul Street Dog." *Interdisciplinary Studies in Literature and Environment* 21, no. 2 (2014): 271–97. https://doi.org/10.1093/isle/isu049.

Fujitani, Takashi. *Splendid Monarchy: Power and Pageantry in Modern Japan*. Berkeley: University of California Press, 1996.

Gandy, Matthew. "Queer Ecology: Nature, Sexuality, and Heterotopic Alliances." *Environment and Planning D: Society and Space* 30, no. 4 (2012): 727–47. https://doi.org/10.1068 /d10511.

Gelvin, James, and Nile Green, eds. *Global Muslims in the Age of Steam and Print*. Berkeley: University of California Press, 2013.

Genç, Ahmet. "Büyük Medeniyetimizin Eyüp'teki İzdüşmeler." In *Tarihi, Kültürü ve Sanatıyla Eyüpsultan Sempozyumu IX. Tebliğler*, 8–9. Istanbul: Eyüp Belediyesi, 2005.

———. "Sunuş." In *1. Eyüpsultan Sempozyumu: Tebliğler*. Istanbul: Eyüpsultan Belediyesi, 1997.

———. "Takdim." In *Tarihi, Kültürü ve Sanatıyla Eyüpsultan Sempozyumu II. Tebliğler*, edited by Osman Sak, 7–8. Istanbul: Eyüp Belediyesi, 1998.

———. "Takdim." In *Tarihi, Kültürü ve Sanatıyla Eyüpsultan Sempozyumu III. Tebliğler 28–30 Mayıs 1999*, edited by Osman Sak, 7. Istanbul: Eyüp Belediyesi, 2000.

Ghabin, Ahmad. "The Well of Zamzam: A Pilgrimage Site and Curative Water in Islam." In *Sacred Waters: A Cross-Cultural Compendium of Hallowed Springs and Holy Wells*, edited by Celeste Ray. New York: Routledge, 2020.

Gimaret, Daniel. "Shirk." In *Encyclopaedia of Islam, Second Edition*, edited by P. Berman, Th. Bianquis, C. E. Bosworth, E. van Donzel and W. P. Heinrichs. Leiden: Brill, 1960.

Ginzburg, Carlo. "Latitude, Slaves, the Bible: An Experiment in Microhistory." *Critical Inquiry* 31, no. 3 (2005): 665–83.

Gökarıksel, Banu. "Beyond the Officially Sacred: Religion, Secularism, and the Body in the Production of Subjectivity." *Social & Cultural Geography* 10, no. 6 (2009): 657–74.

———. "The Intimate Politics of Secularism and the Headscarf: The Mall, the Neighborhood, and the Public Square in Istanbul." *Gender, Place and Culture* 19, no. 1 (2012): 1–20.

Gökarıksel, Banu, and Anna Secor. "'Even I Was Tempted': The Moral Ambivalence and Ethical Practice of Veiling-Fashion in Turkey." *Annals of the Association of American Geographers* 102, no. 4 (2012): 847–62.

———. "Islamic-ness in the Life of a Commodity: Veiling-Fashion in Turkey." *Transactions of the Institute of British Geographers* 35, no. 3 (2010): 313–33.

———. "Post-Secular Geographies and the Problem of Pluralism: Religion and Everyday Life in Istanbul, Turkey." *Political Geography* 46, no. 1 (2015): 21–30.

Göknar, Erdağ. "Reading Occupied Istanbul: Turkish Subject-Formation from Historical Trauma to Literary Trope." *Culture, Theory and Critique* 55, no. 3 (2014): 321–41.

Göktürk, Deniz, Levent Soysal, and İpek Türeli, eds. *Orienting Istanbul: Cultural Capital of Europe?* New York: Routledge, 2010.

Gölpınarlı, Abdülbaki. "Eyüp Sultan ve İstanbul." *Milliyet*, August 15, 1979.

Gordillo, Gaston R. *Rubble: The Afterlife of Destruction.* Durham, NC: Duke University Press, 2014.

Gözaydın, İştar B. *Diyanet: Türkiye Cumhuriyeti'nde Dinin Tanzimi.* Istanbul: İletişim Yayınları, 2009.

Green, Nile. *Bombay Islam: The Religious Economy of the West Indian Ocean.* Cambridge: Cambridge University Press, 2011.

———. "Migrant Sufis and Sacred Space in South Asian Islam." *Contemporary South Asia* 12, no. 4 (2003): 493–509. http://dx.doi.org/10.1080/0958493042000212678.

Gruber, Christiane. "The Arts of Protection and Healing in Islam: Water Infused with Blessing." *Ajam Media Collective*, 2021.

———. "Bereket Bargains: Islamic Amulets in Today's 'New Turkey.'" In *Islamicate Occult Sciences in Theory and Practice*, edited by Liana Saif, Francisca Leoni, Matthew Melvin-Koushki, and Farouk Yahya, 527–606. Leiden: Brill, 2020.

———. "Like Hearts of Birds: Ottoman Avian Microarchitecture in the Eighteenth Century." *Journal18* 11 (2021). www.journal18.org/5689.

———. "A Pious Cure-All: The Ottoman Illustrated Prayer Manual in the Lilly Library." In *The Islamic Manuscript Tradition: Ten Centuries of Book Arts in Indiana University Collections*, edited by Christiane Gruber, 117–53. Bloomington: Indiana University Press, 2010.

———. "The Prophet as a Sacred Spring: Late Ottoman *Hilye* Bottles." In *The Presence of the Prophet in Early Modern and Contemporary Islam*, edited by Denis Gril, Stefan Reichmuth, and Dilek Sarmis, 535–82. Leiden: Brill, 2021.

Guida, Michelangelo. "Nurettin Topçu and Necip Fazıl Kısakürek: Stories of 'Conversion' and Activism in Republican Turkey." *Journal for Islamic Studies* 34, no. 1 (2014): 98–117.

Gül, Murat. *The Emergence of Modern Istanbul: Transformation and Modernisation of a City.* London; New York: Tauris Academic Studies, 2009.

Gürel, Meltem Ö., ed. *Mid-Century Modernism in Turkey: Architecture across Cultures in the 1950s and 1960s.* London: Routledge, 2015.

Güven, Dilek. "Riots against the Non-Muslims of Turkey: 6/7 September 1955 in the Context of Demographic Engineering." *European Journal of Turkish Studies* 12 (2011). https://doi.org/10.4000/ejts.4538.

"Hadith on Mosques: Whoever Builds a Mosque Is Given Paradise." Updated March 31, 2012. www.abuaminaelias.com/dailyhadithonline/2012/03/31/masjid-built-house-jannah/.

Haksöz, Cengiz. "Eating in Gezi, Devoured by Gezi: Food and Resistance in Istanbul Gezi Park Protests." In *Another Brick in the Barricade: The Gezi Resistance and Its Aftermath*, edited by Güneş Koç and Harun Aksu, 55–75. Bremen: Wiener Verlag für Sozialforschung, 2015.

Hamadeh, Shirine. "Splash and Spectacle: The Obsession with Fountains in Eighteenth-Century Istanbul." *Muqarnas* 19 (2002): 123–48.

Hammond, Timur. "Conjunctions of Islam: Rethinking the Geographies of Art and Piety through the Notebooks of Ahmet Süheyl Ünver." *cultural geographies* (2022). https://doi.org/10.1177/14744740221120248.

———. "Heritage and the Middle East: Cities, Power, and Memory." *Geography Compass* 14, no. 2 (2020): 1–13. https://doi.org/10.1111/gec3.12477.

———. "Matters of the Mosque: Changing Configurations of Buildings and Belief in an Istanbul District." *City* 18, no. 6 (2014): 679–90.

———. "Mediums of Belief: Muslim Place Making in 20th Century Turkey." PhD diss., University of California, Los Angeles, 2016.

———. "The Middle East without Space?" *International Journal of Middle East Studies* 49, no. 2 (2017): 319–22.

———. "Papering, Arranging, and Depositing: Learning from Working with an Istanbul Archive." *Area* 52, no. 1 (2020): 204–12. https://doi.org/10.1111/area.12578.

Haraway, Donna. "Situated Knowledges: The Science Question in Feminism and the Privilege of Partial Perspective." In *Simians, Cyborgs, and Women: The Reinvention of Nature*, edited by Donna Haraway, 183–201. New York: Routledge, 1991.

Harmanşah, Ömür. *Place, Memory, and Healing: An Archaeology of Anatolian Rock Monuments*. New York: Routledge, 2015.

Harris, Jonathan. *Constantinople: Capital of Byzantium*. 2nd ed. London: Bloomsbury Academic, 2017.

Hart, Kimberly. *And Then We Work for God: Rural Islam in Western Turkey*. Stanford, CA: Stanford University Press, 2013.

———. "Istanbul's Intangible Cultural Heritage as Embodied by Street Animals." *History and Anthropology* 30, no. 4 (2019): 448–59. https://doi.org/10.1080/02757206.2019.1610404.

Harvey, David. "From Managerialism to Entrepreneurialism: The Transformation of Urban Governance in Late Capitalism." *Geografiska Annaler, Series B: Human Geography* 71, no. 1 (1989): 3–17.

———. "The Urban Process under Capitalism." *International Journal of Urban and Regional Research* 2, no. 1–4 (1978): 101–31.

Haskan, Mehmet Nermi. *Eyüp Sultan Tarihi*. 2 vols. Istanbul: Eyüp Belediyesi Kültür Yayınları, 2009.

———. *Eyüp Tarihi*. 2 vols. Istanbul: Türk Turing Turizm İşletmeciliği Vakfı, 1993.

Hasluck, F. W. "Studies in Turkish History and Folk-Legend." *Annual of the British School at Athens* 19 (1912/1913): 198–220.

Hasluck, Frederick William, and Margaret Masson Hardie Hasluck. *Christianity and Islam under the Sultans*. 2 vols. London: Clarendon Press, 1929.

Haznedaroğlu, Aslıhan. "Kısmet İçin Rüyaya Yatmak: Alata Kolotisi Hakkında." *Kültür Araştırmaları Dergisi* 10 (2021): 97–124. https://doi.org/10.46250/kulturder.950733.

Hendrick, Joshua D. *Gülen: The Ambiguous Politics of Market Islam in Turkey and the World.* New York: New York University Press, 2013.

Henkel, Heiko. "The Location of Islam: Inhabiting Istanbul in a Muslim Way." *American Ethnologist* 34, no. 1 (2007): 57–70.

Herzog, Christoph, and Richard Wittman, eds. *Istanbul-Kushta-Constantinople: Narratives of Identity in the Ottoman Capital, 1830–1930.* London: Routledge, 2019.

Hetherington, Kevin. "Museum Topology and the Will to Connect." *Journal of Material Culture* 2, no. 2 (1997): 199–218.

Hillenbrand, Carole. "Gardens beneath Which Rivers Flow: The Significance of Water in Classical Islamic Culture." In *Rivers of Paradise: Water in Islamic Art and Culture,* edited by Sheila S. Blair and Jonathan M. Bloom. New Haven, CT: Yale University Press, 2009.

Ho, Enseng. *The Graves of Tarim: Genealogy and Mobility across the Indian Ocean.* Berkeley: University of California Press, 2006.

Hoskins, Gareth. "Materialising Memory at Angel Island Immigration Station, San Francisco." *Environment and Planning A: Economy and Space* 39, no. 2 (2007): 437–55. https://doi.org/10.1068/a38174.

Houston, Christopher. "The Brewing of Islamist Modernity: Tea Gardens and Public Space in Istanbul." *Theory, Culture, and Society* 18, no. 6 (2001): 77–97.

———. *Istanbul, City of the Fearless: Urban Activism, Coup D'etat, and Memory in Turkey.* Berkeley: University of California Press, 2020.

———. "Provocations of the Built Environment: Animating Cities in Turkey as *Kemalist.*" *Political Geography* 24, no. 1 (2005): 101–19.

Houtman, Dick, and Birgit Meyer, eds. *Things: Religion and the Question of Materiality.* New York: Fordham University Press, 2012.

Howe, Nicolas. *Landscapes of the Secular: Law, Religion, and American Sacred Space.* Chicago: University of Chicago Press, 2016.

Hull, Matthew S. *Government of Paper: The Materiality of Bureaucracy in Urban Pakistan.* Berkeley: University of California Press, 2012.

İnalcık, Halil. "Istanbul: An Islamic City." *Journal of Islamic Studies* 1, no. 1 (1990): 1–23.

İpşirli, Mehmet. "İstanbul Kadılığı." In *TDV İslam Ansiklopedisi,* 305–7. Istanbul: Türkiye Diyanet Vakfı, 2001.

Isin, Engin, and Ebru Üstündağ. "Wills, Deeds, Acts: Women's Civic Gift-Giving in Ottoman Istanbul." *Gender, Place and Culture* 15, no. 5 (2008): 519–32.

Issa, Rana, and Einar Wigen. "Levantine Chronotopes: Prisms for Entangled Histories." *Contemporary Levant* 5, no. 1 (2020): 1–12. https://doi.org/10.1080/20581831.2019.1710666.

Ivakhiv, Adrian. "Toward a Geography of 'Religion': Mapping the Distribution of an Unstable Signifier." *Annals of the Association of American Geographers* 96, no. 1 (2006): 169–75.

Jacobs, Jane M. "A Geography of Big Things." *Cultural Geographies* 13, no. 1 (2006): 1–27.

Kabadayı, M. Erdem. "Working in a Fez Factory in Istanbul in the Late Nineteenth Century: Division of Labour and Networks of Migration Formed Along Ethno-Religious Lines." *International Review of Social History* 54, no. S17 (2009): 69–90.

Kafadar, Cemal. *Between Two Worlds: The Construction of the Ottoman State.* Berkeley: University of California Press, 1995.

———. "Eyüp'te Kılıç Kuşanma Törenleri." In *Eyüp: Dün/Bugün: Sempozyum, 11–12 Aralık 1993*, edited by Tülay Artan, 50–61. Istanbul: Tarih Vakfı Yurt Yayınları, 1994.

Kafescioğlu, Çiğdem. *Constantinopolis/Istanbul: Cultural Encounter, Imperial Vision, and the Construction of the Ottoman Capital*. University Park: Pennsylvania State University Press, 2009.

———. "Eyüp." In *Encyclopedia of Islam, Three*, edited by Kate Fleet, Gudrun Kramer, Denis Matringe, John Nawas, and Everett Rowson. Leiden: Brill, 2016.

Kafka, Ben. "Paperwork: The State of the Discipline." *Book History* 12, no. 1 (2009): 340–53.

Kahraman, Alim. "Alus, Sermet Muhtar." In *TDV İslam Ansiklopedisi*, 91–92. Istanbul: Türkiye Diyanet Vakfı, 2016.

Kamil, Melih, Zeynep Nayir, H. Şener, F. Yürekli, and H. Yürekli. "The Eyüp Conservation Area." In *Conservation as Cultural Survival*, edited by Renata Holod, 50–52. Philadelphia, PA: The Agha Khan Award for Architecture, 1980.

Kapsız. "Eyüpsultanda Cuma." *Resimli Hayat* (Istanbul), September 29, 1954, 48–49.

Kara, Hatice Fahrünnisa. "Eyüp." In *Dünden Bugüne İstanbul Ansiklopedisi*, 245–50. Istanbul: Türkiye Ekonomik ve Toplumsal Tarih Vakfı, 1993.

———. "Eyüpsultan Tarihi Yerleşme Dokusunda Planlama Süreci ve Planlama—Uygulama İlişkiler." In *1. Eyüpsultan Sempozyumu: Tebliğler*, 121–38. Istanbul: Eyüpsultan Belediyesi, 1997.

———. "İstanbul Metropoliten Alan Gelişme Sürecinde Bir Dini, Kültürel Sosyal Yerleşim Merkezi—Eyüp." PhD diss., İstanbul Teknik Üniversitesi, 1994.

Kara, İsmail. *Cumhuriyet Türkiye'sinde Bir Mesele Olarak İslam 1*. Istanbul: Dergah Yayınları, 2016.

———. *Cumhuriyet Türkiye'sinde Bir Mesele Olarak İslam 2*. Istanbul: Dergah Yayınları, 2016.

———. *Din ile Modernleşme Arasında: Çağdaş Türk Düşüncesinin Meseleri*. Istanbul: Dergah Yayınları, 2003.

Karaman, Ozan. "Urban Neoliberalism with Islamic Characteristics." *Urban Studies* 50, no. 16 (2013): 3412–27.

Karateke, Hakan T. "Interpreting Monuments: Charitable Buildings, Monuments, and the Construction of Collective Memory in the Ottoman Empire." *Wiener Zeitschrift für die Kunde des Morgenlandes* 91 (2001): 183–99.

Kasaba, Reşat, and Sibel Bozdoğan, eds. *Rethinking Modernity and National Identity in Turkey*. Seattle: University of Washington Press, 1997.

Kaya, Önder. "İstanbul'da Ayazma Kültürü ve Balıklı Ayazması." *Z Dergisi*, 2020. www.zdergisi .istanbul/makale/istanbulda-ayazma-kulturu-ve-balikli-ayazmasi-92.

Kaynar, Hakan. *Projesiz Modernleşme: Cumhuriyet Istanbulu'ndan Gündelik Fragmanlar*. Istanbul: Istanbul Araştırmaları Enstitüsü, 2012.

Keane, Webb. "The Evidence of the Senses and the Materiality of Religion." *Journal of the Royal Anthropological Institute* 14, no. s1 (2008): S110–S127.

Keyder, Çağlar. "A Brief History of Modern Istanbul." In *The Cambridge History of Turkey*, edited by Reşat Kasaba, 504–23. Cambridge: Cambridge University Press, 2008.

Keyder, Çaglar, and Ayşe Öncü. "Globalization of a Third-World Metropolis: Istanbul in the 1980s." *Review* 17, no. 3 (1994): 383–421.

Kezer, Zeynep. *Building Modern Turkey: State, Space, and Ideology in the Early Republic*. Pittsburgh, PA: University of Pittsburgh Press, 2015.

Khalek, Nancy. "Dreams of Hagia Sophia: The Muslim Siege of Constantinople in 674 CE, Abû Ayyûb al-Ansârî, and the Medieval Islamic Imagination." In *The Islamic Scholarly Tradition: Studies in History, Law, and Thought in Honor of Professor Michael Allan Cook*, edited by Asad Q. Ahmad, Behnam Sadeghi, and Michael Bonner, 131–46. Leiden: Brill, 2011.

———. "Medieval Biographical Literature and the Companions of Muḥammad." *Der Islam* 91, no. 2 (2014): 272–94. https://doi.org/10.1515/islam-2014-0012.

Knott, Kim. "Religion, Space, and Place: The Spatial Turn in Research on Religion." *Religion and Society* 1, no. 1 (2010). https://doi.org/10.3167/arrs.2010.010103.

Kocamaner, Hikmet. "Strengthening the Family through Television: Islamic Broadcasting, Secularism, and the Politics of Responsibility in Turkey." *Anthropological Quarterly* 90, no. 3 (2017): 675–714. https://doi.org/10.1353/anq.2017.0040.

Koch, Natalie. *The Geopolitics of Spectacle: Space, Synechdoche, and the New Capitals of Asia.* Ithaca, NY: Cornell University Press, 2018.

Koch, Natalie, Anar Valiyev, and Khairul Hazmi Zaini. "Mosques as Monuments: An Inter-Asian Perspective on Monumentality and Religious Landscapes." *cultural geographies* (2017): 1–17.

Koçu, Reşat Ekrem. "Defterdar Mensucat Fabrikası." In *İstanbul Ansiklopedisi*, 4340–44. Istanbul: Koçu Yayınları, 1966.

———. "Eyyubsultan Kaymağı, Kaymakçı Dükkanları." In *İstanbul Ansiklopedisi*, 5459. Istanbul: Koçu Yayınları, 1971.

———. "Eyyubsultanda Fulya Tarlası, Bağı." In *İstanbul Ansiklopedisi*, 5451–52. Istanbul: Koçu Yayınları, 1971.

Koman, Mahmut Mesut. *Eyüp Sultan, Loti Kahvesi, Çevresi (Le Café de Pierre Loti à Eyüp).* Istanbul: Güler Basımevi, 1966.

Kong, Lily. "Mapping 'New' Geographies of Religion: Politics and Poetics in Modernity." *Progress in Human Geography* 25, no. 2 (2001): 211–33.

Küçükaşçı, Mustafa Sabri. "Zemzem." In *TDV İslam Ansiklopedisi*, 242–46. Istanbul: Türkiye Diyanet Vakfı, 2013.

Küçükerman, Önder. *Feshane, Defterdar Fabrikasi: Türk Giyim Sanayii Tarihindeki Ünlü Fabrika.* Ankara: Sümerbank, 1988.

Kulat, Mehmet Ali. "İstanbul'un Fethini Müjdeleyen Hadisin Değerlendirilmesi." *Diyanet İlmi Dergi* 37, no. 2 (2001): 5–23.

Kuyucu, Tuna. "Ethno-Religious 'Unmixing' of 'Turkey': 6–7 September Riots as a Case in Turkish Nationalism." *Nations and Nationalism* 11, no. 3 (2005): 361–80.

Kuyucu, Tuna, and Özlem Ünsal. "'Urban Transformation' as State-Led Property Transfer: An Analysis of Two Cases of Urban Renewal in Istanbul." *Urban Studies* 47, no. 7 (2010): 1479–99.

Larkin, Brian. "Islamic Renewal, Radio, and the Surface of Things." In *Aesthetic Formations: Media, Religion, and the Senses*, edited by Birgit Meyer, 117–36. New York: Palgrave Macmillan, 2009.

Latour, Bruno. "On Actor-Network Theory: A Few Clarifications." *Soziale Welt* 47, no. 4 (1996): 369–81.

Law, John. "Objects and Spaces." *Theory, Culture, and Society* 19, no. 5/6 (2002): 91–105.

Law, John, and Annemarie Mol. "Situating Technoscience: An Inquiry into Spatialities." *Environment and Planning D: Society and Space* 19, no. 5 (2001): 609–21. https://doi .org/10.1068/d243t.

Lecker, Michael. "Abū Ayyūb al-Anṣārī." In *Encyclopedia of Islam, Three*, edited by Kate Fleet, Gudrun Kramer, Denis Matringe, John Nawas, and Everett Rowson. Leiden: Brill, 2013.

Leder, Stefan. "Riwâya." In *Encyclopedia of Islam, Second Edition*, edited by P. Bearman, Th. Bianquis, C. E. Bosworth, E. van Donzel and W. P. Heinrichs. Amsterdam: Brill, 2012. http://dx.doi.org.libezproxy2.syr.edu/10.1163/1573-3912_islam_COM_0927.

Lees, Loretta. "Towards a Critical Geography of Architecture: The Case of an Ersatz Colosseum." *Cultural Geographies* 8, no. 1 (January 1, 2001): 51–86. https://doi.org /10.1177/096746080100800103.

Leitner, Helga, Eric Sheppard, and Kristin M. Sziarto. "The Spatialities of Contentious Politics." *Transactions of the Institute of British Geographers* 33, no. 1 (2008): 157–72.

Levi-Provençal, E., J. H. Mordtmann, and Cl. Huart. "Abū Ayyūb Khalid b. Zayd b. Kulayb al-Nadjdjārī al-Anṣārī." In *Encyclopedia of Islam, Second Edition*, edited by P. Bearman, Th. Bianquis, C. E. Bosworth, E. van Donzel and W. P. Heinrichs. Leiden: Brill, 2012.

Lewis, Bernard. "Islamic Revival in Turkey." *International Affairs* 28, no. 1 (1952): 38–48.

Lewis, Geoffrey. *The Turkish Language Reform: A Catastrophic Success*. Oxford: Oxford University Press, 1999.

Libal, Kathryn. "'The Child Question': The Politics of Child Welfare in Early Republican Turkey." In *Poverty and Charity in Middle Eastern Contexts*, edited by Michael Bonner, Mine Ener, and Amy Singer, 255–72. Albany: SUNY Press, 2003.

Liebelt, Claudia. "Grooming Istanbul: Intimate Encounters and Concerns in Turkish Beauty Salons." *Journal of Middle East Women's Studies* 12, no. 2 (2016): 181–202.

Lifchez, Raymond, ed. *The Dervish Lodge: Architecture, Art, and Sufism in Ottoman Turkey*, Comparative Studies on Muslim Societies. Berkeley: University of California Press, 1992.

Lory, P. "Shadhiliyya." In *Encyclopedia of Islam, Second Edition*, edited by P. Bearman, Th. Bianquis, C. E. Bosworth, E. van Donzel and W. P. Heinrichs. Leiden: Brill, 2012.

Mahmood, Saba. *The Politics of Piety: The Islamic Revival and the Feminist Subject*. Princeton, NJ: Princeton University Press, 2005.

Majeska, George. "Russian Pilgrims in Constantinople." *Dumbarton Oaks Papers* 56 (2002): 93–108. https://doi.org/10.2307/1291857.

Mandaville, Peter. *Transnational Muslim Politics: Reimagining the Umma*. London: Routledge, 2001.

Mardin, Şerif. *Religion and Social Change in Modern Turkey: The Case of Bediuzzaman Said Nursi*. Albany: State University of New York, 1989.

Martin, Deborah G. "'Place-Framing' as Place making: Constituting a Neighborhood for Organizing and Activism." *Annals of the Association of American Geographers* 93, no. 3 (2003): 730–50.

Massey, Doreen. *For Space*. London: SAGE Publications, 2005.

———. "Places and Their Pasts." *History Workshop Journal* 39 (1995): 182–92.

———. *Power-Geometries and the Politics of Space-Time*. Heidelburg, Germany: University of Heidelberg, 1999.

————. *Space, Place, and Gender*. Minneapolis: University of Minnesota Press, 1994.

Mazumdar, Shampa, and Sanjoy Mazumdar. "In Mosques and Shrines: Women's Agency in Public Sacred Space." *Journal of Ritual Studies* 16, no. 2 (2002): 165–79.

Mazzarella, William. "Culture, Globalization, Mediation." *Annual Review of Anthropology* 33 (2004): 345–67.

McFarlane, Colin. "On Context." *City* 15, no. 3–4 (2011): 375–88.

McGregor, Richard. "Grave Visitation/Worship." In *Encyclopaedia of Islam, Three*, edited by Kate Fleet, Gudrun Kramer, Denis Matringe, John Nawas, and Everett Rowson. Leiden: Brill, 2016.

McKittrick, Katherine. *Dear Science and Other Stories*. Durham, NC: Duke University Press, 2021.

Meeker, Michael. "Once There Was, Once There Wasn't: National Monuments and Interpersonal Exchange." In *Rethinking Modernity and National Identity in Turkey*, edited by Reşat Kasaba and Sibel Bozdoğan, 157–91. Seattle: University of Washington Press, 1997.

Mehmed Emin, Hafız. *El-Âsar ül-Mecidiye fi l-Menakıb il-Halidiye*. Istanbul: Mahmud Bey Matbaası, 1314 [1896/97].

Menon, Kalyani. *Making Place for Muslims in Contemporary India*. Ithaca, NY: Cornell University Press, 2022.

Mestyan, Adam. "Upgrade? Power and Sound During Ramadan and 'Id al-Fitr in the Nineteenth-Century Ottoman Arab Provinces." *Comparative Studies of South Asia, Africa and the Middle East* 37, no. 2 (2017): 262–79. https://doi.org/10.1215/1089201x-4132893.

Meyer, Birgit. "Introduction: From Imagined Communities to Aesthetic Formations: Religious Mediations, Sensational Forms, and Styles of Binding." In *Aesthetic Formations: Media, Religion, and the Senses*, edited by Birgit Meyer, 1–28. New York: Palgrave Macmillan, 2009.

————. "Mediation and Immediacy: Sensational Forms, Semiotic Ideologies and the Question of the Medium." *Social Anthropology* 19, no. 1 (2011): 23–39.

Miller, Timothy S. "Hospital Dreams in Byzantium." In *Dreams, Healing, and Medicine in Greece: From Antiquity to the Present.*, edited by Steven M. Oberhelman, 199–215. Burlington, VT: Ashgate, 2013.

Mills, Amy. "The Cultural Geopolitics of Ethnic Nationalism: Turkish Urbanism in Occupied Istanbul (1918–1923)." *Annals of the American Association of Geographers* 107, no. 5 (2017): 1179–93. https://doi.org/10.1080/24694452.2017.1298433.

————. "Gender and *Mahalle* (Neighborhood) Space in Istanbul." *Gender, Place and Culture* 14, no. 3 (2007): 335–54.

————. "The Place of Locality for Identity in the Nation: Minority Narratives of Cosmopolitan Istanbul." *International Journal of Middle East Studies* 40, no. 3 (2008): 383–401.

————. "Reading Narratives in City Landscapes: Cultural Identity in Istanbul." *Geographical Review* 95, no. 3 (2006): 441–62.

————. *Streets of Memory: Landscape, Tolerance, and National Identity in Istanbul*. Athens: University of Georgia Press, 2010.

Mills, Amy, and Banu Gökarıksel. "Provincializing Geographies of Religion: Muslim Identities Beyond the 'West.'" *Geography Compass* 8, no. 12 (2014): 902–14.

Mills, Amy, and Timur Hammond. "The Interdisciplinary Spatial Turn and the Discipline of Geography in Middle East Studies." In *Middle East Studies for the New Millennium:*

*Infrastructures of Knowledge*, edited by Seteney Shami and Cynthia Miller-Idriss, 152–86. New York: New York University Press, 2016.

Mitchell, Timothy. "Deterritorialization and the Crisis of Social Science." In *Localizing Knowledge in a Globalizing World: Recasting the Area Studies Debate*, edited by Ali Mirsepassi, Amrita Basu, and Frederick Weaver, 148–70. Syracuse, NY: Syracuse University Press, 2003.

Mittermaier, Amira. "Dreams from Elsewhere: Muslim Subjectivities Beyond the Trope of Self-Cultivation." *Journal of the Royal Anthropological Institute* 18, no. 2 (2012): 247–65.

———. *Dreams That Matter: Egyptian Landscapes of the Imagination*. Berkeley: University of California Press, 2011.

———. "How to Do Things with Examples: Sufis, Dreams, and Anthropology." *Journal of the Royal Anthropological Institute* 21, no. S1 (2015): 129–43.

Mol, Annemarie. *The Body Multiple: Ontology in Medical Practice*. Durham, NC: Duke University Press, 2003.

———. "Ontological Politics. A Word and Some Questions." *Sociological Review* 47, no. 1 (1999): 74–89.

Morgan, David. *The Thing about Religion: An Introduction to the Material Study of Religions*. Chapel Hill: University of North Carolina Press, 2021.

Moser, Sarah. "Islamic Cities." In *The Wiley Blackwell Encyclopedia of Urban and Regional Studies*, edited by Anthony Orum, 1–9. New York: John Wiley & Sons, 2019.

Moulton, Gavin. "Mid-Century Sinan: Vasfi Egeli and the Turkish Republic's First Mosque." *Yıllık: Annual of Istanbul Studies* 3 (2021): 39–68.

Muranyi, M. "Sahâba." In *The Encyclopaedia of Islam, Second Edition*, edited by C. E. Bosworth, E. van Donzel, W. P. Heinrichs and G. Lecomte, 827–29. Leiden: Brill, 1995.

Navaro-Yashin, Yael. *The Make-Believe Space: Affective Geography in a Postwar Polity*. Durham, NC: Duke University Press, 2012.

Necipoğlu, Gulru. "Dynastic Imprints on the Cityscape: The Collective Message of Imperial Funerary Mosque Complexes in Istanbul." In *Cimetières et Traditions Funéraires dans la Monde Islamique*, edited by Jean-Louis Bacque-Grammont and Aksel Tibet, 23–36. Ankara: Türk Tarih Kurumu, 1996.

Nereid, Camilla Trud. "Domesticating Modernity: The Turkish Magazine *Yedigün*, 1933–9." *Journal of Contemporary History* 47, no. 3 (2012): 483–504. https://doi.org/10.1177/0022009412441651.

Nolan, Marry Lee, and Sidney Nolan. "Religious Sites as Tourism Attractions in Europe." *Annals of Tourism Research* 19, no. 1 (1992): 68–78.

Öğüt, Cemal. *Eyyüb Sultan*. Istanbul: Eyüp Belediyesi, 1997.

———. *Eyyûb Sultan: Hz. Hâlid Ebu Eyyûb El-Ensârî*. Istanbul: Eyüp Belediyesi, 2005.

———. *Eyyûb Sultan: Hz. Hâlid Ebu Eyyûb El-Ensârî*. Istanbul: Eyüp Belediyesi Kültür Yayınları, 2012.

Okay, M. Orhan. "Beyatlı, Yahya Kemal." In *TDV İslam Ansiklopedisi*, 35–39. Istanbul: Türkiye Diyanet Vakfı, 1992.

Olson, Elizabeth, Peter E. Hopkins, and Lily Kong. "Introduction—Religion and Place: Landscape, Politics, and Piety." In *Religion and Place: Landscape, Politics, and Piety*, edited by Peter E. Hopkins, Elizabeth Olson, and Lily Kong, 1–20. London: Springer, 2013.

Olson, Elizabeth, Peter E. Hopkins, Rachel Pain, and Giselle Vincett. "Retheorizing the Postsecular Present: Embodiment, Spatial Transcendence, and Challenges to Authenticity among Young Christians in Glasgow, Scotland." *Annals of the Association of American Geographers* 103, no. 6 (2013): 1421–36.

Öncü, Ayşe. "Packaging Islam: Cultural Politics on the Landscape of Turkish Commercial Television." *Public Culture* 8, no. 1 (1995): 51–71.

———. "The Politics of Istanbul's Ottoman Heritage in the Era of Globalism." In *Space, Culture and Power: New Identities in Globalizing Cities*, edited by Petra Weyland and Ayşe Öncü, 233–64. London: Zed Books, 1997.

Örik, Nahid Sırrı. *İstanbul Yazıları*. Edited by Bahriye Çeri. Ankara: Türk Tarih Kurumu Basımevi, 2011.

Orman, İsmail. "Mehmed Reşad Türbesi." In *TDV İslam Ansiklopedisi*, 518–19. Ankara: Türkiye Diyanet Vakfı, 2003.

———. "Zal Mahmut Paşa Külliyesi." In *TDV İslam Ansiklopedisi*. Istanbul: Türkiye Diyanet Vakfı, 2013.

Ozaslan, Nuray. "From the Shrine of Cosmidion to the Shrine of Eyup Ensari." *Greek, Roman and Byzantine Studies* 40, no. 4 (1999): 379–99.

Özcan, Abdülkadir. "Hafîd Efendi." In *TDV İslam Ansiklopedisi*, 111–12. Istanbul: Türkiye Diyanet Vakfı, 1997.

Özcan, Nuri. "Kılıç Alayı." In *TDV İslam Ansiklopedisi*, 407–10. Ankara: Türkiye Diyanet Vakfı, 2022.

———. "Sadettin Heper." In *TDV İslam Ansiklopedisi*, 209–10. Istanbul: Türkiye Diyanet Vakfı, 1998.

———. "Salâ." In *TDV İslam Ansiklopedisi*, 15–16. Istanbul: Türkiye Diyanet Vakfı, 2009.

Özdemir, Gürbüz. "Belediye İktisadi Teşebbüslerinin Özelleştirilmesi." *Sayıştay Dergisi* 71 (2008): 41–74.

Özel, Ahmet Murat. "Adak." In *TDV İslam Ansiklopedisi*, 337–40. Istanbul: Türkiye Diyanet Vakfı, 1988.

———. "Şâzeliyye." In *TDV İslam Ansiklopedisi*, 387–90. Istanbul: Türkiye Diyanet Vakfı, 2010.

Özeren, M. Murtaza. "Kimler Hacı Cemal Öğüt'ün Talebesi Olmamış Ki." *Dünya Bizim*, March 21, 2016. www.dunyabizim.com/portre/kimler-haci-cemal-ogut-un-talebesi-olmamis-ki -h23518.html.

Özkan, Aysun. "Türbe Ziyaretlerinin Psiko-Sosyolojik Boyutu (Eyüp Sultan Türbesi Örneği)." MA thesis, T.C. Marmara Üniversitesi, 2009.

Özkan, Behlül. *From the Abode of Islam to the Turkish Vatan: The Making of a National Homeland in Turkey*. New Haven, CT: Yale University Press, 2012.

Özkırımlı, Umut, ed. *The Making of a Protest Movement in Turkey: #Occupygezi*. New York: Palgrave Macmillan, 2014.

Özsoy, İskender. "Son Eyüp Oyuncakçısı." *Popüler Tarih*, June 2001, 76–79.

Öztürk, Nazif. *Türk Yenileşme Tarihi Çevresinde Vakıf*. Ankara: Türkiye Diyanet Vakfı, 1995.

Özyön, Arzu. "Ziya Şakir (Soku)'Nun Selçuk Saraylarında Ömer Hayyam'ın Hayat ve Maceraları Adlı Romanının Tarihsel Roman Olarak İncelenmesi." *Turkish Studies— International Periodical for the Languages, Literature and History of Turkish or Turkic* 9, no. 3 (2014): 1135–46.

Özyürek, Esra. *Nostalgia for the Modern: State Secularism and Everday Politics in Turkey*. Durham, NC: Duke University Press, 2006.

——. "Public Memory as Political Battleground: Islamist Subversions of Republican Nostalgia." In *The Politics of Public Memory in Turkey*, edited by Esra Özyürek, 114–37. Syracuse, NY: Syracuse University Press, 2007.

Pakalın, Mehmet Zeki. "Kılıç Alayı." In *Osmanlı Tarih Deyimleri ve Terimleri Sözlüğü*, 259–64. Istanbul: Milli Eğitim Basımevi, 1983.

Pamuk, Orhan. *İstanbul: Hatıralar ve Şehir*. Istanbul: Yapı Kredi Yayınları, 2003.

Parlak, Sevgi. "Mihrişah Valide Sultan Külliyesi." In *TDV İslam Ansiklopedisi*, 42–44. Istanbul: Türkiye Diyanet Vakfı, 2005.

——. "Şah Sultan Külliyesi." In *TDV İslam Ansiklopedisi*, 258–60. Istanbul: Türkiye Diyanet Vakfı, 2010.

——. "Sokollu Mehmed Paşa Külliyesi." In *TDV İslam Ansiklopedisi*, 358–59. Istanbul: Türkiye Diyanet Vakfı, 2009.

Parlar, Gündegül. "Eyüp Index." In *Eyüp Sultan Symposia I–VIII: Selected Articles*, 197–217. Istanbul: Eyüp Belediyesi, 2005.

——. "Eyüpsultan Sempozyumları Üzerine Tematik Bir Değerlendirme." In *Tarihi, Kültürü ve Sanatıyla Eyüpsultan Sempozyumu IX: Tebliğler*, 46–65. Istanbul: Eyüp Belediyesi Kültür ve Turizm Müdürlüğü, 2006.

Pedersen, J. "Nadhr." In *Encyclopedia of Islam, Second Edition*, edited by P. Bearman, Th. Bianquis, C. E. Bosworth, E. van Donzel and W. P. Heinrichs. Leiden: Brill, 2012.

Pekin, Ayşe. "İstanbul'un Kutsal Semti: Eyüp." *Skylife*, December 1992, 92–97.

Pellat, Charles. "Manakib." In *Encyclopedia of Islam, Second Edition*, edited by P. Bearman, Th. Bianquis, C. E. Bosworth, E. van Donzel and W. P. Heinrichs. Leiden: Brill, 2012.

Pérouse, Jean-François. "Les non musulmans à Istanbul aujourd'hui: Une présence en creux? Le cas de l'arrondissement de Fatih." *Revue des mondes musulmans et de la Méditerranée* 107–10 (2005): 261–95.

——. "Gouverner Istanbul aujourd'hui." *Rives méditerranéennes* 2 (1999): 71–77. https://doi.org/10.4000/rives.152.

Philliou, Christine. *Turkey: A Past Against History*. Berkeley: University of California Press, 2021.

——. "When the Clock Strikes Twelve: The Inception of an Ottoman Past in Early Republican Turkey." *Comparative Studies of South Asia, Africa and the Middle East* 31, no. 1 (2011): 172–82.

Pierce, Joseph, Deborah G. Martin, and James T. Murphy. "Relational Place-Making: The Networked Politics of Place." *Transactions of the Institute of British Geographers* 36, no. 1 (2010): 54–70.

Pinto, Paulo G. "Pilgrimage, Commodities, and Religious Objectification: The Making of Transnational Shiism between Iran and Syria." *Comparative Studies of South Asia, Africa and the Middle East* 27, no. 1 (2007): 109–25. https://doi.org/10.1215/1089201x-2006-047.

Preziosi, Donald. "Introduction: The Mechanisms of Urban Meaning." In *The Ottoman City and Its Parts: Urban Structure and Social Order*, edited by Irene A. Bierman, Rifa'at Ali Abou-El-Haj, and Donald Preziosi, 3–11. New Rochelle, NY: A.D. Caratzas, 1991.

Prochazka-Eisl, Gisela. "Alus, Sermet Muhtar." In *Encyclopedia of Islam, Three*, edited by Kate Fleet, Gudrun Kramer, Denis Matringe, John Nawas, and Everett Rowson. Leiden: Brill, 2016.

Promey, Sally M. "Religion, Sensation, and Materiality: An Introduction." In *Sensational Religion: Sensory Cultures in Material Practice*, edited by Sally M. Promey, 1–21. New Haven, CT: Yale University Press, 2014.

——, ed. *Sensational Religion: Sensory Cultures in Material Practice*. New Haven, CT: Yale University Press, 2014.

Putnam, Lara. "The Transnational and the Text-Searchable: Digitized Sources and the Shadows They Cast." *American Historical Review* 121, no. 2 (2016): 377–402.

Renard, John. *Friends of God: Islamic Images of Piety, Commitment, and Servanthood*. Berkeley: University of California Press, 2008.

Riedler, Florian. "Public People. Temporary Labor Migrants in Nineteenth Century Istanbul." In *Public Istanbul: Spaces and Spheres of the Urban*, edited by Frank Eckardt and Kathrin Wildner, 233–54. Bielefeld: transcript Verlag, 2008.

Rippin, Andrew. "Ḥawḍ." In *Encyclopedia of Islam, Three*, edited by Kate Fleet, Gudrun Kramer, Denis Matringe, John Nawas, and Everett Rowson. Leiden: Brill, 2013.

Roelcke, Annegret. "Constructing the Capital of Peace: Changing Branding Strategies for Istanbul's Eyüp Quarter." *Middle East—Topics & Arguments* 12 (2019): 110–20. https://doi.org/10.17192/meta.2019.12.7931.

——. "Pre-AKP Urban Rehabilitation Projects for Istanbul's Eyüp Quarter: Contextualising the Narrative of 1994 as Point of Rupture." In *Türkeiforschung Im Deutschsprachigen Raum: Umbrüche, Krisen und Widerstände*, edited by Johanna Chovanec, Gabriele Cloeters, Onur İnal, Charlotte Joppien, and Urszula Woźniak, 207–29. Wiesbaden: Springer VS, 2020.

——. "Two Tales of a Neighborhood: Eyüp as a Stage for the Ottoman Conquest and the Turkish War of Independence." In *Urban Neighbourhood Formations: Boundaries, Narrations, and Intimacies*, edited by Hilal Alkan and Nazan Maksudyan, 75–98. London: Routledge, 2020.

Rose, Gillian, Monica Degen, and Begum Basdas. "More on 'Big Things': Building Events and Feelings." *Transactions of the Institute of British Geographers* 35, no. 3 (2010): 334–49.

Rüstem, Ünver. *Ottoman Baroque: The Architectural Refashioning of Eighteenth-Century Istanbul*. Princeton, NJ: Princeton University Press, 2018.

Sağlam, Nuri. "Ruşen Eşref Ünaydın." In *TDV İslam Ansiklopedisi*, 336–37. Istanbul: Türkiye Diyanet Vakfı, 2012.

Şahin, Haşim. "Menâkıbnâme." In *TDV İslam Ansiklopedisi*, 112–14. Ankara: Türkiye Diyanet Vakfı, 2004.

Said, Edward. *Beginnings: Intention and Method*. New York: Columbia University Press, 1985.

Sajdi, Dana. *The Barber of Damascus: Nouveau Literacy in the Eighteenth-Century Ottoman Levant*. Stanford, CA: Stanford University Press, 2013.

Sakaoğlu, Necdet. "Kılıç Alayları." In *Dünden Bugüne İstanbul Ansiklopedisi*, 555–57. Istanbul: Türkiye Ekonomik ve Toplumsal Tarih Vakfı, 1993.

Şakir, Ziya. *Eyüp Sultan ve Haliç*. Istanbul: Akıl Fikir Yayınları, 2011.

Salvatore, Armando. *The Sociology of Islam: Knowledge, Power and Civility*. Malden, MA: Wiley Blackwell, 2016.

Sand, Jordan. *Tokyo Vernacular: Common Spaces, Local Histories, Found Objects*. Berkeley: University of California Press, 2013.

Sayar, Ahmed Güner. *A. Süheyl Ünver: Hayatı, Şahsiyeti ve Eserleri*. Istanbul: Eren, 1994.

Saygılı, Hasip, and Elif Konar. "Türkiye'nin 1950'li Yıllarına Mizah Gözüğyle Bakmak: Akbaba Dergisi (1952–1960)." *Akademik Tarih ve Düşünce Dergisi* 8, no. 2 (2021): 589–626.

Schielke, Samuli. "Ambivalent Commitments: Troubles of Morality, Religiosity and Aspiration among Young Egyptians." *Journal of Religion in Africa* 39, no. 2 (2009): 158–85.

———. "Being Good in Ramadan: Ambivalence, Fragmentation, and the Moral Self in the Lives of Young Egyptians." *Journal of the Royal Anthropological Institute* 15, no. S1 (2009): S24–S40.

Schielke, Samuli, and Georg Stauth. "Introduction." In *Dimensions of Locality: Muslim Saints, Their Place and Space*, edited by Georg Stauth and Samuli Schielke, 7–21. New Brunswick, NJ: Transaction Publishers, 2008.

Schimmel, Annemarie. *Deciphering the Signs of God: A Phenomenological Approach to Islam*. Albany: State University of New York Press, 1994.

Scott, James C. *Seeing Like a State: How Certain Schemes to Improve the Human Condition Have Failed*. New Haven, CT: Yale University Press, 1998.

Secor, Anna. "2012 Urban Geography Plenary Lecture Topological City." *Urban Geography* 34, no. 4 (2013): 430–44. https://doi.org/10.1080/02723638.2013.778698.

———. "'There Is an Istanbul That Belongs to Me': Citizenship, Space and Identity in the City." *Annals of the Association of American Geographers* 94 (2004): 352–68.

———. "Toward a Feminist Counter-Geopolitics: Gender, Space and Islamist Politics in Istanbul." *Space and Polity* 5, no. 3 (2001): 191–211.

———. "The Veil and Urban Space in Istanbul: Women's Dress, Mobility, and Islamic Knowledge." *Gender, Place and Culture* 1, no. 9 (2002): 5–22.

Şenay, Banu. "The Fall and Rise of the Ney: From the Sufi Lodge to the World Stage." *Ethnomusicology Forum* 23, no. 3 (2014): 405–24.

Sevim, Nidayi. *Medeniyetimizin Sessiz Tanıkları: Eyüp Sultan'da Osmanlı Mezar Taşları ve Ebedi Eyüp Sultan'lılar*. Istanbul: Mephisto Yayınları, 2007.

Shafir, Nir. "The Road from Damascus: Circulation and the Redefinition of Islam in the Ottoman Empire, 1620–1720." PhD diss., University of California, Los Angeles, 2016.

Shiller, Robert J. *Narrative Economics: How Stories Go Viral and Drive Major Economic Events*. Princeton, NJ: Princeton University Press, 2020.

Silverstein, Brian. "Disciplines of Presence in Modern Turkey: Discourse, Companionship, and the Mass Mediation of Islamic Practice." *Cultural Anthropology* 23, no. 1 (2008): 118–53.

———. *Islam and Modernity in Turkey*. New York: Palgrave Macmillan, 2011.

———. "Islamist Critique in Modern Turkey: Hermeneutics, Tradition, Genealogy." *Comparative Studies in Society and History* 47, no. 1 (2005): 134–60.

Şimşek, Erdal. "Eyüp Belediyesi Kültür ve Turizm Müdürü İrfan Çalışan ile . . . Aristokrat Diyarı: Eyüp." *Akit*, August 28, 1995.

Singer, Amy. *Charity in Islamic Societies*. Cambridge: Cambridge University Press, 2008.

"Siyar." In *The Oxford Dictionary of Islam*, edited by John Esposito. Oxford: Oxford University Press, 2003.

Smith, Jonathan Z. "Religion, Religions, Religious." In *Critical Terms for Religious Studies*, edited by Mark C. Taylor. Chicago: University of Chicago Press, 1998.

———. *To Take Place: Toward Theory in Ritual*. Chicago: University of Chicago Press, 1992.

Smith, Sarah-Neel. *Metrics of Modernity: Art and Development in Postwar Turkey.* Berkeley: University of California Press, 2022.

Spadola, Emilio. "On Mediation and Magnetism: Or, Why Destroy Saint Shrines?" In *Muslim Pilgrimage in the Modern World*, edited by Babak Rahimi and Peyman Eshaghi, 223–39. Chapel Hill: University of North Carolina Press, 2019.

Starrett, Gregory. "The Political Economy of Religious Commodities in Cairo." *American Anthropologist* 97, no. 1 (1995): 51–68.

Sümertaş, Firuzan Melike. "From Antiquarianism to Urban Archaeology: Transformation of Research on 'Old' Istanbul Throughout the Nineteenth Century." PhD diss, Boğaziçi University, 2021.

Tağmat, Çağlar Derya. "Fetih Derneği ve İstanbul'un Fetihin 500. Yılı." *Tarih Kültür ve Sanat Araştırmaları Dergisi* 3, no. 4 (2014): 46–60.

Tambar, Kabir. *The Reckoning of Pluralism: Political Belonging and the Demands of History in Turkey.* Stanford, CA: Stanford University Press, 2014.

Taneja, Anand Vivek. *Jinnealogy: Time, Islam, and Ecological Thought in the Medieval Ruins of Delhi.* Stanford, CA: Stanford University Press, 2017.

———. "Saintly Animals: The Shifting Moral and Ecological Landscapes of North India." *Comparative Studies of South Asia, Africa and the Middle East* 35, no. 2 (2015): 204–21.

Tanman, M. Baha. "Kılıç Kuşanma Törenlerinin Eyüp Sultan Külliyesi ile Yakın Çevresine Yansıması." In *Tarihi, Kültürü ve Sanatıyla Eyüpsultan Sempozyumu II Tebliğler*, edited by Osman Sak, 76–93. Istanbul, 1998.

———. "Musiki Tarihimizde Onemli Yeri Olan Bahariye Mevlevihanesi'nin Tarihçesi ve Sosyokültürel Çevresi." *Darülelhan Mecmuası* 8 (2017): 13–22.

Tanpınar, Ahmet Hamdi. *Saatleri Ayarlama Enstitüsü.* Istanbul: Dergah Yayınları, 2017.

Tee, Caroline. "The Gülen Movement and the AK Party: The Rise and Fall of a Turkish Islamist Alliance." In *Turkey's July 15th Coup: What Happened and Why*, edited by M. Hakan Yavuz and Bayram Balcı, 150–72. Salt Lake City: University of Utah Press, 2018.

Thum, Rian. *The Sacred Routes of Uyghur History.* Cambridge, MA: Harvard University Press, 2014.

———. "What Is Islamic History?" *History and Theory* 58, no. 4 (2019): 7–19. https://doi.org /10.1111/hith.12133.

Till, Karen E. "Memory Studies." *History Workshop Journal* 62, no. 1 (2006): 325–41.

———. *The New Berlin: Memory, Politics, Place.* Minneapolis: University of Minnesota Press, 2005.

———. "Places of Memory." In *A Companion to Political Geography*, edited by John Agnew, Katharyne Mitchell, and Gerard Toal, 289–301. Malden, MA: Blackwell Publishers, 2003.

Tlili, Sarra. *Animals in the Qur'an.* Cambridge: Cambridge University Press, 2012.

Tolia-Kelly, Divya P. "Locating Processes of Identification: Studying the Precipitates of Re-Memory through Artefacts in the British Asian Home." *Transactions of the Institute of British Geographers* 29 (2004): 314–29.

Tonga, Necati. "Türk Edebiyatı Tarihinde Mühim Bir Mecmua: Akbaba (1922–1977)." *Turkish Studies: International Periodical for the Languages, Literature and History of Turkish or Turkic* 3, no. 2 (2008): 665–79.

Topal, Alp Eren. "Political Reforms as Religious Revival: Conceptual Foundations of *Tanzimat.*" *Oriente Moderno* 101, no. 2 (2021): 153–80. https://doi.org/10.1163/22138617 -12340261.

Tse, Justin K. H. "Grounded Theologies: 'Religion' and the 'Secular' in Human Geography." *Progress in Human Geography* 38, no. 2 (2014): 201–20. https://doi.org /10.1177/0309132512475105.

Tsing, Anna. *Friction: An Ethnography of Global Connection.* Princeton, NJ: Princeton University Press, 2005.

Tuan, Yi-Fu. *Space and Place: The Perspective of Experience.* Minneapolis: University of Minnesota Press, 1977.

Tuğal, Cihan. "The Appeal of Islamic Politics: Ritual and Dialogue in a Poor District of Turkey." *Sociological Quarterly* 47 (2006): 245–73.

———. *Passive Revolution: Absorbing the Islamic Challenge to Capitalism.* Stanford, CA: Stanford University Press, 2009.

Turam, Berna. *Between Islam and the State: The Politics of Engagement.* Stanford, CA: Stanford University Press, 2007.

———. *Gaining Freedoms: Claiming Space in Istanbul and Berlin.* Stanford, CA: Stanford University Press, 2015.

———. "Ordinary Muslims: Power and Space in Everyday Life." *International Journal of Middle East Studies* 43, no. 1 (2011): 144–46.

———. "The Primacy of Space in Politics: Bargaining Rights, Freedom and Power in an Istanbul Neighborhood." *International Journal of Urban and Regional Research* 37, no. 2 (2013): 409–29. https://doi.org/10.1111/1468-2427.12003.

Türeli, İpek. "Heritagisation of the 'Ottoman/Turkish House' in the 1970s: Istanbul-Based Actors, Associations and Their Networks." *European Journal of Turkish Studies* 19 (2014).

———. *Istanbul, Open City: Exhibiting Anxieties of Urban Modernity.* New York: Routledge, 2018.

Türkmenoğlu, Şener. *Eyüp: Bir Semte Gönül Vermek.* Istanbul: ABC Yayın Grubu, 2005.

———. *Son Yüzyılın Hikayesi Eyüp: Yaşayanların Dilinden.* Istanbul: Yayın Dünyamız Yayınları, 2018.

Uludağ, Süleyman. "Basiret." In *TDV İslam Ansiklopedisi*, 103. Istanbul: Türkiye Diyanet Vakfı, 1992.

———. "Nefis." In *TDV İslam Ansiklopedisi*, 526–29. Istanbul: Türkiye Diyanet Vakfı, 2006.

Ünver, A. Süheyl. "İstanbul'da Sahâbe Kabirleri." In *İstanbul Risaleleri*, 221–73. Istanbul: Istanbul Büyükşehir Belediyesi Kültür İşleri Daire Başkanlığı, 1993.

———. "İstanbulun Bazı Acı ve Tatlı Sularının Halkça Maruf Şifa Hassaları Hakkında." *Türk Tıb Tarihi Arkivi* 5, no. 18 (1940): 90–96.

Urfalıoğlu, Nur. "Sebil." In *TDV İslam Ansiklopedisi*, 249–51. Istanbul: Türkiye Diyanet Vakfı, 2009.

Uslu, Aysel. "An Ecological Approach for the Evaluation of an Abandoned Cemetery as a Green Area: The Case of Ankara/Karakusunlar Cemetery." *African Journal of Agricultural Research* 5, no. 10 (2010): 1043–54. https://doi.org/10.5897/AJAR09.200.

Üstündağ, Ayda. *Dedem Ziya Şakir.* Istanbul: Akıl Fikir Yayınları, 2011.

Vakkasoğlu, Vehbi. "Öğüt, Cemal." In *TDV İslam Ansiklopedisi*, 23. Istanbul: Türkiye Diyanet Vakfı, 2007. https://islamansiklopedisi.org.tr/ogut-cemal.

Vatin, Nicolas. "Aux Origens du Pèlerinage à Eyüp des Sultans Ottomans." *Turcica: Revue d'Etudes Turques* 27 (1995): 91–99.

Vatin, Nicolas, and Thierry Zarcone. "İstanbul'da bir Bektaşi Tekkesi: Karyağdı (Eyüp) Tekkesi." *Türk Kültürü ve Hacı Bektaş Veli Araştırma Dergisi* 11 (1999): 143–54.

Vejdani, Farzin. *Making History in Iran: Education, Nationalism, and Print Culture*. Stanford, CA: Stanford University Press, 2015.

Vicini, Fabio. "'Do Not Cross Your Legs': Islamic Sociability, Reciprocity and Brotherhood in Turkey." *La Ricerca Folklorica* 69, no. 1 (2014): 93–104.

———. *Reading Islam: Life and Politics of Brotherhood in Modern Turkey*. Leiden: Brill, 2019.

Voll, John Obert. "Renewal and Reformation in the Mid-Twentieth Century: Bediuzzaman Said Nursi and Religion in the 1950s." In *Globalization, Ethics and Islam*, edited by Ian Markham and Ibrahim Özdemir, 48–62. New York: Ashgate Publishing, 2005.

Vryonis, Speros. *The Mechanism of Catastrophe: The Turkish Pogrom of September 6–7, 1955, and the Destruction of the Greek Community of Istanbul*. New York: Greekworks.com, 2005.

Walton, Jeremy F. *Muslim Civil Society and the Politics of Religious Freedom in Turkey*. Oxford: Oxford University Press, 2017.

———. "Practices of Neo-Ottomanism: Making Space and Place Virtuous in Istanbul." In *Orienting Istanbul: Cultural Capital of Europe?*, edited by Deniz Göktürk, Levent Soysal and İpek Türeli, 88–103. New York: Routledge, 2010.

Wheatley, Paul. *The Places Where Men Pray Together: Cities in Islamic Lands, Seventh through the Tenth Centuries*. Chicago: University of Chicago Press, 2001.

White, Charles. *Three Years in Constantinople; or, Domestic Manners of the Turks in 1844*. Vol. 3. London: Henry Colburn, Publisher, 1846.

White, Jenny B. *Islamist Mobilization in Turkey: A Study in Vernacular Politics*. Studies in Modernity and National Identity. Seattle: University of Washington Press, 2002.

———. "Milli Görüş." In *Islamic Movements of Europe: Public Religion and Islamophobia in the Modern World*, edited by Frank Peter and Rafael Ortega, 14–23. London: I.B. Tauris, 2014.

Wilford, Justin. *Sacred Subdivisions: The Postsuburban Transformation of American Evangelicalism*. New York: New York University Press, 2012.

Wilson, M. Brett. *Translating the Qur'an in an Age of Nationalism: Print Culture and Modern Islam in Turkey*. London: Oxford University Press, 2014.

———. "The Twilight of Ottoman Sufism: Antiquity, Immorality, and Nation in Yakup Kadri Karaosmanoğlu's Nur Baba." *International Journal of Middle East Studies* 49, no. 2 (2017): 233–53. https://doi.org/10.1017/s0020743817000034.

Wolper, Ethel Sara. *Cities and Saints: Sufism and the Transformation of Urban Space in Medieval Anatolia*. University Park: Pennsylvania State University Press, 2003.

———. "Khiḍr and the Changing Frontiers of the Medieval World." *Medieval Encounters* 17, no. 1–2 (2011): 120–46. https://doi.org/10.1163/157006711x561730.

———. "Khidr and the Politics of Place: Creating Landscapes of Continuity." In *Muslims and Others in Sacred Space*, edited by Margaret Cormack, 147–63. Oxford: Oxford University Press, 2013.

Woodall, G. Carole. "'Awakening a Horrible Monster': Negotiating the Jazz Public in 1920s Istanbul." *Comparative Studies of South Asia, Africa and the Middle East* 30, no. 3 (2011): 574–82. https://doi.org/10.1215/1089201x-2010-035.

Woods, Orlando. "Converting Houses into Churches: The Mobility, Fission, and Sacred Networks of Evangelical House Churches in Sri Lanka." *Environment and Planning D: Society and Space* 31, no. 6 (2013): 1062–75. https://doi.org/10.1068/d7912.

Yalçın, Hülya. "Eyüpsultan'da Nezih Eldem'in İzleri." *Mimarlık* 407 (2019): 40–44.

Yanık, Lerna K. "Constructing Turkish 'Exceptionalism': Discourses of Liminality and Hybridity in Post-Cold War Turkish Foreign Policy." *Political Geography* 30, no. 2 (2011): 80–89.

Yavuz, M. Hakan. "Political Islam and the Welfare (Refah) Party in Turkey." *Comparative Politics* 30, no. 1 (1997): 63–82.

———. "Turkish Identity and Foreign Policy in Flux: The Rise of Neo-Ottomanism." *Critique: Critical Middle Eastern Studies* 7, no. 12 (1998): 19–41.

Yıldırım, Muhammed Emin. *İnsani İlişkilerde İlahî Ölçü*. Istanbul: Siyer Yayınları, 2004.

Yılmaz, Hale. *Becoming Turkish: Nationalist Reforms and Cultural Negotiations in Early Republican Turkey, 1923–1945*. Syracuse, NY: Syracuse University Press, 2013.

Yolcu, Mehmet Ali. "Kutsalın Yeniden Üretimi: Kutsal Su İnançları ve Hacıbektaş Zemzem Çeşmesi." *21. Yüzyılda Eğitim ve Toplum Eğitim Bilimleri ve Sosyal Araştırmalar Dergisi* 3, no. 8 (2014): 93–102.

Yorgason, Ethan, and Veronica della Dora. "Geography, Religion, and Emerging Paradigms: Problematizing the Dialogue." *Social & Cultural Geography* 10, no. 6 (2009): 627–37.

Yosmaoğlu, İpek K. "Chasing the Printed Word: Press Censorship in the Ottoman Empire, 1876–1913." *Turkish Studies Association Journal* 27, no. 1/2 (2003): 15–49.

Yüce, Nuri. "Ağaoğlu, Ahmet." In *TDV İslam Ansiklopedisi*, 464–66. Istanbul: Türkiye Diyanet Vakfı, 1998.

Yurdagür, Metin. "İ'la-yi Kelimetullah." In *TDV İslam Ansiklopedisi*, 62–63. Istanbul: Türkiye Diyanet Vakfı, 2000.

Zaman, Taymiya. "An Islam of One's Own." *Comparative Studies of South Asia, Africa and the Middle East* 40, no. 1 (2020): 214–19.

Zarcone, Thierry. "Stone People, Tree People and Animal People in Turkic Asia and Eastern Europe." *Diogenes* 52, no. 3 (2016): 35–46. https://doi.org/10.1177/0392192105055168.

Zencirci, Gizem. "From Property to Civil Society: The Historical Transformation of *Vakıfs* in Modern Turkey (1923–2013)." *International Journal of Middle East Studies* 47, no. 3 (2015): 533–54.

Zürcher, Erik. *Turkey: A Modern History*. 3rd ed. London: I.B. Tauris, 2004.

# INDEX

Page numbers in *italics* signify photos or maps.

Founded in 1893,
UNIVERSITY OF CALIFORNIA PRESS
publishes bold, progressive books and journals
on topics in the arts, humanities, social sciences,
and natural sciences—with a focus on social
justice issues—that inspire thought and action
among readers worldwide.

The UC PRESS FOUNDATION
raises funds to uphold the press's vital role
as an independent, nonprofit publisher, and
receives philanthropic support from a wide
range of individuals and institutions—and from
committed readers like you. To learn more, visit
ucpress.edu/supportus.

Made in the USA
Middletown, DE
05 September 2024

60383494R00146